ELECTRIC AUTOMOBILES

Energy, Environmental, and Economic Prospects for the Future

WILLIAM HAMILTON
General Research Corporation
Santa Barbara Division

McGRAW-HILL BOOK COMPANY

Bogotá □ Düsseldorf □ Johannesburg □ London
New York □ St. Louis □ San Francisco □ Auckland
Madrid □ Mexico □ Montreal □ New Delhi
Panama □ São Paulo □ Singapore
Sydney □ Tokyo □ Toronto

Library of Congress Cataloging in Publication Data

Hamilton, William, date
  Electric automobiles.

  "The work upon which this publication is based was performed pursuant
to contract EY-76-C-03-1180 with the Energy Research and Development
Administration."
  Includes bibliographies and index.
  1. Automobiles, Electric.   I. Title.
TL220.H35   388.34   79-15650
ISBN 0-07-025735-3

234567890 HDHD 89876543210

The work upon which this publication is based was performed pursuant to
Contract EY-76-C-03-1180 with the Energy Research and Development
Administration.

The editors for this book were Tyler G. Hicks and Susan Thomas and the
production supervisor was Thomas G. Kowalczyk.

Printed and bound by Halliday Lithograph.

CONTENTS

TABLE OF CONTENTS (Continued)

FIGURES

FIGURES (Continued)

FIGURES (Continued)

TABLES

TABLES (Continued)

TABLES (Continued)

TABLES (Continued)

TABLES (Continued)

SUMMARY

Scope of this report

Electric cars of the future offer exciting prospects for conserving petroleum and improving the environment. This report measures those prospects and the other advantages and disadvantages of electric cars. To do so, it details the prospective technical features and costs of electric cars, their ability to meet the needs of drivers, their competitive position in the auto marketplace, and the effects they could have on the use of fuels and energy, on air pollution, on noise and other environmental problems, on resources of materials for batteries, and on the economy.

The battery problem ...

It is clear that batteries are the key obstacle to practical electric cars. Electric motors and controllers are highly developed: they are extremely quiet and reliable, and reasonably light and inexpensive. Since the beginning of the century, in contrast, it has been the batteries that have limited the range and speed of electric cars, and kept them more expensive than automobiles with internal-combustion engines.

... and possible solutions

New kinds of batteries, however, offer prospects of greater improvements in the next decade than in the past seventy-five years. Improved lead-acid, nickel-zinc, and lithium-sulfur batteries represent the range of future possibilities. They could double, triple, or even quadruple the amount of energy storage provided by the golf-cart batteries now commonly used in electric cars. Their developers also expect increases of 50-150% in operating life and corresponding reductions of cost. Since a variety of promising approaches to an improved battery are under active development, it seems likely that at least one will succeed, even though most past forecasts have proven overoptimistic.

Future ranges: up to 450 km

Electric cars suitable for mass production by 1985 or 1990 could offer adequate speed and acceleration for freeway driving, with ranges between recharges of about 150, 250, and 450 kilometers for future lead-acid, nickel-zinc, and lithium-sulfur batteries, respectively. These estimates come from parametric models which were constructed to show the weight and performance of four-passenger subcompact electric cars with different batteries and different design ranges. Even with the most advanced batteries, the electric cars will be up to twice as heavy as their conventional counterparts because of the battery and the extra structure required to support it.

Urban travel: seldom over 220 km

Compared to these ranges, the usual needs of drivers are surprisingly modest. An analysis of the data from extensive travel surveys in Los Angeles and Washington indicates that a range of only 75 kilometers between recharges would entirely suffice for the urban driving of secondary drivers (those drivers reporting least travel at households with more than one driver) on 95% of the days they drive. This is within the reach of today's electric cars. For drivers at single-driver households, about twice as much range (150 kilometers) would be necessary to complete all urban travel on 95% of driving days. For urban driving by primary drivers at multi-driver households (or for average drivers of new cars nationwide, not just in urban areas), a range of about 220 km would be necessary. These are well within reach of cars with future batteries. But trips too long for future electric cars, though infrequent, are still important: over 60% of households with cars reported one or more such trips in a recent year, mostly for recreation and vacation. The average number of long trips at such households was five per year, totaling 5,000 kilometers. In comparison, average travel per automobile in the United States is only about 16,000 kilometers per year.

Applicability to urban driving: high

Though electric car owners might have to sacrifice some travel or use a different mode for long trips, electric cars could reasonably be applied very widely, especially for urban driving. Roughly three-quarters of US cars are in urban areas. They are about equally divided in three groups: secondary cars at multi-car households, primary cars at multi-car households, and only cars at one-car households. In each group, most of the cars are at single-family households, where it would be easiest to provide electrical outlets for recharging at overnight parking places. Though most cars are parked off the street at night, such statistics as are available suggest that a substantial minority is parked on the street and would consequently be inaccessible to recharging.

Costs: also high

Even without a battery aboard, an electric car will generally be heavier than a conventional car, because of the extra structure required to support the battery. Largely as a result, the initial cost will generally be higher. A parametric cost model for future electric cars showed that the total costs (initial plus operating and maintenance) would also be generally higher, partly due to this higher initial cost and partly due to the costs of batteries. Electric cars will probably last longer (we assume 20% longer) than conventional cars, and be much cheaper to maintain and repair; but those advantages are not enough to make electric cars less expensive overall. Only at the shortest practical design ranges and with the less-expensive future batteries are electric cars likely to equal conventional cars in overall costs. Depending on the type of battery and design range, gasoline prices would have to rise 50-150% to make conventional cars as expensive as the longer-range electric cars. Improvements in battery life beyond those projected in this study are unlikely by themselves to equalize costs.

Market share: modest

Though improved electric cars would be widely applicable, they are unlikely to capture as much as 10% of the new-car market in this century because they will be more expensive and less capable than conventional cars unless real prices for gasoline increase greatly. They would be most competitive in cost and most capable of meeting travel needs if designed and sold as second cars, but only about ten percent of second cars are purchased new.

Energy efficiency: competitive

Despite the inherent efficiency of electric drive, electric cars would at best be competitive with conventional cars in terms of overall energy use, if oil were the basic source of energy. If coal were to be the source of both electricity and (synthetic) gasoline, however, substantially less would be required for electric cars than for conventional cars.

Recharge power: available

In practice, of course, what fuels are used to recharge electric cars will depend on the facilities available at powerhouses. Accordingly, a detailed model of supply and demand for electricity in future years was constructed and operated for the 228 largest electric utilities in the contiguous United States. It showed

that facilities which would otherwise be idle, mostly late at night when demand
is low, would be adequate for recharging tens of millions of electric cars. It
appears unlikely that the use of electric cars will ever be limited by the capacity
of electric utilities unless historical patterns of supply and demand change drastically. In future years, moreover, the importance of oil-fired facilities for overnight recharging is expected to diminish rapidly.

Petroleum savings: potentially immense

Potential savings of petroleum through the wide use of electric cars are immense
If electric cars were first utilized in those regions of the US using least petroleum
for electric power, up to 30% of US automobiles could be electrified with virtually no use of petroleum in 1980, and up to 60% in 2000. If all cars were electrified in the year 2000, petroleum use for automobiles would be cut 83%. Most
energy for recharging would then come from coal and nuclear power plants. The
resulting reduction in total national use of petroleum would be under 20%, however; automobiles now account for only 28% of national petroleum consumption,
and are expected to require even less after average fuel economy rises in line with
Federal standards.

Air pollution: mixed effects

The effects of electric cars on urban air pollution would be mixed: reduced
emissions from automobiles would be accompanied by increased emissions from
power plants burning fossil fuels. A computer model was used to project emissions from all sources for the 24 largest urban areas in the United States, with and
without electric cars, for 1980-2000. The projections show that the emissions from
conventional automobiles, which are being reduced over 90% by Federal regulation, will no longer be the major source of urban air pollution in future years.
Emissions from power plants are also under relatively tight controls. As a result,
the projected effects of electric cars tend to be dominated by other sources. Complete electrification of automobiles would, on the average, cut urban emissions
of hydrocarbons and carbon monoxide by roughly half. Emissions of sulfur
oxides would rise some 20%, however, due to generation of recharging power, and
most damage recently attributed to air pollution has been attributed to sulfur
oxides.

Traffic noise: reduced

Because electric cars are inherently quiet, they could help to reduce traffic
noise, the primary noise problem in the United States. Important reductions in
the number of people affected by traffic noise are already expected as trucks,
buses, and motorcycles complying with recent Federal regulations replace older,
noisier vehicles. Regulations have yet to be adopted for automobiles, but further
reduction is likely due to quieting of conventional cars. Even after these improvements, wide use of electric cars would produce additional benefits, reducing the
impact to 27% of recent levels, in comparison with a reduction to 41% which may
be achieved without electric cars.

Other environmental impacts: minor

In other much-discussed aspects of environmental pollution and health, electric cars would have only minor effects. They would slightly increase thermal
pollution due to power plants and add a little to the problems of health and safety
associated with coal and nuclear power plants. On the other hand, they could
eliminate the use of most lubricating oil in automobiles and end the indiscriminate

dumping of oil drained from auto engines into the environment. They would make hulks of abandoned autos more valuable and more likely to be recycled, but existing economic forces are expected to eliminate auto hulks from the environment soon in the absence of electric cars.

Battery materials: not necessarily abundant

The wide use of electric cars would considerably affect the demand for materials used in batteries. While electrifying 10% of the personal cars in the United States in this century would probably raise no serious problem, electrifying all US cars could be difficult with any of the representative future batteries (lead-acid, nickel-zinc, or lithium-sulfur). Given this objective, the identified reserves of battery materials are no more abundant than those of petroleum for meeting world demand through 2000. New discoveries, however, are likely to increase the identified reserves of battery materials as the demand increases. Uncertainties are greatest for lithium, partly because it may also be in great demand for use in fusion power plants. Alternative future batteries based on such abundant materials as sodium, sulfur, and chlorine could effectively eliminate problems of inadequate resources.

The economy: little affected

Aside from extra costs for motorists, the wide use of electric cars would have little economic impact in the United States. Only about 3% of US jobs would be affected by a complete switch to electric automobiles. Even if the transition were completed in only twenty years, the annual changes would be very small. In proportion to the higher costs of electric cars, total employment in manufacturing, selling, and servicing automobiles would be increased. Though some battery materials might be imported, their cost would be offset by savings on importation of petroleum in a few years at most.

Petroleum saving versus limited range and higher cost

In conclusion, a national shift to electric cars in order to conserve petroleum and improve the environment would be far more costly than already-adopted moves to low-pollution, fuel-efficient conventional automobiles. Though future electric cars will be capable of most auto travel, they would nonetheless entail sacrifices in capability and performance far larger than those resulting from existing regulation of automotive safety, fuel economy, and exhaust emissions. The ratio of benefits to costs would be most favorable for relatively limited use of electric cars, use as secondary cars and at urban one-car households using other modes for out-of-town travel. Overall, the desirability of any deliberate move to electric cars will depend primarily on the importance attached to the problems of importing petroleum.

ACKNOWLEDGMENTS

The study reported here was initiated by the US Energy Research and Development Administration and completed for the US Department of Energy, its successor, under Contract EY-76-C-03-1180. Dr. Daniel P. Maxfield, Chief, Technology Assessment and Implementation Branch, Division of Transportation Energy Conservation, was technical monitor for the Department of Energy. The study was performed during a 30-month period ending in May 1978, by a team working at General Research Corporation in Santa Barbara.

Major contributors included Dr. Michael Collins and Mr. Wayne Carriere, who projected the potential impacts of electric cars on the electric utility system, on energy use, on petroleum use, and on urban air quality; Mr. Richard Curtis, who projected characteristics of future electric cars; Mr. John Brennand, who developed the computer simulation used to estimate the driving range of electric cars; Ms. Susan Pierce, who reduced data from extensive surveys showing driving requirements of typical motorists; Mr. Robert Carr, who projected costs of electric cars; and Ms. Lynn Morecraft, who projected economic impacts of electric cars.

Opinions expressed in this report are those of the author, who served as director of the study and also developed its projections of future battery characteristics, driving requirements, electric car applicability, impacts on traffic noise, and impacts on supplies of materials.

1 INTRODUCTION

Electric automobiles offer exciting prospects for the future. Inherently efficient, reliable, silent, and pollution-free, they could provide high mobility without the environmental damage of the gasoline car. More important still, electric cars could be recharged at night from coal and nuclear generating stations, ending the dependence of automotive travel on petroleum.

In recognition of these prospects, an unprecedented wave of interest in electric automobiles has swept around the world. Industry and government in major industrial nations are developing and demonstrating improved electric vehicles for service as passenger cars, delivery trucks, and buses. In the largest single program to date, the United States Department of Energy is to develop and demonstrate up to 10,000 electric vehicles by 1985, in a $160-million program. Already, electric cars offer speeds sufficient for freeway driving and ranges between battery recharges up to 120 kilometers--over two and a half times the average daily driving per automobile in the US. Such automobiles could be widely useful as second cars at households with a conventional car available for longer trips. The improved storage batteries expected within a decade would multiply the range of electric cars several times over, to suffice for the needs of almost all drivers in the United States.

Yet no electric car is being produced in quantity today anywhere in the world. The most successful effort in recent years to manufacture electric cars was suspended in 1976, after production of less than 2,000 vehicles. Most authorities expect fewer than ten percent of US automobiles to be electric even in the year 2000, far less than necessary to make major reductions in the petroleum consumption or air pollution of the US auto fleet.

The reasons for this are simple. Even with major technological improvements, electric cars in this century seem likely to remain somewhat more expensive and less capable than petroleum-fueled cars. It would be the exceptional individual who would pay more for less car in order to make infinitesimal reductions in the nation's petroleum consumption and air pollution. Incentives for the individual, in short, are lacking despite the potential collective benefits for society from large-scale electrification of automobiles.

Similar situations often arise, in which decisions made by individuals in a free marketplace do not reflect important "external" considerations and consequently lead to a collective result which is undesirable. Two important examples have already been seen in the automotive marketplace. No individual motorist could alone significantly affect air pollution or petroleum consumption by his choice of an automobile, but the collective result of motorists' choices has a great effect on both. In both cases, the importance of these collective external effects is so great that the Government has regulated the free market to exclude automobiles which either emit excessive pollutants or consume excessive fuel.

Given these precedents and the growing burden of oil imports, it seems certain that there will be a continuing debate of national policy regarding electric cars. The principal issue will be to what extent the nation should promote electric cars over petroleum-fueled cars. Government-sponsored R&D is only one possible means for doing so; direct subsidy of electric cars is another. Alternatively, the competitive position of electric cars in the marketplace could be indirectly enhanced through heavy taxation of petroleum-based automotive fuel, through gasoline rationing, or through outright limitations on the use of conventional cars. Almost any level of electric car use could be attained, given Government action strong enough to compensate for the limited performance and added expense which at present keep the sales of electric automobiles small.

The focus of the debate over electric cars should be whether the benefits from their use will outweigh their additional costs and other disadvantages. This raises a host of very difficult questions. How great a reduction of oil imports is required to justify the extra dollar cost of using electric cars? Will reductions in air pollution justify part of this extra cost? Will limitations on mobility be even more important than added dollar costs to the motorist? In weighing benefits and costs such as these against one another, there can be no definitive conclusion: subjective judgments are required at every step of the evaluation.

The underlying benefits and costs themselves, however, are much less subjective and contentious. For the most part, they can be projected in quantitative terms, by methods which can be widely acceptable. To do so is essential if any policy debate is to be soundly grounded. If the probable magnitudes of petroleum savings or extra costs associated with electric cars are unknown, the importance of them surely cannot be judged effectively.

The object of this report is to present quantitative estimates of the benefits and costs to be expected from large-scale use of electric automobiles in the United States. It is intended to support balanced decisions, not to advocate a particular policy about electric cars. In recognition of the many uncertainties about the future prospects of electric cars, it investigates a spectrum of possibilities rather than a single prediction for the future.

In approaching the prospects for electric cars, this report starts at the cars themselves: their capabilities, their costs, and their potential usage. After a review of today's state of the art which demonstrates the crucial importance of improved batteries, it projects characteristics of representative improved batteries for the future. The range, speed, energy requirements, and other characteristics of future electric cars are next estimated; in comparison with the actual driving requirements of motorists, they show the impressive extent to which the cars will be applicable to typical needs. The dollar costs of acquiring and operating electric cars are then projected and compared with the costs of competitive conventional automobiles. Thus the principal impacts of electric cars on individual motorists are quantified: loss of mobility due primarily to the limited range of the electric car, plus higher costs stemming from the weight and expense of the propulsion battery.

The report then turns to the societal benefits and costs of electric cars: their probable impacts on electric power generation, on energy and petroleum use, on environmental quality, on the economy, and on materials resources. In the analysis, impacts are calculated for assumed usages of electric cars ranging from relatively low to relatively high, to show effects which might result from different levels of governmental emphasis on electric cars. At the core of the analysis is the electric utility system, which must provide the energy required to recharge electric cars. It is the utility system which determines the mix of petroleum, coal, and nuclear energy used for recharging, and the extent to which increased emissions of air pollutants from power plants will offset decreased emissions from conventional automobiles. In this part of the analysis, the principal advantages of electric automobiles are brought forward: reductions in petroleum use, reductions in air pollution, and reductions in traffic noise. At the same time, the important potential limitations on the use of electric autos are quantified. The electric utility system of the future has some limit on its capacity for generating recharge power, and known resources and reserves of materials limit the number of propulsion batteries which could be built.

The principal assumption underlying this report is that overall, conditions will remain much as they are today: though major trends will continue, there will be no abrupt changes or surprises such as drastic increases in the price of gasoline, rationing of gasoline, unavailability of sufficient gasoline or electricity to satisfy demand, or sharp limitations on the use of conventional automobiles.

The pace of technological progress, however, is assumed to remain rapid. In consequence, current programs of research and development for storage batteries are assumed to produce improved batteries for electric cars. For conventional cars, continued improvements in emissions of air pollutants and in fuel economy are anticipated in accord with current regulations, and regulations of noise emissions are also expected. These and other changes in conventional cars are especially important because it is the differences between the electric and the conventional car which lead to both individual and societal impacts. Direct comparisons are necessary at every step in evaluating prospects for electric cars. As conventional cars are improved, the potential benefits of electric cars are correspondingly reduced. If gasoline cars of the future use half as much fuel as those at present, for example, then the maximum saving of petroleum by electric cars will be half what it otherwise could have been.

Only battery-electric passenger cars were considered in this study. Passenger cars constitute, of course, by far the largest single class of highway vehicles in the United States. Though commercial delivery trucks and vans are promising candidates for electric drive, they were not included; nor were personal trucks, vans, and recreational vehicles. Hybrid-electric vehicles, which remove range limitations by adding an internal-combustion engine to the basic battery-electric drive, were not considered either, though it is possible they may prove desirable.

Overall, the study dealt only with electric cars in the United States in this century. Most calculations were focused on three particular years: 1980, 1990, and 2000. Scenarios for the year-by-year introduction of electric cars were not hypothesized; though scenarios may be important in formulating acceptable public policy, they are relatively inconsequential in estimating quantitative impacts.

Each of the succeeding sections of this report follows the same plan. Each offers its most important results in the first page or two, explaining their place in the overall analysis of electric cars and summarizing the steps by which they were developed. The remainder of the section then describes these steps in detail, presenting supporting data and intermediate results. The object of this arrangement is to make key results easily accessible, and to assist readers with special interests in locating relevant materials. The last section, Section 17, offers general conclusions drawn from overall consideration of the findings of the individual sections.

References are listed separately at the end of each section.

2 THE STATE OF THE ART

The point of departure for all projections about future electric cars is the state of the art--what is technically possible now. The state of the art is probably best demonstrated by electric cars which have actually been built and tested in recent years. True, they do not demonstrate all the technology which may actually be within reach today. Nor do they necessarily show the combinations of technical possibilities which would give the highest performance, or the lowest cost, or the optimum combination of performance and cost for typical users. But these are minor drawbacks: above all, existing electric cars are explicit, tangible demonstrations of techniques and accomplishments which provide the basis for future development and improvement.

The electric automobiles described in Table 2.1 and illustrated in Fig. 2.1 are prominent representatives of achievements in the last decade. They exemplify many of the prospects which have excited the current interest in electric cars: useful ranges, speeds adequate for freeway driving, interior accommodations sufficient and convenient for urban travel, and even styling possibilities ranging from the conventional to the futuristic. At the same time, these electric cars also reveal the key limitations of present-day electric vehicles: much less range, speed, and acceleration than offered by even the most modest of conventional cars.

In this section, the individual cars of Table 2.1 are first described and discussed. Then the critical factors underlying the design of electric cars with present-day batteries are considered. A few simple calculations show why the cars of Table 2.1 are as they are, and why batteries are the principal problem in improving electric cars. Finally, the limitations on driving range with today's batteries are estimated. They suggest that the cars of Table 2.1 have made the most of the batteries now available, and that major improvements will come primarily from improved batteries, rather than innovative automotive design.

TABLE 2.1

REPRESENTATIVE ELECTRIC CARS, 1967-77

| 2-Passenger Cars | Curb Weight, kg | Battery Weight, percent | Range, km* | | Acceleration Time* (0-50 km/hr), seconds |
			Constant 50 km/hr	Urban Driving**	
Ford Comuta (1967)	544	32	41	38	12.9
GM-512 (1968)	567	26	91	60	12.5
Citicar (1974-76)	626	37	75	47	19.9
ESB Sundancer (1970)	726	47	173	105	12.5
CDA Town Car (1976)	1339	37	204	101	13.1
4-Passenger Cars					
Ripp-Electric (1974)	1314	44	156	121	14.9
EVA Metro (1975)	1429	33	68	35	16.1
Mars II (1967)	1860	47	181	107	15.6

* Estimate
** SAE Test Procedure J227a, Schedule C

a.   Sebring-Vanguard CitiCar

b.   ESB Sundancer

Figure 2.1.   Recent Electric Cars

9

c.   CDA Town Car

d.   EVA Metro

Figure 2.1.   (Continued)

2.1 RECENT ELECTRIC CARS

The cars of Table 2.1 were inspired in large measure by two recent waves of interest in electric automobiles. The first wave arose in the mid-1960's, when the importance of automotive smog was first widely recognized and efforts to alleviate it began. Before the potentials for cleaning up the exhaust of conventional automobiles were fully appreciated, many people reasoned that pollution-free electric cars might be required to restore reasonable air quality in major urban areas. The second wave of interest arose during the oil embargo and gasoline shortages of 1973-74, when the unreliability and cost of foreign supplies of oil and the rapid depletion of domestic petroleum reserves became painfully evident.

In both cases, bills for developing and promoting electric automobiles were introduced in the US Congress. In the sixties, none were passed into law, but after the oil embargo the Electric and Hybrid Vehicle Research, Development, and Demonstration Act of 1976 eventually emerged. During the late 1970's and early 1980's, the resulting activity should produce storage batteries and electric cars with important improvements. For the moment, however, it is too early for any of these cars to have made their debut; in consequence, all of the cars of Table 2.1 are the work of industry or dedicated individuals.

Cars selected for inclusion in Table 2.1 are important because they exhibit both technical capability and actual offerings for sale. Some were designed from the ground up to utilize electric propulsion as effectively as possible, while others are conversions of conventional automobiles benefiting from the low cost and proven performance of mass-produced vehicles and components. They illustrate a wide range of approaches not only to technical problems of design and construction, but to the potential marketplace where electric cars must ultimately compete. Range and performance figures in Table 2.1 are interpolations and extrapolations from reported tests and data, which were measured or calculated under a variety of different conditions and are not directly comparable.[1] They were developed by use of the computer simulation described in Sec. 4 and Appendix A. They are in reasonable agreement with test of existing electric cars and vans reported subsequently and summarized in Fig. 2.2.[2] Individual comparisons between these tests and the estimates of Table 2.1 are not possible because the published test results do not identify individual vehicles by name or maker.

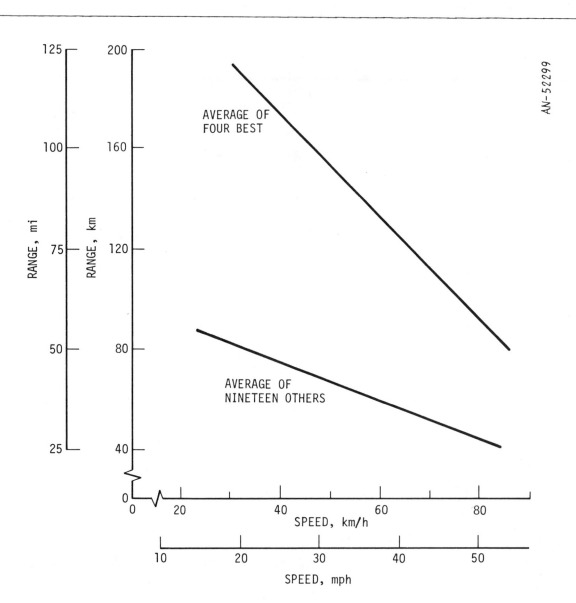

Figure 2.2.   Range Versus Speed of Electric Vehicles Tested in 1975-77 (from Ref. 2)

Two-passenger electric cars have received the most serious attention in the past decade, though most conventional cars carry four passengers or more. All the two-passenger cars in Table 2.1 were designed from scratch for battery-electric propulsion; none are conversions, with the design compromises which result as batteries are fitted into the available space and the structure loaded beyond the expectations of its designers. Nevertheless, these two-passenger cars reflect a considerable spectrum of design approaches and service objectives.

Both Ford Motor Company and General Motors seriously investigated electric cars during the mid-60's concern over automotive air pollution and the best methods for alleviating it. The first two cars of Table 2.1 reveal the similarity of approaches and objectives of these large auto makers.[3,4] Both cars basically accommodated only two passengers, though the Ford Comuta provided space behind the two primary passengers for two small children. Neither offered sufficient performance for use on high-speed highways and freeways. The GM 512 was expressly designed to operate only in areas or on streets where there were no large vehicles. The Ford Comuta, built in England where cars were smaller, was considered to be capable of mingling with ordinary street traffic though its size and speed were substantially the same as the GM 512. Both cars carried the propulsion batteries underneath the bench seat provided for the occupants, and both used chopper-controlled DC series-wound traction motors mounted behind the rear axle, as in Fig. 2.3. Both cars had fiberglass bodies with steel structure, and both were designed with an eye to inexpensive production though neither was a manufacturing prototype. The Comuta employed separate drive motors for each rear wheel rather than a differential. The GM 512 used a single motor of special construction with coaxial drive shafts for the two rear wheels. In comparison with the Comuta, the 512 reflected greater emphasis on efficiency and performance. Aside from the specially designed coaxial motor, it employed tires especially constructed to provide exceptionally low rolling resistance. It also used a specially-built

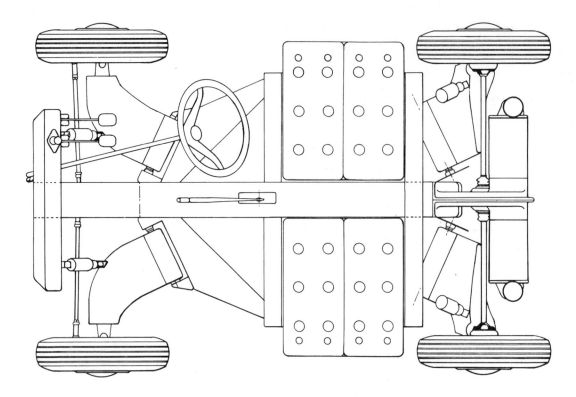

Figure 2.3. Layout of the Ford Comuta

---

battery which provided high energy density, deep-discharge capability, and a low physical profile suited to the under-seat mounting.

The Sebring-Vanguard CitiCar was manufactured and sold for several years immediately following the oil embargo and shortages of 1973 and 1974.[5] The total number produced, in several models, approached 2,000. In concept, the CitiCar resembled the Ford and GM cars: it was very small, offered performance insufficient for freeway or highway use, and was arranged with batteries under the single bench seat and a DC series-wound, rear-mounted traction motor. Unlike the Comuta and 512, however, the CitiCar was conceived for production in very low volume with minimum tooling, and was the work of a fledgling manufacturer. It used off-the-shelf components and a primitive contactor controller providing only three selectable levels of power. Its structure was aluminum tubing, with body panels of ABS plastic. Though owners generally liked the CitiCar, Consumers Union twice rated it "not acceptable" for lack of capability, comfort, convenience, and safety, and on account of brake failure in tests which appeared to be due to inadequate design.[6,7]

The ESB Sundancer and the CDA Town Car, the remaining two-passenger cars of Table 2.1, were developed by a major manufacturer of storage batteries and a trade association promoting the uses of copper [8,9] (in propulsion motors and brake drums). Both were intended to demonstrate the highest possible technical performance, but under different conditions. The Sundancer was designed and built to provide the "most favorable operating environment for the propulsion battery...with minimum aerodynamic, chassis, and inertial losses." A very small car with a battery weighing nearly as much as the rest of the automobile, the Sundancer was not intended for ordinary driving; it provided little luggage space and was hard to get in or out of. The Town Car, on the other hand, offered doors designed for exceptional access to the interior, good comfort and convenience, adequate space for parcels, and provisions for crash safety. Both of these cars had a front-mounted DC motor driving the front wheels, and a single longitudinal box girder as the principal structural member. Batteries were housed inside the girder on a roll-out tray, as shown in Fig. 2.4. Both were designed for very high electromechanical efficiency, with low rolling resistance from the tires and low aerodynamic drag. The Sundancer used the same specially-built tires as the GM 512. Two Sundancers were built, one with contactor speed control and the other with chopper speed control of the series-wound traction motor. The Town Car used a shunt motor with several different controllers combining contactor switching of battery voltage with chopper control of the motor field and armature. The Sundancer used a two-speed transmission, the Town Car a single-speed transmission.

All the four-passenger cars of Table 2.1 were conversions of conventional mass-produced automobiles. The Ripp-Electric, a very sophisticated conversion of a Datsun 1200, was built by a private individual for his own use.[10] Its series-wound DC motor replaced the original

15

Figure 2.4. Batteries Housed in a Structural "Tunnel"

internal-combustion engine in the front of the car, with drive through the
original clutch and four-speed manual transmission to the rear wheels.
Twenty 29-kg (65-pound) batteries were mounted in the available spaces
in the original engine compartment and luggage compartment. Heavy-duty
suspension components and tires were substituted for the original equipment to handle the battery weight, which was almost equal to that of the
entire original car. The transformerless charger and transistor controller
of this car weighed only 18 kg (39 pounds). The charger operated at an
average efficiency of 95%, far above the 65-75% of most available battery
chargers. The controller was capable of effective regenerative braking
down to almost zero speed, almost entirely avoiding loss of energy in the
friction brakes during stops. No other cars of Table 2.1 but the Mars II
included regenerative braking (though it was later added to the Town Car).

The Electric Vehicle Associates Metro and the Mars II of Electric Fuel Propulsion were both conversions of Renault automobiles offered by small manufacturers to the public.[11,12] Both drove the rear axle through the original transmission, a three-speed automatic for the Metro and a four-speed manual for the Mars II. Both used DC series traction motors mounted in place of the original gasoline engines. The spaces originally provided for engine and luggage were filled with the propulsion motor, controller, and batteries. The longer range of the Mars II was in part due to the larger battery with which it was equipped. The advantage of the additional range was offset by poor handling resulting from the "excessive weight and adverse weight distribution" of the lead-acid batteries.[13] In all, the car was encumbered with twenty batteries weighing almost 42 kg each.

The electric cars in Table 2.1 have certainly demonstrated the potential of useful range: as much as 120 kilometers in urban driving and 200 kilometers at a constant moderate speed. In comparison, the average automobile in the United States is only driven about 50 kilometers per day. These cars also exhibited adequate speed for highway travel: except for the three neighborhood cars which begin Table 2.1, all the rest could reach or exceed the legal speed limit in the United States, 88 kilometers per hour. Beyond this, the cars have shown that comfort, convenience, simplicity of operation, and a wide range of styling are all within reach of the recent state of the art. On a preliminary basis, at least, these cars demonstrate that electric automobiles could be widely useful.

On the other hand, they also indicate that electric cars are heavy and sluggish in comparison with conventional gasoline automobiles. Gasoline engine systems suitable for these cars would weigh no more than the electric motors and controllers with which they were actually equipped. Thus the entire weight of batteries is extra weight which comparable conventional cars would not carry. In the case of the Sundancer and the Mars II, the battery weight added 88% to the car weight without batteries—

which would be nearly the weight of the same car with a gasoline engine. Except for the GM 512, which used special batteries to achieve high performance with low weight (batteries which have never been offered for sale), the other cars carry batteries adding 47% or more to their basic weight. The sluggishness of the cars, partly the result of the battery weight, is evident in the time required to accelerate from zero to fifty km/hr (31 mph). These times, from 12.5 to 19.9 seconds, are similar to those in which conventional standard and subcompact cars ordinarily accelerate from zero to almost twice the speed (97 km/h, or 60 mph). Thus the electric cars achieved only about half the acceleration of conventional cars.

The cars of Table 2.1 demonstrate that there are a variety of designs and components which are promising and likely to prove acceptable. This has certainly been true of conventional internal-combustion cars, which are presently offered with front and rear-wheel drive, front and rear-mounted engines, longitudinal and transverse engine orientation, diesel and gasoline engines, and so on. Similarly, the electric cars included both front and rear drive and motor placement, with batteries under the seats, in central structural tunnels, or under front and rear decks, together with a variety of speed controls, a variety of motors, automatic and manual transmissions offering one to four speeds, and so on.

The cars of Table 2.1 also reflect different design objectives. It is these as much as technical factors which determine differences among the cars. None of the designers attempted to compete in range or acceleration with internal-combustion cars. All offered less payload: the three conversions retained four-passenger seating but sacrificed luggage space, while the two-passenger cars sacrificed half the usual passenger capacity in order to obtain small size, convenience in urban use, and the lower cost of a smaller vehicle. The two-passenger cars, which received so much attention in the last decade, alone offered costs potentially lower than those of conventional cars offered in the marketplace. They also offered much less capability, but the four-passenger cars, which offered interior accommodations similar to those of conventional cars, offered lower range and speed at higher cost than their conventional competitors.

With improvements in automotive technology, in electric motors and controllers, and in propulsion batteries, the cars of the future should do much more than those of the past decade. The important factors in car design and ultimate limitations on performance are reviewed in the remainder of this section. In subsequent sections, detailed projections are made for future batteries and improved electric cars which would use them.

2.2   UNDERLYING DESIGN CONSIDERATIONS

The basic electric propulsion system is illustrated in Fig. 2.5. It includes the battery in which all propulsion energy is stored, a controller which regulates and conditions the electric power supplied by the battery, a motor to convert the electric power into rotary motion, a transmission to match the speed of the rotary motion to that of the axle, and a differential which balances the power supplied to each driven wheel.

In designing an electric car, the battery is first chosen to supply sufficient energy for a required driving range and sufficient power for required acceleration and hill-climbing, at the lowest possible cost.

Once the battery is chosen, the remaining elements of the propulsion system are selected and matched for optimum performance—that is, the most favorable combination of low weight, high efficiency, and low cost. In this selection, as the recent cars of Table 2.1 illustrate, there are many reasonable possibilities.

Two of the major components of Fig. 2.5, the transmission and differential, may actually be eliminated. The transmission ordinarily

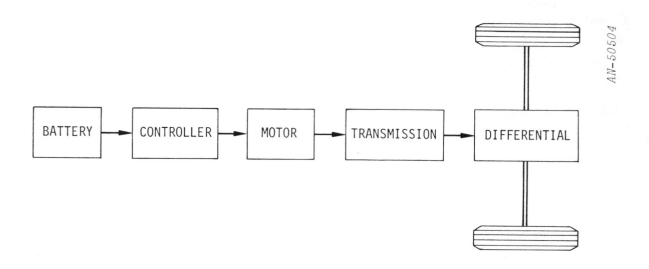

Figure 2.5. The Basic Electric Propulsion System

---

reduces the speed of the motor by one of several selectable ratios. It
is unnecessary if the motor is initially designed to operate over a speed
range which is wide enough and low enough. In the design process, the
weight, cost, and losses of the transmission must be compared with the
extra weight, extra cost, and reduced efficiency of a motor designed
for a wider, lower range of speeds. The differential may also be eliminated,
by the use of separate motors for each driven wheel. Again, the weight and
cost of the differential must be compared with the extra weight and cost
of the two-motor system, which also may require two transmissions.

Motors and Controllers

The controller and the motor may be built in various ways, but in
each case they must be appropriately matched. DC commutator motors have
been most popular to date, but the brushes require occasional maintenance
and limit the practical operating speed. AC brushless motors require virtually

no maintenance and can operate at much higher speeds, enabling more power to be extracted from a given weight of motor. Offsetting these advantages, however, is their requirement for a relatively complex and expensive controller, which must electronically perform switching functions analogous to those of the brushes and commutator of the DC motor.

The controller for DC motors has historically been a simple arrangement of contactors in which large electromechanical switches connect batteries and resistors in various combinations to regulate power input to the motor. Contactor controllers have been simple and inexpensive, but they do not provide continuously variable control and they do require some maintenance. Semiconductor "chopper" controllers interrupt the current from the battery at a high frequency with a variable "on" time, enabling continuous control of average power with high efficiency. Semiconductor inverters convert DC power from the battery to AC power which is usually variable in both frequency and voltage. Either silicon-controlled rectifiers (SCRs) or large transistors may be used in semiconductor choppers and inverters, which require few electromechanical components and may be designed for very long life with little or no maintenance. The SCR circuits, the usual choice to date, have been relatively heavy and expensive; transistor systems made possible by improved semiconductor technology promise major reductions in both weight and cost.

Though electric motors and controllers have not been optimized for automotive use or automotive mass production, they nevertheless perform very well today. An engineer of the Ford Motor Company put it this way:

> The traction motor and electrical controls required for
> electric vehicle propulsion have reached a very high
> degree of sophistication and present almost no problems--
> technical or economic--to hinder electric vehicle develop-
> ment.[14]

Nevertheless, it does not appear that electric motors and controllers will be either cheaper or lighter than comparable ICE (internal-combustion-engine) systems for automotive propulsion unless they provide substantially lower output power. Table 2.2 summarizes characteristics of electric motors and controllers suitable for propulsion of a subcompact automobile. Table 2.3 offers for comparison the characteristics of several ICE engine systems. Both tables include examples of both current and future technology.

In Tables 2.2 and 2.3, the output per kilogram of today's commutator motor with chopper controller is only 60% of that for a typical V-8 automotive engine, and the future electric motor-controller systems are not dramatically better. Though they match or surpass recent automotive diesel systems, they fall far short of improved gasoline and diesel systems which may be achieved in the future.

The cost of the current V-8 system in Table 2.3 was estimated to be about $6 per kW, substantially less than the costs of any electric motor-controller system in Table 2.2.[14] In both cases, costs are factory costs; they are roughly half the final sales price paid by the consumer. The efficiencies of the electric systems are dramatically higher than those of the ICE systems, but this is only part of the story. Losses in the storage battery, the charger, and the power plant have not yet been considered (nor have losses in refining and transporting petroleum, though they are generally much smaller). Efficiencies shown are for operation at rated speed and load; they drop substantially at lower speeds and loads.

Batteries

Unlike electric motors and controllers, batteries do present major problems to hinder the development of electric vehicles. With the batteries now available, designing an electric car is much like what designing a conventional automobile would be if a tankful of gasoline weighed over 60 kg per liter (500 pounds per gallon), roughly 85 times its actual weight. Besides weight, the available power and the cost of energy stored also pose difficulties. A few simple calculations, described in the following paragraphs, lead to the comparisons of battery-electric and conventional power systems in Table 2.4.

22

TABLE 2.2

AUTOMOTIVE ELECTRIC MOTORS
(30 kW or 40 hp output; with controller)

	Weight, kg		Typical Efficiency, percent	Specific Output, kW/kg	Specific Cost Dollars/kW
	Motor	Controller			
DC Commutator Motor-SCR chopper	114	41	85	.19	13
AC Induction Motor-2-phase inverter	27	82	85	.27	17
Ford Disc Motor-SCR Chopper	44	68	84	.27	11

Source: Ref. 14

TABLE 2.3

AUTOMOTIVE INTERNAL-COMBUSTION ENGINES
(with battery and pollution controls)

1975 Engines	Weight, kg	Maximum Efficiency, percent	Specific Output, kW/kg
150-hp (112-kW) V-8	291	27	.39
80-hp (60-kW) Diesel	255	32	.23
150-hp (112-kW) Advanced Rotary Engines			
Stratified Charge	186	29	.60
Diesel	289	35	.39

Source: Ref. 15

TABLE 2.4

TYPICAL CHARACTERISTICS OF BATTERY-ELECTRIC

AND CONVENTIONAL POWER SYSTEMS

	Electric Drive[*]	ICE Drive[**]
Mechanical Energy Output per kg of Energy Storage, MJ	.085	7.2
Mechanical Power Output per kg of Power System, kW	.062	.325
Cost of Mechanical Energy Output, cents per MJ[†]	6.02	2.8

[*]1976 premium golf-car batteries, DC traction motor and chopper controller (85% efficiency)

[**]Gasoline in tank, typical 1975 V-8 engine (20% efficiency)

[†]For gasoline at $.20 per liter ($.75 per gallon), electricity at $.04 per kWh.

Combustion of a kilogram of gasoline releases about 48 MJ of energy as heat. In average driving, the efficiency of the ICE system is likely to be little more than 20%, rather than the 27% maximum shown in Table 2.3. As a result, about 9.6 MJ of mechanical energy are available from a kilogram of gasoline. Even if the gasoline tank adds a third to the gasoline weight, 7.2 MJ remains available per kilogram of gasoline and tank.

The batteries used in almost all of the electric cars of Table 2.1 are premium golf-car batteries. The ESB EV-106, the battery used most, weighs 29.5 kg, provides about 6 volts, and can supply 75 amperes for 106 minutes before the output voltage drops below 5.25 volts. If discharged over a nominal period of two hours, it delivers about 27 watt-hours per kilogram, or .1 MJ/kg. With a motor-controller system of 85% efficiency, .085 MJ of mechanical energy may be obtained from each kilogram of battery. This is little more than 1% of the mechanical energy available from a kilogram of gasoline in a tank. Put another way, today's golf-car batteries weigh 85 times as much as a tank of gasoline providing equal energy to the drive wheels.

The power output of a battery is also limited. Golf-car batteries have an internal resistance of roughly 1 milliohm per 2-volt cell. Maximum power output is obtained with an equal load resistance, at a current of some 1000 amps and a cell terminal voltage of near 1 volt. Since each golf-car battery has three cells, maximum battery output is roughly 3 kW (1000 amps at 3 volts) or about 100 W/kg.

With a motor-controller operating at 85% efficiency, the battery can then provide only .085 kW/kg of mechanical power. The current V-8 ICE system, in comparison, can produce .39 kW/kg, or 4.6 times as much. And allowances for the additional weights of the motor and controller have yet to be included.

At .23 kW/kg, the motor and controller weigh 4.34 kilograms per kilowatt of electrical output. At 85% efficiency, 1.18 kilowatts of electrical input is required per kilowatt of output. The weight of battery required to produce 1.18 kW is 11.8 kg. Thus the battery-motor-controller combination weighs 16.0 kg/kW, and provides .062 kW/kg. If the weight of the V-8 ICE system is increased 20% to allow for a reasonable amount of gasoline and the necessary tank, its mechanical output is reduced to .325 kW/kg. This is 5.25 times that of the electrical system.

Besides limiting the energy and power available for electric propulsion, storage batteries make a major contribution to the cost of energy. Though its list price is considerably higher, the EV-106 golf-car battery is often purchased for a little over $40. Considering its salvage value, a net cost of $40 is reasonable. Discharged at the two-hour rate, the battery yields about .8 kWh, so its cost is about $50 per kWh of capacity, a common target in battery development programs. Since the life of the EV-106 is roughly 400 deep discharges, it can deliver at most 320 kWh during its life-time. The average battery depreciation is thus 12.5¢ per kilowatt-hour of output (3.5¢/MJ).

With battery charger efficiency of 90% and battery efficiency of about 75%, 1.48 kWh of electricity is required from the wall outlet for each kWh of battery output. At 4¢/kWh, about the national average for residential electricity, the electric power costs about 4.9¢/kWh of battery output, less than one-third of the total cost of 18.4¢/kWh for both power and battery depreciation. With a controller and motor operating at 85% efficiency, total cost is 21.7¢/kWh (6.02¢/MJ) of mechanical energy output.

For gasoline selling at 75¢/gal (19.8¢/liter), the cost of its 48 MJ heat energy is 26.7¢/kg. At 20% efficiency, the ICE system delivers 9.6 MJ/kg, so the overall cost of mechanical energy from gasoline is 10.1¢/kWh (2.8¢/MJ), less than half that of mechanical energy from the electric propulsion system.

Overall, electric propulsion systems are relatively limited as to the power and total energy which they can provide. At the same time, they provide this energy at relatively high cost. The end result is that present-day electric cars tend to provide less driving range, acceleration, payload, and accommodations than gasoline cars, at higher cost. Only if sacrifices in range and payload are considerable can overall energy requirements be reduced sufficiently to make today's electric cars less expensive than gasoline cars.

2.3   BASIC LIMITATIONS OF ELECTRIC CARS

The energy content of today's premium golf-car battery is about
.1 MJ/kg (in a two-hour discharge). If all this energy were used to lift
the battery itself, it would suffice for a vertical ascent of 10.2 km.

In practice, of course, only a fraction of car weight can be devoted
to battery, as the examples of Table 2.1 indicate. With a reasonable payload, perhaps 40% of car weight could be battery. Then battery energy of
.1 MJ/kg would suffice to lift the car vertically only 4 km if used with
100% efficiency. Motor-controller efficiency of 85% and transmission/
differential efficiency of 94% leads to only 80% efficiency overall,
however, which would limit the hypothetical vertical rise to a maximum of
3.2 km (10,500 feet).

The rolling resistance of a well-designed automobile can be as low
as about 1% of its weight, most of this due to the tires. At speeds low
enough so that aerodynamic drag is insignificant, the electric car could
thus travel 100 times as far on a level road as its hypothetical vertical
ascent, or 320 km. In practice, however, no one would drive such distances
at very low speed. In highway driving at a speed usually between 50 and
90 km/hr (35-55 mph), depending on car design, aerodynamic drag becomes equal
to rolling resistance. At this nominal speed, the potential range in highway
driving would be halved, to about 160 km.

Though this sort of calculation is simplistic, it is in reasonable
agreement with the performance of the longest-range electric cars of Table
2.1 and Fig. 2.2. The implication, borne out by detailed study of the individual cars themselves, is that the best of them have made good use of the
level of technology recently available. Significant technological advances,
not just new designs, will thus be necessary to improve electric cars substantially.

At the nominal highway speed, half the energy of the battery could be
used to traverse 80 km of road while the other half was used to reach an

elevation of 1600 m. In slow ascents of much shorter, steeper grades, relatively little distance would be traveled and much less energy would be used in overcoming rolling resistance and aerodynamic drag, so that the maximum ascent could be nearly 3000 m.

Table 2.5 summarizes these simple limitations on electric cars. They apply only for today's golf-car batteries, of course; if battery energy were to be doubled or quadrupled, the limits would rise proportionately.

TABLE 2.5

PRESENT LIMITATIONS OF ELECTRIC AUTOS

(with 1978 premium golf-car batteries
constituting 40% of car weight)

Maximum Range	
at low speed	320 km
at nominal highway speed	160 km
Maximum Ascent (change in altitude)	
at low speed	3,200 m
at nominal highway speed	1,600 m

2.4 OPPORTUNITIES FOR IMPROVEMENT

Though recent electric cars demonstrate the impressive potential of electric propulsion for useful travel, present technology clearly places them at a major disadvantage in performance and cost in comparison with conventional cars and their internal-combustion engines. Interest and activity are high, however, in vehicle and propulsion technology. Major improvements may be expected as a result.

There are three major areas for possible improvement in electric cars: batteries, propulsion systems, and the remainder of the vehicle. All promise valuable gains, but it is battery improvements which are critical to improving the competitive position of electric cars. Lighter-weight, lower-cost, lower-drag vehicles with tires of lower rolling resistance are highly desirable, but they would enhance the performance and economy of conventional and electric cars alike, little affecting the relative disadvantage of electric cars. Electric propulsion systems are already so effective that even if their weight, cost, and losses all were cut in half, improvements in electric cars would be relatively modest. For major improvements in performance and cost relative to conventional cars, then, better batteries will be crucial.

Future batteries, future auto technology, and their combined potential for improving the competitive position of electric cars are investigated in the following pages in quantitative detail. So also are the needs of typical drivers, since the performance advantages of conventional cars are vital only to the extent that they are used and enjoyed.

SECTION 2 REFERENCES

1. John Brennand, et al., <u>Electric and Hybrid Vehicle Performance and Design Goal Determination Study</u>, SAN/1215-1, General Research Corporation, August 1977.

2. <u>State-of-the-Art Assessment of Electric and Hybrid Vehicles</u>, NASA TM-73756, National Aeronautics and Space Administration, Lewis Research Center, Cleveland, September 1977.

3. L. Martland, A. E. Lynes, and L. R. Foote, <u>The Ford Comuta - An Electric Car for Use in City and Suburb</u>, SAE Paper 680428, May 1968.

4. James J. Gumbleton, et al., <u>Special Purpose Urban Cars</u>, SAE Paper 690461, May 1969.

5. Sebring-Vanguard, Inc., Sebring, Florida, Various brochures.

6. <u>Survey of 195 Electric Car Owners</u>, J. D. Powers & Assoc., January 1976-January 1977.

7. "The Electric Citicar," <u>Consumer's Review</u>, October 1976.

8. R. S. McKee, Boris Borisoff, F. Lawn, and J. Norberg, <u>Sundancer: A Test Bed Electric Vehicle</u>, SAE Paper 720188, January 1972.

9. Michael Pocobello and Dan Armstrong, <u>The Copper Electric Town Car</u>, SAE Paper 760071, February 1976.

10. W. E. Rippel and H. A. Frank, <u>Evaluation of W. Rippel's Electric Datsun 1200</u>, Jet Propulsion Laboratory, Report 900-759, Pasadena, October 1976.

11. Electric Vehicle Associates, Inc., brochure.

12. R. H. Aronson, <u>The MARS II Electric Car</u>, SAE Paper 680429, May 1968.

13. J. E. Greene, <u>A Summary Report on the Experimental Evaluation of the MARS II Electric Automobile</u>, Cornell Aeronautical Laboratory, VK-2623-K-2, Buffalo, New York, February 1969.

14. Lewis E. Unnewehr, <u>Electric Vehicle Systems Study</u>, presented at 3rd International Electric Vehicle Symposium, Washington, February 1974.

15. <u>Should We Have a New Engine? An Automobile Power Systems Evaluation</u>, Vol. II, Technical Reports, Jet Propulsion Laboratory, California Institute of Technology, Pasadena, 1975.

3   FUTURE BATTERIES

As Sec. 2 has shown, better batteries are crucial to the improvement and eventual success of the electric automobile. Projection of the characteristics of future batteries is thus the essential starting point for analyzing the prospects of future electric cars.

Though there are great uncertainties, the projected batteries in Table 3.1 cover the likely range of possibilities, from low through medium to high performance. Also included, as a point of reference, is one of today's premium golf-car batteries--the same battery used in most existing electric automobiles and discussed at some length as an example in Sec. 2. A graphical portrayal of projected battery performance appears in Fig. 3.1. It elaborates the single values of energy and power density in Table 3.1, showing how energy output varies with power output or the corresponding time of discharge of the battery.

The prospects of Table 3.1 are truly exciting: increases in energy density by a factor of nearly five, plus major increases in life. Together they might multiply the range of electric cars nearly fivefold and cut battery depreciation in half, dramatically relieving the principal disadvantages of electric drive.

Because the performance of future batteries may be as uncertain as it is important, this section begins with a discussion of the battery forecasting problem: how it was approached in this study, and why it may have arisen in the past. Then the prospects for future propulsion batteries are summarized from a review of the literature. From these prospects, the representative examples of Table 3.1 are next developed and discussed. The major assumptions are presented and the uncertainties discussed. Projections and predictions from the recent literature are frequently included to illustrate the range of opinion and uncertainty about the results of battery research and development.

TABLE 3.1

REPRESENTATIVE BATTERY CHARACTERISTICS

	Recent	Projected		
	Lead-acid 1976	Lead-acid 1985	Nickel-zinc 1985	Lithium/Aluminum metal sulfide 1990
Energy Density, Wh/kg (2-hour discharge) MJ/kg	27 .10	46 .17	77 .28	115 .41
Power Density, W/kg (peak)	100	150	200	150
Energy Efficiency, percent	75	75	70	70
Life, deep-discharge cycles	400	1000	600	800
Initial User Cost, $/kWh (1976 dollars)	50	40	60	50

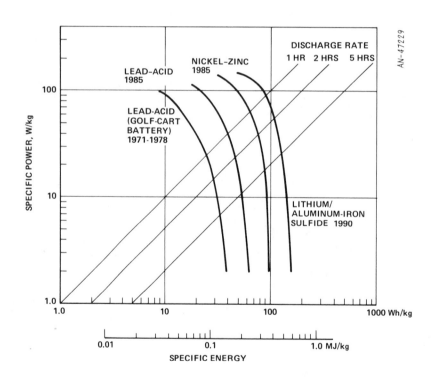

Figure 3.1. Power and Energy Densities of Representative Batteries

3.1 THE FORECASTING PROBLEM

Accurate forecasts of progress in battery development have apparently been either difficult or impossible. Far more than in most other fields, the literature abounds with predictions and projections which subsequently proved wrong.

In most cases, the errors were on the optimistic side. Where much progress was foreseen, little was actually achieved, at least so far as practical new batteries are concerned. Superficially, it might therefore seem that the best forecast would be simply a continuation of the status quo. But this too seems unrealistic in view of today's accelerating pace of battery development, the continued optimism of prominent authorities in the field, and the many different approaches which are now being pursued. Perhaps it is this abundance of prospects which is most heartening: with so many different approaches receiving serious attention, surely at least one will succeed. And only one breakthrough would be required to transform the prospects of electric cars.

To analyze the resultant prospects for electric cars, it would be possible to deal separately and completely with each promising type of battery. In practice, however, this is undesirable because there are too many batteries in the race which are too much alike from the standpoint of electric car development. Regardless of their internal workings, batteries of similar size, performance, and cost will lead to cars of similar capabilities and similar impacts on energy and the environment. Individual consideration of every promising battery would lead to a voluminous collection of performance and impact calculations differing little from one another. For the most part, any differences would be insignificant in relation to uncertainties in the projected performance of the batteries themselves.

This analysis takes an intermediate path in projecting battery and car characteristics for the future. It deals at length only with three prospective batteries, which are selected to represent low, medium, and high levels of future performance. Furthermore, it deals with these representative batteries in the simplest way, at the least level of detail necessary for reasonable calculations of electric car capabilities and impacts. It

33

focuses specifically on the capacity, life, and cost of representative batteries. To obtain reasonable values of these simple descriptors, it briefly reviews the published literature rather than reinvestigating in depth the problems and opportunities of the various battery development projects which are now underway.

Though reviewing the literature leads to useful estimates of battery characteristics, it has an even more important function: revealing the different opinions about probable characteristics held by different people, at different times. This sheds some light on an important question: how reliable are projections of future battery characteristics? Were it not for the need to address this question, it would suffice simply to quote projected characteristics for future batteries from a single source, such as the battery development program of the Department of Energy.

In reviewing the literature on battery development, it is especially useful to note some of the forecasts made in past years which have gone conspicuously awry. The projection of battery characteristics and development schedules has not been revolutionized by any new technique, data, or procedure, so the projection to be presented here is doubtless subject to the same weaknesses and uncertainties which have become clear over the years in previous forecasts and predictions.

The simple descriptions of future batteries to be developed in the remainder of this section treat the battery as a "black box." The minimum possible attention is paid to the inner workings of the battery; instead attention is confined to those overall descriptors which bear on the performance of the electric automobile. As a result, relatively little will be said about the practical problems in improving batteries, and the possible reasons for past overoptimism and present uncertainties about better batteries. Though these alone could easily fill volumes, only a brief review can be offered here of the nature of the electric storage battery and the possible reasons for persistent overoptimism about future improvements.

Basically, a battery is an electrochemical system for storing energy in chemical form and releasing it as electricity upon connection of an external electrical load. In primary batteries (such as flashlight dry cells), the chemical reaction is not reversible: once the energy of the chemicals manufactured into the battery is released, the life of the battery is over. Secondary batteries (storage cells), in contrast, can be electrically recharged: passage of an electric current from an external source through the battery regenerates the chemical compounds inside which store the energy, returning the battery more or less to its original fully-charged condition. Because they provide electric energy at much less overall expense, secondary batteries are almost without exception the only reasonable candidates for electric propulsion of automobiles.

The basic chemical components of a battery are two active materials and an electrolyte. During discharge, these components react to form new chemical compounds, releasing energy which is available as electricity for external use. In some ways the process is parallel to energy storage in gasoline. When gasoline is burned with oxygen from the air, it also forms new chemical compounds and liberates energy. The energy released, however, is in the form of heat, not electricity, which is an important disadvantage. Transforming heat to mechanical energy for automotive propulsion is relatively complex and inefficient. Moreover, the chemical products of the reaction are not contained and reused; instead, they are discharged as pollutants into the atmosphere.

The simplest secondary batteries are easily demonstrated. Two strips of lead immersed in a beaker of dilute sulfuric acid become a lead-acid battery when "formed" and charged by repeated passage of an electric current from one plate to the other. The chemical reactions are identical to those in the lead-acid batteries which are used by the millions for automotive starting, lighting, and ignition; for golf cars and mine locomotives, for stand-by power in telephone exchanges, and a host of other applications. The simple cell in the beaker, however, is a very long way from practical application. It demonstrates the potential of the lead-acid system, but is shows little of the practical problems involved in manufacturing batteries with high capacity per unit weight and long service life.

In a practical lead-acid battery, the active materials are not thin layers developed electrically on sheets of solid lead; this would be impractical. Instead, the active materials are spongy masses into which the electrolyte penetrates, reaching the immense surface areas necessary for rapid chemical action and release of stored energy. The active materials are held in place by lead grids, into which they are applied as a paste during manufacturing. The lead in the grid is not intended to enter into the chemical reactions of the battery; its function is to support the active materials in place, and to conduct electricity to or from them. The plates are placed close together to minimize the total volume of the battery and the weight of electrolyte required. Porous separators are placed between them to hold the active material in place and prevent internal short circuits which could discharge electrically the stored energy in the battery. The plates and separators are placed in a container which retains the electrolyte, supports the internal components, and protects them from unwanted external effects. Finally, conductors are provided to connect positive and negative plates with one another and with terminals accessible from outside the container.

In recent lead-acid batteries, the weight of the substances actually reacting during full discharge to produce electricity may be well under twenty-five percent of total battery weight. Additional active materials and electrolyte, plus grids, connectors, terminals, and container, make up all the rest. They are thus crucial in determining the battery's weight and cost. But their weight and cost are not easy to reduce, because they are also crucial to the service life of the battery.

During a single discharge or recharge, active materials in considerable volume are transported through the electrolyte and separators as ions moving between positive and negative plates. New compounds are simultaneously formed or reformed at the plates and in the electrolyte. For long life, these processes must be so accurately reversible that even after hundreds or thousands of cycles, recharging will still make the original quantities of active material available for use, in the same accessible physical form and location.

The difficulties in this are numerous. The compounds formed during cycling do not occupy the same volumes as those they replace, nor do they assume precisely the same shape. Surface area gradually decreases and active material is gradually dislodged from the plates or even deposited in the separators, diminishing capacity and eventually leading to short circuits between adjacent plates. Active material may be deposited on plates in a crystalline form highly resistant to further utilization ("sulfation"). At the same time, there may be undesired chemical reactions: corrosion of grids, for example, which weakens them and raises their electrical resistance and consequent losses. Moreover, plates, grids, connectors, and containers are all subject to mechanical failure induced by the vibration and shock of normal vehicular service--or by overcharging or excessive depth of discharge.

Developers of improved lead-acid batteries address all these problems, and more. Unfortunately, the obvious steps to reduce weight and cost also reduce service life, so their task is not easy. Developers of other advanced batteries begin by selecting new active materials from the host of possible combinations which are generally more energetic and potentially capable of storing more energy per unit weight. But to make the potential a reality, all the practical problems--support, separation, containment, interconnection--must be solved afresh, and the more reactive the materials of the battery, the more difficult it may be to contain and separate them, and to prevent corrosion and dissolution.

It is relatively easy to choose an electrochemical couple, to calculate its theoretical energy density, to add an allowance for extra active material, electrodes, separators, conductors, and containers, and thereby to arrive at an attractive projection of energy density. On the other hand, it is impossible to foresee all the practical problems which will limit the performance and life of these components, or the methods by which these problems may be solved--let alone predict the weight and cost. Especially where service life is concerned, theory is incomplete and experiment is exceptionally demanding. Controlled life tests require expensive equipment and may take months or even years to reveal the effects of a single simple change in battery material, design, or manufacturing procedures.

This may be the basic source of overoptimism about batteries: it is so much easier to foresee the potential performance than the implicit practical problems.

3.2   FUTURE BATTERY POSSIBILITIES

Sources of Information

The prospects for battery-electric automobiles were investigated in the mid-sixties and again in the mid-seventies by the United States Congress in connection with bills for electric car research and development.[1,2] Statements made to Congressional committees by acknowledged experts provide a fruitful source of battery information; but even more important, the public and government interest manifested in the hearings led to a number of informative technical symposia.[3-6] Many of the papers at these symposia specifically addressed the probable characteristics of future batteries.

The recent acceleration of research on electric vehicles and batteries is evident in a collection of three bibliographies published in 1970.[7] During the period 1926-66, citations appeared at an average rate of 41 per year. From 1966 to 1968 the rate tripled, to 136 per year. And from 1968 to 1970 it doubled, to 267 per year.

Especially during the past 10 years, systematic review of battery and electric car prospects has been popular. Twenty such reviews of US battery and car status were examined for this report,[8-27] as were ten reviews of foreign status.[28-37]

Numerous papers on individual types of batteries have also appeared during the past decade, along with review papers on groups of closely related types. An assortment of both types of papers was examined for data not presented in the broader surveys of electric vehicle and battery prospects.[38-60] Finally, individuals involved in battery R&D programs were contacted directly to obtain supplementary appraisals, opinions, and technical data.

Although a considerable part of the literature was surveyed, this brief review neither covers all important publications of the decade nor arrives at any new conclusion. To do so would probably be impossible. As one observer noted in 1968 after the first recent resurgence of interest in electric cars, "A fantastic number of technical papers has resulted... In fact, it is almost impossible to say anything on the subject which has not already been printed."[15]

Battery Descriptors

The purpose of the battery projections developed here is to support analysis of the impacts of the wide use of electric cars. Accordingly, it is not necessary to give highly detailed descriptions of future batteries. The descriptors that bear strongly on impact calculations include:

- Specific energy. Energy per unit weight available from the battery

- Specific power. Power per unit weight available from the battery

- Operating life. Number of deep discharge cycles obtainable before battery energy storage falls below a given fraction of its rating; or number of years of service expected in automotive propulsion

- Cost. Initial cost to the user

- Energy efficiency. Ratio of energy provided by the battery during discharge to energy required to restore the battery to its fully charged condition

- Key materials. Quantities of potentially scarce or imported materials required per unit of battery capacity

The first two descriptors are required to determine the range of the electric car in urban driving, and to assure that it can keep up with traffic. The next two descriptors are required to estimate the life-cycle cost of the battery, which can be a critical factor in the life-cycle cost of the entire electric car. The next-to-last descriptor is required for calculations of the overall energy requirements of the electric car. The last descriptor is required to determine the adequacy of materials production and resources for large numbers of electric cars.

Certain additional descriptive data is required for batteries with special requirements such as operation at elevated temperatures, which can influence both life-cycle cost and energy efficiency.

The Future State of the Art

Possible storage batteries are commonly identified by their active materials and electrolytes. The number of interesting possibilities is large. As shown in Table 3.2, 26 different cells were found worthy of individual description, discussion, and comparison in a recent review. Since authoritative summaries of cell and battery construction and operation abound in the literature, no attempt will be made here to describe all the promising possibilities.[10,21,25,27]

To proceed beyond surveys such as that of Table 3.2, it is necessary to quantify battery system prospects according to the descriptors listed above. A major step in this direction is provided by a recent survey which produced Table 3.3.[27] For the eight systems of Table 3.2 judged most promising, it provides both recent and projected estimates of energy and power density, cycle life, and cost.

Important information, nevertheless, is missing in Table 3.3: the dependence of energy density on power density. For most battery systems, the total amount of energy available decreases as it is withdrawn more rapidly. A recent graphic summary of this dependence is reproduced in Fig. 3.2.[25]

TABLE 3.2

SELECTED CANDIDATE SECONDARY BATTERIES

Battery	Major Factors Affecting Possible Use	Near-Term Prospects 0-5 Years	Long-Term Prospects 5-15 Years
Lead-Acid	Low cost; better energy density and life needed	Excellent	Good
Nickel-Zinc	Need improved cycle life	Fair	Good
Zinc-Bromine	Need separator for long activated stand	Poor	Fair
Nickel-Iron	Uncertain cost	Good	Good
Nickel-Cadmium	High cost, limited cadmium supply	Poor	Very Poor
Nickel-Hydrogen	Cost and hydrogen tank weight	Good	Good
Zinc-Chlorine Hydrate	Weight, cost and reliability	Poor	Fair
Zinc-Air	Weight, cost and life	Poor	Poor
Aluminum-Air	Rechargeable aluminum electrode	Poor	Fair
Iron-Air	System complexity, cost, life	Fair	Good
Lead-Air	Weight and life	Very poor	Very poor
Sodium-Sulfur	Solid separator, life, cost	Fair	Good
Sodium-Phosphorus/Sulfur	Solid separator, life, cost	Poor	Fair
Sodium-Selenium	Limited selenium supply, cost, improved energy density	Very Poor	Poor
Lithium-Sulfur	Improved sulfur electrode, life	Poor	Good
Lithium-Chlorine	Improved energy density	Poor	Good
Lithium-Tellurium Tetrachloride	Improved energy density	Poor	Good
Lithium-Selenium	Limited selenium supply, cost, improved energy density	Poor	Fair
Aluminum-Chlorine	Improved aluminum electrode	Poor	Good
Lithium-Phosphorous/Sulfur	Improved sulfur electrode, life	Poor	Good
Magnesium-Chlorine	Requires more basic research	Very poor	Poor
Calcium/Barium-Chlorine	Requires more basic research	Very poor	Poor
Calcium-Nickel Fluoride	Improved solid electrolyte doping, better electrode geometry	Very poor	Fair
Lithium-Sulfur Dioxide	Cost, high rate capability	Poor	Poor
Lithium-Lamellar Structure	Cost, high rate capability	Poor	Poor
Antimony Redox	Requires more research and development	Poor	Fair

Source: Ref. 21.

TABLE 3.3

POTENTIAL ELECTRIC VEHICLE BATTERIES

Batteries			Current (January 1976)				Projected			
Systems	Electrolytes	Temp. °C	Wh/kg	W/kg (peak)	Cycle Life	Cost $/kWh	Wh/kg	W/kg (peak)	Cycle Life	Cost $/kWh
Near Term (1-2 years)										
Lead-Acid (SOA)	Aq. H_2SO_4	Room Ambient	30	50	700	100	50	150	>1000	60
Ni-Fe	Aq. KOH	Room Ambient	44	110	<800	1800	60	150	>1000	120
Intermediate Term (3-5 years)										
Lead-Acid (Advanced)	Aq. H_2SO_4	Room Ambient	–	–		–	50	150	>1000	60
Ni-Zn	Aq. KOH	Room Ambient	77	110	200	800	110	150	>1000	50
Long Term (5 years)										
(Zn,Fe)-Air	Aq. KOH	Room Ambient	80-120	40	<150	2000	90	80	>1000	60
Li-metal sulfide	Aq. $ZnCl_2$	Room Ambient	<66	<60	<100	<2000	130	150	>1000	50
Li-MS	LiCl-KCl eutectic	400-450	100	120	<250	<2000	150	300	>1000	40
Na-S	β-alumina	300-350	90	100	<200	<2000	170	200	>1000	40

Source: Ref. 27

43

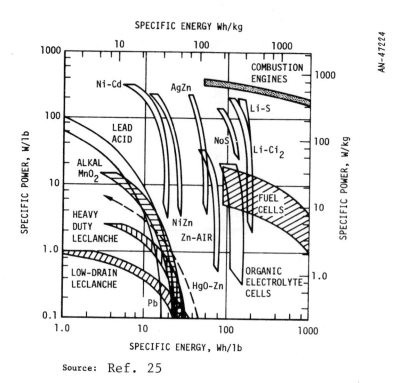

Source: Ref. 25

Figure 3.2. **Performance Capability of Various Battery Systems**

Figure 3.2 shows specific power versus specific energy for various battery systems, both secondary and primary. In addition, it shows specific power versus specific energy for typical combustion engine systems and for fuel cells. In the range of 10 to 50 W/kg, a power level at which electric car batteries are frequently operated, it is clear that, for lead-acid batteries, the available energy is less than that obtainable at very low power by a factor of 2 or more.

The broad bands for each battery system in Fig. 3.2 are usually interpreted as representing the range of design alternatives for given electrochemical couples. A single trace for a particular battery may also be presented in the same format. With technological advance, such traces and the bands including them tend to move up and to the right, yet there seems to have been relatively little change over the years.

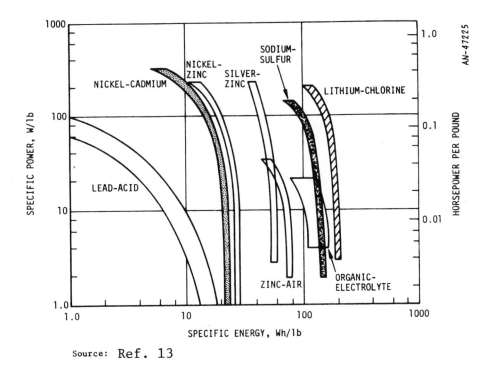

Source: Ref. 13

Figure 3.3. Specific Power versus specific Energy for Batteries

---

Figure 3.3 is a similar chart published in 1967 in the
then-definitive study of electric vehicle prospects carried out by a
distinguished panel of experts.[13,14] It was used to display the prospects
of future battery systems and, with an overlay (Fig. 3.4), to show how
battery characteristics were related to range at constant speed for a
hypothetical electric car. The reasoning is so graphic and persuasive
that it has become a regular part of surveys of battery and electric
car prospects.

Evidently there is little difference between Figs. 3.2 and 3.3.
Neither, unfortunately, includes the lithium-metal sulfide battery
systems which figure prominently in Table 3.3. These are included,
however, in another recent survey devoted entirely to high-temperature
batteries.[47] It provides the specific power-specific energy relations
of Fig. 3.5, which suggests that some of the lithium systems may be almost
as dependent on discharge rates as are lead-acid batteries.

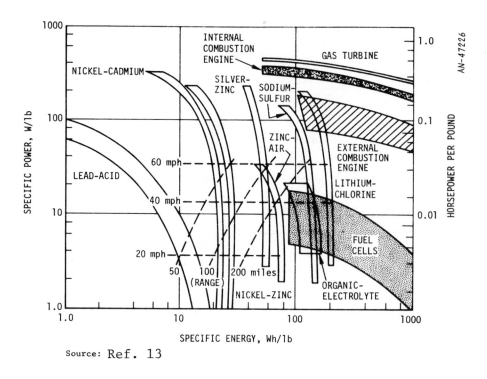

Source: Ref. 13

Figure 3.4. Vehicle Requirements and Motive Power Source Requirements

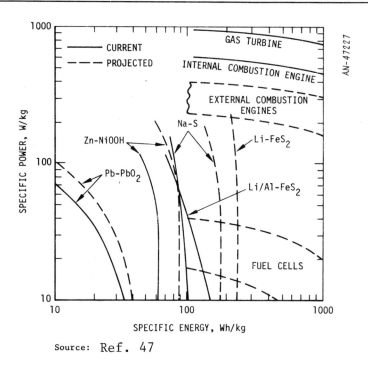

Source: Ref. 47

Figure 3.5. Specific Energy Versus Specific Power for Various Systems

Another important piece of information lacking in Table 3.3 is energy efficiency. Since energy efficiency depends on usage, and particularly on the manner of recharging, accurate estimates can generally be made only for specific combinations of battery charging and conditions of use. The literature frequently provides efficiency estimates; though their conditions are not fully defined, they usually are in the range of 70-80% except for the nickel-iron systems, which are likely to be perhaps 15% less, and for the metal-air systems, which may be 30% less.

It is implicitly assumed in Table 3.3 that the future batteries included are relatively likely to achieve the indicated performance--that is, likely relative to the many systems which are not included. But even though all the included developments may be judged reasonably likely, their probabilities of success are almost surely unequal. At least one survey has offered subjective estimates of the probability of success, as shown in Table 3.4.[22]

The prognosis of Table 3.3 comes from a government source, but there is little reason to expect that industry would view future prospects very differently. An industry viewpoint of less recent origin, presented in Table 3.5, differs only in its omission of the metal-air battery systems.[24] It is interesting that the metal-air systems were included in Table 3.4 with high estimated probability of success--and that both Tables 3.4 and 3.5 originated within the same company, though several years apart. It is also to be noted that the projections of Table 3.5, advanced in 1974, have already proven overoptimistic.

R&D Programs

Those battery systems being actively investigated appear most likely to be developed successfully for vehicular use. Thus the allocation of R&D effort by battery system is important in considering and selecting battery systems for impact calculations. In this section, the thrust of propulsion battery R&D is briefly summarized for the US and several foreign nations.

TABLE 3.4

FUTURE BATTERY SYSTEMS AND PREDICTED PROBABILITY OF SUCCESS

Battery	Projected Energy Density Wh/kg	Projected Power Density W/kg	Anticipated Probability of Success[*]
Nickel-zinc	90	80	60%
Zinc-air	100	100	60%
Sodium-sulfur	175-330	200-350	25%
Lithium-sulfur	250-350	550-800	20%
Lithium-chlorine	330-450	200-400	1%

[*] That is, for the system to be available commercially at the indicated values and at prices competitive per energy unit to the industrial type lead-acid battery.

Source: Ref. 22.

TABLE 3.5

ENERGY SOURCE COMPARISON
(PROJECTED CHARACTERISTICS AND AVAILABILITY)

Battery	Wh/kg	W/kg	$/kWh	Cycle Life	Projected Availability
GROUP I					
Lead-acid	35-40	55	20-50	300-200	Now
Nickel-iron	44-66	132	20-30	300-400	1976
Nickel-zinc	66-88	165	20-25	250-350	1977
GROUP II					
Zinc-chlorine (hydrate)	132	132	10-20	500[*]	1978-79
Lithium-sulfur	132-176	220	15-20	1000[*]	1980-85
Sodium-sulfur	176-220	220	15-20	1000[*]	1980-85

[*] Nominal life based on current experimental models.

Source: Ref. 24.

Estimated funding for US battery R&D in 1972 and 1975 is shown
in Table 3.6, by battery type. Even after allowance for inflation, a
considerable increase is evident. In 1975 about half the funding came
from industry, with the remainder primarily from the Federal government.
While the industrial effort was spread across the entire set of systems
tabulated, government support was heavily concentrated in high-temperature
battery development.

Since 1975, government battery R&D has been expanded in both breadth
and total volume. It is actively pursuing all the systems in Table 3.6.
These are the systems (singled out earlier in Table 3.3) judged most promising at the Department of Energy, the agency responsible for battery
development.

TABLE 3.6

BATTERY R&D FUNDING IN THE USA

Battery System	Millions of Dollars	
	1972	1975
Lead-acid	} 1.0-1.5	2.3
Nickel-iron		.5
Nickel-zinc	} 1.5-2.0	1.3
Metal-air		2.15
Zinc-chlorine		.5
Lithium/Aluminum- metal sulfide	} 1.5-2.5	5.0
Sodium-sulfur		3.2
TOTAL	4.0-6.0	15.0

Sources: Ref. 19 and N. P. Yao, Argonne National Laboratories (private
communication)

Now, as in 1972, battery development is pursued for either or both of two reasons: load-leveling for electric utilities, and propulsion of on-the-road vehicles. In many instances it is impossible to identify a research effort with one or the other of these eventual applications, since the same technological developments often serve both almost equally. In Table 3.6, funding is for both.

In Japan there have been two programs of importance for electric vehicle development in the past decade. In 1968, an electric vehicle committee was formed with membership drawn from electric power companies, electric machinery companies, automobile companies, and battery companies.[28,29] Nineteen electric vehicle prototypes were operated, most with lead-acid or nickel-cadmium batteries. One, however, employed a nickel-zinc alkaline battery rated at 45 Wh/kg (20-hour discharge). In 1971, a government-sponsored program was formed with a budget of about $18 million for a five-year period.[30,34] About $7 million was allocated to battery development, and the remainder to vehicle systems. During the first three years, advanced lead-acid, metal-air, and sodium-sulfur batteries were built and tested. Results of tests in 1974, and goals subsequently adopted for 1977, are summarized in Table 3.7. Considerable improvement in cycle life is sought; the 1974 tests showed lifetimes of generally fewer than 100 cycles, except for the lead-acid batteries.[36]

A program of action for electric vehicles was reported on to the government of France several years ago.[35] Aimed at improving environmental quality, reducing air pollution, and improving urban circulation through the use of electric vehicles, it called for employment of nickel-zinc and zinc-air batteries until 1990, with sodium-sulfur batteries and fuel cells thereafter. Specific battery development goals are summarized in Table 3.8. A more recent report of status and prospects in France un-equivocally endorses the circulating zinc-air battery and the sodium-sulfur beta-alumina batteries as the principal contenders for energy

TABLE 3.7

BATTERY DEVELOPMENT GOALS,
JAPANESE NATIONAL ELECTRIC VEHICLE PROJECT (1971-1977)

Battery Type	Developer	Module Size (kWh)	1974 Achievement Sp. Energy[8] (Wh/kg)	1977 Goal Sp. Energy* (Wh/kg)	Cycle Life
Pb-Acid (Multilayer Electrode)	Japan Storage Battery	1.80	70		
Pb-Acid (Porous Sheet Electrode)	Shin-Kobe Electric	1.68	64	>50	>500
Pb-Acid (Bipolar, Circulating System)	Yuasa	2.00	61		
Zn-Air (Fixed Electrolyte)	Japan Storage Battery	1.25	123		
Zn-Air (Circulating Electrolyte)	Sanyo Electric	2.40	91	>80	200-300
Fe-Air	Matsushita	1.56	88	>70	200-300
Na-S	Yuasa (Toshiba)	2.81	90	NA	NA

---

*Specific Energy values correspond to a 5-hour discharge rate for Pb-acid and Na-S batteries and a 7-hour discharge rate for metal-air batteries.

Source: Ref. 36

TABLE 3.8
BATTERY DEVELOPMENT GOALS RECOMMENDED IN FRANCE

Type	Specific Energy, Wh/kg*	Specific Power, W/kg	Cycle Life	Energy Efficiency, percent	Development Time, year
Nickel-zinc	70	250	500	70	2
Zinc-air	120	100	800	50	6-8
Sodium-sulfur	200	200	1000	80	10-15

---

*Two-hour rate

Source: Ref. 35

storage in future electric vehicles.[56] The French government identified
no foreseeable electric vehicle market in France, however, and subsequently
curtailed its support for battery research and development.

In West Germany, a study of the potential feasibility and desirability of electric automobiles was completed in 1975 and, together with a
recommended development program, submitted to the government.[33] A plot
of its more promising battery systems is reproduced here as Fig. 3.6.
Though nickel-zinc batteries are not shown, a thorough report on a prototype vehicle propulsion battery yielding 45 Wh/kg at the two-hour rate
was given in early 1975.[40] It concluded that only further testing in
vehicles was required to prove the desirability of this battery. A more
recent survey from Germany, however, complains there has been "little
information officially published"--but finds in this "lack of information"
a certain "indication of progress."[37]

Considerable activity has been reported in other nations. Nickel-
zinc, nickel-iron, and iron-air batteries are under development in Sweden.[48]
The sodium-sulfur battery development in Great Britain has already begun
road testing in vehicles and has been judged "ahead of the programs in
the US" with respect to "development of an economically viable product."[48]
One important factor in viability is, of course, the cost of competing
fuels. In Europe, where governmental action raises gasoline prices
through heavy taxation rather than lowering prices through controls,
gasoline prices are two to three times those now prevailing in the US.

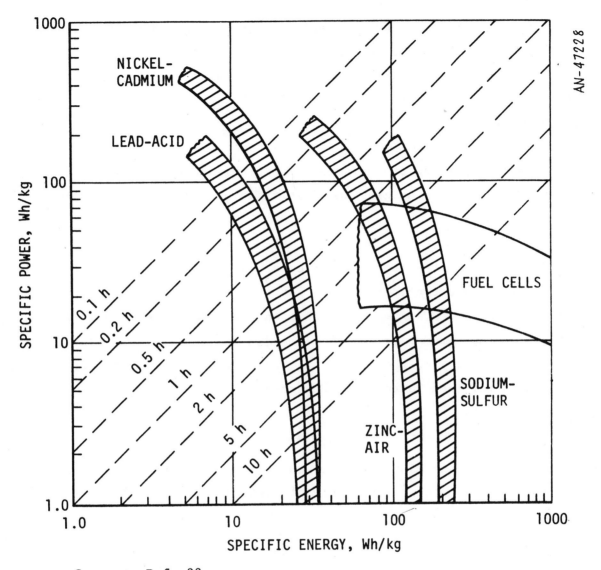

Source: Ref. 33

Figure 3.6. Battery Performance Foreseen in West Germany

3.3 REPRESENTATIVE FUTURE BATTERIES

Representative future batteries are selected and characterized in this section. The selection and characterization is intended to show the range of electric car performance which the future may bring, and to serve as a basis for calculating the impacts accompanying the wide urban use of such cars.

Characteristics of the selected batteries were summarized in Table 3.1 and Fig. 3.1. Their origins and justifications are explained below.

Selection

The object of selecting particular batteries is to support realistic and relevant impact calculations. For this purpose only a few representative examples are needed, examples which span the spectrum of possibilities. To the extent that groups of future batteries are similar according to the descriptors of Sec. 3.2, there is little to be gained in lengthy recalculation of impacts for each battery in the group.

The characteristics of batteries affect impacts primarily in these ways:

- By determining the reasonable driving ranges of the cars, and hence their degree of applicability to the needs of urban drivers

- By determining energy consumption through their efficiency and through the weight they add to the basic automobile

- By determining requirements for particular materials not ordinarily used in cars which may be in limited supply

- By determining an important part of the initial and life-cycle costs of owning an electric car

Selection of representative batteries for impact calculations should span the spectrum of these possibilities, rather than enumerate systems which--even though they might be considered very likely to be developed--differ very little in energy capacity or cost.

At the low-performance end of the battery spectrum are lead-acid systems. There are two possibilities for selection as representative: the existing golf-cart batteries now widely used in electric automobiles, and advanced propulsion batteries being developed expressly for automotive use. Both are included in Table 3.1. The existing golf-cart battery, though developed for another purpose, is the best production battery available today for electric cars; it serves as a firm reference to which possible improvements in batteries may be compared. The advanced lead-acid battery, though it has yet to be developed, promises so much more in energy density and operational life that it would drastically improve the range and economy of electric automobiles; thus it deserves separate consideration.

At the other end of the spectrum of future performance, as shown in Figs. 3.2-3.6, are the high-temperature systems, such as those based on sodium-sulfur and lithium/aluminum-metal sulfide. As Fig. 3.5 shows, the lithium systems seem ultimately to offer the greater potential. Moreover, as Table 3.6 makes clear, in the United States the lithium systems have recently been ahead in the competition for financial support. In most respects influencing impacts, there is little to distinguish this system from the sodium-sulfur system: goals for energy and power density, life, and cost are reasonably similar--at least in relation to current uncertainty about when and if the goals for either of these systems will be attained. Accordingly, the lithium/aluminum-metal sulfide system is selected here as representative of the high-temperature, advanced-battery systems.

This leaves one or more representatives of the mid-range of performance to be selected. The leading candidates from Tables 3.3 and 3.6 are nickel-iron, nickel-zinc, zinc-air, and zinc-chlorine. Among these systems, nickel-zinc is nearest to midway in energy and power density between lead-acid and lithium/aluminum-metal sulfide. Moreover, nickel-zinc systems have been frequently recognized as the leading contender for intermediate performance in the intermediate term. An independent observer (at NASA) of the battery development scene stated that nickel-zinc batteries are "the most likely candidate to replace lead-acid."[23] The nickel-zinc development work by Gould, Inc., has led the vice-president and president of that company to optimistic predictions:

> I'm confident, however, that the technology exists to solve the nickel-zinc cycle-life problem, and undoubtedly nickel-zinc will become an important new battery for electric vehicle application.[24]

> I'd say we have a 75% chance of being able to produce these [nickel-zinc batteries] commercially within three years.[41]

Officials at DOE, equally encouraged, also foresee high probabilities of success in their current development of improved nickel-zinc batteries.[*] A study for the government of France foresaw nickel-zinc batteries reaching a life of five hundred 80% discharges in two years, and an involved researcher commented that it was reasonable to assume future lifetimes of 1000 cycles, with energy densities fifty to a hundred percent greater than lead-acid batteries.[35,56] A nickel-zinc battery developed in Germany several years ago needed only vehicular testing to confirm its worth.[40] In Japan, a nickel-zinc battery was undergoing road test several years ago.[29]

Given the high levels of interest, optimism, and activity which are evident world-wide in nickel-zinc batteries, selection of this system to represent the mid-range of future battery performance seems most appropriate.

Among the candidate battery systems of Table 3.3 which were not selected, the nickel-iron and metal-air batteries seem initially less desirable because of their lower energy efficiency. In other present or prospective performance characteristics, they offer only one unique feature from the standpoint of impact calculation: they employ materials which are more abundant than those of the selected batteries. The zinc-

---

[*] Private communication, N. P. Yao, Argonne National Laboratories, 1976.

chlorine system also uses plentiful materials, and it does not labor under an efficiency disadvantage; but its development status in Table 3.3 is clearly less advanced: despite appealing projected performance, its current levels in the table come nowhere near those of nickel-zinc.

Lead-Acid Batteries

Projected power and energy density are shown in Fig. 3.7 for a representative lead-acid battery which could be available in quantity around 1985. For comparison, other curves are presented in Fig. 3.7 to describe current production batteries and high-energy prototypes which have actually been operated in electric cars. Also shown are goals of recent government development efforts. These were adopted in 1976 by the Energy Research and Development Administration (ERDA) for batteries to be in pilot production in 1978-80.

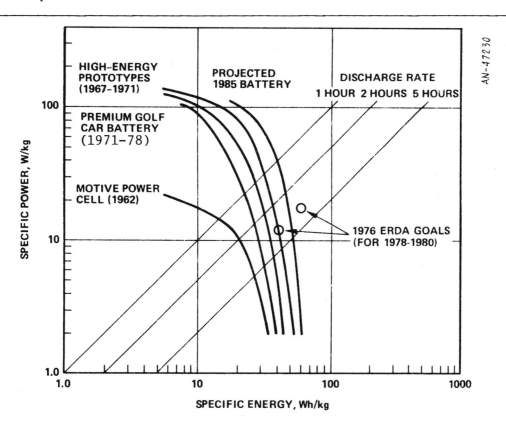

Figure 3.7. Performance of Lead-Acid Propulsion Batteries

The currently available motive power cell in Fig. 3.7 is intended for industrial truck service. It provides very long service life, 1500-2000 deep-discharge cycles, but at relatively low energy and power density. Despite a relatively high cost due to high materials cost per kWh of storage and limited production volume, its long service life makes it economical overall. Its low power and energy densities, however, almost preclude its use in an automobile of reasonable performance. The source of the curve shown in Fig. 3.7 is a data sheet dated 1962.[61]

The premium golf-car battery in Fig. 3.7 is the ESB EV-106. At a cost of lower cycle life it provides much higher energy and power density than the motive power cell.* The premium battery of a leading competitor, Gould, Inc., offers virtually equal performance.[62] The EV-106 battery was introduced in 1971.

High-energy prototype batteries for golf car and electric car service were developed and tested in electric cars in 1969 and 1971. The lower performance battery prototype described in Fig. 3.7 is the ESB LEV-115, a laminar-grid design for which very high cycle life has been reported.[39] This battery has not been commercially marketed, apparently because premium batteries have captured a disappointingly small share of the golf-car market. The higher performance prototype battery was developed by Delco specifically for use in an experimental urban electric car, the GM 512 discussed in Sec. 2.1.[64,65] Though it is described as a deep-cycle battery, its life has not specifically been reported.

As shown in Fig. 3.7, the power versus energy density projected for the representative 1985 battery is somewhat beyond that of the prototypes built five years ago, falling midway between the goals set by DOE in its current procurements for development of an "improved state-of-the-art" battery and for development of an "advanced" lead-acid

---

*Private communication, J. F. Norberg, ESB, Inc., Philadelphia, 1976.

battery for automotive propulsion.[*] It follows projections developed in
some detail at ESB in 1975 as a basis for a proposal to improve lead-
acid battery performance to a high level for automotive propulsion.[**]
These projections explored the possible improvement of two different battery
designs, one based on the pasted-plate construction of the EV-106 golf-
car battery, the other based on the tubular-plate construction of the
motive power cell. It appeared that either approach could reach the level
of performance indicated in Fig. 3.7 and at the same time extend life to
1000 deep cycles.

The energy and power densities of Fig. 3.7 are somewhat optimistic
in that they include no weight allowance for battery mounting or thermal
management. It appears, however, that under 5% of battery weight will
suffice. In the recent Town Car built for the Copper Development Association,
for example, the battery tray weight for 490 kg of golf-car batteries was
only 6.8 kg (1.4%).[†] A roller system facilitating quick battery change
added 10.4 kg (2.1%). Even during range testing, battery temperature in
this car never rose substantially above ambient, demonstrating that forced
cooling is not necessary. Insulation to keep battery temperature up for
good performance in cold climates seems desirable, however. To keep the
490 kg of batteries at 25°C in an ambient of 0° with no other heat than
that released in the battery during typical charge-discharge cycling would
require about 7 kg of inexpensive fiber insulation (1.4% of battery weight).
Air flow from car motion could provide the necessary cooling in hot weather.

According to a standard reference on lead-acid batteries, "A fair
average for the efficiency of the lead battery under ordinary operating
conditions is about 75 percent."[65] This level has been assumed in Table 3.1

_____

[*] Private communication, N. P. Yao, Argonne National Laboratory, May 1976.
[**] Private communication, J. F. Norberg, ESB, Inc., Philadelphia, March 1976.
[†] Private communication, Dan Armstrong, Triad Services, Dearborn, Michigan,
August 1977.

for the 1985 battery, though in practice it seems certain to vary substantially depending on conditions of charging and discharging. Figures 3.8 and 3.9 show how the voltage and current of typical lead-acid cells vary with charging and discharging. Evidently the difference between charging and discharging voltage--sometimes termed the voltage efficiency of the cell--varies greatly depending on the rate of charge or discharge and the state of charge. The average voltage during charging will depend importantly upon the characteristics of the battery charger used, as well as the depth to which the battery has been discharged. Discharge voltage will similarly depend on rate and state of discharge.

Additional inefficiency arises from the need for overcharge--returning to the battery more ampere-hours than were taken out during discharge. Since individual cells of a battery differ, most must be overcharged if the least efficient cell is to be brought up to full charge. If it is not fully charged, it may be fully discharged or even reversed if the battery is deeply discharged, leading to premature failure.

A standard reference says that "normally, a 10 to 20 percent overcharge is recommended to assure full charge of all cells and to prevent battery sulfation."[22] Assuming the lesser figure, and using a typical voltage efficiency figure, leads to an estimate for overall energy efficiency of 77-78 percent, close to the figure of 75 percent adopted for the representative 1985 battery.[66] Considerably higher figures might be attained if full or equalizing charges were not administered every day; this might be possible in automotive service where the full range of the car was seldom used. On the other hand, lower figures could easily result under charging systems which may be employed to speed charging or to prolong battery operating life. In an experimental evaluation of alternative charging systems, energy efficiencies as low as 60 percent were reported during the working life of the battery.[67] Charging methods in this study included the currently popular modified-constant-potential method and two methods dependent on measurement of gas evolution

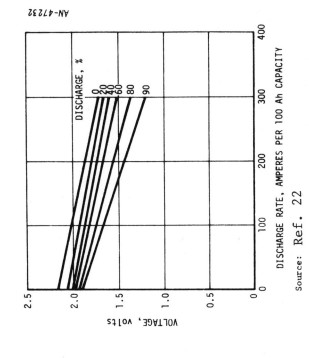

AN-47232

DISCHARGE, %

0
20
40
60

80

90

DISCHARGE RATE, AMPERES PER 100 Ah CAPACITY

Source: Ref. 22

Figure 3.9. Lead-Acid Battery Discharging
Voltage Per Cell Versus Discharge Rate

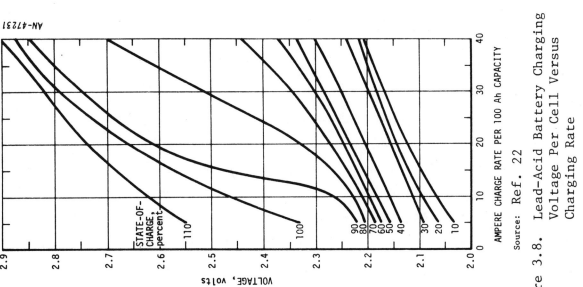

AN-47231

STATE-OF-
CHARGE,
percent

110

100

90
80
70
60
50
40

30

20

10

AMPERE CHARGE RATE PER 100 Ah CAPACITY

Source: Ref. 22

Figure 3.8. Lead-Acid Battery Charging
Voltage Per Cell Versus
Charging Rate

(which accompanies overcharge and excessively rapid charge). In only
one of six reported cases did measured energy efficiency reach the value
of 75 percent assumed for the representative 1980 battery.

The operating life of a lead-acid battery may depend more on how it is
charged and maintained than how it is discharged. Achievement of the thousand-
cycle life assumed here for the representative 1985 battery will require
battery charging equipment which ensures proper treatment depending on
battery age and conditions of daily use. The assumption of 1000-cycle
life is based on the goals adopted in 1976 for ERDA-supported battery
development, the recent ESB study and proposal for major improvements in
automotive propulsion batteries, and a second, independent opinion from
another major battery manufacturer.*

Further assumptions about battery life are necessary for automotive
propulsion, since shallow rather than deep cycling is to be expected.
Average daily driving in the US is about 50 km (30 mi). Future lead-
acid battery cars are likely to have a range capability of 100-150 km
(60-95 mi), however, in order to be able to handle occasional driving
days which require much more than the average. For a maximum range of
150 km, the average daily driving would result in an average cycle depth
of only 33 percent. Accordingly, life must be estimated at this and
other cycle depths which may be typical in the future.

Figure 3.10 presents the relationship assumed here for the future
lead-acid battery between cycle depth and operating life. Also shown
is the relationship which corresponds to a constant total energy output
from the battery during its life, independent of cycle depth. This
relationship is frequently assumed, since little is available from which
to derive an empirically based relation. It appears that for lead-acid

---

*Private communication, Warren Towle, et al., Globe-Union, Inc., February
1976.

62

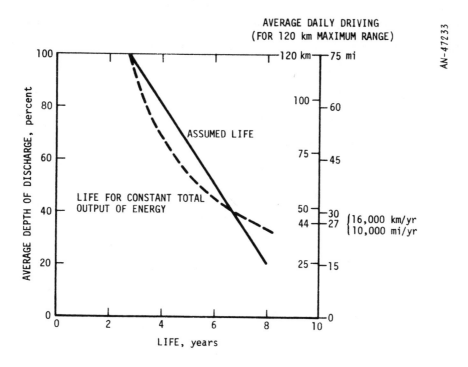

Figure 3.10. Assumed Life of Representative 1985 Lead-Acid Battery in Automotive Service

batteries of this type, however, very deep cycling is especially detrimental to battery life, so that initial reductions in cycle depth from the nominal 100 percent depth may improve life more than proportionately. Eventually, however, further decreases in cycle depth will not prolong the life of the battery, because failure mechanisms such as corrosion, which continues even without cycling, become the limiting factor. Thus the simple linear relationship assumed in Fig. 3.10 departs as might be expected from the constant-energy-output assumption.

At an average daily use of 50 km (30 mi), battery life in a car with 120-km range would be about 7 years for either the assumed linear relation between life and cycle depth or the constant-energy-output relation. The linear relation would be slightly more conservative for longer-range cars, and slightly less so for shorter-range cars.

The recent actual cost of the premium golf-car battery of Fig. 3.7 to the user (who might typically buy in quantities of 10 to 20 batteries in order to outfit an electric car) is in the range $40-$55, or $1.36-$1.87 per kg. The cost per kilogram of the representative 1985 battery is expected to be in the same range (in 1976 dollars), assuming mass production.[*] (The golf-car battery is now manufactured on a much smaller scale.) Owing to the higher energy content per pound of the 1985 battery, its price per kWh is considerably lower; even at $1.87 per kg, the upper end of the price range for current batteries, it would be only about $40. The initial goal of the DOE development was set in 1976 at $50 for 1980 batteries.

About 22 kg of lead and .5 kg of antimony are required for the current golf-car battery per kWh of capacity (at the two-hour rate of discharge).[*] The 1985 battery would require approximately 13 kg of lead and .2 kg of antimony per kWh of capacity, assuming a low-antimony design. Supply of other battery materials is unlikely to pose problems, even with general use of electric cars.

Nickel-Zinc Batteries

Power density versus energy density is shown in Fig. 3.11 for several nickel-zinc propulsion batteries. The West German "DAUG" battery (a prototype built by the Deutsche Automobilgesellschaft Forschungslaboratorium) was ready for road tests in vehicles in 1975.[40] The other two batteries were projected by Gould, Inc., in 1974 as objectives of an active nickel-zinc development program.[68] Possible production dates for these batteries were recently estimated as 1977 and 1979.[**] The 1977 projection is very close to that shown in Fig. 3.5 as a future possibility. Also shown for comparison in Fig. 3.11 is the goal set in 1976 for ERDA development of nickel-zinc batteries to be in pilot production in 1980.[†]

---

[*] Private communication, J. F. Norberg, ESB, Inc., Philadelphia, 1976.

[**] Private communication, R. Fedor, M. Obert, and C. Menard, Gould, Inc., April 1976.

[†] Private communication, N. P. Yao, Argonne National Laboratories, May 1976.

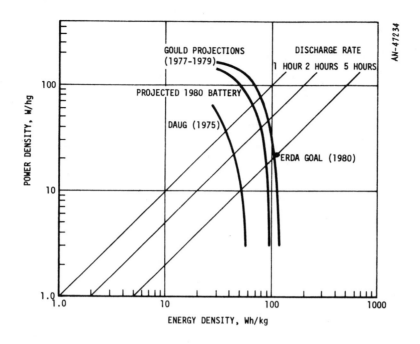

Figure 3.11. Performance of Nickel-Zinc Propulsion Batteries

The lower in performance of the two Gould projections has been
adopted for this study as descriptive of the representative nickel-zinc
battery which could be in mass production in 1985. It lies between the
reported DAUG achievement and the ambitious ERDA goal, in the range
which Gould suggests may be more cost-effective.

The energy efficiency estimated previously by Gould for the nickel-
zinc battery in automotive service was 70%.[68] This is bracketed by reported
observations of energy efficiency on the DAUG battery: 72.3% for a ten-
hour discharge and 65% for a two-hour discharge.[40] The latter is closer
to the conditions of automotive service. A 17% overcharge is recommended
for the DAUG battery in contrast to the 10% overcharge assumed for the
1980 lead-acid battery. The higher efficiency of the lead-acid battery--
75%--may be attributable to this difference.

The cycle life of the representative 1985 nickel-zinc battery is projected to be 600 cycles, midway between current laboratory accomplishments and optimistic long-range projections. DAUG reports less than 20% capacity loss for small nickel-zinc cells after 400 deep-discharge cycles. Gould projected, from laboratory tests, a 400-cycle life (to 60% capacity) for the 1979 battery.[68] A French study and projection foresaw a 500-cycle life within reach of a two-year development program.[35] A French developer stated that "it is reasonable to assume that lifetimes in excess of 1000 cycles under practical conditions will be eventually obtained."[56] The ambitious goal of the DOE development effort is 1000 cycles.

With shallower cycling, the cycle life of the 1985 nickel-zinc battery is assumed to be inversely proportional to cycle depth. This amounts to assuming that the total number of kilowatt-hours which the battery will deliver over its life is independent of cycle depth. As yet, supporting data for this or any other similar assumption has apparently not been published. Informally, however, Gould engineers indicate that overall energy output will be substantially greater for shallower discharges than for full discharges, so the constant-energy assumption appears conservative.

The cost goal for the Gould nickel-zinc development is the same cost per kilowatt-hour of capacity as for lead-acid batteries designed for comparable service. In Table 3.5, this cost for lead-acid batteries is $20-$50 per kilowatt-hour. The upper figure is close to the 1974 estimate for future nickel-zinc batteries provided by Gould, assuming recycling and a 2:1 ratio of user cost to manufacturing cost.[68] In Table 3.5, possibilities of lower cost than for lead-acid batteries are clearly implied. A French investigator, however, states "...a major difficulty is system capital cost, which will be at least 50% higher per watt-hour than that of lead-acid."[56] This, however, neglects the salvage value of the used battery, which is considerable due to the amount of valuable nickel present. It should be noted that though nickel electrodes are well-developed and understood (for the common nickel-cadmium battery),

66

there may be room for improvement. A new method of manufacture is claimed for the electrodes of the DAUG battery which reduces nickel use and cost by about half for a given capacity. For the representative 1985 nickel-zinc battery, a user cost of $60 per kilowatt-hour is projected, 50% above that for the 1985 lead-acid battery.

About 3.3 kg of nickel, 3.5 kg of zinc, and .05 kg of cobalt are required per kWh of nickel-zinc battery capacity.[*] Other battery materials are unlikely to be scarce.

Lithium/Aluminum-Iron Sulfide Batteries

Figure 3.12 shows specific power versus specific energy for various high-temperature lithium cells.[**] It also shows specific power and energy projections for a complete lithium/aluminum-iron sulfide battery, packaged for use in an electric car.

The lowest performance curve in Fig. 3.12 describes cells recently tested at Argonne National Laboratories. It is essentially identical to the curve in Fig. 3.5 for current $Li/Al-FeS_2$ cells.

The highest performance curve in Fig. 3.12 is projected for cells with molten lithium cathodes rather than solid lithium-aluminum cathodes. Eventually, if the difficult engineering problems in such cells are solved, they may provide very high performance. The level shown is like that for similar cells in Fig. 3.5, except for limited high-power capability.

The performance of lithium/aluminum-metal sulfide cells is expected to be improved considerably during the next few years. Figure 3.12 also shows an intermediate level of cell performance considerably higher than that of the current cells. This level is expected to be reached in 1981.[**]

---

[*] Private communication, Richard Steiner, Gould, Inc., April 1977.

[**] Private communication, A. A. Chilenskas, Argonne National Laboratories, July 1976.

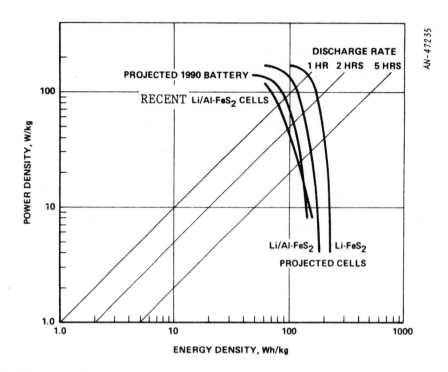

Figure 3.12. Performance of Lithium-Iron Sulfide Propulsion Batteries

Tables 3.9 and 3.10 show steps in the expected development leading to such cells, together with anticipated cell characteristics other than specific energy and power.

Table 3.10 makes it clear that the weight anticipated for an assembled battery is considerably higher than that of its cells alone. This extra weight is required for a package providing proper thermal control plus support structure and interconnections for charging and discharging. Figure 3.13 shows conceptually how the individual cells of the 1981 battery might be connected and maintained at operating temperature. In addition, a steel outer enclosure is required for structural support and assurance against spilling battery materials in the event of accidents.

The weight goal for the hardware required to assemble the cells into the complete battery package is 100 kg for 1981 in Table 3.10, or 33%

TABLE 3.9

PERFORMANCE GOALS FOR INDUSTRIALLY FABRICATED Li/Al-FeS$_2$ CELLS

Performance Goal	1976	1978	1981
Specific Energy, Wh/kg	75	100	160
Peak Power,[*] W/kg	75	100	200
Energy Efficiency, percent	70	70	75
Lifetime[**]			
Deep discharges[***]	200	400	800
Automobile cycles	600	1,200	2,400
Equivalent kilometers	32,000	64,000	129,000
Years of use	2	4	8

---

[*] 15-second pulse; cell discharged to 50% capacity at approx. 4-hr rate.

[**] Lifetime based upon a deep discharge equivalence of 160 km; automobile cycles based upon 5 cycles/week at 32 kilometers/cycle and one cycle/week at 160 km/cycle (16,000 km/year)

[***] Deep discharge is equivalent to 70% utilization of the active electrode materials.

Source: Ref. 52

TABLE 3.10

PERFORMANCE GOALS FOR Li/Al-FeS$_2$ BATTERIES

	1978	1981
Cell Weight, kg	300	300
Battery Weight, kg	400	400
Battery Output at Terminals		
Energy, kWh at approx. 4-hr rate	30	49
Peak Power, kW (15-second pulse)	29	59

Source: Ref. 52

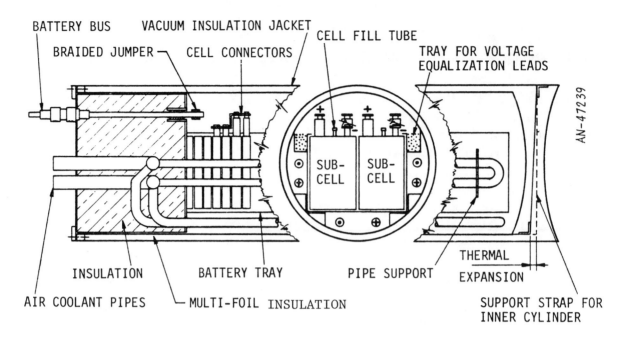

BATTERY BUS
VACUUM INSULATION JACKET
BRAIDED JUMPER
CELL CONNECTORS
CELL FILL TUBE
TRAY FOR VOLTAGE EQUALIZATION LEADS

SUB-CELL   SUB-CELL

AN-47239

INSULATION
BATTERY TRAY
PIPE SUPPORT
THERMAL EXPANSION

AIR COOLANT PIPES
MULTI-FOIL INSULATION
SUPPORT STRAP FOR INNER CYLINDER

Source: Ref. 52

Figure 3.13. Sectional View of 30 kWh Li/Al-FeS$_2$ Vehicle Battery

---

of cell weight. This is enough so that hardware weight must be factored into the cell performance shown in Fig. 3.12 in order to get reasonable estimates for a complete high-temperature battery system. The 1990 battery projection shown in Fig. 3.12 is based on the assumption that hardware will add only 25% to basic cell weight, reducing specific energy and power by 20% relative to that for the 1981 Li/Al-FeS$_2$ cells. This may be optimistic, but optimism is warranted since no adjustments of specific energy and power were made for lead-acid and nickel-zinc batteries, though hardware might add 5% to their weight.

Given the 25% addition to cell weight for associated hardware, the energy density and power density stated in Table 3.1, 115 Wh/kg at the two-hour rate and 160 W/kg peak, may be calculated from the 1981 goals for cells in Table 3.9.

The goal for energy efficiency of the Li/Al-FeS$_2$ cell shown in Table 3.9 for 1981 is 75%. This presumes that operating temperature is maintained exogenously in the proper range, about 380°-450°C. In a vehicular battery, however, the energy required to maintain this temperature will be part of the total required recharging energy. If it exceeds internal cell losses during normal operation, recharge requirements will be increased, reducing the apparent efficiency of the battery system below the basic 75% cell efficiency.

The rate of heat loss estimated for the complete battery system of Table 3.10 was 250 W, or 6 kWh (21.6 MJ) per day.[52] In the absence of internal heat release, the battery temperature would drop about 3°C per hour, or 72°C per 24-hour day.* Without use, deliberate battery heating would be required from its stored energy after about 24 hours. In ordinary use, however, there will be heat released internally each day owing to cell losses while the battery is being charged and discharged. If this is sufficient, it alone will maintain battery operating temperature in the desired range. Otherwise, supplementary energy for this purpose must be drawn from the source of recharge power.

Thus the basic cell efficiency of 75% represents an upper limit on the overall efficiency of the lithium/aluminum-metal sulfide battery system. The lower limit, of course, is zero since over 20 MJ of energy per day must be supplied to maintain battery temperature during prolonged periods when the car is not driven at all.

On an average day, cars are driven about 50 km. At .5-.8 MJ per km, appropriate to advanced electric cars, some 25 to 40 MJ of battery output will be required. Given a fixed energy loss of 20 MJ per day through the insulation, battery system efficiency will be from 44 to 67 percent.

---

*Private communication, A. A. Chilenskas, Argonne National Laboratory, 1977.

Precise figures depend on a number of factors such as:

- Car design range and test weight, which determine energy required per km

- Battery size, insulation efficiency, and resultant rate of heat loss

- The distribution of daily driving distance, which determines the frequency and amount of energy inputs required solely to maintain battery temperature

At the current preliminary stage of battery enclosure design and optimization, it seems inappropriate to model these factors in detail. Instead, it is simply assumed that enclosure performance will be substantially improved and that the average efficiency of the battery system will be 70% by 1990, when volume production is first assumed.

A life goal of 800 deep-discharge cycles, or 8 years in typical automotive use, is advanced in Table 3.10. Though this requires that recent lifetimes be quadrupled, it is a goal already based on considerable experience and testing. Though optimistic, it is adopted in Table 3.1. It is further assumed that within the maximum life of eight years, cycle life is inversely proportional to cycle depth, as for the nickel-zinc battery. Again, insufficient information is available to substantiate this or any alternative assumptions.

The cost goal for the $Li/Al-FeS_2$ batteries has been stated elsewhere as \$20-\$40 per kWh of capacity.[51] This is an OEM price (a selling price for large quantities direct from the manufacturer), not a user cost. A detailed study of manufacturing costs for similar cells for the utility load-leveling application arrived at an estimated selling price of \$29.16 per kWh including a reasonable allowance for return on invested capital.[50] A reduction of about 10% may be possible owing to a new manufacturing technique utilizing lithium sulfide, a cheaper source of lithium, rather than metallic lithium in initial cell construction.[51] The cost of the necessary battery hardware is expected to raise the total price per kilowatt hour for the vehicle battery to the vicinity of \$35/kWh.

Assuming a 50% markup for resale to the car owner, the value implicit in the lowest recent selling prices for current lead-acid batteries, leads to a price of $50/kWh.

Materials required per kWh of battery capacity include 380 g of lithium, 270 g of molybdenum (used as the positive current collector), 90 g of cobalt (used in the positive electrode), and 50 g of yttrium (used in insulators).[*]

Assumptions and Conditions

For all the representative batteries, it is assumed that three potential problems will be fully resolved: maintenance, safety, and size.

Most electric vehicles to date have required substantial routine maintenance of their batteries. At intervals of a week or two, it has been necessary to check the electrolyte level in every cell, adding water as necessary. In the larger cars with batteries of fifty to sixty cells, this has been no small undertaking. Moreover, it has required ready access to the top of each cell, which has imposed requirements and limitations on placing and mounting the battery in the vehicle. In addition, cleaning of the battery compartment, terminals, and cell covers has been necessary to minimize the corrosion which can result when droplets of electrolyte containing sulfuric acid are discharged through the individual cell caps of the battery.

For future batteries, it is assumed that this maintenance will be virtually eliminated, either by sealed construction in the case of the high-temperature battery, or by a single-point watering and venting system for the aqueous-electrolyte batteries. In this system, water would be conveyed as needed to individual battery cells from a single reservoir which might be filled once a month. Vapors from individual cell vents would be ducted to a single point for discharge outside the battery

---

[*]Private communication, J. E. Battles, Argonne National Laboratory, April 1977.

compartment without danger of corrosion. Such systems have been introduced by both German and Japanese battery makers.

The safety problem to be solved is battery integrity in crashes. Partly this is a problem for the automotive designer who provides the battery compartment and surrounding structural protection. Partly, however, it is the function of the battery case itself to prevent discharge of hazardous materials in a crash. The electrolytes of the lead-acid and nickel-zinc batteries are mildly corrosive and could be harmful. The molten salt electrolyte of the high-temperature battery system is much more dangerous: it is almost red-hot, and it may also react chemically with materials outside the battery.

Finally, it is assumed that the physical size of future batteries will be roughly equal to the size of present golf-car batteries of equal weight. Otherwise, it might be the space available in a practical electric car, rather than the weight-carrying capability, which would limit the maximum usable battery capacity and maximum car range. This assumption implies that the energy density per unit <u>volume</u> will be improved in future batteries about as much as is the capacity per unit <u>weight</u> shown in Table 3.1. This improvement is among the goals and expectations of the developers of all three representative future batteries, though in the past it has received relatively little attention in the literature.

Aside from these assumptions about maintenance, safety, and size, a number of favorable conditions are implicit in the characteristics which have been projected for representative future batteries. Under less favorable conditions, battery output and life would be impaired.

First, the batteries were assumed to be fully charged. At lower levels of charge, less power is usually available. Figure 3.14 shows this effect for existing lead-acid batteries, which when 80% discharged

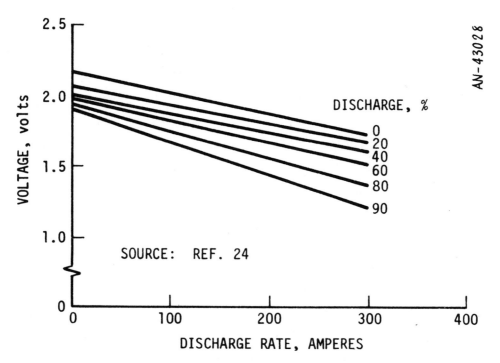

Figure 3.14. Lead-Acid Electric Vehicle Batteries, Voltage and Current Versus Percentage of Discharge for a 100-AH Battery Discharged at 6-hour Rate at 77°F

provide about 30% less voltage (and power) at 300-amp output current than would be available at full charge. Similar data has yet to be published for nickel-zinc and lithium battery systems, but there will probably be a similar effect. If the vehicle design includes a motor and controller designed to withdraw power from the battery at the maximum rate possible with a full charge, then the reduction in battery capability with discharge will be readily apparent. Many designs, however, provide motors and controllers which themselves limit vehicle performance, so that decreasing battery capability would only become apparent near full discharge.

Also implicit in the performance projections is like-new condition of the battery. As batteries age with use (or abuse), they lose both energy storage capability and power output capability. This would reduce the driving range of an electric car, and could reduce acceleration and hill climbing ability for cars designed to utilize the full power of the fully-charged battery. Little information is available for lead-acid batteries on this topic, probably because different mechanisms limit battery life depending on conditions of use. Generally, life is defined in terms of capacity reduction to 80% of rated capacity, but how actual capacity varies during life and how it is related to rated capacity is not always clear. For recent golf-car batteries, actual capacity commonly exceeds rated capacity for a substantial portion of cycle life, falling below the rating and approaching the 80% end-of-life figure only late in life.

Good care and treatment of the battery is also assumed in the projected lifetimes. This means that any necessary watering or other maintenance is provided, that very deep discharges and associated cell reversals are infrequent or entirely avoided, and that charging follows a favorable schedule. Very high rates of charging and either repeated overcharge or undercharge are harmful and impair the life of lead-acid batteries. This may also be expected for nickel-zinc batteries. "Smart" battery chargers which may be developed with modern integrated-circuit electronics should do much to assure long life if used regularly. For the lithium/ aluminum-metal sulfide battery, in which cells can tolerate no overcharge without permanent loss of capacity, a very sophisticated battery charger is essential. It will have to monitor the state of each individual cell and control individual charging currents accordingly to insure full charge without overcharge of any cell.

Alternatives and Uncertainties

The selections and projections of representative future battery systems offered here must be treated with caution and understanding. Other battery systems may prove preferable, and other levels of performance (even under ideal conditions) are very likely. To place these possibilities in proper perspective, this section offers comments and projections about the other promising systems of Table 3.3 which were not selected as representative future prospects.

Unfulfilled expectations for the first of these systems, nickel-iron, began with the first electric cars. In this instance, the authoritative predictions of a battery breakthrough were advanced by no less a figure than Thomas A. Edison. A history of early automotive development notes that although the electric auto was considered the ideal automobile for city use at the turn of the century,

> The weight of storage batteries remained inordinately heavy
> for the horsepower generated, and they still deteriorated
> rapidly. For years Thomas A. Edison had been rashly promising
> that he would soon develop an improved storage battery that
> would make the electric more practical than the gasoline
> automobile. At first Edison had been taken seriously, but
> by 1908 he was being ridiculed for his persistent failures.
> As Motor Age commented in 1908, "Mr. Edison's bunk has come
> to be somewhat of a joke--a real joke."[69]

History records that Edison did not succeed in making the electric car more practical than the gasoline; by the 1920s, electric cars were all but extinct in the marketplace. Yet Edison's nickel-iron battery was nevertheless a significant development, used extensively in ships, railway carriages, mine locomotives, and industrial tractors; and at the same time that Motor Age derided Edison's failure, an authoritative treatise on self-propelled vehicles reported that

> In relation to its weight, however, the Edison cell is
> very much more powerful than the average of other types...
> The average lead-acid cell yields between 4 and 6 watt-
> hours per pound weight [8.8-13.2 Wh/kg]. The Edison battery,
> on the other hand, yields 14 watt-hours per pound weight
> [30.9 Wh/kg].[70]

Futhermore, current authorities see prospects for nickel-iron rivaling or surpassing those of lead-acid systems, as shown in Tables 3.3 and 3.6. A continued development program at Westinghouse reportedly has demonstrated, in prototype batteries which have been road tested, the performance potential anticipated in Table 3.3.[*]

Another promising system of Table 3.3 not selected here is the metal-air system. In 1966, in a widely read article, an authoritative observer noted that

> The battery problem is the principal obstacle that has discouraged serious consideration of the electric automobile all these years....
>
> The innovation that now makes the electric automobile thinkable is a device called the air battery....
>
> Experiments have already demonstrated that with zinc as the fuel this potentially inexpensive device can store and deliver more than 50 watt-hours of electricity per pound of battery [110 Wh/kg]...
>
> It can safely be predicted that before long this development will produce metal-air batteries with an energy density of 60 watt-hours per pound [132 Wh/kg] or even higher.[8]

A year later, experts making predictions before a congressional committee were equally optimistic:

> ...zinc-air rechargeable batteries should offer advantages in performance, weight, volume, and material costs...
> ...continued development...should lead within the next couple of years to truly economically feasible batteries for electric vehicles.[71]
>
> In our judgment the zinc-air battery project is well ahead of every other advanced project and stands a good chance of success.[72]
>
> We are expecting commercial availability of these zinc-air batteries in the early 1970s.[73]

---

[*] Private communication, Frank Pittman, Westinghouse R&D Center, Pittsburgh, 1976.

But the intervening years since these predictions have not yet brought a satisfactory metal-air battery. The Japanese government development program has tested both iron-air and zinc-air batteries with what must be considered disappointing results: lives of less than 100 cycles.[36] Nevertheless, success is still viewed as just around the corner, both in the US and abroad. A development program at Westinghouse reports laboratory cell lifetimes near 500 cycles.[*] The Japanese government program went on to seek a 200-300 cycle life at a small sacrifice in performance, as shown in Table 3.7. In France, interest and optimism have been high, and one authority reported that prototype batteries have demonstrated low costs, high energy and power densities, and life of over 600 cycles. He concluded that

> The primary power system can therefore at this point be regarded as being out of the laboratory stage...Passage from the present state of research to the required engineering objectives is no longer dependent on the successful resolution of fundamental engineering problems.[56]

Perhaps success _is_ just around the corner.

The zinc-chlorine system is another promising prospect of Table 3.3 which was not selected for impact calculation. Yet, for it too, success has seemed just around the corner for some time. A zinc-chlorine battery system was installed in a subcompact automobile in 1972, providing power for over 240 km of non-stop driving at an average speed of 80 km/hr. The results were presented in a paper optimistically titled "A Zinc-Chloride Battery--The Missing Link to a Practical Electric Car."[46] No further automotive demonstrations have been reported, however, and despite development progress generally, auto applications were recently seen as coming after use in delivery vans in the late seventies, and after utility load-leveling in the early 80's.[**]

---

[*] Private communication, E. Buzzelli, Westinghouse, Inc., May 1976.
[**] Private communication, P. C. Symons, Energy Development Associates, February 1976.

The sodium-sulfur system is the remaining entry in Table 3.3 which was not selected here for impact calculations. Work on this system has a long history, including well-publicized efforts at the Ford Motor Company to develop a practical battery for automotive propulsion. In 1967 success seemed just around the corner:

> We believe that, within the next decade, research and development now being conducted by Ford and others will make it possible to produce marketable electrical vehicles much superior to any that can be built today.
>
> Our sodium-sulfur battery is now in an advanced stage of laboratory development. Its technical feasibility and excellent performance have been demonstrated...[73]

This remains a fair description of the current status of sodium-sulfur battery development. A recent survey put the situation this way:

> The progress in the last seven or eight years has been very good...The prospects for continued progress look bright, but during this period, the difficult materials and seals problems must be solved, and the cost problems must be squarely faced.[47]

These problems which must now be faced are not new; they were apparent from the outset, and indeed have been critical in other battery development programs. Yet expert opinion remains sufficiently optimistic to justify further work, with reasonable hope for successful sodium-sulfur systems within the next few years.

In summation, the forecasts and predictions of authoritative persons in battery development have frequently proved overoptimistic. Moreover, there is no assurance that the projections advanced here for representative future batteries will prove more realistic than the previous projections discussed in this section. The optimistic remarks quoted earlier to support selection of the nickel-zinc system, for example, are remarkably like those quoted above for several systems which were not selected.

Battery experts themselves well know the uncertainties in their predictions. One of them put it this way some years ago:

> In conclusion, a word of caution is warranted regarding the development of new systems. Long experience has shown there are many problems and pitfalls in moving from the small test tube cell of the research laboratory to a practical battery of commercial usefulness.[12]

In view of all this, the selections and projections of representative batteries offered here should be regarded as just that: <u>representative</u> of what may be achieved. They constitute a reasonable basis for analyzing the impacts of electric car use, not a reliable prediction of battery development.

SECTION 3 REFERENCES

1. *Electric Vehicles and Other Alternatives to the Internal Combustion Engine*, Joint Hearings before the Committees on Commerce and Public Works, US Senate, 90th Congress, on S.451 and S.453, March 14-17 and April 10, 1967, US Government Printing Office, Washington, 1967.

2. *Electric Vehicle Research, Development, and Demonstration Act of 1975*, Hearings before the Subcommittee on Energy Research, Development, and Demonstration of the Committee on Science and Technology, US House of Representatives, on H.R. 5470, Washington, June 3-6, 1975.

3. *Symposium on Power Systems for Electric Vehicles*, Law School, Columbia University, New York, April 6-8, 1967.

4. *Proceedings of the First International Electric Vehicle Symposium*, Phoenix, Arizona, Nov. 5-7, 1969, Electric Vehicle Council, New York, 1969.

5. *Proceedings of the Second International Electric Vehicle Symposium*, Atlantic City, New Jersey, Nov. 8-10, 1971, Electric Vehicle Council, New York, 1971.

6. *Proceedings of the Symposium and Workshop on Advanced Battery Research and Development*, March 22-24, 1976, Argonne National Labs., Argonne, Ill., ANL-76-8.

7. *Electric Vehicles, A Bibliography*, Electric Vehicle Council, New York, December 1970.

8. G. A. Hoffman, "The Electric Automobile," *Scientific American*, Vol. 215, October 1966, pp. 34-40.

9. V. R. Cooper, *Power Plants for Electric Terrestrial Vehicles*, AIAA Paper 66-980 presented at the Third Annual Meeting of the American Institute of Aeronautics and Astronautics, Boston, Nov. 29-Dec. 2, 1966.

10. J. Werth, *Electric Vehicular Power*, AIAA Paper 66-977, presented at AIAA Third Annual Meeting, Boston, Nove. 29-Dec. 2, 1966.

11. _Development of Electrically Powered Vehicles_, Bureau of Power, Federal Power Commission, Washington, Feb. 1967.

12. O. T. Ferrell, _Power Systems for Electric Vehicles_, in Ref. 5, 1967.

13. _The Automobile and Air Pollution: A Program for Progress_, Report of the Panel on Electrically Powered Vehicles to the US Department of Commerce, Washington, October 1967.

14. D. V. Ragone, _Review of Battery Systems for Electrically Powered Vehicles_, SAE Paper 680453, May 1968.

15. E. S. Starkman, _Prospects of Electric Power for Vehicles_, SAE Paper 680541, Society of Automotive Engineers, West Coast Meeting, San Francisco, August 1968.

16. _Prospects for Electric Vehicles: A Study of Low-Pollution-Potential Vehicles--Electric_, National Air Pollution Control Administration Publication APTD 69-52, US Department of Health, Education, and Welfare, Raleigh, North Carolina, 1969.

17. R. C. Shair, _Battery Systems for Electric Cars_, in Ref. 6, p. 416, 1969.

18. C. C. Christianson, _Batteries for Electric Vehicles_, in Ref. 7, 1971.

19. J.H.B. George, _Electrochemical Power Sources for Electric Highway Vehicles_, Arthur D. Little, Inc., C-74692, Cambridge, Mass., June 1972.

20. _An Evaluation of Alternative Power Sources for Low-Emission Automobiles_, Report of the Panel on Alternate Power Sources to the Committee on Motor Vehicle Emissions, National Academy of Sciences, Washington, April 1973.

21. S. Gross and S. W. Silverman, _Study of Batteries for Electric Vehicles_, Boeing Aerospace Company Final Report, Project 72-8, Seattle, Wash., March 1973.

22. G. A. Mueller, ed., _The Gould Battery Handbook_, Gould, Inc., Mendota Heights, Minn., 1973.

23. H. J. Schwartz, _Electric Vehicle Battery Research and Development_, NASA Lewis Research Center, NASA TM X-71471, October 1973.

24. E. E. David, _A Battery Manufacturer's Point of View_, presented at the Third International Electric Vehicle Symposium, Washington, Feb. 19-20, 1974.

25. N. P. Yao and J. R. Birk, _Battery Energy Storage for Utility Load Leveling and Electric Vehicles: A Review of Advanced Secondary Batteries_, IECEC Paper 759166, Newark, Delaware, August 1975.

26. _Should We Have a New Engine? An Automobile Power Systems Evaluation_, Jet Propulsion Laboratory, California Institute of Technology, Pasadena, August 1975.

27. A. R. Landgrebe, _Secondary Batteries for Electric Vehicles_, in Ref. 8.

28. Y. Miyake, _Development of Electric Vehicles in Japan_, SAE Paper 690072, Society of Automotive Engineers, International Automotive Engineering Congress, Detroit, Jan. 1969.

29. M. Iragaki, _Electric Vehicle Development in Japan_, in Ref. 6, p. 434.

30. _Development Program of Electric Car in Japan_, Agency of Industrial Science and Technology, Ministry of International Trade and Industry, April 1971.

31. J. P. Gomis, J. F. Laurent, and P. Lassere, _Accumulators for Electric Vehicles_, presented at Electric Vehicle Study Days, Brussels, March 13-14, 1972.

32. M. Poehler, _Batteries for Electric Road Vehicles_, presented at Electric Vehicle Study Days, Brussels, March 13-14, 1972.

33. H. G. Müller, et al., _Elektrische Angetriebene Kraftfahrzeuge_, (Studie der GES in Auftrag des Ministers für Verkehr der Bundesrepublik Deutschland), GES – Gesellschaft für Elektrischen Strassenverkehr, Düsseldorf, 1 August 1973.

34. Gene E. Smith, _Development of Electric Vehicles in Japan_, Paper 7473, presented at the 3rd International Electric Vehicle Symposium and Exposition, Washington, Feb. 1974.

35. _Pour Un Developpement des Véhicules Électriques_, (Rapport remis au government le 15 Novembre 1974), La Documentation Francaise, Paris, 1974.

36. N. P. Yao, _Battery Development in Japan_, in Ref. 8.

37. G. Lander and E. Voss, _Batteries for Electric Vehicles in Western Europe_, in Ref. 8.

38. A. C. Simon and S. M. Calder, _The Lead-Acid Battery_, in Ref. 8.

39. J. C. Duddy and J. B. Ockerman, _Laminar Plate Lead Acid Batteries for Electric Vehicles_, in Ref. 7.

40. G. Kucera, H. G. Plust, C. Schneider, _Nickel-Zinc Storage Batteries as Energy Sources for Electric Vehicles_, SAE Paper 750147, Society of Automotive Engineers, Automotive Engineering Congress and Exposition, Detroit, February 1975.

41. D. Fisher, "Gould 'Breakthrough' Lifts Hopes for Electric Cars," _Los Angeles Times_, Jan. 31, 1975, p. 12, part III.

42. Statement by Dr. Edward E. David, Executive Vice President of R&D, Gould, Inc. in Ref. 4, 1975, p. 105.

43. _The Zinc-Chloride Battery_, Leaflet of Energy Development Associates, Madison Heights, Michigan, 1974.

44. P. C. Symons, _Performance of Zinc Chloride Batteries_, presented at the 3rd International Electric Vehicle Symposium, Washington, Feb. 1974.

45. P. C. Symons, _Batteries for Practical Electric Cars_, SAE Paper 730253, Society of Automotive Engineers, International Automotive Engineering Congress, Detroit, Jan. 1973.

46. C. J. Amato, _A Zinc-Chloride Battery--The Missing Link to a Practical Electric Car_, SAE Paper 730248, Society of Automotive Engineers, International Automotive Engineering Congress, Detroit, Jan. 1973.

47. E. J. Cairns and J. S. Dunning, _High-Temperature Batteries_, in Ref. 8.

48. P. A. Nelson, _Comparison of US and European High-Temperature Battery Programs_, in Ref. 8.

49. H. Shimotake, M. L. Kyle, V. A. Maroni, and E. J. Cairns, _Lithium/ Sulfur Cells and Their Potential for Vehicle Propulsion_, in Ref. 6, p. 392.

50. W. L. Towle, et al., _Cost Estimate for the Commercial Manufacture of Lithium-Iron Sulfide Cells for Load-Leveling_, ANL 76-12, Argonne National Laboratory, Argonne, Ill., March 1976.

51. R. O. Ivins, et al., <u>Design and Performance of Li-Al/Iron Sulfide Cells for Utility Energy Storage and Electric Vehicles</u>, presented at the 27th Power Sources Symposium, Atlantic City, June 1976.

52. A. A. Chilenskas, et al., <u>Design and Testing of Lithium/Iron Sulfide Batteries for Electric-Vehicle Propulsion</u>, presented at the Fourth International Electric Vehicle Symposium, Dusseldorf, August 1976.

53. J. Werth, I. Klein, R. Wylie, <u>The Sodium Chloride Battery</u>, presented at the meeting of the Electrochemical Society, Dallas, October 1975.

54. J. T. Kummer and N. Weber, <u>A Sodium-Sulfur Secondary Battery</u>, SAE Paper 670179, Society of Automotive Engineers, Automotive Engineering Congress, Detroit, January 1967.

55. S. A. Weiner, <u>The Sodium-Sulfur Battery: A Progress Report</u>, in Ref. 8.

56. A. J. Appleby and J. P. Gabano, <u>Current Status and Prospects of the Zn-Air and Na-S Batteries in France,</u> in Ref. 8.

57. A. J. Appleby, J. P. Pompon, and M. Jacquier, <u>Zinc-Air Batteries in Vehicular Applications</u>, in Ref. 7, paper 7430.

58. R. Vignaud, <u>L'Accumulateur Zinc-Air</u>, presented at Electric Vehicle Study Days, Brussels, March 1972.

59. L. A. Herédy, H. L. Recht, and D. E. McKenzie, <u>The Atomics International Sodium-Air Cell</u>, in Ref. 5, 1967.

60. G. L. Holleck and J. R. Driscoll, <u>Sulfur-Based Lithium-Organic Electrolyte Secondary Batteries</u>, Report ECOM-74-0072-6, US Army Electronic Commanc, Ft. Monmouth, Va., Nov. 1975.

61. Exide data sheet S-132 and catalog section 20.20, ESB Inc., Philadelphia.

62. <u>Battery Performance Data: Powerbreed 220 Electric Vehicle Battery</u>, Gould, Inc., St. Paul, Minnesota

63. J. Gumbleton, et al., <u>Special Purpose Urban Cars</u>, SAE Paper 690461, May 1969.

64. D. C. Sheridan, et al., <u>A Study of the Energy Utilization of Gasoline and Battery-Electric Powered Special Purpose Vehicles</u>, SAE Paper 760119, presented at Automotive Engineering Congress and Exposition, Detroit, Feb. 1976.

65. G. W. Vinal, <u>Storage Batteries</u>, Fourth Edition, John Wiley & Sons, Inc., New York, 1955.

66. <u>Chargers and Charging for Lead-Acid and Nickel-Iron Batteries</u>, Exide Power Systems Division, ESB, Inc., Philadelphia, 1970.

67. E. G. Siwek and J. L. Weininger, <u>A System Evaluation of Lead-Acid Battery Chargers</u>, Final Report ILZRO Project, No. LE-205, International Lead Zinc Research Organization, New York, 1975.

68. <u>Impact of Future Use of Electric Cars in the Los Angeles Region</u>, EPA-460-3-74-020, US Environmental Protection Agency, Washington, October 1974.

69. James J. Flink, <u>America Adopts the Automobile, 1985-1910</u>, The MIT Press, Cambridge, Mass., 1970.

70. J. E. Homans, <u>Self-Propelled Vehicles: A Practical Treatise on the Theory, Construction, Operation, Care and Management of all Forms of Automobiles</u>, Theo. Audel & Co., New York, 1908.

71. Statement of Dr. Stewart M. Chodosh, Battery Manager, Leesona Moos Laboratories, in Ref. 3, p. 290-1, 1967.

72. Statement of Charles Avila, President, Boston Edison Co., in Ref. 3, p. 353, 1967.

73. Statement of Dr. Frederick de Hoffman, Vice President, General Dynamics, in Ref. 3, 1967.

74. Statement by Michael Ference, Jr., Vice President, Scientific Research, Ford Motor Company, in Ref. 3, 1967.

75. R. Wolf, J. Heurtin, and M. Cochat, <u>Experiments on a Trial Series of Electric Vehicles</u>, presented at the Third International Electric Vehicle Symposium, Washington, Feb. 19-20, 1974.

4   FUTURE ELECTRIC CARS

Though improved batteries may be more important, improvements in
auto technology can also substantially enhance the performance of electric
cars. These prospects are illustrated by the representative future electric
cars described in Table 4.1. The characteristics of these cars were developed with the aid of a computer model of urban driving. They show that
dramatic improvements are in sight from the combination of improved batteries
with improved automotive technology. Relative to cars employing current
US auto technology and golf-car batteries, also included in Table 4.1, the
"advanced" electric cars could provide up to six times as much driving
range, with lower dollar costs and lower energy use at the same time.
Moreover, significant improvements can be made even without the most optimistic future battery, the high-temperature lithium system. Even the improved lead-acid battery could easily double the range of electric cars,
and at the same time cut their overall cost per kilometer by almost 25%.

The recent-technology car of Table 4.1 uses the premium golf-car
battery of Secs. 2 and 3, together with "weight-conscious" car designs
like those of the down-sized domestic automobiles of 1977-79. The improved-
technology cars employ the improved lead-acid or nickel-zinc batteries of
Sec. 3 with the weight-conscious car designs. The advanced-technology
cars are somewhat optimistic, primarily in that they use the high-performance lithium battery system; their automotive technology is simply
that expected for US automobiles in the 1980s after another round of
improvement.

The applications in Table 4.1 are drawn from Sec. 5, where they
are discussed in detail. Similarly, the costs shown are from Sec. 7.

The two-passenger cars of Table 4.1 are unlike anything now available.
The four-passenger cars, however, are comparable to prospective domestic
subcompacts in interior accommodations and overall size. They could be
manufactured, except for the battery-electric drive system, from essentially

88

TABLE 4.1

REPRESENTATIVE FUTURE ELECTRIC CARS

Application	Number of Passengers	Technology	Battery	Nominal Range, km	Curb Weight, kg	Battery Fraction	Life-Cycle Cost*, ¢/km	Energy Use, MJ/km**
Extra or Secondary Car	2	Recent	Lead-Acid	65	1,271	0.42	10.0	0.900
Secondary Urban Car	2	Improved	Lead-Acid	75	835	0.29	7.2	0.662
		Improved	Ni-Zn	75	700	0.21	8.1	0.644
		Advanced	Li/Al-FeS$_2$	100	568	0.19	6.9	0.554
Secondary Urban Car	4	Recent	Lead-Acid	75	2,128	0.41	14.0	1.307
		Improved	Lead-Acid	100	1,359	0.30	9.4	0.889
		Improved	Ni-Zn	100	1,111	0.22	10.3	0.835
Urban Car	4	Improved	Lead-Acid	150	1,747	0.38	10.7	1.062
		Improved	Ni-Zn	150	1,254	0.27	10.7	0.904
General Use Car	4	Improved	Ni-Zn	250	1,747	0.38	12.9	1.138
		Advanced	Li/Al-FeS$_2$	250	1,033	0.27	9.3	0.752
			Li/Al-FeS$_2$	450	1,501	0.4	12.4	0.954

*12 year, 193,000 km life.

**Input to battery charger (with 90% charger efficiency).

the same materials, by the same techniques, at the same factories as conventional subcompacts. Thus the automotive assumptions implicit in Table 4.1 are relatively conservative, anticipating no performance or production innovations beyond those already anticipated for conventional subcompacts—which are expected to improve considerably as increasingly stringent requirements for fuel economy constrain the manufacturers.

The principal source of projections for conventional cars underlying Table 4.1 is a comprehensive study recently made by the Federal Government's Interagency Task Force on Motor Vehicle Goals Beyond 1980.[1] The work of the Task Force brought together in a single place projections of a breadth and depth unequaled in other publicly-available sources. It provided the primary reference not only for projecting characteristics of future cars, but for projecting their costs and some of their impacts on the economy and the environment as well.

The representative cars in Table 4.1 were selected from the parametric analysis of future electric automobiles which is described in this section. The key parameter in designing electric cars is the fraction of weight to be devoted to the battery. All else follows from the choice of battery fraction: driving range, overall weight, and the attendant dollar costs and energy requirements. For each of the major possibilities--either two or four-passenger cars, with one of the representative batteries from Sec. 3-- car characteristics were calculated for battery fractions ranging from as low as 10% to as high as 50%, encompassing the range which has proven desirable and practical in the past.

This section begins with a review of the technology levels projected for conventional cars by the Interagency Task Force. Future batteries, motors, and controllers are chosen for each overall level of electric car technology. Next, the levels of interior accommodation and acceleration to be offered to the consumer are selected. Then the major components of the automobile are analyzed. Equations are developed to relate weights of structure and propulsion equipment to the battery fraction. Electric drive efficiencies are estimated, as are losses in tires and aerodynamic drag. The computer model used to evaluate range and energy use for different levels of technology and battery fraction is described together with conditions for evaluation and results of model runs. Then the representative cars of Table 4.1 are selected. Finally, one of them is chosen as a reference and used to illustrate the sensitivities of its calculated characteristics to various changes in assumptions about batteries, automotive technology, and driving conditions.

4.1 CONCEPTUAL DESIGNS FOR FUTURE ELECTRIC CARS

The work of the Interagency Task Force on Motor Vehicle Goals Beyond 1980 is the most recent and comprehensive documentation of present and prospective automotive technology. This is the starting place for projecting future electric automobiles. It provides information about virtually every aspect of automotive design except electric propulsion. From this information consistent conceptual designs of electric cars may be projected and compared with their conventional internal-combustion-engine (ICE) counterparts.

Conceptual designs for future ICE cars were analyzed by the Task Force for all combinations of the various choices boxed in Fig. 4.1--864 in all. The choices include accommodations comparable to those now prevalent, but the choices of acceleration performance in Fig. 4.1 correspond only to average and low acceleration by present standards. This reflects the prospect that with the increased fuel economies required by law, together with the lower maximum speed limits of recent years, acceptable acceleration capability will be somewhat less than in the past. The "level I" safety and emissions choices in Table 4.1 correspond to those required in 1975-76. The higher levels may ultimately be required by government regulation.

The design concepts for future electric cars shown in Fig. 4.2 were chosen in a similar manner. They differ from those of Fig. 4.1 primarily in that choices relevant or important to ICE cars have been replaced

CONSUMER CHOICES		COMPONENT DESIGN ALTERNATIVES			SAFETY/EMISSIONS CRITERIA*	
INTERIOR VOLUME	ACCEL. TIME, 0 TO 96 km/hr	STRUCTURE	ENGINE	TRANSMISSION	SAFETY	EMISSIONS
3 CHOICES	2 CHOICES	3 CHOICES	4 CHOICES	2 CHOICES	2 CHOICES	3 CHOICES
4 PASSENGER		TYPICAL	AVG '75	TYPICAL '75	LEVEL I	LEVEL I
	15 sec		TOP '75			LEVEL II
5 PASSENGER		WEIGHT CONSCIOUS		UPGRADED	LEVEL II	
	20 sec		DIESEL			
6 PASSENGER		INNOVATIVE	ADVANCED			LEVEL III

AN-49898

ENGINE: AVG '75 - AVERAGE FUEL ECONOMY PERFORMANCE FOR 1975 FLEET
           TOP '75 - BEST FUEL ECONOMY PERFORMANCE FOR 1975 FLEET

TRANSMISSION: TYPICAL '75 - 3-SPEED AUTOMATIC
               UPGRADED - TORQUE CONVERTER, 4-SPEED LOCK-UP

STRUCTURE: CURRENT - AVERAGE '75

            WEIGHT CONSCIOUS - FIRST STEP IN SIGNIFICANT WEIGHT
            REDUCTION WITHOUT SACRIFICING INTERIOR SPACE

            INNOVATIVE - SECOND STEP IN WEIGHT REDUCTION, UTILIZING
            10% TO 15% PLASTIC/ALUMINUM SUBSTITUTION

*SAFETY   LEVEL I: 48 km/h FRONTAL
            LEVEL II: 64 km/h FRONTAL; 32 km/h SIDE

EMISSIONS   LEVEL   I: 1.5-HC/15.0-CO/3.1-NO_x(gm/mi)
            LEVEL II: 0.41-HC/3.4-CO/2.0-NO_x(gm/mi)
            LEVEL III: 0.41-HC/3.4-CO/0.4-NO_x(gm/mi)

Source: Page 4-3, Reference 1.

Figure 4.1. Design Elements for Future ICE Cars

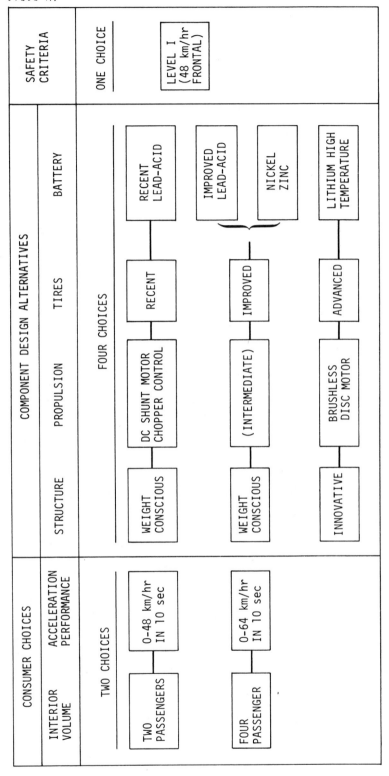

Figure 4.2. Design Elements for Electric Cars

with entries important for electric cars. In addition, entries are grouped into only three sets of choices, to minimize the number of different cases for the parametric analysis.

In view of the potentially high cost of electric cars with large passenger capacity and high acceleration, the consumer choices in Fig. 4.2 are limited to relatively small, slow cars. Among component design alternatives, only the two lighter-weight structural levels of Fig. 4.1 are included. Because of the high cost of structural weight to an electric car, it would be unlikely that the heavier recent structural technology would ever be employed. It was considered only briefly, as a part of sensitivity studies showing the effects of specific changes in one of the four choices shown.

Associated with the structural types are combinations of propulsion, tires, and batteries appropriate for future years. They match possible advances in propulsion and in low-loss tires with the improved batteries described in Sec. 3. Only one level of safety is shown, Level I, but Level II of Fig. 4.1 was included in the sensitivity studies.

All together, eight different conceptual designs are implied by the choices in Fig. 4.2. For each of these overall weight, driving range, and energy consumption were calculated as a function of battery weight. Throughout this calculation, acceleration capability and passenger capacity were held constant.

Three levels of technology are represented in these design concepts:

- Recent technology, summarized in the upper row of component choices in Fig. 4.2, was available several years ago and could have been offered today in electric cars had decisions to produce them been made and carried out.

- Improved technology, summarized in the middle row of component choices in Fig. 4.2, will be available when (and if) the improved lead-acid and nickel-zinc batteries of Sec. 3 become available. In small quantities, this might be as early as 1980; in large quantities, it might be around 1985.

- Advanced technology, indicated in the lower row of component choices in Fig. 4.2, couples innovative auto technology not expected until the 1980s with an electric motor specifically designed for automotive use, advanced low-loss tires, and the highest-performance battery projected in Sec. 3. Again, availability depends on the battery, which may be produced in small quantities in the early 80s, and in large quantitites by 1990.

The design concepts of Fig. 4.2 are developed in more detail in the following subsections.

4.2 CAPACITY AND PERFORMANCE

The interior volume of the four-passenger electric cars for the future was assumed to be the same as that selected by the Interagency Task Force for its representative future ICE subcompact. In terms of the "roominess index" employed by the Task Force, this implies an average value essentially the same as that of the recent Fiat 128 or Volkswagen Rabbit.[2]

Since no two-passenger automobiles were analyzed by the Task Force, it was simply assumed that the rear seat space of the four-passenger car would be eliminated for this design. Size and weight were adjusted accordingly.

The acceleration performance selected for the four-passenger electric cars is substantially less than the lowest level shown in Table 4.1. Because high acceleration capability adds costly weight to electric cars and is wasteful of battery capacity, the level selected was the minimum considered acceptable for operation on freeways. Though comprehensive data is unavailable, a recent review showed that in Los Angeles, almost 60% of access ramps

95

to freeways were at freeway crossings above surface streets, and that such ramps were typically 150 to 300 meters in length with four to six percent grades.[3] The acceleration performance sufficient to go from 0 to 64 km/h (40 mph) in 10 seconds on a level road suffices for accelerations up these ramps to a speed of about 64 km/h during merging with freeway traffic. Since accident statistics show rapid increases as differences in vehicle speeds increase, entry into the freeway at any lower speed would be relatively hazardous. It should be noted that electric cars capable of 0-64 km/h in 10 seconds will require about 25 seconds for acceleration from zero to 96 km/h (60 mph), considerably longer than the 15-20 seconds for future ICE cars indicated in Table 4.1.[4]

Unlike gasoline engines, automotive electric motors will probably offer a peak power output which is two or three times the rated continuous power output. For occasional bursts of acceleration, the peak output will be available. For extended hill-climbing, however, only the continuous rating will be available. The capability of 80 km/h or more on 6% freeway grades, then, could only be maintained for a few minutes, perhaps two or three kilometers. Because the electric cars have limited range and are usually intended for urban driving, this should be sufficient on almost all occasions. It would be costly and of relatively little advantage to insist on continuous hill-climbing capability of this sort, with a resultant increase in capability for short-term accelerations beyond that for the four-passenger car in Fig. 4.2.

The two-passenger electric cars of Fig. 4.2 are conceived as low-cost cars of limited utility. They are not intended for freeway operation and they do not offer the acceleration capability needed for up-hill on-ramps. The acceleration of 0-48 km/h in 10 seconds shown in Fig. 4.2 is in line with measurements for representative light urban traffic. To keep up with moderate or heavy traffic, even lower levels would suffice: 0-35 km/h in 10 seconds.[3]

4.3 PARAMETRIC WEIGHT

The object of this analysis is to show possibilities for future electric cars as a function of battery weight. Since battery weight determines car range, total weight, cost, and energy use, it is necessarily a critical parameter in any analysis. Eventually, it may be set at that figure offering the best possible compromise between driving range and cost. For the moment, however, a wide range of possibilities must be carried through the analysis. In all cases, of course, the capacity and acceleration performance of the cars are to be held constant at the levels of Fig. 4.2.

A simple parametric model was constructed to estimate the weight of the electric car and its principal components for each level of technology, each level of capacity and performance, and each selection of battery weight. The essential assumptions of the model are these:

- There is a fixed weight for passenger compartment, seats, instruments, heating and ventilation, body panels, and the like which depends only on the selected payload and is independent of the amount of battery carried.

- The remaining structural and chassis weight is proportional to the gross vehicle weight--the weight with the maximum design payload aboard. This weight would include the structure, suspension, tires, wheels, and other components which must carry the fixed weight including maximum payload, the propulsion system, and the battery.

- The propulsion weight is proportional to the test weight of the car, that is, the curb weight plus a nominal payload. Generally, propulsion power output is proportional to propulsion weight, and acceleration performance is proportional to output power. This assumption, then, is equivalent to assuming constant acceleration performance.

- Battery weight is some fraction of curb weight which may be varied over a wide range.

With these simple assumptions, the curb weight of an electric automobile may be analyzed and represented parametrically as summarized in Table 4.2. The first quantity of the table, the maximum design payload, is that appropriate for either the two-passenger or four-passenger cars. So also is the next quantity, the fixed weight, which depends on the payload and is independent of battery, propulsion, and other structural and chassis weight. The gross vehicle weight is simply the curb weight plus the maximum design payload. The test weight is the curb weight plus a payload of 136 kilograms (300 pounds), the conventional assumption for the weight of two average occupants. The weights of remaining structure and chassis, propulsion, and battery are assumed proportional to the gross, test, and curb weights of the vehicle as indicated above, with coefficients of proportionality a, b, and c which are to be determined. Coefficients a and b reflect the assumed levels of structural technology and propulsion technology in Fig. 4.2. Coefficient c is to be chosen within a reasonable range. Initially, values of c from .1 to .5 were considered.

Combining the formulas at the right of Table 4.2 and solving for curb weight leads to the equation at the bottom. This equation accomplishes the desired objective: expressing the curb weight of the electric car in terms of the amount of battery selected, assuming constant passenger capacity and acceleration performance.

To apply this equation, it is necessary to select specific values for maximum design payload and for the coefficients a and b which show the dependence of structure and chassis weight on gross weight and the dependence of propulsion weight on test weight. The values selected for this analysis appear in Tables 4.3 and 4.4.

The fixed weights of the electric cars include the maximum design payload, the "upper body" weight which depends only on payload and is independent of battery and propulsion weight, and any extra weight for safety provisions in excess of those assumed in level I of Fig. 4.1,

TABLE 4.2

PARAMETRIC REPRESENTATION OF WEIGHT

Symbol	Definition	Formula
$W_{PL,max}$	Maximum design payload	–
W_F	Fixed weight (including $W_{PL,max}$)	–
W_G	Gross vehicle weight	$W_G = W_C + W_{PL,max}$
W_C	Curb weight	(see below)
W_T	Test weight	$W_T = W_C + 136$ kg
W_S	Structure and chassis weight	$W_S = a \cdot W_G$
W_P	Propulsion weight	$W_P = b \cdot W_T$
W_B	Battery weight	$W_B = c \cdot W_C$

$$W_C = \frac{(W_F - W_{PL,max}) + a\, W_{PL,max} + 136b}{1 - (a + b + c)}$$

TABLE 4.3
FIXED WEIGHTS

	Two-Passenger Cars			Four-Passenger Cars		
	Recent	Improved	Advanced	Recent	Improved	Advanced
Maximum Design Payload, kg	227	204	204	454	408	408
Upper Body, kg	340	289	250	445	378	326
Safety Level II, kg (optional)	43	39	39	58	52	52

TABLE 4.4

VARIABLE WEIGHTS

Weight Fraction	Two-Passenger Cars			Four-Passenger Cars		
	Recent	Improved	Advanced	Recent	Improved	Advanced
$a = W_S/W_G$ (structure and chassis fraction)	.258	.239	.230	.258	.239	.230
$b = W_P/W_T$ (propulsion fraction)	.068	.057	.047	.120	.101	.083
$c = W_B/W_C$ (battery fraction)	---------------------0.1 to 0.5----------------------					

which is implicit throughout this parametric analysis. The fixed weights employed in the analysis are summarized in Table 4.3. The maximum design payloads for four-passenger cars are simply those assumed by the Interagency Task Force; for the future cars, they are ten percent less (900 vs 1000 lbs) than for the actual recent cars. Half these payloads were assumed for the two-passenger cars. The upper body weights were derived from information collected and projected by the Task Force. The extra weights for Safety Level II were set equal to those of the Task Force for the four-passenger cars and reduced to 75% for the two-passenger cars.

The basis for choosing upper body weights in Table 4.3 was the apportionment of weight presented in Table 4.5 for a weight-conscious ICE subcompact. The listed component weights were apportioned as shown to the upper body fixed weight, the structure and chassis weight which depend on gross vehicle weight, and the propulsion weight. Also indicated is the weight of propulsion energy storage (or gasoline in its tank), which would correspond to the battery weight in the electric car.

TABLE 4.5

APPORTIONMENT OF WEIGHT FOR "WEIGHT-CONSCIOUS" ICE SUBCOMPACT CAR

Component	Weight, kg	Upper Body, kg	Structure & Chassis, kg	Propulsion, kg	Energy Store, kg
Body and frame	497	344	153		
Heater	9	9			
Electrical	23	18		5	
Steering	14	7	7		
Suspension	45		45		
Wheels and tires	61		61		
Brakes	45		45		
Axle and propshaft	27		22	5	
Engine	133			133	
Exhaust	14			14	
Transmission	27			27	
Fuel system and fuel	45				45
TOTALS	940	378	333	184	45

Source: Ref. 1

The body and frame weight was divided between upper body and dependent structure weight in accord with a recent study showing that about 70% of this weight was independent of propulsion and energy storage weight.[5] The electrical system weight was partly apportioned to the propulsion system, since it consists primarily of battery weight and one battery function is starting the internal combustion engine. This portion of battery weight would presumably increase when propulsion size increased. The remainder, which provides for lighting, ventilation, and accessories, should be independent of propulsion weight. Steering weight was divided equally in two parts, the steering wheel and column which would be essentially independent of gross vehicle weight, and the lower portion which would depend directly on gross vehicle weight. The axle and propeller shaft were apportioned partly to dependent structure, partly to propulsion, since their function and size depend both on load to be carried and on propulsive power to be transmitted to the wheels.

The total weight of upper body shown in Table 4.5, 378 kilograms, is the value assumed for the "improved" four-passenger electric car in Table 4.3. The upper body weights for the four-passenger cars with "recent" and "advanced" technology were scaled directly from this in accord with the findings of the Task Force. For the two-passenger cars, 75% of these upper body weights were chosen. This is a rough estimate, based on the consideration that the rear seat space accounts for considerably less than half of the upper body weight for the four-passenger cars, even though it accounts for half the passenger capacity.

The basis for choosing the structure and chassis coefficient "a" in Table 4.4 was also the apportionment of weight presented in Table 4.5 for the weight-conscious ICE subcompact. Table 4.5 shows that in the ICE subcompact, 333 kilograms of structure and chassis weight were dependent on gross vehicle weight. With a curb weight of 940 kg and maximum design payload of 454 kg, this gives a = .239 for the ICE car of Table 4.5. Accordingly, this value was used for the "improved" electric car in Table 4.4. (Here only, the maximum design payload for subcompact cars hypothesized by the Interagency Task Force was 454 kilograms; elsewhere, it was stated to be 408 kilograms.) The "innovative" ICE car of the Task Force had 10% less curb weight than the weight-conscious car, while the "recent-technology" car had 20% more curb weight. Assuming the same 454-kilogram payload and the same percentage of curb weight in the structure and chassis weight which depends on gross vehicle weight, additional values of coefficient "a" may be computed as shown in Table 4.4. The same coefficients were assumed to apply to both two-passenger and four-passenger electric cars.

102

The propulsion fractions in Table 4.4 are derived in the next section, which also considers efficiency and weights of propulsion components appropriate to the levels of technology assumed for the electric cars.

Because it is based on conventional cars, in which weight is less important than in electric cars, the weight model should generally be conservative. It omits, however, any provision for battery size as opposed to weight. The energy and power densities per unit volume of different types of future batteries are expected to be similar, as noted in Sec. 3.2; in consequence, it is not necessary that the parametric model distinguish among them in this respect. For moderate battery volumes, like those typically assigned to compartments for automotive internal-combustion engines, the model should yield reasonable weights. For higher-volume batteries required for very long design ranges, the model may tend to underestimate the structural weight required to support and contain the battery. Accurate representation of this situation would depend significantly on battery placement (whether in single or multiple packages, for example, in a longitudinal tunnel through the passenger compartment, or underneath the seats, or over the front and rear axles, or under the door sills, or in some combination of these possibilities). The most desirable placement, however, or its dependence on battery size and weight, have not yet been established, so more detail here could be premature.

4.4 PROPULSION COMPONENTS

Components for propulsion of the electric car include an electric motor and its associated controller, a transmission, and an axle and drive shaft assembly. The controller regulates and conditions the flow of power from the battery to the motor in accord with commands from the driver. The transmission matches the shaft speed of the motor to the requirements of the axle. For optimum performance, the controller, motor, and transmission should be designed for one another.

Table 4.6 shows the propulsion components assumed for each level of electric car technology, together with their specific weights and average efficiencies. The specific weights relate component weight to rated power output, which in the case of the motors and controllers is a peak or short-term rating for accelerations and short hill-climbs. The efficiencies shown are averages, based on analyses of real components, which may be expected in stop-start city driving or in constant-speed highway driving. To introduce more detail here would require detailed descriptions of future motors and controllers which have not yet been developed.

TABLE 4.6

SPECIFIC WEIGHTS AND EFFICIENCIES OF PROPULSION COMPONENTS

Technology	Component	Specific Weight, kg/kW	Average Efficiency, percent	
			City	Highway
Recent	DC series-wound traction motor with transistor chopper	4.6	80	85
Improved	Improved transistor-controlled traction motor	3.8	82.5	87.5
Advanced	Brushless variable-reluctance "disc" motor with 3-phase semiconductor controller	3.0	85	90
Recent	Manual transmission and clutch	0.55		
Improved, Advanced	Manual transmission and clutch	0.47	94	96
Recent	Axle and driveshaft	0.110		
Improved, Advanced	Axle and driveshaft	0.097		

The motor-controller combinations of Table 4.6 were based on a study of prospective motor weight and cost made at the Ford Motor Company in 1973.[4] In the years since then, high-power, high-current transistors have been developed which promise to replace the SCR's of the study, eliminating heavy commutation circuitry. Accordingly, controller weights were assumed to be about half those of the Ford study, but motor descriptors from the study were unchanged. The recent-technology motor in Table 4.6 is a conventional direct-current, series-wound traction motor controlled by a transistor chopper. Operation of the motor at low speeds, where efficiency is relatively low, is unnecessary because a multispeed transmission and clutch are included in the propulsion system. The improved-technology motor and controller are simply assumed to be midway in weight and efficiency between the recent and advanced components. They might employ improved transistor choppers and traction motors with field and/or armature current control. The advanced-technology motor is a brushless design of ultimate mechanical simplicity. It is light and efficient, even for relatively low design speeds, needs virtually no maintenance, and is especially suitable for inexpensive high-volume production. It requires, however, a relatively sophisticated controller. Though this system is not fully developed for production, laboratory models have been tested with excellent results.

The inclusion of a transmission and clutch is not necessary in electric cars but is usually advantageous. Electric motors which operate efficiently at very low speeds are both heavy and expensive. With a multispeed transmission, motor speed and efficiency may be kept relatively high even when the car is moving slowly. The weight and cost of the transmission and clutch are usually less than the reductions in motor weight and cost which they permit. The manual transmission assumed is the most efficient type available. Given the limited capacity of storage batteries, use of the most efficient transmission possible is desirable.

The weights and efficiencies of the transmissions and axles in Table 4.6 were taken from the work of the Interagency Task Force and from other studies which support the high overall efficiencies shown.[4,6]

To derive the propulsion coefficients for four-passenger electric cars, it was assumed that required motor output was 23 watts for each kilogram of car test weight. This figure was found adequate in the Ford study of electric drive for acceleration from 0 to 64 km/h in 10 seconds, as required here for electric cars.[4] Adding the weights per kilowatt of Table 4.6 for a given technology level, adjusting for transmission and axle losses, and then multiplying by 23 watts per kilogram yields the values of coefficient "b" which appear in Table 4.4. For two-passenger cars, coefficients were based on a figure of 13 watts per kilogram; this was derived from the ratio of acceleration requirements for the two- and four-passenger cars, assuming similar histories of motor power during acceleration.

4.5 ROAD LOAD

On a level road at constant speed, the propulsion system must supply power to the driven wheels equal to the road load, which is composed of aerodynamic drag and the rolling resistance of tires, wheels, and wheel bearings. Minimization of road load is as important as minimization of weight in designing an electric car for long range between recharges.

The aerodynamic drag assumed for future electric cars is shown in Table 4.7. The drag coefficient, C_D, relates drag to body shape; for US automobiles it has typically been around 0.5, and for European automobiles about 0.46.[7] The value assumed for the four-passenger car, 0.35, is near the historical minimum for production automobiles.[8] The value for the two-passenger car, 0.4, need not be as low because this car is intended for lower-speed operation and is less sensitive to drag. Wind-tunnel tests have suggested that drag coefficients under .25 are theoretically possible, so future cars may surpass the assumptions of Table 4.7.[9] Theoretical possibilities, however, must be tempered with many real-world requirements often omitted from wind-tunnel tests, such as impact-resistant bumpers, external rear-view mirrors, convenient door handles, and underbody treatment giving reasonable access for maintenance to propulsion and running gear.

The frontal areas of Table 4.7 are primarily determined by the requirement for two-abreast seating in both the two-passenger and four-passenger cars. The values shown were taken from a review of actual electric car designs and are adequate for comfortable seating, but not commodious. The two-passenger CDA Town Car (see Table 2.1) had a frontal area of 1.69 m^2. The Honda Civic, among the smallest of recent ICE cars, has a frontal area of 1.58 m^2.[10]

The rolling resistance assumed for future electric cars is shown in Table 4.8. It includes contributions from both tires and wheel bearings, though that of tires is an order of magnitude larger. Good current radial-ply tires are assumed for the "recent" level of technology.[11,12] Reductions of 10% and 20% (at 80 km/h) are assumed for future radial-ply tires. Again, there is a considerable range of possibilities, with many factors to be considered beside efficiency. These include durability, tread life, noise, harshness of ride, and suitability for existing designs of wheel rims, among others. The values in Table 4.8 are relatively conservative; though testing methods have yet to be standardized, recent measurements suggest that the radial-ply tires of some manufacturers already offer rolling resistances well below those shown.[13] Because coefficient C_2 is quite small, rolling resistance rises less than 3% at speeds under 88 km/h. Overall rolling resistances from Table 4.8 are about 1% to 1.3% of vehicle weight.

TABLE 4.7

AERODYNAMIC DRAG

	Drag Coefficient C_D	Frontal Area A
Two-Passenger Car	0.4	1.67 m^2
Four-Passenger Car	0.35	1.858 m^2

Drag Force $F_a = \frac{1}{2} \rho V^2 \cdot C_D A$ newtons,

where V is velocity (m/s)

ρ is air density (1.225 kg/m^3 at sea level)

TABLE 4.8

ROLLING RESISTANCE

	C_1	C_2
Recent technology	.127	.000116
Improved technology	.118	.000108
Advanced technology	.108	.000099

Rolling Resistance $F = (C_1 + C_2 V) \cdot W_T$ newtons,

where V is velocity (m/s)

W_T is test weight of car (kg)

Figure 4.3 summarizes road loads for future electric cars as a function of speed and test weight. The curve applies to both the two-passenger and four-passenger cars, since their products of drag coefficient and frontal area are almost equal. Evidently tire rolling resistance exceeds aerodynamic drag in most low-to-moderate-speed urban driving.

If a particular weight is assumed, the total power required to propel a car at constant speed may be calculated, as shown in Fig. 4.4 for one of the representative future cars of Table 4.1. The power required for ascending a six percent grade far exceeds that for cruising on a level road. Given the 23 W/kg peak motor power required for acceleration from 0-64 km/h in 10 seconds, about 42 kW is available at the driving wheels, enough to maintain the 88-km/h speed limit on maximum freeway grades of 6%. The power continuously available, assumed to be forty percent of this, is 17 kW, substantially more than needed to cruise at the legal maximum on level roads.

4.6   CALCULATION OF DRIVING RANGE AND ENERGY REQUIREMENTS

A computer simulation was developed and operated to calculate the range and energy usage of the future electric cars in urban driving. The simulation, called ELVEC, uses the car weights and road load equations of Secs. 4.3 and 4.5 to calculate moment-by-moment power requirements for following a specified urban driving cycle. It transforms these into battery power outputs by using the propulsion efficiencies of Sec. 4.4. It utilizes a model of battery discharge, the "fractional depletion" model, to determine the number of driving cycles--and hence the range between recharges--possible with the batteries described in Sec. 3. It also estimates the recharging energy requirements from the battery output, the battery efficiencies of Sec. 3, and a given efficiency for the battery charger.

The ELVEC simulation was run with battery fraction as a parameter for each of the eight design concepts for future electric cars (see Fig.

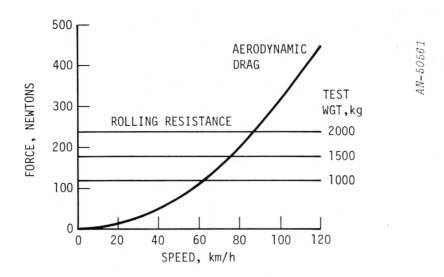

Figure 4.3. Road Load for Improved-Technology Car

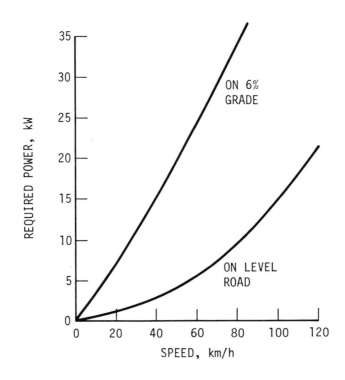

Figure 4.4. Power Required at Constant Speed
(four-passenger, improved electric
car, 1747 kg curb weight, 136 kg payload)

4.2). The resultant driving ranges and energy outputs from the propulsion battery are shown in Figs. 4.5 and 4.6 as a function of battery fraction. In all cases, the battery chargers were assumed to be 90% efficient, a reasonable achievement for future years but far above the 65-75% typically attained by chargers built in recent years.

Figure 4.5 shows that the design range of the electric car depends strongly on battery fraction. There are practical limits, however. If the battery is too small, it cannot provide sufficient output power to meet the acceleration requirement. If too large, its weight or bulk may be too great to carry in a car of reasonable proportions. Moreover, energy use and purchase price both rise rapidly as battery fraction and curb weight increase.

Reasonable design ranges are indicated in Fig. 4.7, which is simply the parametric results replotted to show curb weight as a function of range. At the dashed extremities of the curves, either the battery is too small to meet acceleration power requirements or the battery fraction exceeds 42% of curb weight, a reasonably high figure in previous electric cars. Within these limits, the choice of battery fraction can vary with the design range of the cars by a factor of about two (almost three for the nickel-zinc battery car). The most appropriate choice of design range depends on driving requirements, to be discussed in Sec. 5, and associated costs, to be discussed in Sec. 7. It also depends on energy use, which is shown as a function of range in Fig. 4.8.

The calculation of the minimum battery fraction sufficient for meeting acceleration requirements was based on a maximum battery power density of 80% of the value shown in Table 3.1 for each battery type. As batteries age and are partially discharged, their maximum power output dwindles; the 80% factor was introduced in recognition of this fact, though details of the actual diminution remain to be determined for the future batteries.

111

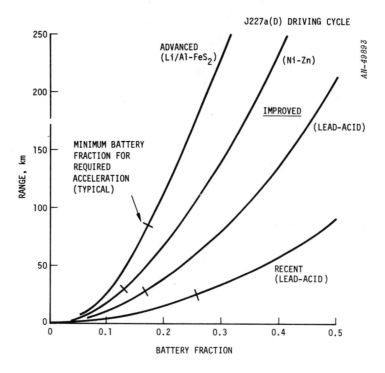

a. Two-Passenger Cars

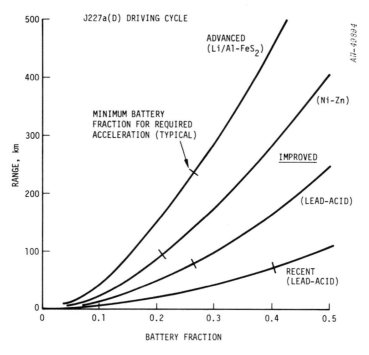

b. Four-Passenger Cars

Figure 4.5. Range Versus Battery Fraction

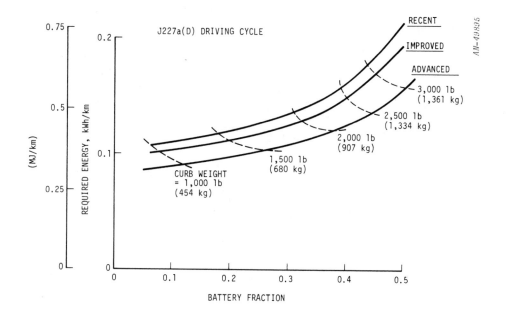

a. Two-Passenger Cars

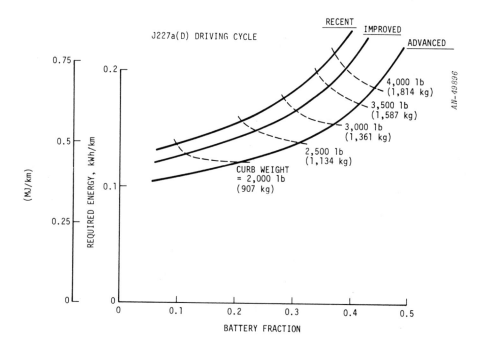

b. Four-Passenger Cars

Figure 4.6. Energy Use Versus Battery Fraction

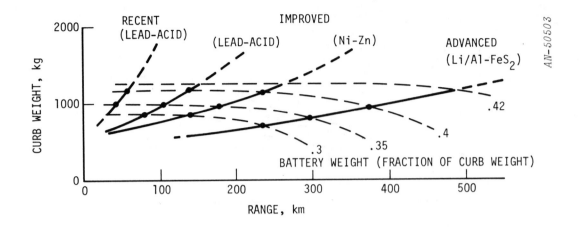

a. Two-Passenger Cars

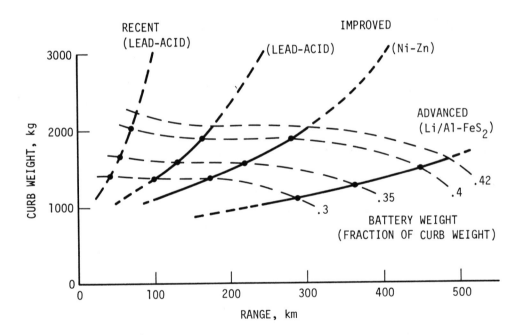

b. Four-Passenger Cars

Figure 4.7. Curb Weight Versus Range

114

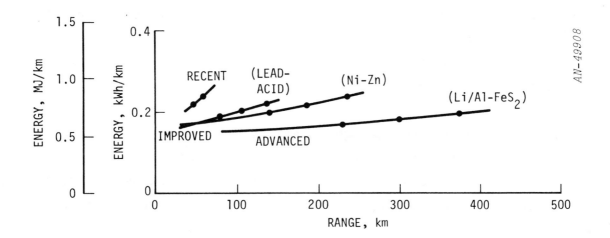

a. Two-Passenger Cars

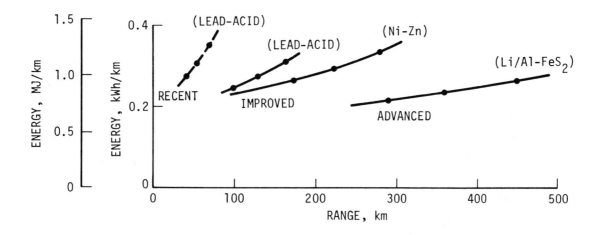

b. Four-Passenger Cars

Figure 4.8. Recharge Energy Versus Range

The driving cycles used in calculating ranges were urban cycles recommended by the Society of Automotive Engineers for the evaluation of electric vehicles. Four such cycles have been defined, as shown in Fig. 4.9. The most demanding, described by schedule "D", was used to calculate the urban range of the four-passenger car. The D cycle requires a top speed of 72 km/h and covers about 1.6 km.

The schedules for the SAE cycles are written in terms of speeds and times that can readily be followed by a driver on a test track. Though a linear increase of speed during the acceleration time (constant acceleration) is often assumed, other profiles of acceleration which reach the specified cruise speed at the end of the acceleration time are acceptable. An exponentially decreasing acceleration profile is a desirable alternative because it requires constant power rather than the linearly increasing power necessary for constant acceleration. The exponentially decreasing profile illustrated in Fig. 4.9 was used in simulating the future electric cars. It reduces the peak power required by about 35%, thus avoiding the high power outputs which would reduce the overall energy output of the battery.

The ELVEC simulation effectively integrates the equation of motion of the electric car following the specified driving cycle. This equation is simply

$$F_P = F_A + F_R + M_e A$$

where

F_P = propulsive force applied via driven wheels

F_A = aerodynamic drag force

F_D = rolling resistance

M_e = effective mass (including rotating components)

A = acceleration

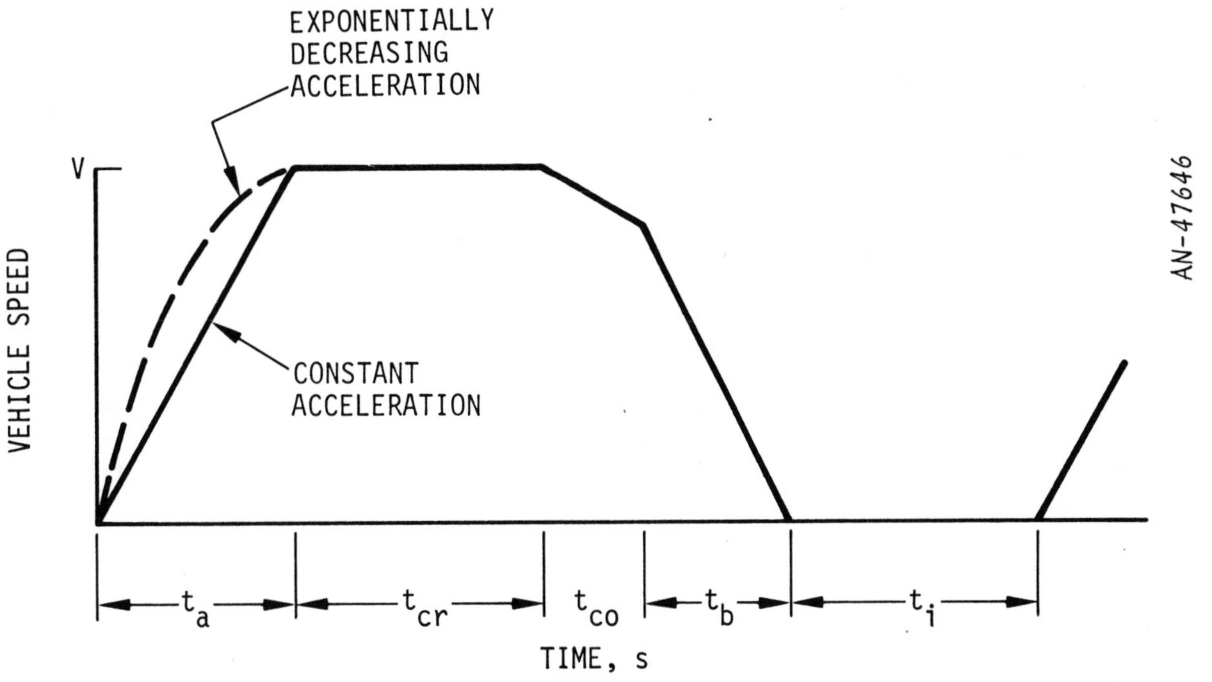

TEST PARAMETER	SAE SCHEDULE (all times in seconds) A	B	C	D
MAXIMUM SPEED (V). km/h	16 ± 1.5	32 ± 1.5	48 ± 1.5	72 ± 1.5
ACCELERATE TIME (t_a)	4 ± 1	19 ± 1	18 ± 2	28 ± 2
CRUISE TIME (t_{cr})	0	19 ± 1	20 ± 1	50 ± 2
COAST TIME (t_{co})	2 ± 1	4 ± 1	8 ± 1	10 ± 1
BRAKE TIME (t_b)	3 ± 1	5 ± 1	9 ± 1	9 ± 1
IDLE TIME (t_i)	30 ± 2	25 ± 2	25 ± 2	25 ± 2
TOTAL TIME	39 ± 2	72 ± 2	80 ± 2	122 ± 2

Figure 4.9. SAE J227a Driving Cycle Schedules

In this equation, the acceleration is that required to meet the driving schedule. The aerodynamic drag and rolling resistance are calculated as in Tables 4.7 and 4.8. The propulsive force is determined for each increment of time, multiplied by speed to give the instantaneous propulsive power required, and divided by the propulsion system efficiency to yield the required battery output power.

The effective mass M_e is nearly the test mass of the car (the curb weight plus the 136-kg test payload representing two average male adults). It includes a small adjustment for the rotating components of the car, the wheels, axles, transmission, clutch, and motor, which must be spun up as the car is accelerated over the road. An empirically-determined formula was used for this adjustment to M_e, which typically was 4% or less of the curb weight of the car.

To calculate the range of the electric car, it is necessary to estimate how many times the battery can meet the output power requirements of the driving cycle. This estimate was based on the fractional depletion model, the simplest of several models of battery discharge which are available in ELVEC. For lead-acid batteries it has been shown to give accurate results. For the future batteries, insufficient test data has been published either to calibrate the other models or to verify the accuracy of any of them.

The fractional depletion model is built around estimates of specific power versus specific energy such as those shown in Fig. 3.1. It assumes that the fraction of battery capacity which is depleted during a time interval Δt is

$$f = p \cdot \Delta t / e$$

where

p = specific power required from battery during time interval Δt
e = specific energy of battery at specific power output p

During each increment of a driving cycle, the specific power required, p, is determined from the total output required from the battery and the battery weight. The associated specific energy is determined from the estimates plotted in Fig. 3.1, and the fraction of battery depleted is found from the equation above. The sum of depletions during each increment of the cycle equals the total depletion per cycle. The reciprocal of this, rounded down to the nearest integer, is taken as the range of the car in driving cycles, and multiplied by the length of the cycle to give the urban driving ranges shown in Figs. 4.4-4.7.

For constant-speed driving, the fractional depletion model obviously gives reasonable results. It reduces to a determination of the required power for steady-speed cruise and the determination from Fig. 3.1 of the time during which the battery can provide that power. For stop-start driving it has an obvious disadvantage: it cannot represent the phenomenon of recuperation, well-known for lead-acid batteries, in which the battery "recovers" capability if allowed to stand unloaded for a time after being heavily loaded. Nevertheless, the fractional depletion model proved to be nearly as effective in estimating the urban ranges of actual electric cars as a more elaborate model which explicitly provided for recuperation.

It should be recognized that the computer model is simply a substitute for actual range tests, and even in real-world tests there is considerable variation of electric car range. The condition of the battery (state of charge, age, temperature, recent cycling history) is seldom constant from test to test. Neither is a host of other conditions. Rolling resistance, for example, may decline considerably over the life of a tire. The condition of the road surface and the type of pavement further influence rolling resistance. And in any car, gasoline or electric, the habits of the driver strongly influence fuel economy and, consequently, range per refueling or recharging.

4.7 SPECIFIC FUTURE ELECTRIC CARS

At this point it was necessary to choose some specific examples of electric cars from the parametric results of the preceding section. To make further analyses of performance and impact for the whole range of possibilities treated so far would have been an endless task. Accordingly, examples were selected which are representative of future possibilities giving a combination of good service and reasonable cost in important applications. These representative examples were summarized at the beginning of this section in Table 4.1.

As Sec. 5 will show, the least demanding application for electric propulsion is as urban secondary cars. These are cars at urban households which also have a conventional (primary) car which can be used for long trips or large loads. With ranges of 55-75 km, electric secondary cars would be adequate for 95% of the travel days at a typical multicar household. For "only" cars, those at one-car urban households, corresponding ranges would be 85-150 km. And for primary urban cars, those used for the most demanding travel days at multicar households, ranges of 110-220 km are needed. With the greater capability, 220 km, the electric car would be adequate for 95% of general use, not just urban use, in the most demanding service--that usually exacted from new cars, which are driven considerably farther per year than the average of cars of all ages.

These applications and associated upper ranges were the basis for the selection of specific cars shown in Table 4.1. They appear to represent a reasonable compromise between cost and capability. On the one hand, it would clearly be desirable to increase ranges so as to cover driving requirements on say 98% of driving days instead of only 95%. On the other hand, this would increase required range thirty to forty percent. Much larger cars and batteries would be necessary, with attendant cost increases which could be a cent per km or more over the life of the car. Is a little extra travel on one day out of twenty worth paying an extra cent for every kilometer driven? No one can anser that general question

120

with assurance today. Implicit in the use of the 95% criterion for choosing ranges here, however, is the answer "no." The issue is discussed further in Sec. 8.1.

Several of the representative cars have ranges greater than the 95th percentile requirement of their application. In all such cases but one, the indicated range is the minimum at which the required acceleration can be achieved. In the remaining case, the improved four-passenger car with nickel-zinc battery for general use, the 250 km range was chosen to enable direct comparisons with the 250-km advanced car, and also with the 150-km improved car with lead-acid battery, which happens to have the same battery fraction and curb weight.

Among the representative future cars of Table 4.1, the most interesting is probably the improved four-passenger car with battery fraction of .38. With future lead-acid batteries, this car's range of 150 km would suffice for urban use as either a secondary or only car. With future nickel-zinc batteries, its range of 250 km would be adequate for general use, even in replacing new cars. The chances for successful development of one or both of these batteries seem good.

In comparison, the other cars of Table 4.1 seem likely to be less significant. The advanced lithium battery car is less likely to be achieved, though it would be even more widely useful if successfully developed. The smaller cars and the cars of lesser range, on the other hand, are of limited importance because their applications are much more restricted.

For these reasons the improved four-passenger car with battery fraction of .38 was singled out for special attention. Section 4.8 shows the effects on its range and energy use of changing various assumptions. Figures 4.10 and 4.11 present breakdowns of its nominal weight and energy use.

The weight of the improved four-passenger car is apportioned as shown in Fig. 4.10. For comparison, the figure also shows the weight apportionment for the weight-conscious ICE car which was used as a basis for the parametric modeling of electric car weight. The great difference between the two cars arises in the weight of battery which must be carried in the electric car to give adequate operating range: 664 kg, as opposed to the 45 kg for fuel and tank carried in the ICE car. To support this battery, the electric car requires an additional 182 kg of structure. The two cars have identical passenger compartments and upper body weights, and the propulsion weights are also nearly equal. The output of the electric propulsion components is a little less, however, and in the heavier electric car it leads to relatively low acceleration capability. Overall, the electric car weights 86% more than its ICE counterpart (15% more without battery), provides only about half the acceleration capability, and is limited to 150-250 km range, depending on battery.

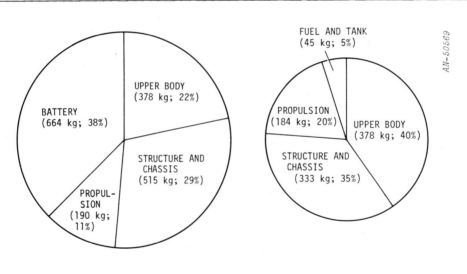

"IMPROVED" ELECTRIC SUBCOMPACT

- 1747 kg CURB WEIGHT
- 43.3 kW PEAK POWER AVAILABLE
  (23 W PER kg OF TEST WEIGHT)
- 250 km RANGE (NICKEL-ZINC BATTERY)
- 150 km RANGE (LEAD-ACID BATTERY)

"WEIGHT CONSCIOUS" ICE SUBCOMPACT

- 940 kg CURB WEIGHT
- 53 kW CONTINUOUS POWER AVAILABLE
  (49.3 W PER kg OF TEST WEIGHT)
- UNLIMITED RANGE (WITH REFUELING)

Figure 4.10. Curb Weights of Comparable Electric and ICE Cars

Figure 4.11 shows the energy flow in this car during urban driving. About 1 MJ of energy input to the battery charger is required for each km of travel. Some 30% is lost in the charger and battery. The remainder passes through the propulsion system, which applies about half of the original megajoule to the driving wheels as mechanical energy. Most of this mechanical energy goes to overcoming tire and aerodynamic losses; only about a third of it (a sixth of the total energy input) is dissipated in the brakes.

Regenerative braking, which has so far not been considered, would recover part of the energy lost in the brakes. Because the performance estimates made so far do not include regenerative braking, they tend to be conservative. Offsetting this, however, are various assumptions which tend to be optimistic. Probably the most important of these is that the batteries will meet the performance projections of Sec. 3. Even if the projections are met by the battery when new, degradation of performance with aging and when partially discharged seems inevitable. No allowance has been made for this degradation. On the other hand, the performance of ICE cars is invariably specified for new condition, and is also degraded under most actual conditions of use.

4.8 ALTERNATIVES

So far, this report has evaluated the range and energy use of electric cars only in a single driving cycle (SAE J227a, schedule D). Under other driving conditions, range and energy use may be substantially different. Furthermore, they may also be substantially affected by changes in assumptions about battery and automotive technology, by the inclusion of regenerative braking, and by the inclusion of provisions for more safety in crashes.

The effects of a number of changes in driving conditions and technological assumptions are shown quantitatively in Table 4.9. The reference car to which the percentage changes refer is the improved four-passenger electric car of Table 4.1 with battery fraction 0.38 and nickel-zinc

123

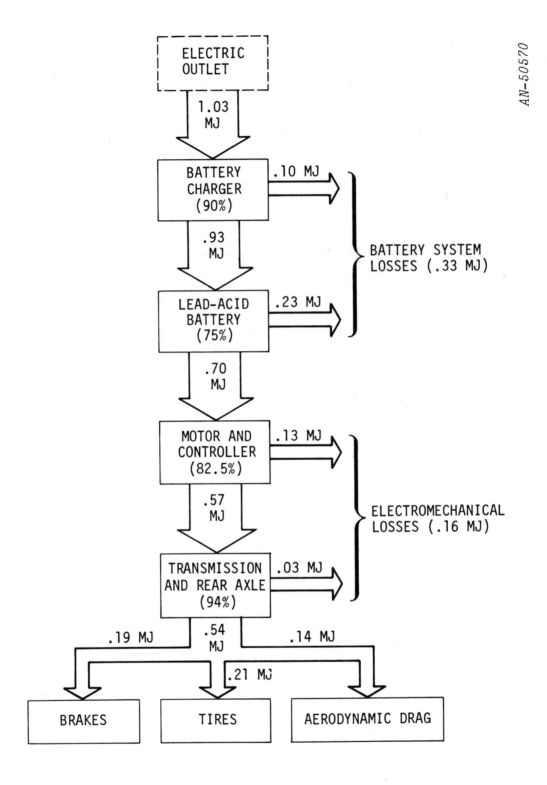

Figure 4.11. Energy Flow in the Improved Four-Passenger
Electric Car (per km of urban driving)

TABLE 4.9

EFFECTS OF CHANGED CONDITIONS AND ASSUMPTIONS

Condition	Urban Range		Energy Use	
	km	Change, percent	MJ/km	Change, percent
Reference Case (Improved four-passenger car with Ni-Zn battery, 136-kg payload, in SAE J227a(D) cycle)	255	0	1.12	0
Other Driving Cycles:				
Federal Urban Cycle	249	-3	1.10	-2
FAKRA	236	-7	1.22	10
SAE J227 Metropolitan	246	-4	1.13	1
SAE J227 Residential	326	28	.91	-18
SAE J227a(C)	283	10	1.05	-6
Constant-Speed Driving				
65 km/h	510	100	.67	-40
88.5 km/h	360	41	.89	-21
115 km/h	233	-9	1.20	7
Other Payloads				
0 kg	274	7.4	1.07	-4
408 kg	223	-13	1.26	12
Other Batteries				
Improved Lead-Acid	149	-42	1.05	-5
Advanced Li/Al-FeS$_2$	414	62	1.31	17
Other Automotive Technology				
Recent Domestic (1975-6)	180	-29	1.50	34
Advanced	308	21	.95	-15
Regenerative Braking	328	28	.90	-19
Safety Level II	245.7	-4	1.15	3

battery. The effects of changed conditions were computed by reruns of the ELVEC simulation. The energy usage shown is that required as input to the battery charger, assuming a charger efficiency of 90% and the battery efficiencies in Table 3.1.

In Table 4.9, the first three alternatives are different driving cycles: the Federal urban cycle in which conventional ICE cars are evaluated, the FAKRA urban cycle commonly used in Germany, and an SAE urban cycle which was recently superseded by schedule D of recommended test procedure J227a. The ranges of the reference car in these cycles differ little though the cycles themselves differ considerably. The Federal urban cycle is 1,372 seconds long, almost ten times the length of the reference cycle, with very little constant-speed driving; its maximum speed is 91 km/h. The FAKRA cycle, in contrast, is about half as long as the reference cycle and includes a maximum speed of only 50 km/hr.

Two other driving cycles are also included in Table 4.9, both better suited to cars intended for low-speed neighborhood use than general urban driving. The second of these, schedule C of SAE J227a, is described in Fig. 4.9. Its maximum speed is only 48 km/h. The Residential schedule of J227, which it supersedes, is similarly undemanding. On both these driving cycles, range is substantially increased and energy use substantially reduced.

In constant-speed driving, even larger range increases and reductions in energy use could be obtained because there would be no loss in braking (Fig. 4.11). At the legal speed limit, range would be 41% greater than in the reference case, and energy use 21% less.

In actual use, stop-start driving to the full range of the car as in the reference case is probably unlikely--at the average speed of 48 km/h implicit in the reference driving cycle, it would take well over 5 hours to travel 255 km. On the other hand, a typical day's travel will not all

126

be constant-speed driving on a level, windless road where a maximum range of 360 km or more, depending on speed, might be obtained. Some figure between these two values would probably be achievable in actual itineraries.

In comparison with constant-speed driving, changes in payload affect range and energy use relatively little. The values shown in Table 4.9 are for extremes: zero and maximum design loads.

If other batteries were substituted for the nickel-zinc batteries of the reference cars, range changes could be very great. The basic energy use of the vehicle would be unaffected, however, so changes in energy use per km would arise only from different battery efficiency. The alternatives for propulsion batteries appearing in Table 4.9 are those selected to represent the future range of possibilities in Sec. 3. There are, of course, many other possibilities, but probably none of them which are reasonably likely would result in a range beyond the 414 km of the table.

The use of other levels of automotive technology would considerably affect both the range and energy use of the car, through changes in weight, propulsion efficiency, and tire losses. A reversion to the technology of recent standard domestic sedans is unlikely, but the resultant figures in Table 4.9 illustrate how much more favorable today's efficient, weight-conscious automotive technology is for electric automobiles. Reaching the "advanced" level of technology in the mid-1980's seems nearly certain for the structure of the future electric car, but the higher efficiency and lighter weight of the "advanced" motor and controller are less sure.

In Fig. 4.12, the effects on range of three specific technical varia-tions are shown separately. These variations are expressed as percentage changes of the reference car losses shown in Fig. 4.11. Their relative importance in Fig. 4.12 reflects the stop-start reference driving cycle. In constant-speed driving, aerodynamic losses would be relatively more important, while electrical and mechanical losses would be less so. In

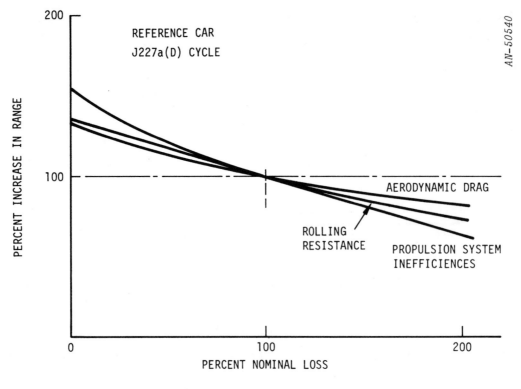

Figure 4.12. Effect of Varied Losses

constant-speed driving, average power requirements are less and the losses
in motor and controller would also be a smaller percentage of this lower
power.

The effects of regenerative braking shown in Table 4.9 are probably
an upper bound on real-world possibilities. They were computed under
several optimistic assumptions. First, it was assumed that with no penalty
in propulsion weight, regeneration at all speeds down to zero could be
achieved with the same efficiencies attained by the propulsion system in
ordinary driving. Actually, however, few regenerative braking systems have
ever recovered energy efficiently at low car speeds. Second, it was
assumed that all the energy returned to the battery would subsequently be
withdrawable for propulsion, despite the assumed battery efficiency of 70%.
This assumption was made in deference to test results for lead-acid battery
systems, which indeed show that regeneration permits as much (or even more)
extra energy to be withdrawn from the battery as is returned through braking.
This is no violation of the principle of conservation of energy; instead,

it results from the partial utilization of active material during rapid discharge of the battery. More of the active material is apparently made accessible for discharge by the periodic reversals of battery current due to regenerative braking. A portion of the extra energy output is thus supplied eventually from the charger (a factor not included in the energy use estimate of Table 4.9). If this effect applies at all to nickel-zinc batteries, it may well be much less pronounced than in lead-acid batteries, since the accessibility of active material in the nickel-zinc battery seems to be less reduced by heavy current drains.

If its cost is reasonable, the addition of regenerative braking to the reference car would surely be desirable. Its practical effect, however, would probably be relatively modest. Its efficiencies would surely be less than those implicit in the example of Table 4.9. Furthermore, it affords little or no benefit in highway driving at relatively constant speed, and highway driving is likely to be a major part of the long travel days which would tax range capability.

Finally, Table 4.9 shows the effects of increased safety on the range and energy use of the reference car. Safety Level I is implicit in all the future electric cars considered thus far. It provides protection against 48 km/h frontal crashes into fixed barriers and represents today's level of required performance. Safety Level II provides protection against 64 km/h frontal crashes and 32 km/h side impacts as well, and might become a requirement for automobiles of the future.

The additional weight due to Safety Level II is estimated at 52 kg for the reference car. This is effectively fixed weight, requiring an accompanying 27-kg addition to the structural weight of the car which depends on gross vehicle weight. The weight of the battery in the reference car was held constant, so the car offering Safety Level II in Table 4.9 has a curb weight of 1,826 kg, versus 1,747 kg for the reference car. Its range and energy use are moderately affected. So also is its acceleration capability.

Specific requirements for accessory power have not yet been included in the analysis, though a weight allowance of 18 kg for an accessory battery is included in the upper body weights of all the future cars. In the reference car, a nickel-zinc battery weighing 18 kg could provide over 5 MJ (1400 watt-hours) of energy for such accessories as power steering and brakes (assumed necessary in a car of this weight), lights, windshield wipers, and the like. This would be adequate in most cases, but for high-power accessories such as an air conditioner or auxiliary electric heater, it would be necessary to draw power from the propulsion battery. This would reduce vehicle range.

Typical requirements for today's accessories are shown in Table 4.10. The minimum likely total, for power steering, power brakes, and intermittent brake lights (assuming braking as required in the SAE J227a (D) cycle), is 90.1 watts. This could be provided for over 15 hours by the accessory battery, far longer than likely to be required. Driving the maximum range of the reference car on the "D" cycle requires only 5.4 hours; driving the maximum range at a steady 88.5 km/h (the legal limit) takes only 4.1 hours. With the addition of headlights, the accessory battery would provide 5.7 hours of operation; with headlights and windshield wipers, 4.7 hours.

TABLE 4.10

POWER REQUIRED FOR TYPICAL RECENT ACCESSORIES

Power Steering	70 W
Power Brakes	10
Brake Lights	48
Headlights	154
Wipers	55
Radio	31
Blower	144
Air Conditioner	2050

Source: Ref. 6

130

It is also probable, of course, that more efficient accessories could be developed. Quartz-halogen headlights, for example, provide several times as much light per watt of electric power. Overall, then, no adjustments to the range of the reference car seem needed to account for basic accessories.

For forced ventilation, auxiliary electric heating, and air conditioning, however, substantial additional power might be required from the propulsion battery, since no reasonable accessory battery would suffice. The requirement for an air conditioner in Table 4.10, about 2 kW, is an upper bound; it is sufficient for recent domestic full-sized sedans. Full-time operation of such an air conditioner from the propulsion battery would reduce the range of the reference car by some 15% and increase energy use per km correspondingly. The penalty would be less for a smaller car and for part-time operation of the air conditioner, which would be thermostatically controlled and cycle on and off except under the most adverse conditions. Nevertheless, on those occasions demanding nearly the full range of the car in hot weather, it would be necessary for drivers to choose between air conditioning and a reduction of up to 15% in the day's travel.

Whether auxiliary heating will be required is dependent on climate. In mild areas, waste heat from the motor and controller would suffice to maintain comfortable interior temperatures in ambient temperatures of 5-10° C (40-50° F). The losses of the motor and controller in the urban driving cycle are about 1.6 kW; they appear as heat which could largely be recovered to warm the passenger compartment. An auxiliary gasoline heater would be effective in very cold climates. A 2-kW resistance heater would provide auxiliary heating sufficient for temperatures of -5° C to 0° C, but better performance with less power would probably be obtained from electric seat heaters or from operation of the air conditioner in reverse as a heat pump.

In any case, auxiliary electric heating would be likely to limit travel only on that small proportion of driving days in which very long trips and cold weather occur together.

There remains another interesting alternative to the reference car of Table 4.9: a car offering acceleration comparable to that of conventional internal-combustion automobiles. This is primarily a prospect for cars using the nickel-zinc battery, which affords a relatively high peak power density. The car described in Table 4.11 takes advantage of it, and at the same time offers a choice of maximum ranges through use of either a full battery or half battery.

In comparison with the reference car, this high-performance car offers the same battery weight (with full battery) but a larger motor and controller. This gives acceleration near the low end of the range exhibited by current ICE cars. With half the battery removed, however, the reduced weight of the car allows acceleration typical of recent conventional cars. This high-performance car also benefits from two optimistic assumptions: high-efficiency regenerative braking and improved tires with 15% less rolling resistance than those of the reference car, more than offsetting its extra propulsion and structure weight.

This is only one exmaple, of course, of the myriad ways in which future technological possibilities might be tailored to maximize the market appeal of electric cars. Government and industry may be expected to explore many of these possibilities in the marketplace as their technology becomes available. In this study, however, other factors as yet uninvestigated require consideration next: the adequacy of future electric cars to meet the requirements of typical driving, and their cost relative to that of conventional ICE cars.

TABLE 4.11

A HIGH-PERFORMANCE ELECTRIC CAR
WITH NICKEL-ZINC BATTERY

	Half Battery	Full Battery
Battery Weight, kg	332	664
Curb Weight, kg	1,470	1,802
Payload, kg	740	408
Range, km		
on SAE J227a (D) cycle	172	350
at 88.5 km/h	186	393
Energy Use, MJ/km		
on SAE J227a (D) cycle	.75	.85
at 88.5 km/h	.76	.82
Acceleration Time, seconds	15.7	18.9
(for 0-96 km/sec acceleration)		

SECTION 4 REFERENCES

1. *The Report by the Federal Task Force on Motor Vehicle Goals Beyond 1980*, Vol. 2, Task Force Report (Draft), US Department of Transportation, September 2, 1976.

2. *Automotive Design Analysis, Report of a Panel of the Interagency Task Force on Motor Vehicle Goals Beyond 1980*, Interim Report, R. Strombote, US Department of Transportation, Chairman, August 1976.

3. J. R. Brennand et al., *Electric and Hybrid Vehicle Performance and Design Goal Determination Study*, General Research Corporation CR-1-734, August 1977.

4. L. Foote, et al., *Electric Vehicle Systems Study*, Ford Motor Company Report No. SR-73-132, October 1973.

5. D. G. Adams et al., *High Strength Materials and Vehicle Weight Reduction Analysis*, Chrysler Corporation, SAE Paper No. 750221, February 1975.

6. D. Sheridan, et al., *A Study of the Energy Utilization of Gasoline and Battery - Electric Powered Special Purpose Vehicles*, General Motors Corporation, SAE No. 760119, February 1976.

7. W. H. Hucho, et al., *The Optimization of Body Details - A Method for Reducing the Aerodynamic Drag of Road Vehicles*, SAE Paper No. 760185, February 1976.

8. A. Morelli, et al., *The Body Shape of Minimum Drag*, SAE Paper No. 760186, February 1976.

9. S. F. Hoerner, *Fluid Dynamic Drag*, Second Edition, Published by the authors, Brick Town, New Jersey, 1965.

10. *Electric Vehicle Design*, Technical Proposal No. E(04-3)-1213, AMF Advanced Systems Laboratory, April 1976.

11. D. Tenniswood and H. Graetzel, *Minimum Road Load for Electric Cars*, SAE Paper No. 670177, January 1967.

12. S. K. Clark, et al., *Rolling Resistance of Pneumatic Tires*, Michigan University Report No. DOT-TSC-OST-74-33, May 1975.

13. Glenn D. Thompson, et al., *Variations in Tire Rolling Resistance*, LDTP-77-5, US Environmental Protection Agency, Ann Arbor, Michigan, October 1977.

5   BASIC DRIVING REQUIREMENTS

Section 4 has shown that as the range between recharges of electric cars is increased, battery weight and curb weight both increase rapidly. As will be demonstrated in Sec. 7, initial and life-cycle costs will rise correspondingly. This makes it important to design the electric car for the minimum range sufficient for its intended application. Extra range which would be infrequently used may not be worth its relatively high extra cost to most motorists. Nor, for that matter, may seldom-needed speed or passenger capacity be worth its extra costs.

To determine the minimum requirements for range, speed, and capacity in typical kinds of driving, it is necessary to make a detailed new analysis of existing travel data. For previous applications of this data, it has been unnecessary to determine such things as the frequency with which daily driving exceeds a given range. For electric cars, however, with a limited range between overnight recharges, this is a critical consideration.

The range and capacity required for urban use shown in Table 5.1 were derived from extensive origin-destination travel surveys made some years ago in Washington and Los Angeles. These requirements would suffice for all travel on 95% of driving days for three distinct groups of cars. Primary cars include the single car driven most at each multicar household. Secondary cars include all other cars at these households. "Only" cars include all remaining cars, which are at one-car households. In addition to the ranges and capacities shown, speeds sufficient for freeway driving are required by all three groups if needs on 95% of driving days are to be met.

If required ranges were chosen to suffice on 98% rather than 95% of driving days, the values in Table 5.1 would be increased by 30-40%.

The requirements in Table 5.1 for general-use cars reflect needs of interurban and rural driving as well as urban driving. They are based

135

TABLE 5.1

REQUIRED RANGE AND CAPACITY

(for 95% of driving days)

	Range, km	Capacity, persons
Urban Use		
Secondary Car	55–75	3-4
Only Car	85–150	3-4
Primary Car	110–220	4
General Use		
Average Car (16,000 km/yr)	130	4
New Car (28,000 km/yr)	220	4

on much less detailed data and depend on the average distance a car is driven in a year, which is much greater for new cars than average cars.

Overall, the requirements of Table 5.1 are remarkably modest. They are all well within the reach of the cars of Sec. 4 with nickel-zinc or lithium batteries, and even the car with improved lead-acid batteries could meet all requirements save those for urban primary cars or new general-use cars.

Long trips, which are largely weekend and vacation trips, average about 1,000 km (round-trip distance) and are largely beyond the foreseeable capabilities of electric cars. Though they are relatively infrequent, occurring on less than one percent of driving days, they account for about one-sixth of annual driving per car.

This section describes the derivation of basic driving requirements and discusses their interpretation. Because driving requirements are crucial to the desirability of electric cars but little has been published on the subject, this derivation and its sources of data are presented in detail. The basic approach relies entirely on travel actually reported by various groups of people, and emphasizes the sacrifices in this travel which cars of limited capability might impose. In Sec. 8, Marketability, the travel sacrifices detailed here are considered in relation to the costs of electric cars from Sec. 7.

5.1   URBAN DRIVING

Origin-Destination Surveys

The most detailed information available on driving patterns comes from home-interview, origin-destination travel surveys which were conducted in the 1960s for most cities in the United States. In the larger cities each such survey involved lengthy interviews at tens of thousands of households. The interviews recorded details of every trip taken by each member of the household on the survey day: place and time of origin and destination, purpose of trip, mode of travel, passengers carried, use of freeway, and so on. In addition, the surveys recorded characteristics of individual travelers (age, sex, occupation, position in household, etc.) and characteristics of the household itself (type of housing unit, household income, number of automobiles available, number of drivers).

These origin-destination surveys serve as the basic source of data for comprehensive transportation planning and analysis in urban areas. For such analysis, the basic unit of travel is the individual trip; consequently, statistics abound in published reports on the frequency of trip-making and the distribution of trip distances for various purposes.

For electric cars, however, the basic analytic unit should be the entire day's travel. Since recharging will generally be done overnight, the critical question is whether the range of the electric car between recharges suffices for all the trips taken in an entire day, not just a single trip from that day. To develop such information, reprocessing of basic survey data at the individual-trip level is necessary if differences among important driver groups are to be distinguished.

Origin-destination data available from the fifteen largest urban areas of the United States are described in Table 5.2.[1] Since the labor of reprocessing individual trip data from such surveys is considerable, only two regions were investigated in this study: Los Angeles, California, and Washington, D.C.

TABLE 5.2

MAJOR URBAN ORIGIN-DESTINATION SURVEYS (from Ref. 1)

Region	Survey Year	Survey Year Population, millions	Number of Samples, thousands	Sample Rate, percent of households
New York	1963	17.8	57.2	1
Los Angeles	1967	10.2	33.0	1
Chicago	1970	6.9	21.7	0.9
San Francisco	1965	4.3	53.1	4
Detroit	1964	4.3	46.8	4
Philadelphia	1960	4.0	65.6	4/10*
Boston	1963	3.4	48.0	3/7*
Washington, D.C.	1968	2.8	30.0	4
Pittsburgh	1967	2.5	30.0	4
Cleveland	1963	2.2	173.5	25/33*
Minneapolis-St Paul	1970	1.9	6.0	1
Dallas-Ft. Worth	1964	1.8	34.2	4
St. Louis	1965	1.8	15.8	3
Baltimore	1962	1.6	27.1	5/10*
Denver	1971	1.5	16.0	3

* suburbs/city

Los Angeles was chosen for analysis because of its size, the relatively recent year of its survey, and its historic dependence on automotive travel. Furthermore, an earlier investigation of the Los Angeles data provided a substantial starting point for more thorough processing.[2] Washington was chosen because its survey was made at about the same time as the Los Angeles survey and because it differs from Los Angeles in potentially significant ways: it is much smaller, and much more dependent on public transportation.

The survey regions encompassed the complete urban areas, both cities and suburbs. The Los Angeles region covered 23,000 km^2 (9,000 square miles) in five counties, with 127 cities, four Standard Metropolitan Statistical Areas, nine million people, three million occupied housing units, and almost four million automobiles. The survey was conducted at a representative one-percent sample of housing units, about thirty thousand in all.[3] The Washington region included the District of Columbia, the three adjacent counties in Virginia, and the developed or developing portions of four additional counties in Virginia and Maryland, with nearly three million people. Again, thirty thousand households were interviewed--about four percent of all households in this smaller urban area.[4]

Processing of Data from Washington and Los Angeles

The processing in this study of origin-destination data is summarized schematically in Fig. 5.1. For each urban area, computer tapes were obtained which described all individual trips reported on the survey day. These individual trip descriptions were condensed and aggregated into new files containing whole-day travel descriptors rather than individual trip descriptors. The aggregated files for the two urban areas were written in the same format, so that distributions of travel characteristics could be developed from them by a single program.

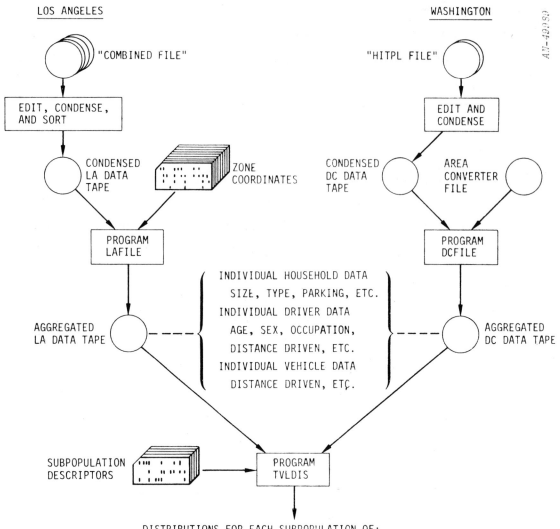

Figure 5.1. Processing of Origin-Destination Data

In the initial condensation, the files obtained from the two urban areas were edited into a format suitable for the computer in use, condensed by elimination of data not subsequently required, and sorted (in the case of Los Angeles) to group all trip records for each individual household. In the aggregation to whole-day travel descriptors, the lengths of the individual trips were determined from the origins and destinations, and added to give the entire day's travel for individual drivers and vehicles. Other information for whole travel days was also recorded: whether freeways were used, the maximum number of passengers carried, and so on.

In the final step of the processing, the aggregated data were stratified to produce distributions of driver travel, driver characteristics, and household characteristics. The distributions included either all drivers or specific subpopulations of drivers described by input cards. This made it possible to search for those drivers having limited travel patterns especially suited to the capabilities of electric cars. Almost two dozen separate subpopulations were investigated for each of the two urban areas.

Individual trip distances in this processing were computed from locations of trip origin and destination which were stated on the data tapes in terms of traffic zone numbers. Each surveyed region had been divided into over a thousand of these traffic zones. Coordinates of zone centroids were obtained and used to estimate airline travel distance, "as the crow flies," for each trip. The airline distances were converted to approximate over-the-road distances by multiplying by 1.27 (that is, $4/\pi$). This is the average factor by which over-the-road distances via a rectangular grid of roadways differ from airline distances between points of origin and destination chosen at random. Use of a detailed network model to estimate over-the-road travel distances would have been preferable, but was beyond the resources of this study. The approximation used here to obtain over-the-road travel was validated in a preliminary analysis of Los Angeles data by comparison with independent measures of total vehicular travel.[2]

Trips beginning and ending in the same zone were assigned a nominal distance based on the nearness of the centroids of adjacent zones, an approximation which little affects overall results because intrazonal travel was small (about 3% of total travel distance in Los Angeles, and under 1% in Washington).

For both survey regions, the numbers of reported trips from the data tape were adjusted upwards according to factors developed by the organizations which made the surveys. Since the surveys usually queried a single member of a household about all trips by all members of that household made on the previous day, it was expected that some trips would be forgotten by survey respondents. In Los Angeles, comparisons of reported trips with traffic counts made on the survey day indicated substantial underreporting, as did comparisons with other independent estimates of travel. Accordingly, some types of reported trips were weighted by a factor greater than one in survey processing, thereby adjusting the total number of trips and the total amount of travel upwards to correspond with independent observations.[5] The upward adjustment was greatest, up to 80%, for the short shopping and recreational trips considered most likely to be underreported by survey respondents. Work trips were not adjusted upward at all. Overall, the number of trips reported in Los Angeles was adjusted upwards by 27%, and the total travel distance by 22%. In Washington, the upward adjustments were less than half as large.

Results

The adjusted distributions of travel reported by all drivers on the survey days are shown in Fig. 5.2. Evidently, there was considerably less travel per driver in Washington. Furthermore, the difference is greater at the longer ranges, as might be expected from the smaller size of the Washington region, which limits opportunities for long urban trips in a single day.

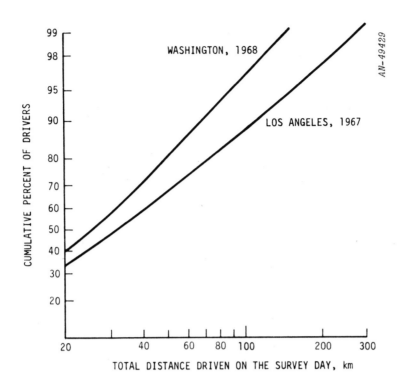

Figure 5.2. Distributions of Driver Travel, Los Angeles and Washington

---

The average distances per driver in Fig. 5.2, 50 km for Los Angeles and 33 km for Washington, appear to be in reasonable agreement with measures of total travel developed elsewhere from survey data. Analysts in Los Angeles employed a network model which showed about 44 km of auto travel per car in the area.[2] Multiplied by 1.09, the number of cars reported per driver reporting travel in the survey, this gives about 48 km of auto travel per driver. Analysts in Washington estimated internal auto travel from airline trip distances to be 36 km per resident auto, using a factor of 1.35 to convert airline to over-the-road distance.[6] In this study, the Washington distribution of Fig. 5.2 gave an average travel per car driven of 34.5 km, based on a slightly smaller conversion factor. Though encouraging, this comparison must remain incomplete because the percentage of cars not driven on the survey day was not available.

A number of important limitations apply to the travel distributions developed here from the survey data. First, the distributions are limited to urban travel, that is, trips beginning and ending within the survey area. Distances could not be computed for trips crossing the boundary of the region, which amount to roughly 1% of all trips recorded. Second, drivers who reported no trips on the survey day are not included, since the data files obtained from both Los Angeles and Washington were trip-oriented and did not present information about drivers not reporting any trips. Previous processing of other files from Los Angeles, however, indicated that this number of drivers was not large: only about 6% of all drivers in the region.[2] Third, travel by drivers who shared a single car was deliberately eliminated from all distributions except that of Fig. 5.2. In Los Angeles, only 12% of drivers reporting trips came from households where sharing a vehicle was necessary, while in Washington, 91% of cars driven on the survey day were driven by only one driver. As automobile ownership continues to rise, even fewer drivers will share single cars and limit their travel patterns accordingly. Fourth, the travel distributions apply to weekday travel only, since weekend travel was unavailable for Washington. For Los Angeles, a brief analysis of weekend travel showed little difference from weekday travel. This is to be expected since the survey data includes only urban travel and not the longer trips common on weekends.

A basic assumption is required in using distributions like those of Fig. 5.2 to specify range requirements which would avoid frequent inconvenience for drivers. The data and the distributions describe the travel by many drivers on a single day, whereas a range requirement must match the distribution of travel by a single driver on many days. To assume that the two distributions are practically the same is likely to be unsatisfactory for the group of drivers described in Fig. 5.2, simply because the group is not homogeneous. Certain subgroups of drivers—heads of households or the elderly, for example—might be expected to travel long distances more or less frequently than the average driver. Only if distributions are compiled for homogeneous groups of drivers

144

will each driver have equal probability of traveling less than a given distance in a single day, making the basic assumption valid.

Almost two dozen distinct groups of drivers were investigated for both Los Angeles and Washington, as shown in Tables 5.3 and 5.4. Initially, drivers were grouped according to age, sex, and type of dwelling, but for the most part, there was relatively little difference in travel from group to group. Groups reporting markedly more or less travel than average seemed likely to have high percentages of primary or secondary drivers. Accordingly, a group called "secondary" drivers was singled out for separate investigation. By definition, a secondary driver was a driver from a household with more than one driver who reported less travel on the survey day than the driver reporting most travel at the household. Those drivers traveling most at multidriver households were separated into a second separate group called "primary." The remaining drivers, those at households with only one driver on the survey day, were called "only" drivers.

Distributions of reported driving distance for these three groups are shown in Figs. 5.3 and 5.4. Of all groups examined, the secondary and primary driver groups exhibited the extremes of total travel, while only drivers were very close to the average for all drivers with cars available. To test the homogeneity of the primary and secondary groups, the drivers in each group reporting travel in the highest decile were separated and compared with other drivers. They differed little so far as driver characteristics or household characteristics were concerned, suggesting that the drivers reporting high travel distances were not a separate subgroup.

The distributions of reported driving indicate the percentage of urban driving days for which cars of a given range would be entirely adequate. On other days, depending on the details of the travel, these cars might be useful for only a part or even none of the travel. To investigate these possibilities, two additional distributions were computed. One shows the percentage of total driving that was reported by drivers who drove less

TABLE 5.3

FULL-DAY AUTO USE REPORTED BY DRIVERS, LOS ANGELES, 1967

Class of Drivers	Percent of Drivers With Cars	Driver Travel, km			Percent Using Freeway	Percent Carrying at Most N Passengers		
		Median	Average	95th Percentile		N = 1	N = 2	N = 3
All Drivers		32	50	156	33	82	91	96.2
Drivers with Cars	100	33	51	160	35	85	92	96.7
Only Drivers with Cars	40	30	47	150	33	88	94	97.5
At Single Family Housing Units	23	32	49	151	34	86	93	96.7
Primary Drivers with Cars	31	58	78	218	52	79	89	95.3
At Single Family Housing Units	25	60	79	218	52	77	88	94.7
Secondary Drivers with Cars	27	20	28	77	20	84	92	96.8
At Single-Family Housing Units	22	21	28	78	20	82	91	96.5
At Single-Family Units with Off-Street Parking	20	21	29	79	20	83	92	96.7
At Other Housing with Off-Street Parking	3	20	28	74	22	93	97	98.6
At Households with No One Under 22 Years	15	19	26	71	21	94	99	99.6
At Households with a Spouse	24	20	28	70	20	82	91	96.4
At Households with Spouse and Housewife	12	20	28	77	16	74	87	94.5
Drivers with Cars, Male	57	40	59	183	43	87	93	97.4
Drivers with Cars, Female	40	26	39	118	23	80	91	95.7
Drivers with Cars, 15-25 Years	26	34	51	156	36	83	92	96.9
Drivers with Cars, 25-45 Years	58	36	54	164	38	80	89	95.3
Drivers with Cars, 45-65 Years	26	29	47	158	30	93	97	99.0
Drivers with Cars, Over 65 Years	7	22	40	153	18	92	97	99.2
Drivers with Cars, At Single-Family Units	72	30	53	164	35	83	91	96.0
Drivers with Cars, At Flats and Apartments	22	30	47	146	35	91	96	98.7

Source: 1967 Origin-Destination Survey, Los Angeles Regional Transportation Study

146

TABLE 5.4

FULL-DAY AUTO USE REPORTED BY DRIVERS, WASHINGTON, D.C., 1968

Class of Drivers	Percent of Drivers With Cars	Driver Travel, km			Percent Using Beltway	Percent Carrying at Most N Passengers		
		Median	Average	95th Percentile		N = 1	N = 2	N = 3
All Drivers		25	33	88	9	85	93	97.1
Drivers with Cars	100	26	34	94	10	87	94	97.5
Only Drivers with Cars	44	24	32	85	9	89	95	98.3
At Single Family Housing Units	20	26	34	91	9	88	94	97.5
Primary Drivers with Cars	29	40	48	110	14	84	92	96.6
At Single Family Housing Units	23	41	48	109	14	83	91	96.2
Secondary Drivers with Cars	26	16	21	55	6	86	94	97.3
At Single-Family Housing Units	21	16	21	56	6	84	93	97.2
At Single-Family Units with Off-Street Parking	*	*	*	*	*	*		
At Other Housing with Off-Street Parking	*	*	*	*	*	*		
At Households with No One Under 22 Years	13	16	20	51	7	94	98	99.1
At Households with a Spouse	20	16	20	55	6	83	92	96.6
At Households with Spouse and Housewife	12	15	19	54	5	77	89	95.2
Drivers with Cars, Male	64	30	37	96	12	90	95	98.1
Drivers with Cars, Female	36	21	27	76	6	81	92	96.4
Drivers with Cars, 15-25 Years	31	26	34	90	11	87	95	98.2
Drivers with Cars, 25-45 Years	63	27	35	97	10	84	92	96.8
Drivers with Cars, 45-65 Years	19	23	30	86	7	93	97	99.2
Drivers with Cars, Over 65 Years	3	17	25	81	4	93	98	99.6
Drivers with Cars, At Single-Family Units	64	27	35	90	10	85	93	97
Drivers with Cars, at Flats and Apartments	31	25	32	84	10	91	96	98.8

*Data unavailable

Source: 1968 Home Interview Survey. Metropolitan Washington Council of Governments

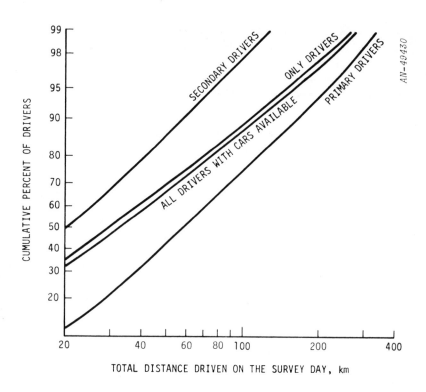

Figure 5.3.   Distributions of Travel by Drivers with Cars Available, Los Angeles

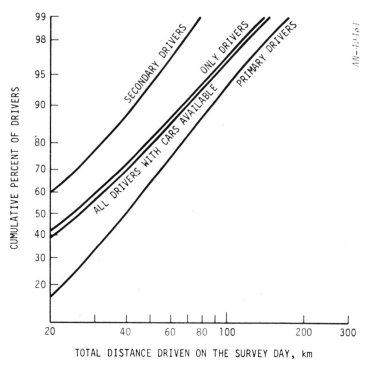

Figure 5.4.   Distributions of Travel by Drivers with Cars Available, Washington

than a given range on the survey day. Even if a car of this range were use-less on all days requiring more travel, it could serve this percentage of total driving distance. The other distribution shows the percentage of total driving that was within a given range, assuming that this entire range is useful on every day requiring longer total range. This is the maximum possible travel which could be served by a car of the given range without rescheduling trips from one day to another. These two distributions are given in Table 5.5 for Los Angeles, along with the distributions plotted in Fig. 5.3.

In Fig. 5.5, the additional distributions are plotted as a function of the percentile range which can be driven in a day. The curves show, for example, that a car capable of the 98th-percentile range for a driver group would be capable of 97-98% of all travel if its entire range could be used every day, and capable of 87-91% of all travel (depending on driver group) if none of its range could be used on days requiring greater range.

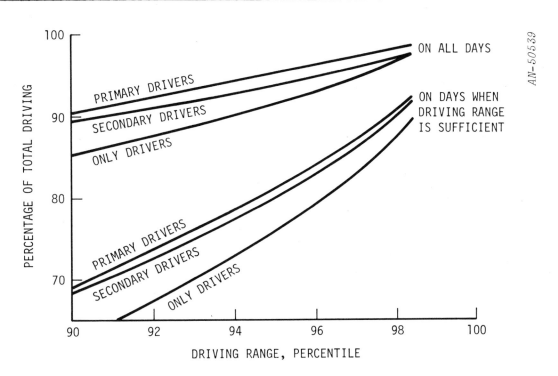

Figure 5.5. Percentage of Total Driving Within a Given Range
(Los Angeles)

TABLE 5.5

DISTRIBUTIONS OF DRIVERS AND DRIVING VERSUS REPORTED DRIVING DISTANCE
(Los Angeles, 1967)

Full-Day Driving, km	Percent of Drivers Reporting Less Than the Specified Driving			Percent of Driving By Drivers Reporting Less Than the Specified Driving			Percent of Driving At Ranges Less Than the Specified Driving		
	Secondary	Only	Primary	Secondary	Only	Primary	Secondary	Only	Primary
10	23.5	17.0	3.3	4.9	2.0	.3	32.2	19.7	12.7
20	49.6	35.4	11.5	18.7	7.9	1.9	54.7	35.4	24.6
30	67.2	50.5	21.8	34.2	15.9	5.2	69.3	47.5	35.3
40	78.1	61.0	32.5	47.7	23.7	10.0	79.0	56.9	44.6
50	85.4	69.5	42.8	59.4	31.8	15.9	85.5	64.2	52.6
60	90.3	75.7	51.7	69.0	39.1	22.2	89.8	70.1	59.4
70	93.6	79.9	59.5	76.6	44.9	28.6	92.6	74.8	64.9
80	95.6	83.9	65.8	82.0	51.3	34.7	94.6	78.7	69.8
90	96.9	86.9	71.1	85.9	56.7	40.5	95.9	81.8	73.8
100	97.6	89.4	75.5	88.3	61.7	45.8	96.9	84.3	77.2
120	98.7	92.4	82.1	92.6	68.7	55.1	98.2	88.1	82.6
140	99.3	94.3	86.6	95.4	73.9	62.6	98.9	90.9	86.7
160		95.9	89.4		79.0	67.9		93.0	89.6
180		96.7	91.8		81.8	73.1		94.4	92.0
200		97.4	93.7		84.7	77.8		95.8	94.0
220		98.1	95.2		87.8	81.8		96.7	95.4
240		98.6	96.2		90.3	84.8			96.5
260		98.8	97.2			88.0			97.3
280		99.1	97.8			90.0			97.9
300		99.2	98.4			92.3			98.5

The amount of travel which could be accomplished by a car of given range probably lies somewhere between the two groups of curves in Fig. 5.5. If the longest travel days consisted of only two or three very long trips, it would be unlikely that the car could be used for any of them and still returned home at the end of the day, so the actual amount would lie near the bottom set of curves. In fact, however, the longer travel days involve more trips than average, though trip length also increases. This is shown in Table 5.6, which shows how the average number of trips and trip length for all drivers in each group compare with averages for those drivers in approximately the top decile of reported range. Since considerable numbers of trips were required to reach the longer full-day distances, it seems likely that much of the range of the car could have been used to make some of the trips and still return the car home.

The upper curves of Fig. 5.5 are interesting in another context. A hybrid-electric car might be driven up to some maximum range each day on energy stored in its battery during overnight recharging. For ranges in excess of this maximum, an internal-combustion engine in the car would provide motive power. In this case, the upper curves show precisely the amount of travel which would be possible solely on stored energy, with gasoline (or other liquid fuel) required only for the remainder.

Minimum Requirements for Range, Speed, and Capacity

A single driver may be a primary driver on one day and a secondary driver on the next. By agreement in a household, however, the primary driver might always use a conventional automobile, leaving cars with lesser capability to satisfy the lesser needs of the secondary drivers for that day. Ranges required by secondary drivers, then, seem likely to represent minimum reasonable targets for a limited-capability car.

If the 95th percentile range is taken as sufficient to avoid frequent inconvenience for drivers, then ranges for limited-performance urban cars could be as small as 55 km in Washington and 75 km in Los Angeles, for cars driven by secondary drivers. Almost a third of urban cars fall in this

151

TABLE 5.6

REPORTED TRIPS AND TRIP LENGTHS, LOS ANGELES

	Average Distance Driven, km	Average Number of Trips	Average Trip Length, km
Secondary Drivers			
All	28.4	4.6	6.2
Those reporting over 60 km	82.8	5.7	14.5
Only Drivers			
All	49.4	5.1	9.7
Those reporting over 110 km	181	9.4	19.2
Primary Drivers			
All	79.2	6.5	12.2
Those reporting over 170 km	193	7.3	26.4

category. Similarly, cars with ranges of 85 and 150 km would suffice for that additional third of drivers who are the only drivers in households. Presumably, these are the first markets in which limited-performance urban cars might find substantial application. To meet the 95th-percentile requirements of primary drivers, ranges of 110 km and 220 km would be needed.

If the 98th instead of the 95th-percentile ranges were taken as necessary, these requirements would increase thirty to forty percent.

Speed requirements depend largely on whether cars are to be used on freeways and other high-speed highways. Frequency of freeway use may be determined directly from the Los Angeles survey, since the data includes whether freeways were used for each reported driver trip. For Washington, the data simply includes whether the Beltway was used--but in Washington at the time of the survey, there was relatively little additional freeway to be considered.

So far as passenger capacity is concerned, the total weight, energy requirement, and cost of a car depend strongly on whether four seats (three passengers in addition to the driver) are provided, or whether two seats are sufficient. Again, the surveys provide directly relevant information, since they show the number of passengers carried in each driver trip.

Tables 5.3 and 5.4 show freeway use and passengers carried on the survey day in addition to measures of distance traveled for each driver group. For distance traveled, one group of drivers (secondary drivers) stood out as requiring relatively little; but for freeway capability and passenger capacity, there seems to be no similarly undemanding group if adequacy on 95% of driving days is assumed as a criterion.

In no group of drivers considered did 95% or more report carrying at most one passenger (besides the driver). In every group, however, at least 95% of drivers reported carrying at most three passengers. Accordingly, two-seat cars appear generally inadequate, while four-seat cars appear generally sufficient.

Freeway use was relatively frequent even in Washington, where little freeway was available at the time of the survey. The Los Angeles data is probably more representative of other cities. In Los Angeles, only two groups of drivers--people over 65 and secondary drivers at husband-housewife households--reported an incidence of freeway use under 20% on the survey day.

Overall, these figures suggest that a two-person car incapable of freeway driving would satisfy the needs of few urban drivers on 95% or more of driving days. With freeway capability and with four-person capacity, however, the car could be widely applicable.

Inferences about requirements for freeway capability and passenger capacity from Tables 5.3 and 5.4 seem less secure than those about driving range. In Washington, for example, it seems almost certain that only those living near the Beltway frequently used it. Accordingly, the various classes of drivers shown would not be homogeneous in this respect, so that it cannot reasonably be assumed that the statistics of the entire group on the survey day would approach the statistics for each single driver throughout several years. The same considerations apply to passengers carried. The larger households associated with a group of drivers may have accounted for all the reports of high car occupancy. Indeed, the groups of drivers likely to come from the smallest households (drivers over 65, drivers from households with no minors) most frequently carried no more than one passenger besides the driver. On the other hand, even in these groups, which seem relatively likely to be homogeneous, two or more passengers were carried over 5% of the time.

"Freeway capability" as used here implies sufficient speed and acceleration for safe freeway operation. This implies a cruising speed at least equal to the legal speed limit (88 km/hr) plus sufficient acceleration for entering the freeway at a safe speed and for maintaining safe speed on customary freeway grades. Acceleration on up-hill on-ramps seems to pose the dominant requirement. Such ramps are relatively common in urban areas, where cars must ascend from surface streets to freeways on viaducts. Capability for acceleration from 0 to 64 km/hr in ten seconds on level ground has been suggested as a reasonable minimum requirement for cars which must enter freeways on uphill ramps.[7]

Minimum requirements from the survey data are summarized in the first part of Table 5.1, which shows range and capacity sufficient for 95% of driving days for secondary, only, and primary urban drivers. The lower limit on required range comes from the Washington data, while the upper limit comes from the Los Angeles data and is in good agreement with other sources of information. While a capacity of three persons (two passengers in addition to the driver) suffices for drivers of secondary and only cars who are older and live in multi-family housing units, four-person capacity is generally needed. In every case, speed and acceleration must be sufficient for freeway use.

If requirements were based on capability sufficient for 98% of driving days, rather than 95%, the ranges in Table 5.1 would increase 30 to 40%. Three-passenger capacity would suffice only for secondary drivers at households without children, and four-passenger capacity only for older drivers and drivers at multi-family housing units. Five- or six-passenger capacity would be necessary elsewhere.

Driving in Other Areas

Average daily driving in most urban areas of the United States has been reported in two national studies.[8,9] Unfortunately, however, their figures appear inconsistent and do not agree with estimates obtained locally for selected regions from other sources. For lack of any better procedure, it seems appropriate to assume that the actual requirements of other urban areas lie somewhere between those of Washington and Los Angeles.

Indeed, there is some question as to whether the Washington result may be misleadingly low, with other cities much nearer the Los Angeles example. Gasoline sales per automobile in the Washington area, for example, were apparently higher than in Los Angeles in the survey years, though the survey data suggests cars in Los Angeles were driven almost 50% farther.[10] On the other hand, the good weather, smaller cars, and extensive freeways of the Los Angeles area all promote higher fuel economy, which would tend to offset higher auto usage.

5.2   GENERAL DRIVING

No origin-destination surveys which detail non-urban as well as urban travel have been processed at the individual-trip level to develop full-day travel ranges. Separate distributions of trip length and trip frequency derived from surveys have, however, been combined at least twice in the past to estimate national distributions of daily driving including rural and interurban travel. In 1971, Kalish synthesized driving distributions comparable to those of Fig. 5.2 from trip frequency and trip distance distributions developed by the Chicago Area Transportation Study from 1957 survey data.[11,12] In 1976, Schwartz developed comparable driving distributions from trip frequency and length distributions compiled by the Nationwide Personal Transportation Study from data obtained in late 1969 and early 1970.[13,14] In both these cases, assumptions were required about the interdependence of the trip frequency and distance distributions employed. The more realistic assumptions appear to be those of Schwartz, who employed a Monte Carlo simulation to develop his results.

The calculated distance distributions of Kalish and Schwartz are presented in Fig. 5.6 together with the distributions from the Los Angeles and Washington origin-destination surveys shown in Fig. 5.2. The agreement is reasonably good, considering that the survey results included no long-distance intercity travel, whereas the simulation results of both Schwartz and Kalish included these long trips. This may account for the substantial differences between survey and simulation results occurring at the very long travel distances.

Both Schwartz and Kalish produced estimates stratified by annual travel distance. In Fig. 5.7, the dependence of Schwartz's results on assumed annual travel is shown by the solid line. Also shown in Fig. 5.7 are the 95th-percentile ranges and associated annual travel distances for the range distributions of Figs. 5.2, 5.3, and 5.4. There is obviously good agreement between the simulation results (and their extrapolations) and the survey results.

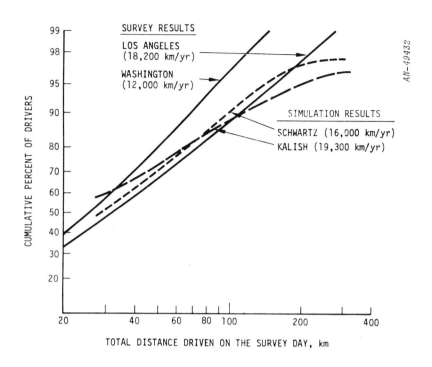

Figure 5.6. Distributions of Driver Travel from Simulations and Surveys

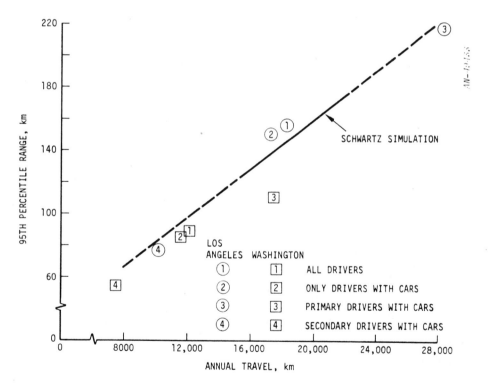

Figure 5.7. 95th-Percentile Driving Distances vs Annual Travel

157

Annual auto use decreases with the auto's age as shown in Table 5.7. At the average for all ages, 18,700 km, the 95th-percentile driving distance estimated by Schwartz is 145 km (Fig. 5.7), quite close to the Los Angeles figures for all drivers and only drivers with cars. At the average for new cars, 28,200 km per year in Table 5.7, the simulated 95th-percentile range is close to that for primary drivers in Los Angeles, while at the average for the oldest cars, 10,500 km per year, the simulation is near the range for secondary drivers in Los Angeles. The implication is that primary cars are new and secondary cars are old. In fact, this is usually the case.[15]

TABLE 5.7

AUTO USE VERSUS AGE

Year of Vehicle Life	Estimated Average Annual Use, 1000 km
1	28.2
2	25.9
3	21.2
4	18.3
5	18.8
6	16.1
7	16.6
8	13.8
9	17.5
10	12.9
11 and beyond	10.5
all years	18.7

Source: US Department of Transportation, Nationwide Personal Transportation Study, Report 2: Annual Miles of Automobile Travel, April 1972

Though the Nationwide Personal Transportation Study found the average annual use of automobiles to be 18,700 km, as shown in Table 5.7, a somewhat lower figure is reported in Highway Statistics, an annual publication by the Department of Transportation. The data from Highway Statistics is particularly useful because it is available for many years and thus reveals the surprising stability of auto use through periods of depression, war, prosperity, and major innovations in both vehicles and highways. It is shown for the years 1936-1975 in Fig. 5.8. Only gasoline rationing in World War II, together with cessation of auto manufacturing and a shortage of autos which persisted until about 1950, have drastically perturbed average use. The effects of higher petroleum prices and gasoline shortages in 1973-74, however, are clearly evident. They suggest that with continued problems of gasoline supply, the slow long-term growth of auto use may be halted in the remainder of this century. There are other deterrents to additional average use as well: the great postwar expansion of the US highway system is over, the number of cars continues to increase, and probable increases in congestion will increase the time required for making any given trip, making travel more demanding and less desirable.

In this study, the average annual use of automobiles will be taken as 16,000 km for calculating costs and impacts of electric cars, in line with the data of Fig 5.8. The difference which would result from using the higher figure of Table 5.7 is generally unimportant. The difference between the two figures is apparently the result of different methods of derivation: the Nationwide Personal Transportation Study interviewed about 6000 households to determine their patterns of travel, while Highway Statistics publishes estimates based on state data derived from traffic counters on major highways, sales of gasoline, and vehicle registrations. Whether either result is much more accurate than the other remains to be demonstrated.

In actuality, of course, the average usage of electric cars in the auto fleet may be quite different from the nominal 16,000 km/yr. Secondary cars, which may be first to be electrified, appear to be driven much less, only about 10,000 km/yr. Moreover, the limited range of the electric car would bar it from most long trips regardless of application. On the other hand,

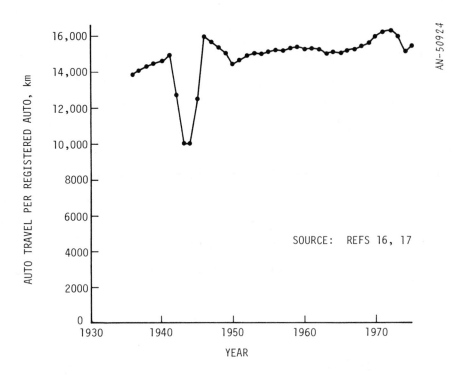

Figure 5.8. Average Travel Per Car, 1935-75

new cars are usually driven much more than the nominal 16,000 km/yr, and despite limited range a new electric car might be used as a matter of preference for many more urban trips than the conventional secondary car it would displace. Actual average usage of electric cars, then, will probably depend not only on regional differences like those between Los Angeles and Washington, but on the ages of the cars, their range capabilities, and the roles for which they are purchased, whether new or used. Estimates of average usage based on these factors were not undertaken in this study due to their uncertainty, their dependence on assumed scenarios for year-by-year sales of electric cars, and the complexities they would introduce into presenting impacts parametrically for levels of use ranging from very low to very high.

5.3 LONG TRIPS

For a further appreciation of the travel which is beyond the reach of electric cars, it is necessary to turn to additional sources of data. One such source, the Nationwide Personal Transportation Study of 1972, was used to generate the distance distributions for general driving discussed in Sec. 5.2; the basic data showed that 0.8% of annual trips exceeded 161 km in length, and accounted for some 17% of annual vehicle miles.[13] Another source is the 1972 Census of Transportation, which yields the information about long trips in Table 5.8.[18] It too includes only trips exceeding 161 km in one-way length, accounting for roughly 16% of total annual auto use. Its terminology differs from that of previously-discussed data, however; in Table 5.8, a trip is a round trip beginning and ending at the home.

It seems unlikely that much of the travel in the long trips of Table 5.8 could be accomplished by electric cars, even the most advanced, unless recharge facilities were widely available at hotels, motels, campgrounds, and the like. 77% of the trips involved overnight travel. Only 22% of the travel involved round-trip distances under 643 km, which itself is more than the longest range of future electric cars considered in Sec. 4.

If electric cars were the only cars available at a household, it appears that most long trips would be made by rental car, or by other modes such as bus, train, and plane, or would simply be sacrificed if the alternatives were expensive or inadequate.

TABLE 5.8

LONG TRIPS (OVER 161 km), 1972

Fraction of US households with car or truck reporting one or more long trips	62%
Average number of trips per household reporting trips	5.0

Distribution of Trips and Trip Distance

Round-trip length, km	Percent of Trips	Percent of Total Distance
322-643	49	22
644-965	22	17
966-1289	10	11
1290-1609	5	7
1610-3220	8	18
Over 3220	4	25
Outside US	2	–
Average round-trip distance		1,000 km
Average total trip distance per household reporting trips		5,000 km

Distributions of Trips by Type and Purpose

Vacation trips	30%
Weekend trips	45%
Overnight Trips	77%
Visit friends and relatives	36%
Business and conventions	28%
Outdoor recreation	9%
Sightseeing and entertainment	11%
Other	16%

Source: 1972 Census of Transportation[16]

SECTION 5 REFERENCES

1. <u>Urban Origin-Destination Surveys</u>, Federal Highway Administration, US Department of Transportation, July 1975.

2. W. Hamilton, <u>Impact of Future Use of Electric Cars in the Los Angeles Region</u>, EPQ-460/3-74-020, US Environmental Protection Agency, Washington, October 1974.

3. <u>LARTS Base Year Report: 1967 Origin-Destination Survey</u>, Los Angeles Regional Transportation Study, December 1971.

4. <u>The Home Interview Survey - What and Why</u>, National Capital Region Transportation Planning Board, Washington, D.C., February 1968.

5. <u>Los Angeles Regional Transportation Study: 1967 Distribution Documentation</u>, California Department of Transportation, September 1, 1973.

6. <u>Home Interview Survey Accuracy Checks</u>, Technical Report No. 5, Metropolitan Washington Council of Governments, National Capitol Region Transportation Planning Board, July 1971.

7. N. Rosenberg, et al., <u>Institutional Factors in Transportation Systems and Their Potential for Bias Toward Vehicles of Particular Characteristics</u>, Transportation Systems Center, US Department of Transportation, Cambridge, Mass., August 1977.

8. <u>1970 National Highway Needs Report to Congress</u>, House Public Works Committee, US Department of Transportation, Federal Highway Administration, 1970.

9. <u>1974 National Transportation Study</u>, US Department of Transportation, Office of Transportation Planning Analyses, 1975.

10. <u>Highway Statistics 1968</u>, US Department of Transportation, Washington.

11. Stanley J. Kalish, <u>The Potential Market for On-the-Road Electric Vehicles</u>, Electric Vehicle Council/Copper Development Association, New York, May 1971.

12. <u>Chicago Area Transportation Study</u>, Vol. I, December 1959.

13. H. J. Schwartz, <u>The Computer Simulation of Automobile Use Patterns for Defining Battery Requirements for Electric Cars</u>, Paper 211.1(E) presented at Fourth International Electric Vehicle Symposium, Dusseldorf, August-September 1976.

14. R. H. Asin, <u>Purposes of Automobile Trips and Travel</u>, Report No. 10, Nationwide Personal Transportation Study, US Department of Transportation, Federal Highway Administration, May 1974.

15. G. G. Udell, et al., <u>Just How Big is the Consumer Market for Electric Vehicles?</u>, Paper 7471, Third International Electric Vehicle Symposium, Washington, D.C. 1974.

16. US Department of Transportation, <u>Highway Statistics: Summary to 1975</u>, US Government Printing Office, Washington, 1976.

17. D. B. Shonka, A. S. Loebl, and P. D. Patterson, <u>Transportation Energy Conservation Data Book: Edition 2</u>, ORNL-5320, Oak Ridge National Laboratory, October 1977.

18. <u>National Travel Survey: Travel During 1972</u>, TC72-N3, US Bureau of the Census, Washington, D.C.

6   APPLICABILITY OF ELECTRIC CARS

The key limitation of electric cars has always been range between recharges. More than anything else, this has restricted the applicability of electric cars to the travel of most motorists.

Section 5, however, has shown that the usual needs of major groups of drivers are surprisingly moderate, and far below the capabilities of conventional cars. Electric cars of relatively modest ranges would suffice for all the travel of major groups of drivers on 95% or more of their travel days. Moreover, Sec. 4 has shown that improvements expected in battery and auto technology during the coming decade should easily enable electric cars to reach or exceed these ranges.

Figure 6.1 shows how the applicability of electric cars increases as range between recharges increases. Applicability is here expressed in terms of the percentage of US urban autos which could be replaced by electric cars with no sacrifice of urban travel on 95% or more of travel days. It should not be confused with marketability, which is discussed in Sec. 8. Marketability also depends strongly on the cost of electric cars and on the competition from conventional cars. Applicability does not reflect these factors.

In Fig. 6.1, applicability is estimated separately for two different groups of drivers: those at single-family housing units, and those at multifamily units. For each, a band of possibilities is shown. At the upper edge of the band, electric cars are assumed applicable to the functions of automobiles at all housing units. At the lower edge, electric cars are assumed applicable only at those housing units with off-street parking.

Now and for a long time to come, recharging of electric cars will almost entirely be done overnight. Off-street parking is almost essential for this purpose because large amounts of electric power are involved.

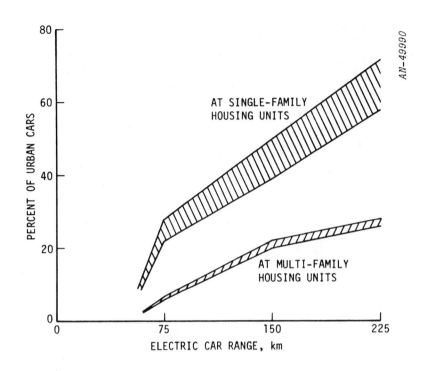

Figure 6.1. Applicability of Electric Cars in Urban Areas, 1974

The more realistic estimates of applicability, then, are those at the lower edges of the bands in Fig. 6.1.

Furthermore, the off-street parking at multifamily housing units is much less likely to be easily outfitted for recharging. The provision of a secure, individually-metered outlet at each space in parking lots or garages could be a major undertaking in both expense and effort. At single-family housing units, in contrast, adding a recharging outlet would be much easier and in many cases would be unnecessary. Accordingly, electric cars are likely to be applied initially primarily at single-family housing units.

Still, the potential is immense. Some 70% of US automobiles are in urban areas, and of these urban cars about 22% are secondary cars at single-family houses with off-street parking. Electric cars with ranges of only 55-75 km would be applicable at such units. With ranges of 85-150 km, they could also be applied as only cars at single-car urban households, and with greater ranges still as primary cars. Once ranges reach 220 km, the electric cars become applicable to general driving. In each case, the majority of cars are at single-family units, where recharging would be easiest to arrange.

Perhaps 25% of urban cars are parked on the street overnight and are poor candidates for early electrification, though available data is incomplete and the actual number might be as low as 15% or as high as 48%. For these cars, electrification would require systems of battery exchange, quick-charge stations, or daytime recharging in parking lots and garages at businesses and shopping areas. Such systems appear economically infeasible, however, until large numbers of electric cars are already in operation.

In this section, the requirements of recharging and the various possible facilities for recharging are first reviewed. Then the proportions of cars with and without access to off-street parking are estimated and the derivation of Fig. 6.1 detailed. Finally, projections are advanced for the future US auto fleet so that the percentages of Fig. 6.1 may be transformed into absolute numbers of automobiles which might be electrified by the year 2000.

6.1 INSTALLATIONS FOR RESIDENTIAL RECHARGING

As was shown in Sec. 4, a typical requirement for recharge energy is 1 MJ/km. For average driving of 16,000 km/yr, or 44 km per day, overnight recharge will require 44 MJ, or 12 kilowatt hours, per average driving day.

The relation of this recharging requirement to the electric energy used for typical appliances is apparent from Table 6.1. It is 10% above that for a water heater, the biggest energy user among present appliances, and almost three times as much as electric lighting. Even at half this level of use, the electric car would be a major factor in household electricity cost.

TABLE 6.1

USE OF ELECTRIC ENERGY IN HOUSEHOLDS

	Annual Energy Use, kWh[*]	Annual Energy Cost, dollars[**]	Average Daily Energy Use, MJ
Electric Car	4,440	178	44
Water Heater	4,040	162	40
Kitchen Range and Oven	3,061	122	30
Room Air Conditioner	2,387	95	24
Lighting	1,870	75	18
Freezer	1,534	61	15
Refrigerator-Freezer	1,268	51	13

[*] Assumes 1 MJ per km is required for an electric car driven 44 km per day. Other estimates from Ref. 1.

[**] Assumes electricity at 4 cents per kWh.

The expense of electricity for recharging a single electric car will be sufficiently great that unmetered service is inappropriate. This poses problems in parking lots and garages at multi-family housing units, where installation of individual meters may be as expensive as providing the recharge outlets themselves.

In many cases, installation of high-capacity electrical outlets for residential recharging of electric cars will be desirable or even essential. Table 6.2 shows the approximate capacity of typical outlets for recharging in periods of one, eight, and twelve hours. The energy available is in MJ and consequently is approximately equal to the urban driving, in km, which would be possible with that much recharging. It is clear that for a full recharge of a long-range car, both the 12-hour period and the highest-capacity outlet (of the type usually provided for electric ranges) would be necessary. It would also allow significant amounts of driving to be obtained from even a one-hour charge, extending the effective range of the car on travel days involving several home-based trips with an opportunity for recharge in between.

TABLE 6.2

CAPABILITY OF RESIDENTIAL ELECTRIC OUTLETS FOR RECHARGING

Outlet Type	Rating	Maximum Recharge Power, kW		Recharge Energy, MJ		
		Initial	Average[*]	1 hour	8 hours[*]	12 hours[*]
Household	120V, 15A	1.8	1.1	6.5	31	47
Heavy-Duty	120V, 20A	2.4	1.4	8.6	41	62
Dryer	240V, 30A	7.2	4.3	26	125	185
Range	240V, 50A	12.0	7.2	43	207	311

[*]Assumes full recharge with a declining rate averaging 60% of the initial rate.

In Table 6.2, the maximum power available from the outlet is assumed to be used throughout the one-hour charging period. For the other periods, a full charge is assumed beginning at maximum power and tapering to about 20% during the final hour of charge. This approximates a typical recharge profile for lead-acid batteries, in which the average power is only 60% of the maximum power.[2] Use of full outlet power requires, of course, that no other load be placed on the circuit at the same time. In effect, this may require a separate circuit solely for charging.

Although many cars are parked overnight in garages already equipped with outlets for electric dryers or other appliances which could be used for a battery charger, new installations are likely to be required for electric cars at many overnight parking places. Representative costs of electrical installations which might be needed are shown in Table 6.3.[3] The range circuit with weatherproof receptacle would provide both high capability and a desirable measure of safety, since the ground-fault interrupter would disconnect electrical power almost instantly at any dangerous leakage of electric current from the circuit to ground. At a house with adequate service to begin with, this would cost roughly $150-$250,

TABLE 6.3
REPRESENTATIVE COSTS OF INSTALLING RESIDENTIAL
WIRING FOR RECHARGING

Job	Estimated Cost, 1977 dollars[*]
Average light fixture	$20
Dryer circuit	45
Range circuit	65
Service and panel, 100A	250
200A	450
Weatherproof receptacle with ground fault interrupter at panel	75

[*] Assumes average runs of non-metallic sheathed cable. For other methods of wiring, as may be required by building codes, costs are increased 8% to 90%.

Source: Ref. 3

depending on the local building codes and lengths of wiring runs. At houses without sufficient capacity available, installation of higher-capacity service would also be necessary, more than doubling the cost.

It is not absolutely necessary than an electric car be fully recharged at the end of each day's driving. So long as reduced range is tolerable, so is partial recharge, so long as the battery is fully charged roughly once per week to equalize charges on individual cells. Even if only 120-volt outlets were available, then, recharging sufficient for much travel could be obtained. On the other hand, cars to be recharged must be reasonably accessible to the electric outlet, so recharging of cars parked on the street would generally be infeasible.

Provision of recharge power is clearly easiest at single-family housing units with off-street parking. In multifamily units with parking lots or garages, provision of individually-metered outlets would require the owner to undertake a major new electrical installation. Probably owners would be reluctant to make such investments unless electric cars were relatively common. Applicability of electric cars is likely to begin, then, at the single-family houses.

While recharging at residences is possible whenever the electric car is not elsewhere, overnight recharging seems almost certain to be most common. Many more cars are parked at residences overnight than during the day. Furthermore, electric utilities have much more reserve capability for generating electricity at night than during the day and early evening. Preferentially lower rates for electricity are available today in many communities for such large appliances as water heaters, which store sufficient hot water so that additional heating can often be conveniently deferred until late at night. In the future, peak pricing of electricity is expected to become much more common, with very attractive rates available for late-night use. With nighttime prices of electricity as low as 20% or less of peak-hour prices, there will be strong incentives to recharge at night.

6.2 OTHER PROVISIONS FOR RECHARGING

If electric cars become common, it seems certain that new facilities and services will appear to accommodate them with recharges away from home base. At the very least, service trucks which supply gasoline to stranded motorists with empty tanks will also supply quick partial recharges for those with fully-discharged batteries. Provision of recharge outlets at daytime parking places on streets and in parking lots at businesses and stores could become common. So could battery service stations, at which batteries could be given a quick charge or even exchanged for fully-charged units.

Recharging outlets at metered parking on streets or in lots, at stores and shopping centers, and at employee parking lots could do much to increase the effective range of electric cars. The only real deterrent is cost. As Table 6.2 suggests, each outlet involves a substantial initial expense and during the year can supply electricity of still greater value. The cost of both the installation and the electricity should be borne by the user, who will be reluctant so long as home recharging suffices. Home recharging entails minimal charges for additional installations and is likely to benefit from the most favorable nighttime rates for electric power. Only if it is insufficient for needed travel is the operator of an electric car likely to bear the added cost and effort of additional daytime recharges. With this sort of prospective limitation on demand, businesses and communities may restrict their offerings of daytime recharge power to a relatively few of the parking spaces they control.

Recharging at battery service stations is another possibility, one which seems more likely to become common. It is possible to recharge a propulsion battery to a major fraction of its capacity in an hour or less. Exact times and amounts depend on the type of battery, but in the past at least one lead-acid battery has been offered for electric cars which could be recharged 80% in just 45 minutes.[4] If future batteries equal this performance, a battery service station could almost double the effective daily range of an electric car by a quick recharge during a lunch hour, a business meeting, or a shopping excursion.

For quick recharges, special high-capacity facilities may be essential. The 250-km reference car of Sec. 4, for example, requires about 250 MJ for a full battery recharge. An 80% recharge in 45 minutes would require an average power of 74 kW, over ten times the average for overnight recharge.

Again, the principal obstacle is likely to be cost. Electricity for quick recharges may be bought at high peak-hour rates and may subject the station operator to high standby charges for making the power available.

In addition, service charges will be necessary to cover costs of providing and operating necessary facilities. These charges seem unlikely to be less than those for a typical sale of gasoline, which takes much less time and ties up equipment and facilities much less than would a 45-minute recharge. The average markup on gasoline sold in service stations of both the self-service and full-service type is now about $1.00 for a representative transaction (a markup of 10¢ per gallon on a sale of 10 gallons). For a quick recharge of 200 MJ, a one-dollar markup would increase electricity costs by almost 50% over the average rate paid by residential users (about 4 cents per kWh or 1 cent per MJ). Drivers of electric cars would be likely to incur the expense and inconvenience of quick charges only when essential to their travel plans. With electric cars achieving the ranges projected in Sec. 4, this would be infrequent. In consequence, quick-recharge stations are unlikely to be anywhere near as prevalent as is today's gasoline station.

A final possibility is battery exchange at a battery service station. With proper design, a propulsion battery can be removed from a car and replaced with another in two or three minutes. The effect is to make refueling as quick and easy as for conventional automobiles. If battery exchange stations were as common as gasoline stations, the range limitations of electric cars could become inconsequential.

Costs of battery exchange, however, seem likely to be greater than for home recharge of a battery kept permanently in the car. The battery exchange stations require facilities, personnel, and an inventory of spare batteries which are unnecessary with home recharging. The costs of an exchange are not likely to be less than for filling up with gasoline, and leasing of batteries to users, with the attendant overhead, is essential. Otherwise, the user could not safely trade his battery for another, which might be near the end of its life and consequently of much less value. A British study estimated that the total cost of battery exchange would be twice that of petroleum (excluding taxes) for a given driving distance.[5]

In view of the cost and inconvenience of battery exchange in comparison with home recharge, its potential extent seems limited. Even a subscriber to the service with a leased battery would ordinarily find it easier and cheaper to recharge at home overnight. Without frequent exchanges, exchange stations could not be nearly as numerous in relation to automobiles as gasoline stations are now. In consequence, exchange stations will probably appear only after electric cars have already become common, and probably only at specific locations where motorists are likely to need the additional range afforded by the exchange privilege.

6.3   AVAILABILITY OF OFF-STREET PARKING

Since off-street parking is required for residential recharging, it is necessary next to estimate the number of cars with access to off-street parking. The estimates must also distinguish between cars at single-family units and at multifamily units, where recharging facilities may be more difficult to obtain, and between cars serving the three major classes of drivers in Sec. 5: secondary, primary, and only drivers.

One of the few sources of data on off-street parking is the Annual Housing Survey of the Bureau of the Census and the Department of Housing and Urban Development.[6] Recently-published reports of the Survey summarize this information for owner- and renter-occupied units, together with the availability of cars at these units. The <u>availability</u> of cars refers to the number of cars reported in response to survey questions about the number of cars available for use at the housing units. The numbers presumably exclude cars not in running order, business cars garaged at home but not available for private use, etc.

All housing units in Survey reports are broken down according to whether they are occupied by owners or renters. Furthermore, detailed tabulations are available only for certain types of housing units. "Specified owner-occupied" units are owner-occupied single-family homes on ten acres or less, with no business on the property. "Specified renter-occupied" units include most renter-occupied units, but exclude single-family renter-occupied units on ten acres or more.

As Table 6.4 indicates, these two classes of occupied units amount to substantially less than the national total--about 15% less. The remaining units are largely rural single-family rentals, single-family owner-occupied homes on ten acres or more, or with a business on the property, and owner-occupied multifamily housing units. To include the units omitted in the two classes for which parking availability is published, it is necessary to extrapolate from Table 6.4. The results of such an extrapolation are summarized in Table 6.5.

The extrapolation was made in three steps. First, specified renter-occupied housing units were simply scaled up, assuming that the added units were like those tabulated, to give totals for all renter-occupied housing units. The necessary scaling factor is very near 1 for this step. Second, single-family units which were renter-occupied were subtracted from the renter categories and added to specified owner-occupied units to approximate all single-family housing units. For this step, the single-family renter-occupied units were assumed to have the same numbers of cars per unit, and the same availability of off-street parking, as the specified renter-occupied units. This tends to underestimate the number of cars, but to overestimate the availability of parking, since rented single-family units probably have more cars and less off-street parking than multi-family units. Third, the renter-occupied housing units found in the first step were scaled up to include owner-occupied multifamily housing units. The owner-occupied units were assumed to have the same auto availability and parking availability as specified renter-occupied units, again a conservative assumption.

The results of this expansion are shown in Table 6.5 for various geographic breakdowns, including single SMSAs (Standard Metropolitan Statistical Areas) which constitute major parts of the survey regions for Los Angeles and Washington discussed in Sec. 5. The estimated total number of cars available at all occupied units in Table 6.5 is about 3 1/2% below that reported in the Annual Housing Survey in Table 2.3. For the numbers in SMSAs, however, the underestimate is less: only 2 1/2%. These

175

TABLE 6.4

REPORTED AVAILABILITY OF CARS AND OFF-STREET PARKING, 1974

	Housing Units, thousands	Percent Units with:				Cars Available		Units with Parking, percent
		No Car	1 Car	2 Cars	3 or More Cars	Total, thousands	Per Unit	
All Occupied Housing Units	70,830	17	48	28	7	88,197	1.25	-*
Specified Owner-Occupied**	36,154	8	45	37	10	53,681	1.48	75†
Specified Renter-Occupied††	24,292	31	50	17	2	22,065	.91	91§
Occupied Units in SMSAs	48,674	18	46	30	7	61,129	1.26	-
Specified Owner-Occupied	25,057	8	42	40	10	38,637	1.54	77
Specified Renter-Occupied	18,800	32	49	17	2	16,710	.89	92
Occupied Units Outside SMSAs	22,156	15	54	25	6	27,070	1.22	-
Specified Owner-Occupied	11,097	11	51	30	8	15,042	1.36	69
Specified Renter-Occupied	5,491	25	54	18	2	5,355	.98	87

*Not tabulated

**Includes only one-family homes on ten acres or less with no business on property

†With garage or carport on property

††Excludes one-family homes on ten acres or more

§Off-street parking facilities included in rent

Source: US Bureau of the Census, Annual Housing Survey: 1974, Parts A and C

TABLE 6.5

ESTIMATED AVAILABILITY OF CARS AND OFF-STREET PARKING

	United States	Outside SMSAs	In SMSAs			Los Angeles Long Beach SMSA	Washington DC SMSA
			Total	In Central Cities	Outside Central Cities		
Population, thousands	211,391	56,427	154,964	-	-	6,926	3,015
Occupied Housing Units, thousands	70,830	19,586	48,674	22,566	26,109	2,520	981
With Parking, percent	83	77	85	86	84	94	71
Single Family, percent	63	75	61	52	70	61	56
With Parking, percent	78	73	80	80	79	94	54
Multifamily, percent	37	25	39	48	30	39	44
With Parking, percent	91	87	92	93	91	94	93
Persons Per Unit	2.98	2.88	3.18			2.75	3.07
Cars Available (estimate), thousands	85,178	23,321	59,628	23,278	36,778	3,243	1,302
Percent of US Total	100	27	70	27	43	4.6	1.5
Cars Per Occupied Housing Unit	1.20	1.19	1.23	1.03	1.41	1.28	1.33
Cars as Percent of Available Cars							
At 1 Car Units	39.4	44.1	36.9	43.7	32.5	37.1	32.1
Single-Family	24.0	32.9	21.5	22.7	20.8	20.4	14.9
Multi-Family	15.4	11.2	15.4	21.1	11.8	16.7	17.2
At 2 Car Units	45.6	42.2	47.3	43.0	50.2	45.9	48.0
Single-Family	35.0	34.5	36.7	31.5	39.9	34.1	35.3
Multi-Family	10.5	7.5	10.6	11.4	10.3	11.8	12.7
At 3 or More Car Units	15.1	14.0	15.8	13.3	17.3	17.0	19.9
Single-Family	13.0	12.5	13.7	11.1	15.3	14.5	16.9
Multi-Family	2.1	1.5	2.1	2.2	2.0	2.5	3.0
Cars with Parking, percent*	56-83	65-77	52-85	62-86	58-84	67-97	47-71

*Assumes each housing unit with parking has either 1 space (lower limit) or as many spaces as cars available (upper limit).

177

underestimates appear insignificant relative to other uncertainties involved in using the data.

The principal uncertainty is in the meaning of "units with parking" in Tables 6.4 and 6.5. For single-family units, the Annual Housing Survey asked whether there was a garage or carport on the property. It did not determine the availability of other off-street parking, which might be in yards or driveways. At multifamily units, the Survey determined only whether parking facilities were included in the rent. The availability of other facilities, or the nature and location of facilities included in the rent, were not reported.

The figures for units with parking in Tables 6.4 and 6.5 are thus far from definitive. They do not show yard or driveway parking which may be available at single-family units, and they do not show the number of off-street parking spaces available per unit at either single-family or multi-family housing units. No better figures, however, were located for use in this analysis.

The lower portion of Table 6.5 shows the percentage of the total cars in each column which are at one-car, two-car, and three-car housing units. It also shows percentages at single- and multi-family housing units, so they may be combined directly with the percentages of these types of units having off-street parking.

It is especially noteworthy in Table 6.5 that in Washington, only 54% of single-family units had a garage or carport. This is much less than in Los Angeles, where 94% reported having a garage or carport, or in the United States as a whole, where 78% reported having a garage or carport. The implication is that the applicability of electric cars may be much less in areas like Washington than in auto-oriented regions like Los Angeles.

It is also possible that single-family units in Washington frequently provide off-street parking in yards and driveways rather than in garages or carports. Unfortunately, the Washington origin-destination survey discussed in Sec. 5 (unlike the Los Angeles survey) did not record the availability of off-street parking at residences, and an effort to locate other relevant descriptive data was unsuccessful.

6.4   PRESENT APPLICABILITY OF ELECTRIC CARS

The applicability of electric cars as of 1974 may be simply estimated from the auto and parking availability data in Table 6.5. Table 6.6 divides cars available at residences according to their location (urban or rural), their function (secondary, only, or primary car), and the type of unit at which they are parked. The table shows a range of values for each entry, corresponding to cars at units with parking available and cars at all units. Only cars are, of course, those at one-car households in Table 6.5; primary cars are the first cars at two- and three-car households; and secondary cars are all other cars.

TABLE 6.6

AVAILABILITY OF CARS BY FUNCTION, 1974

	Percent Urban Cars*		Percent Non-Urban Cars**	
	At Single-Family Units	At Multi-Family Units	At Single-Family Units	At Multi-Family Units
Secondary Cars	22–28[†]	6.2–6.7[††]	19–26[†]	4.1–4.8[††]
Only Cars	17–22	14–15	24–33	10–11
Primary Cars	18–23	5.5–6.0	16–21	3.7–4.3

*In SMSAs

**Not in SMSAs

[†]First figure only includes cars at units with garage or carport. Second figure includes cars at units without garage or carport.

[††]First figure only includes cars at units with off-street parking included in rent. Second figure includes cars at units without off-street parking included in rent.

179

Figure 6.1 draws on Table 6.6 to illustrate the applicability of electric cars in urban areas as a function of range. Applicability is assumed to begin at 50 km, the 95th-percentile range required for secondary cars in the Washington area, and rise linearly to 75 km, the range required in Los Angeles. The implicit assumption is that range requirements in other urban areas are evenly distributed between those of Washington and Los Angeles. Additional cars are assumed to become applicable as only cars for ranges exceeding 75 km in Washington, increasing to the 150-km range requirements for only cars in Los Angeles. At this point, the percentages of cars shown in Fig. 6.1 include all secondary and only cars, leaving primary cars to be added. The applicability of electric cars as primary cars is assumed to begin at 150 km range, the requirement for Washington, and to be complete at 225 km range, about the range required in Los Angeles.

The lower edges of the bands shown in Fig. 6.1 correspond to the assumption that electric cars may be used only at units with parking available as defined in Tables 6.4, 6.5, and 6.6. At single-family units, this should be conservative since it does not include off-street parking in yards and driveways which might suffice for overnight recharging. On the other hand, the lower edges of the bands in Fig. 6.1 may overestimate applicability at ranges in excess of 150 km. At these ranges, primary cars are being added at multi-car households; that is, more than one electric car per household is being introduced. The lower edges of the bands assume that units with parking available have as many spaces as are needed for both primary and secondary cars. In fact, some units--particularly at multi-family structures--may have only a single parking place available off-street, preventing recharge of primary cars in addition to secondary cars. If this were true in every case, the lower edges of the bands shown in Fig. 6.1 would be horizontal at ranges beyond 150 km.

Figure 6.1 indicates that electric cars are widely applicable, even with moderate range capability. The majority of cars in each use category (secondary, only, primary) are at single-family housing units where the provision of individually-metered recharging outlets would be relatively easy. With 150 km range capability, something approaching half of urban cars could be electrified with little limitation on urban travel and reasonably easy provision of overnight recharge.

6.5   PROJECTED APPLICABILITY OF ELECTRIC CARS

To project the availability and applicability estimates of Table 6.6 and Fig. 6.1 into the future on an absolute basis, it is necessary to project the total number of cars which will be available at residences in the United States. It is also necessary to determine the percentages of these cars which will be urban and non-urban, along with possible changes in the relative numbers of secondary, only, and primary cars.

The projections in Table 6.7 are simple extrapolations and inter-polations of widely available projections for population, households, and motor vehicles. The population figures are recent Series II projec-tions of the US Bureau of the Census. So also are the numbers of house-holds and persons per household, but they had to be extrapolated for the final year, 2000. The driving-age population per registered motor vehicle was assumed to follow authoritative forecasts advanced by the Federal Highway Administration for 1980 and 1990; again, extrapola-tion to 2000 was required. Motor vehicle registrations were deduced from driving-age populations per registered motor vehicle and overall driving-age populations. Car registrations were assumed to be 80% of motor vehicle registrations, as projected by the Federal Highway Administration. The number of cars available was taken to be in the same ratio to registrations as was reported in 1974.

In 1974, as shown in Table 6.4, 88.2 million cars were available at occupied housing units. This was 84% of the 105 million cars registered during 1974 in the United States. Registrations are expected to be about 10% higher than the average number of cars actually in use during the year, for two reasons: first, cars whose owners move during the year may be

TABLE 6.7

PROJECTIONS OF POPULATION, HOUSEHOLDS, AND CARS AVAILABLE

	Actual					Projected			
	1950	1960	1970	1974	Annual Growth, percent	1980	1990	2000	Annual Growth, percent
Entire United States									
Population, millions[1]	152	181	205	212	1.4	223	245	262	.8
Driving Age Population, millions[1]	111	124	146	157	1.5	172	191	204	1.0
Households, millions[1]	42.9	53.0	63.5	69.9	2.1	79.4	94.3*	101*	1.4
Persons per Household	3.52	3.38	3.20	2.97	-.7	2.81	2.60	2.60*	-.5
Motor Vehicle Registrations, millions[1]	49.3	73.9	108	130	4.1	150*	171*	185*	1.4
Driving Age Population per Registered Motor Vehicle[2]	2.25	1.68	1.35	1.21	-2.6	1.15	1.12	1.10*	-.4
Car Registrations, millions[1]	40.3	61.7	89.3	105	4.1	120*	137*	148*	1.3
Percent of Motor Vehicle Registrations[2]	82	83	82	81	-	80	80	80*	-
Cars Available[3]	-	-	78.0	88.1	-	102*	116	126	1.4
Cars Available per Household	-	-	1.23	1.25	-	1.28*	1.23*	1.25*	0.0
SMSAs									
Number[1]	168	209	243	264	-	-	-	-	-
Population, millions[1]	84.5	113	137	151	2.4	165*	191*	212*	1.3
Available Cars, millions[3]	-	-	53.9	61.1	-	73*	89*	99*	1.9
Percent of US Population[1]	56.1	63.0	68.6	72.8	-	74*	78*	81*	-
Percent of US Available Cars	-	-	69	69	-	72*	76*	79*	-

*GRC projection

Sources:

1 - US Bureau of the Census, Statistical Abstracts of the United States: 1976, Tables 3, 14, 49, 52, 988

2 - Gary Maring, Highway Travel Forecasts, Federal Highway Administration, November 1974

3 - US Bureau of the Census, Annual Housing Survey, 1974, Part A, Table A-1

registered in more than one state; and second, some cars are junked during the year.[7] There remains a further difference of about 6%, which is presumably accounted for by cars in fleets which were not available at residences for use. Police cars, government-owned cars, rental cars, and many business cars may be in this category. Some 12% of US autos are in fleets of four or more; it seems plausible that half of them would not be available at residences for personal use.

At the bottom of Table 6.7, separate projections are advanced for urban cars--that is, cars in Standard Metropolitan Statistical Areas. There are, of course, many smaller urban areas which are not in SMSAs. It is assumed, however, that driving patterns for such cars may be more demanding than for cars in SMSAs, since smaller urban areas do not provide a complete range of shopping or services, necessitating trips to larger centers.

Projecting the population in SMSAs is difficult because the long-standing trend to urbanization in the United States has been slowing recently. The projected percentages in Table 6.7 are simply extrapolations of the actual percentages recorded in 1950-1970. The other figures for SMSAs follow these percentages and the projections for the entire United States.

It is noteworthy in Table 6.7 that the independent projections of cars available and households lead to only small changes in the number of cars available per household. On the one hand, there is a trend toward more automobiles per person of driving age; on the other hand, there is an offsetting downward trend in household size. The overall result is a change in number of vehicles per household so small through the year 2000 that it is ignored here in the projection process. That is, the proportions of secondary, only, and primary cars are assumed to remain constant through this century at the levels of Table 6.6.

Given this assumption and the basic projections of Table 6.7, Table 6.8 offers projected applicability of electric cars in future years. These projections are not market projections, nor are they projections of the expected numbers of electric cars in future years. Instead, they show the percentage and number of US automobiles which might reasonably be electrified without major sacrifice of travel, given the range and recharge availability shown.

In the earliest year of Table 6.8, it is certainly reasonable to assume 75 km range, since existing technology and batteries are capable of this much. Moreover, overnight recharge is assumed only at single-family urban units with off-street parking, i.e., garage or carport, where the necessary electric outlets are likely to be available already or could be provided at minimum expense. For 1990, achieving the 150 km range would require the successful development of an advanced lead-acid battery (or some other improved battery), coupled with improved automotive technology. Even with recharge only at single-family units with garage or carport, this nearly doubles the number of cars which could be applicable. In

TABLE 6.8

PROJECTED APPLICABILITY OF ELECTRIC CARS, 1980-2000

Year	Assumed Car Range, km	Assumed Availability of Overnight Recharge	Electric Car Applicability	
			Percent of US Cars	Number of Cars, millions
1980	75 km	Single-family urban units with off-street parking	16%	16
1990	150 km	Single-family urban units with off-street parking	30%	34
2000	225 km	All single-family units with off-street parking	58%	73
		All units with off-street parking	82%	104

184

2000, the achievement of 225 km range would require the successful development of a nickel-zinc, lithium-sulfur, or other battery system with substantially higher energy density than expected for improved lead-acid batteries. Because such cars have sufficient range for general use, including non-urban use, availability of recharge is assumed at all single-family units with garage or carport, not just urban units. Again, the percent applicability almost doubles. The final step in Table 6.8 assumes recharge at all housing units with off-street parking, whether single-family or multi-family. Furthermore, it assumes sufficient parking places at each unit for all cars at the unit. It is a relatively high estimate, since the provision of recharge power at multi-family parking lots and garages may be slow in coming, while not every unit with several cars has enough off-street parking places to accommodate them.

SECTION 6 REFERENCES

1. _Energy Efficiency Program for Appliances_, Midwest Research Institute, Kansas City, Missouri, February 1977.

2. G. A. Mueller, Ed., _The Gould Battery Handbook_, Gould, Inc., Mendota Heights, Minn., 1973.

3. _Building Construction Cost Data 1977_, 35th Edition, Robert Shaw Meens Company, Inc., Duxbury, MA 1976.

4. R. R. Aronson, _The MARS II Electric Car_, paper 680429, Society of Automotive Engineers, New York, 1968.

5. R. Weeks, _A Refueling Infrastructure for Electric Cars_, TRRL Laboratory Report 812, Transport and Road Research Laboratory, Crowthorne, Berkshire, 1978.

6. _Annual Housing Survey: 1974 United States and Regions_, Series H-150-74, Current Housing Reports, US Government Printing Office, Washington, 1976.

7. A. S. Loebl, _Transportation Energy Conservation Data Book: Supplement III_, ORNL-5248, Oak Ridge National Laboratory, May 1977.

7   COSTS OF FUTURE CARS

Estimated costs of conventional and electric subcompact cars are presented in Table 7.1. The electric cars are representative future cars derived from the parametric models of Sec. 4 and further described in Table 4.1. The internal combustion engine (ICE) car is a projected conventional design for 1980 which was the basis for estimating characteristics of the electric cars. Both initial and life-cycle costs shown in Table 7.1 are based on an assumption of mass production (hundreds of thousands of units per year).

It is clear in Table 7.1 that improved and advanced technology promise major decreases in the life-cycle costs of electric cars at the same time that they improve range. Nevertheless, the initial costs of electric cars seem sure to remain substantially higher than those of comparable conventional subcompacts, primarily because of the weight and cost of the battery. Except in the case of advanced technology, the electric cars even without battery cost more than the conventional vehicle because of the weight of additional structure and propulsion required by the battery.

For this reason, design range is a critical determinant of the costs of electric cars. As range increases, battery, structure, and propulsion weight all increase too. The design ranges shown for the nickel-zinc and lithium battery cars in Table 7.1 are both relatively low. If they were increased to 250 and 450 kilometers, near the upper limit of practical designs, life-cycle costs per kilometer would increase 21% and 33% over the figures shown.

An important assumption favoring electric cars in Table 7.1 is a 20% longer life than conventional cars. The inherent longevity of electric drive would actually support far greater lifetimes. Most cars, however, seem to be discarded not because they are unrepairable, but because bodies are rusted, damaged, and worn in the course of normal use, and in addition are obsolescent in styling and technology. The extra two years of life

TABLE 7.1

INITIAL AND LIFE-CYCLE COSTS OF REPRESENTATIVE FUTURE CARS

	Subcompact ICE Car	Four-Passenger Subcompact Electric Cars			
		Recent Technology	Improved Technology		Advanced Technology
Range, km	–	75	150	150	250
Battery type	–	Lead-Acid	Lead-Acid	Ni-Zn	Li/Al-FeS$_2$
Inital Cost, dollars	3,700	6,240	5,670	5,440	4,800
Vehicle	3,700	4,990	4,390	3,770	3,100
Battery	–	1,250	1,280	1,670	1,700
Life-Cycle Cost, ¢/km[1]	9.5	14.0	10.7	10.7	9.3
Vehicle	2.0	2.3	2.1	1.8	1.5
Batteries	–	3.3	1.0	1.7	1.2
Fuel[2]	1.2	1.5	1.2	1.0	.8
Repairs and maintenance	1.8	.7	.7	.7	.7
Replacement tires	.2	.3	.3	.2	.2
Insurance	1.0	1.0	1.0	1.0	1.0
Garages, parking, tolls, etc.	1.4	1.4	1.4	1.4	1.4
Licensing, registration, taxes	.5	.9	.7	.6	.6
Cost of capital[3]	1.4	2.6	2.3	2.2	1.9

[1] ICE car life: 10 years, 161,000 km
Electric car life: 12 years, 192,000 km

[2] ICE car: fuel economy 12.3 km/liter (29 mpg); fuel 13.4¢/liter (50.7 ¢/gal). Road use tax of 3.6 ¢/liter (13.6 ¢/gal) included elsewhere, with other taxes.
Electric car: electricity 4¢/kWh. Road use tax included with other taxes.

[3] 100% financing assumed at 10% annual interest.

is a compromise assumption. Electric cars also benefit from low maintenance costs, which are based on studies showing that 62% (or more) of maintenance costs for conventional cars arise in the engine and its fuel, ignition, cooling, and exhaust systems. The costs of the motors and controllers for the electric cars are near those of the internal-combustion systems they replace, and overall costs are insensitive to their precise values.

The cost categories and many of the basic entries in Table 7.1 were derived from historical data reported in DOT studies of the costs of owning an automobile. Only one important category is added: cost of capital. One hundred percent financing of all capital investment is assumed in Table 7.1. This is necessary to reflect properly the relatively higher investments in vehicle and battery required for electric cars. One relatively minor cost is omitted: that of the battery charger and any extra wiring required to bring electricity to the recharging site.

Prices for fuel--gasoline (and oil) for the conventional car, electricity for the electric car--were assumed to be at levels prevalent in 1977. If gasoline prices were to increase substantially while electricity prices remained unchanged, the extra costs of electric cars might partially or entirely disappear. With gasoline at 30¢ per liter ($1.13 per gallon) including tax, the life-cycle cost of the conventional subcompact would be 10.7¢ per kilometer, equal to that of the two electric cars with 150-kilometer range. For longer-range cars, gasoline prices would have to rise substantially more to equalize costs.

This section begins with a description of parametric models of initial and life-cycle costs for future cars. These cost models are based on the parametric weight model described in Sec. 4. Then initial and life-cycle costs resulting from the models are presented as a function of range for the electric cars. Finally, the effects of changes in important assumptions about costs are illustrated. Further discussion of the relation between range, utility, and cost, as well as the most desirable design range, is presented in Sec. 8.

7.1   THE PARAMETRIC MODEL OF COST

Since the future electric cars hypothesized in Sec. 4 were analyzed parametrically, for several values of the fraction of curb weight devoted to battery, costs were analyzed similarly. Initial cost estimates were based on a further breakdown of the component weights of cars developed in Sec. 4. Operating costs were based on published studies of the costs of operating conventional cars. In all cases, costs were adjusted to constant 1977 dollars.

Initial Cost

Initial costs were calculated from component weights of electric cars as shown in Table 7.2. Specific values of weights were obtained from the parametric weights calculated in Sec. 4.

In Table 7.2, "initial cost" means the manufacturer's suggested retail price. This was assumed to be a constant factor times the average variable cost of manufacturing the car. This assumption, and the numerical value of 1.97, are in accord with the analysis of the Interagency Task Force on Motor Vehicle Goals Beyond 1980, which also provided the basis for the parametric weight analysis of Sec. 4.[1-4]

To obtain the suggested retail price for a given average variable cost of manufacturing, an "allocation factor" was first applied to account for average fixed cost and return on equity. An allocation factor of 0.64 was used, based on that of a large, efficient manufacturer. The allocation factor was next multiplied by a "market adjustment factor" appropriate to small cars. Automobile manufacturers generally attribute a larger share of the fixed cost and return on equity to larger, more expensive models. A market adjustment factor of 0.76, the lowest used by the Interagency Task Force, was applied here. Together, these factors increase the average variable cost by about 49%, in effect multiplying it by 1.49. The factor of 1.49 was further increased to account for dealer

TABLE 7.2

Initial Cost = 1.97 x (average variable cost)

Average variable cost equals the sum of costs for:

Upper body	$43.96 + 2.69 (W_F - W_{PL,max})$
Structure and chassis	$-37.51 + 1.526 \cdot a_1 W_G$
	$-101.12 + 2.19 \cdot a_2 W_G$
Drive train	$85.59 + 0.838 (b_2 W_T + a_3 W_G)$
Motor and controller	$C_{MC} \cdot b_1 W_T$

where

W_F, $W_{PL,max}$, W_G, and W_T are electric car weights defined in Tables 4.2 and 4.3

$a_1, a_2, a_3, b_1,$ and b_2 are weight coefficients defined in Table 7.3

C_{MC} is motor and controller cost per kg: \$2.90, \$3.16, and \$3.33 for the recent, improved, and advanced levels of technology.

---

markup and inflation since the base year (1975). In 1975, dealer markups ranged from 15.6% on a subcompact to 30.1% on a full-sized automobile.[5] A markup of 19%, in accord with Ref. 1, was assumed. The upward adjustment for inflation was 11.5%.[6] Together, these additional adjustments result in the factor of 1.97 shown in Table 7.2.

The average variable cost was estimated as the sum of costs for the components shown in Table 7.2, which were defined and described in Sec. 4. The cost estimating relationships shown were derived by regression analysis of detailed data in the Vehicle Configuration Reports of Appendix G, Ref. 3. They are valid only for automobiles in the weight ranges considered here. The structure and chassis weight depending on gross vehicle weight (coefficient a in Sec. 4) was divided into two parts (coefficients a_1 and a_2 of Table 7.3) for cost estimation. Similarly, the propulsion

TABLE 7.3

WEIGHT COEFFICIENTS FOR CALCULATING INITIAL COST OF ELECTRIC CARS

Component	Weight Coefficient	Two-Passenger Cars			Four-Passenger Cars		
		Recent	Improved	Advanced	Recent	Improved	Advanced
Structure and Chassis	a	.258	.239	.230
Chassis less drive train	a_1				.117	.110	.110
Structure	a_2	(same as four-passenger cars)			.114	.110	.101
Drive Train	a_3				.027	.019	.019
Propulsion System	b	.068	.057	.047	.120	.101	.083
Motor and Controller	b_1	.060	.050	.040	.105	.088	.070
Transmission, Axle	b_2	.008	.007	.001	.015	.013	.013

system of Sec. 4 was separated into drive train weight (coefficients b_2 and a_3) and motor-controller weight (coefficient b_1), so that different costs per unit weight could be applied. These separations were based, as were the overall weight estimates by category, on the work of the Interagency Task Force.

The costs for the motor and controller were derived from the detailed study by the Ford Motor Company which was used to estimate the weights of these components in Sec. 4.[7] Since that study was completed in 1973, there has been an important innovation in controller technology: the substitution of high-power transistors for the silicon-controlled rectifiers (SCRs) ordinarily used to switch battery power. The larger transistors require lighter, less complex control circuitry, a fact which was included in the weight estimates of Sec. 4. Potentially, the cost of controllers may also be reduced. At present, however, such transistors are developmental items produced in very small quantity, at costs ranging from very low to very high. The costs of units sufficiently reliable for automotive use, manufactured in quantity, have yet to be determined. Accordingly, the costs for SCR controllers described in the Ford study were used as the basis for the cost estimates presented in Table 7.2, adjusted only for inflation since 1973.

No costs were included for battery chargers, or for the costs of additional wiring required to bring electric power to the charging site (discussed in Sec. 6.1). The cost of a future on-board battery charger with sufficient capacity for overnight full recharge is expected to be less than that of the controller, however, which in turn is only a small part of the overall initial cost of the electric car. In the past, battery chargers have been heavy, costly, and inefficient. In the future, however, electric cars will probably use sophisticated semiconductor chargers which eliminate the costly transformers now employed, weigh very little, and operate at efficiencies at least as high as the 90% assumed here, in contrast to the 65-75% typical of recent charging equipment.[8] The Ripp-Electric of Table 2.1, for example, employs an advanced 300-amp, 120-volt chopper control with regenerative braking and a 2 kW transformerless charger with a reported efficiency of 95%, all contained in a package weighing just 18 kg.[9]

The cost of batteries was estimated from the battery weights assumed in the parametric modeling and the costs of Table 3.1. To apply the costs per kilowatt hour of capacity presented in Table 3.1, battery capacity was estimated at a nominal two-hour discharge rate from the given weight.

Operating Cost

The estimates of operating cost were based on the cost categories and data developed in a recent study of the costs of operating an automobile made by the US Department of Transportation.[10] Where necessary, additional categories appropriate to electric cars were included. The components of estimated operating costs are shown in Table 7.4.

The life of initial and replacement batteries, and the cost of replacement batteries, were estimated in accord with the projections of Sec. 3. The life of the future lead-acid battery was taken from Fig. 3.10, given an average depth of discharge appropriate to the assumed annual use and the maximum range of the car. The life of the current lead-acid battery was assumed to be only 40% of that in Fig. 3.10. For nickel-zinc and lithium/aluminum-metal sulfide batteries, lifetime energy output was assumed to be independent of cycle depth up to a maximum life of eight years, as described in Sec. 3.3. The resultant estimates of battery life and depreciation may be somewhat optimistic; under one common method of rating batteries, for example, cycle life is measured at discharges to only 80% rather than 100% of rated capacity. For practical electric cars, however, the depth of discharge in average daily driving will be well under 50%, and as low as 10% for the longest-range designs. Under these conditions the life of future batteries is so uncertain, and relevant data is so scarce, that there is almost no factual basis for improving the estimation of battery life and depreciation employed here.

194

TABLE 7.4

COMPONENTS OF OPERATING COST

Batteries: Cost and life in accord with Sec. 3 (Table 3.1, Fig. 3.10)

Repairs and maintenance: Subcompact ICE car: 1.75 cents per km

Two-passenger electric car: .67 cents per km

Four-passenger electric car: .74 cents per km

Replacement Tires: $4 \cdot (26.46 + .0207 \cdot W_C / 63,000)$ dollars per km

where W_C = curb weight of car

Insurance: $223 + $138 per year

Garaging, parking, tolls, etc.: $223 per year

Titling, registration, licensing, etc. $(8.36 + .0105 \, W_C)(L + .053 \, C)$ dollars

where L = life in years, C = initial cost

Road tax: $(0.143 + .00019 \, W_C)$ cents per km

Electricity: 4 cents per kWh

Gasoline and oil: 1.19 cents per km

Cost of capital (car less batteries):

$$n \left(\frac{Pi(1+i)^n}{(1+i)^n - 1} \right) - P \text{ dollars}$$

where

P = initial cost of car (less battery)

i = interest rate (10% per annum)

n = life of vehicle, years

Cost of capital (batteries):

$$Ny \left(\frac{Bi(1+i)^y}{(1+i)^y - 1} + Si \right) - B \text{ dollars}$$

where

N = number of batteries used in car life

B = battery cost less salvage value

S = battery salvage value

y = battery life

The costs of repairs and maintenance were estimated for subcompact ICE cars simply by adjusting the DOT figures for this category upward to account for inflation since 1976. For two-passenger electric cars, maintenance per kilometer of travel was assumed to be 38% of this figure. For four-passenger electric cars, 38% of the slightly higher figure from the DOT data for compact automobiles was used, since the electric cars are generally heavier than the subcompact ICE car. The reduction to 38% reflects the elimination of most of the parts and labor required for repair and maintenance of conventional cars because they are required by the internal-combustion engine, whereas the electric motor and controller which replace it should require little or no service during the life of the automobiles. A previous analysis of parts sales and labor requirements for repair and maintenance of conventional cars, based on 1972 data, produced the results in Tables 7.5 and 7.6. It concluded that 72% of labor hours and 62% of parts sales were required for the engine and its fuel, ignition, cooling, and exhaust systems, none of which are present in an electric car.[11] Recent figures for on-the-road failures of autos, summarized in Table 7.7, corroborate these high percentages: 84% of failures serviced by the major agencies in the Washington, D.C. area (not including flat tires, dead batteries, or running out of gasoline) were due to the engine and its subsystems.[12] The lowest of these figures, 62%, was used in the cost model because overall maintenance appears to be declining despite added requirements for pollution control devices. Since 1972, innovations such as electronic ignition have reduced engine maintenance requirements for conventional cars, and proposed limitations of adjustments which could increase pollutant emissions suggest that this trend will continue.[13] Maintenance of the remainder of the conventional car has also been substantially reduced: in the 1978 model year, for example, chassis lubrications are recommended by manufacturers at intervals as long as three years or 36,000 kilometers.[14]

TABLE 7.5

AUTOMOTIVE PARTS SALES

Source: Ref. 11

Lines Related to Internal Combustion Engines	Percent Share of Market	Lines Not Related to Internal Combustion Engines	Percent Share of Market
Batteries	8.6	Tires	33.2
Spark Plugs	5.9	Chemicals (50%)	2.15
Mufflers, Pipes, etc.	5.5	Brake Lining and Lined Shoes	3.7
Filters	4.3	Shock Absorbers	3.0
Chemicals (50%)	2.15	Paint and Body Supplies	2.0
Ignition Parts	2.8	Chassis Parts	0.7
Fan Belts, Radiator and Heater Hose	2.4	Gasket and Oil Seals (40%)	0.44
Remanufactured Units	1.9	Brake Parts	1.0
Motor Parts	0.7	Front End Parts	0.9
Anti-Freeze/Coolant	1.5	Wipers and Blades	0.9
Gasket and Oil Seals (60%)	0.66	Equipment	0.9
Clutch Assemblies, Parts, etc.	1.0	Lamp Bulbs, Flashers and Sealed Beams	0.8
Engines (Small) and Parts	0.9	Bearings (Anti-Friction)	0.8
Grease and Oil (80%)	0.48	Tools (Small Hand)	0.8
Carburetors and Parts	0.6	Wire and Cable Products	0.7
Bearings (Motor)	0.6	Grease and Oil (20%)	0.6
Fuel Pumps and Parts	0.6	Wheels and Rims	0.6
Piston Rings	0.5	Tools (Power)	0.3
Thermostats	0.5	Automatic Transmission and Parts	0.3
Brass Fittings and Fuel Lines	0.3	All Other Lines (50%)	2.45
All Other Lines (50%)	2.45		
Total*	44.34	Total*	55.94

*Does not add to 100% due to rounding.

TABLE 7.6

AUTO REPAIRS AND SERVICE

Source: Ref. 11

	Percent of Cars Serviced Per Year	Labor Time, Hrs.	Percent of Total Repair Costs
Tune-Up*	66	2.1	33.4
Periodic Maintenance*	160	0.5	19.2
Brakes Relined	20	2.0	9.6
Exhaust System*	20	0.5	2.4
Wheels Balanced	16	0.8	3.1
Front Wheels Aligned	16	1.2	4.6
Headlight Beams Aimed	11	0.3	0.7
Cooling System*	11	0.35	0.9
Carburetor Overhauled or Replaced*	7	1.2	2.0
Generator Repaired	7	1.1	1.9
Voltage Regulator Adjusted or Replaced*	7	0.45	0.8
Body Repair	7	0.4	0.7
Fuel Pump Replaced*	6	0.35	0.5
Automatic Transmission Repaired	5	0.8	0.9
Major Engine Overhaul*	5	14.5	17.5
Fuel Pump Repaired*	4	0.35	0.3
Shock Absorbers Replaced	3	1.0	0.7
Standard Transmission Repaired*	2	0.7	0.3
Power Steering Repaired*	1	0.5	0.1
Standard Steering Repaired	1	0.9	0.2
Total	375		98.8**

----

*Repairs directly related to internal combustion engines, with the exception of Periodic Maintenance, which is approximately 60% internal-combustion-engine-related and 40% non-engine-related.

**Does not add to 100% due to rounding

TABLE 7.7
ON-THE-ROAD FAILURES OF AUTOMOBILES
Source: Ref. 12

Cause of Failure	Frequency, Percent
Engine	8.6
Fuel System	13.6
Cooling system	27.3
Ignition system	18.2
Starting/charging system	16.4
Total – Engine Systems	84.1
Transmission	5.7
Driveline	1.7
Brakes	1.2
Suspension	1.4
Electrical System	3.5
Other	2.0
Total – Remainder of Car	15.5

Because electric cars are substantially heavier than conventional cars offering similar accommodations for passengers, a cost estimating relationship for tires was used which reflects the weight of the car. The relationship is based on data for radial-ply tires with a life of 63,000 kilometers.

Costs of insurance, garaging, parking, tolls, and so on in Table 7.4 are assumed to be the same for both conventional and electric cars, and come directly (with adjustment for inflation) from the DOT data.[10] For titling, registration, and licensing costs, the simple cost estimating relationship shown in Table 7.4 was derived to reflect the fact that these costs depend both on weight and on initial vehicle cost, both of which tend to be higher for electric cars. The data on which the relationship is based are given for the different sizes of cars covered in the DOT report.[10]

The road user tax in Table 7.4 is paid by drivers of conventional automobiles through state and federal gasoline taxes. These taxes provide for the construction and maintenance of roads and highways, and must presumably be paid in some manner by operators of electric cars. Since consumption of gasoline depends on vehicle weight, drivers of heavier conventional vehicles pay more road use tax than do drivers of light vehicles per kilometer of travel. The cost estimating relationship in Table 7.4 reflects this prospect, and provides for electric cars to pay a tax per kilometer equal to that now collected from typical conventional cars of equal weight.

A cost of four cents per kilowatt-hour of electricity was assumed throughout for electric cars. This is near the national average price paid for electricity in 1976. Exact prices for electric cars depend strongly both on location and on conditions of use, since reduced rates for high-usage households are commonplace. The regional variation alone led to residential bills for 500 kWh in January of 1976 ranging from $5.42 in Seattle to $36.64 in New York City (1.1 to 7.3 cents per kWh).[15] Widespread use of electric cars could also reduce the average national cost of producing a kilowatt-hour of electric power by a few percent. Whether the users of electric cars would be sold their electricity at the average cost, the marginal cost, or some other price remains to be determined. The assumption here of average cost avoids any implicit subsidy of electric cars.

Prices of gasoline and oil in Table 7.4 reflect an assumption of improved fuel economy for the conventional car, 12.3 kilometers per liter (29 miles per gallon), and a gasoline price of 13.4 cents per liter excluding state and federal taxes (50.7 cents per gallon). Typical taxes were included in the road use tax estimated previously. The conventional car was assumed to require one liter of engine oil per 119 liters of gasoline.

A cost of capital was included as shown in Table 7.4 even though it is not a part of the DOT cost estimates. In an electric car, substantially higher investments are required both because the cars themselves tend to be more expensive and because batteries add an additional capital requirement. The costs of this capital must be paid somehow, whether through financing charges on borrowed money or interest loss and opportunity cost on savings invested. It was assumed here that all capital required during the life of the car was borrowed at an annual rate of 10%. The formula shown in Table 7.4 for the cost of the capital is standard.[16] For batteries, revisions were necessary as shown to reflect battery salvage value.

Life Cycle Costs

Life cycle costs were estimated from initial and operating costs
under the following assumptions:

- Straight-line depreciation of vehicle and battery
- Salvage value of vehicle and battery equal to 10% of initial
  cost
- Average annual driving of 16,000 kilometers (10,000 miles)
- Ten-year average life for ICE cars
- Twelve-year average life for electric cars

The ten-year life for conventional cars is typical of actual experience.
The twenty-percent longer life assumed for electric cars reflects the
longevity of the electric propulsion components. The brush-type electric
motors now commonly used are extremely simple in comparison with internal
combustion engines. They require very little maintenance: typically, an
inspection of the brushes each thousand hours, or about once each three
years for average automobile use. Their service life could easily be
ten times that of automotive engines. The advanced brushless motors are
even simpler, and should last even longer. The life of the cars they
power, however, is unlikely to be as long. The wear and tear of ordinary
operation is often a major factor in decisions today whether to repair
or replace used automobiles. Even with the best of care, damage from rust
and accidents will limit actual vehicle life. The twelve-year life assumed
for electric cars gives some recognition to the long life of electric
propulsion components. It is only an assumption, however, which cannot
be further substantiated at present.

7.2 INITIAL AND LIFE CYCLE COST VERSUS RANGE

The parametric cost model was applied to the eight different electric cars described parametrically in Figs. 4.5-4.8. The resultant initial costs including battery are shown in Fig. 7.1, and the life-cycle costs in Fig. 7.2.

The two-passenger cars are less expensive at the shorter design ranges than the conventional subcompact car, as might be expected from their small size. At the 95th percentile ranges for secondary and only urban cars, life-cycle costs are roughly 20% below those of the conventional subcompact. No low-performance, two-passenger conventional car was costed. Such a car would probably be considerably cheaper, however, than the two-passenger electric cars.

With battery, the four-passenger electric cars are always more expensive than the conventional subcompact, at all design ranges for which performance is sufficient for reasonably safe entry into freeways. If batteries were leased, however, the initial cost of the battery might be avoided. Then the initial costs of the shorter-range cars compare favorably with those of the conventional subcompact. At long design ranges, however, the propulsion weight and the weight of structure dependent on gross vehicle weight must be considerably increased on account of the large battery to be carried. As a result, initial costs without battery exceed those of the conventional subcompact, which are virtually unaffected by changes in design range.

In general, the electric cars offer no prospects of competing simultaneously in capacity, range, and cost with the conventional car, so long as gasoline prices remain as low as they have been recently.

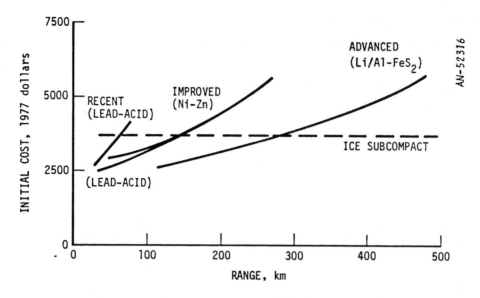

a.   Two-Passenger Electric Car and Subcompact ICE Car

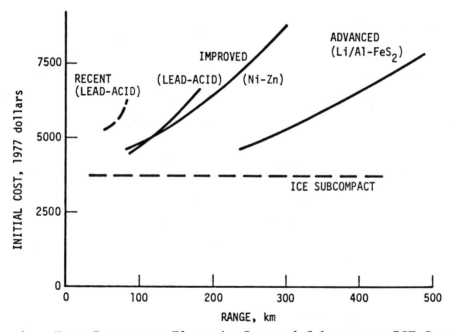

b.   Four-Passenger Electric Car and Subcompact ICE Car

Figure 7.1.   Initial Cost Versus Range

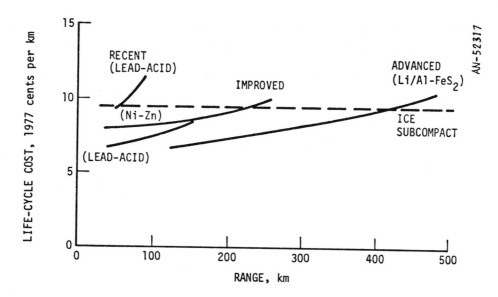

a. Two-Passenger Electric Car and Subcompact ICE Car

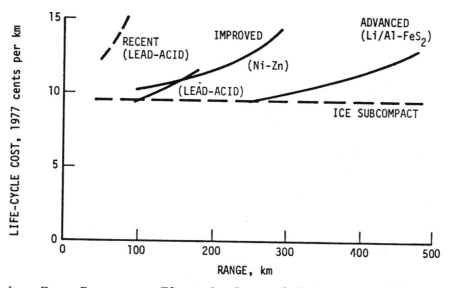

b. Four-Passenger Electric Car and Subcompact ICE Car

Figure 7.2. Life-Cycle Cost Versus Range

205

If gasoline were to become scarce and expensive, the relative position of electric cars would be considerably enhanced. Table 7.8 shows the levels of gasoline cost at which selected electric cars would be equal in life-cycle cost to the conventional car. For the shortest-range electric car with lead-acid battery and the shortest-range advanced electric car, the present price of gasoline already makes the conventional subcompact more expensive. For the other cars of Table 7.8, prices up to about three times that now prevailing for gasoline are required to equalize costs, depending on design range and battery type.

In the past, high proportions of the life-cycle costs of electric cars have been associated with battery depreciation. For the improved and advanced cars of this study, however, major increases in battery lifetime have been assumed in Sec. 3. As a result, further decreases in the life-cycle cost of batteries, whether through lower initial price or still longer life, are unlikely to reduce total costs sufficiently to make the electric cars competitive with the conventional subcompact. Table 7.8 also shows the percentage changes in battery cost per kilometer required to equalize costs of electric and conventional cars. For the higher-cost electric cars, the changes are so great that they are unlikely to come about. Since these are long-range cars, in ordinary use their batteries would seldom be cycled deeply and the battery life implicit in the cost calculation is eight years, the upper limit assumed in Sec. 3 to result from corrosion and other aging effects which are independent of use. Under this assumption, longer cycle life does not affect costs. The changes in Table 7.5 would then have to come entirely from reductions in initial cost, which seem unlikely because they are so large.

The effects on life-cycle cost of changes in other assumptions may be appraised by considering the individual components of life-cycle costs appearing in Table 7.1. There appears to be no single item of cost which alone could be reduced sufficiently to make long-range electric cars competitive.

TABLE 7.8

GASOLINE COST AND REDUCTION IN BATTERY COST TO EQUALIZE

LIFE-CYCLE COSTS OF ELECTRIC AND ICE SUBCOMPACT CARS

Electric Car Application	Technology	Battery	Range, km	Gasoline Cost*		Percent Change in Battery Cost per km
				$/liter	$/gallon	
Urban secondary car	Improved	lead-acid	100	.16	.60	-8
Urban only car	Improved	lead-acid	150	.30	1.13	76
		Ni-Zn	150	.30	1.14	48
General-use car	Improved	Ni-Zn	250	.55	2.09	92
General-use car	Advanced	Li/Al-FeS$_2$	250	.15	.56	-10
			450	.49	1.87	70

*including tax

207

So far, all life-cycle costs have been presented for a nominal annual use of about 16,000 km, near the national average. Because they are capital-intensive, electric cars tend to grow cheaper relative to conventional cars at higher levels of use. The effect, however, is small. It is illustrated in Table 7.9 at 28,000 km/yr, which is near the use of primary cars in Los Angeles, or of new cars nationwide (see Fig. 5.7 and Table 5.7). Conversely, electric cars tend to be relatively more expensive at low annual usage. Table 7.9 also shows life-cycle costs at 10,000 km/yr, approximately the annual use of secondary cars in Los Angeles. At this usage, even the electric cars with the shortest design ranges are more expensive than the ICE subcompact.

TABLE 7.9

LIFE-CYCLE COST VERSUS ANNUAL USE FOR
FOUR-PASSENGER ELECTRIC AND ICE CARS

Technology	Battery Type	Range, km	Annual Use, km*		
			10,000	16,000	28,000
Improved	Lead-Acid	100	12.2	9.4	7.6
		150	13.9	10.7	8.4
Improved	Ni-Zn	150	13.5	10.7	8.8
		250	17.5	12.9	10.2
Advanced	Li/Al-FeS$_2$	250	12.6	9.3	7.1
		450	17.1	12.4	9.1
(Subcompact ICE car)			11.8	9.6	8.0

*Assumed total life: Electric cars - 192,000 km
ICE car   - 161,000 km

SECTION 7 REFERENCES

1. The Report by the Federal Task Force on Motor Vehicle Goals Beyond 1980, Task Force Report (Draft), US Department of Transportation, September 2, 1976.

2. The Report by the Federal Task Force on Motor Vehicle Goals Beyond 1980, Vol. II, Task Force Report (Draft), September 1976.

3. Automotive Manufacturing and Maintenance, Report of a panel of the Interagency Task Force on Motor Vehicle Goals Beyond 1980, Office of the Secretary of Transportation, Washington, D.C., March 1976.

4. National Industrial and Consumer Economics, report to the panel of the Interagency Task Force on Motor Vehicle Goals Beyond 1980, Office of the Secretary of Transportation, Washington, D.C, March 1976.

5. R. Kaiser, Memorandum – Automobile Cost/Price Data from Council on Wage and Price Stability, US Department of Transportation, Transportation Systems Center, Cambridge, MA, November 10, 1976.

6. A. Horowitz and W. Killy III, Report on 1977 Automobile Prices, Council of Wage and Price Stability, Washington, D.C., October 1976.

7. L. E. Unnewehr, et al., Electric Vehicle Systems Study, Ford Motor Company, #SR-73-132, October 1973.

8. Chargers and Charging for Lead-Acid and Nickel-Iron Batteries, ESB, Inc., Philadelphia, 1970.

9. W. E. Rippel, and H. A. Frank, Evaluation of W. Rippel's Electric Datsun 1200, 900-759, Jet Propulsion Laboratory, Pasadena, October 1976.

10. L. L. Liston and C. A. Aiken, Cost of Owning and Operating an Automobile, Department of Transportation, Federal Highway Administration, Washington, D.C., 1976.

11. W. F. Hamilton, et al., Impact of Future Use of Electric Cars in the Los Angeles Region, Vol. 3, EPA-460/3-76-020c, US Environmental Protection Agency, Ann Arbor, 1964, pages 9-33 through 9-40.

12. William Hatch, et al., Analysis of On-Road Failure Data, DOT-HS-802 360, US Department of Transportation, Washington, May 1977.

13. "EPA Proposing No-Tuneup Car," Automotive News, Detroit, August 20, 1977.

14.   <u>1977 National Petroleum News Factbook Edition</u>, McGraw-Hill, Inc., New York, 1977.

15.   <u>Institutional Factors in Transportation Systems and Their Potential for Bias Towards Vehicles of Particular Characteristics</u>, HCP/M1043-01, US Department of Transportation, Transportation Systems Center, Cambridge, MA, February 1978.

16.   E. L. Grant, W. G. Ireson, and R. L. Leavenworth, <u>Principles of Engineering Economy</u>, The Ronald Press Company, New York, 1976.

8   MARKETABILITY OF ELECTRIC CARS

The marketability of future electric cars depends on their advantages and disadvantages for motorists in comparison with those of conventional internal-combustion cars. Marketability begins with applicability as defined in Sec. 6, that is, the ability of electric cars to meet the needs of typical driving. It also depends heavily on the costs of electric cars, and on their overall capabilities, in comparison with what is offered by competing conventional cars.

Quantitative measures of the capability and cost of future electric cars have been derived in Secs. 4 through 7. Though electric cars could meet most of the probable travel needs of future years, they seem certain to offer less capability than conventional cars, at greater cost. Unless today's trends and conditions change drastically, sales of electric cars seem likely to remain small.

New projections of market penetration were not part of this study. Two concurrent studies by other groups, however, independently projected sales of electric cars for the remainder of this century to be modest at best. One projection showed about 3% of US cars in 2000 to be electric, the other up to 9%.

In this section, the advantages and disadvantages of electric cars for the potential buyer are reviewed and summarized. Then market surveys and studies made elsewhere are described and their sales projections for electric cars compared.

8.1   THE ADVANTAGES AND DISADVANTAGES OF ELECTRIC CARS

For the motorist in the market to purchase an automobile, the electric car is a possible alternative to conventional internal-combustion engine cars. Sales of electric cars will depend on the advantages and disadvantages for the motorist relative to future conventional cars.

211

For the individual motorist, the advantages of purchasing an electric car include:

- Reliability. The inherent simplicity and long life of electric propulsion components seem sure to make electric cars more reliable than conventional cars. As a result, the motorist will be less likely to be stranded on the road, or to sacrifice desired trips because of existing or anticipated mechanical trouble. Table 7.7 showed over 80% of on-the-road failures to be engine-related in conventional cars. These could potentially be eliminated in electric cars, but there is little data available on the frequency of ICE car on-the-road failure or the sacrifice of travel due to impending or actual mechanical difficulties. For electric cars, moreover, it is difficult to predict the frequency of failure. Early experience with electric cars has been discouraging; but it seems very likely that in quantity production, the unreliability which has plagued many recent electric cars will be eliminated and the potential of electric drive will be achieved.

- Low Maintenance. Very little scheduled and unscheduled maintenance should be required by electric propulsion systems, reducing maintenance by two-thirds relative to conventional cars. This prospect has already been projected and included in the low costs estimated for maintenance in Sec. 7, but that is not the whole story. There are important disadvantages of maintenance to motorists which are not reflected in simple costs: the difficulty of travel while the car is being serviced or repaired, the difficulty of getting a car to and from the garage, and the nagging certainty of many motorists that the repair work is ineffective and overpriced. The electric car could greatly reduce these disadvantages relative to conventional cars, but again, quantitative measures of the reduction are unobtainable.

- **Independence of Gasoline.** Gasoline has recently been
available in abundant quantities, at prices which are lower
after adjustment for inflation than they were in 1950. The
dependence of the supply of gasoline on imported petroleum,
however, is growing, and the US balance of payments has become a serious problem. As in 1973-74, there is a real risk
of further increases in the price of gasoline, of long lines
at service stations due to inadequate supplies at fixed prices,
and of outright rationing of gasoline. Because it requires no
gasoline, the electric car does not run these risks. Their
actual importance and probability, however, cannot be quantitatively projected.

- **Psychic Benefits.** The driver of an electric car will enjoy
knowing that he is causing much less pollution and using much
less scarce petroleum than the driver of a conventional car.
The actual contribution of the individual to relieving either
the pollution or depletion problem, however, is so small that
it is imperceptible; the benefits from any individual decision
in favor of electric cars must be intangible, or psychic. Other
intangible benefits include the novelty of an electric car,
the prestige which may be associated with it, and the satisfac-
tion of utilizing so elegant a technology.

The disadvantages of electric cars are relatively easier to project
in quantitative terms and to evaluate in terms of a common currency.
They include:

- **Less Capability.** The practical range of electric cars for
daily driving will remain substantially below that of conventional cars, even if the highest-performance batteries now
under intensive development are entirely successful. Acceleration and gradeability will at best match future lower-
performance conventional cars. Accommodations may be designed
to equal those of conventional cars if attendant higher costs
are acceptable.

213

- __Higher Cost__. Initial and life-cycle costs of electric cars
  will be greater than those of comparable conventional cars,
  given existing conditions and trends. Only if either range,
  or passenger capacity, or both are sacrificed are costs
  likely to be competitive. Reductions in battery and motor
  costs beyond those projected here would have relatively little
  benefit for electric cars; doubling or tripling of gasoline
  prices could eliminate or reverse the cost disadvantages, but
  limited range would still restrict the electric car relative
  to the conventional car.

On balance, the disadvantages of future electric cars for the
individual motorist appear strongly to outweigh the advantages. In consequence, it is difficult to foresee electric cars capturing a substantial
share of the automobile market in the United States without major increases
in gasoline prices or government intervention. The disadvantages are summarized in Table 8.1, which shows the extra cost and reduced capability of
representative future electric cars in relation to a subcompact conventional
car representative of prospects for 1980. These are to be weighed against
the uncertain and intangible advantages for the individual motorist noted
above.

For two-passenger electric cars with short range, Table 8.1 shows
substantial negative extra costs--that is to say cost advantages. These
cars offer only half the seating capacity of the conventional compact to
which they are compared, however, and a two-passenger ICE compact designed
for low cost and comparably low performance would probably be equally inexpensive. Only at the very shortest design ranges for a given type of
battery do the four-passenger cars show less cost than the conventional
subcompact. At longer ranges, initial costs exceed that of the conventional subcompact by over a hundred percent, if battery is included, and
life-cycle costs are 36% higher despite the assumption of longer life for
the electric cars. If batteries were leased, the initial cost would not
include the price of the battery and would compare much more favorably;

TABLE 8.1

RELATIVE COST AND CAPABILITY OF REPRESENTATIVE FUTURE ELECTRIC CARS

(Basis: 1980 four-passenger conventional subcompact with $3,700 initial cost, 9.5 cents/km life-cycle cost)

Technology	Battery	Urban Range, km	Extra Initial Cost, percent		Extra Life-Cycle Cost, percent	Loss of Seating Capacity, percent	Travel for Which Range is Inadequate				
							Urban Travel, percent		Long-distance Trips	
			Less Battery	With Battery			Days	Distance	Trips	Distance
Two-Passenger Cars										
Urban Secondary Car										
Improved	Lead-acid	75	-34	-21	-24	50	5	6-21	0	0
	Nickel-zinc	75	-38	-18	-14	50	5	6-21	0	0
	Lithium high-temperature	100	-48	-30	-27	50	2	8-24	0	0
Four-Passenger Car										
Urban Secondary Car										
Improved	Lead-acid	100	5	27	-1	0	2	3-12	0	0
	Nickel-zinc	100	-3	29	8	0	2	3-12	0	0
Urban Only Car										
Improved	Lead-acid	150	19	53	13	0	5	8-24	5	5,000
	Nickel-zinc	150	2	47	13	0	5	8-24	5	5,000
	Nickel-zinc	250	19	107	36	0	1	3-12	5	5,000
Urban Primary Car or General-Use Car										
Improved	Nickel-zinc	250	19	107	36	0	3	3-14	5	5,000
Advanced	Lithium high-temperature	250	-16	30	-2	0	3	3-14	5	5,000
Advanced	Lithium high-temperature	450	-2	97	31	0	0	0-2	(Uncertain)	

215

but conventional cars can be leased, too, so the advantage is not decisive. If cars and batteries were entirely leased, the extra life-cycle costs would remain, requiring lease payments for the electric cars up to 36% higher than those for conventional cars.

The limited range of electric cars makes them inadequate for amounts of travel which are also shown in Table 8.1. Depending on range and intended application, the electric cars might be inadequate on as many as five days out of a hundred for urban travel. Depending on the type of driving, the associated loss of urban travel distance might range up to 24%, as shown in Fig. 5.5. Beyond urban travel, of course, remain longer trips for weekends, vacations, and out-of-town business and recreation. Secondary electric cars at multi-car households would presumably not be used for such travel. Electric cars at one-car households and electric cars serving as primary cars would be inadequate for virtually all this travel, which involves overnight stops away from home and round-trip distances exceeding 300 km. The typical household reporting such trips makes an average of five per year, with distance per trip averaging about 1000 km. Only the long-range version of the advanced-technology car in Table 8.1 seems likely to be useful for any such trips. The range of this car on the highway exceeds 500 km. Though many conventional cars are driven further than 500 km in a single day, reasonable rescheduling of many trips to avoid days exceeding this distance would be possible. If high-powered facilities for overnight recharging were available away from home, this electric car could accomplish a great deal of long-distance travel.

The representative future cars of Table 8.1 are examples of what may be possible in the future. None, however, is necessarily optimum for a given application, offering the most favorable combination of capability and cost. Two nickel-zinc battery cars, for example, are shown for application as the only car at an urban household. With 250 km range, costs are relatively high but travel needs beyond the range of the car are much less than with 150 km range. The same sort of compromise is evident in Table 8.1 for cars with other batteries, in other applications.

Though the optimum design range cannot be precisely determined, the analyses of Secs. 5, 6, and 7 may be combined to indicate that the choices implicit in Table 8.1 are at least reasonable. Figure 8.1 shows how initial and life-cycle costs of the representative future cars depend on the percentile range for the three major applications identified in Sec. 5. Only four-passenger cars are considered here. The increasingly rapid rise of costs as cars exceed the 95th-percentile range is evident. It is less apparent, however, that because the extra costs apply to all travel, but yield relatively little extra travel, the overall costs of each extra unit of travel may be relatively high.

The extra costs of extra travel are illustrated in Fig. 8.2 for four-passenger, improved-technology electric cars at one-driver households. Figure 8.2a shows the added life-cycle cost per kilometer of extra travel as range is extended. The extra costs were taken from Fig. 8.1, while the extra travel was taken from Fig. 5.5, which shows a range of possibilities, depending on the kind of driving done. The extra cost associated with this extra travel consequently extends over a range of possibilities. With lead-acid batteries, these extra costs are far above average costs per kilometer at the 95th-percentile range, two to four times as much, and are rising rapidly with increases in percentile range. For the car with nickel-zinc batteries, however, extra costs are lower and rising less rapidly, because the range capabilities of the car are very much greater. With lead-acid batteries, after all, there is a relatively low percentile range which is the absolute maximum, even at infinite cost, which can be achieved.

In Fig. 8.2b, the added costs are expressed in terms of additional travel days which may be fully accommodated by the increased capability of the car. For the lead-acid battery car, for example, increasing the design range beyond the 95th percentile increases the cost well over $20 for each extra day accommodated. A motorist might choose to pay $20, $30, or $40 per day more for the extra travel capability by purchasing

217

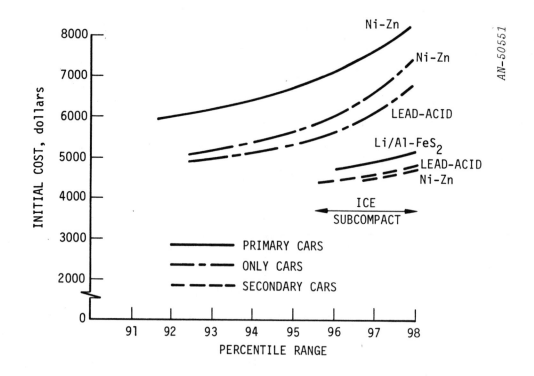

a. Initial Costs

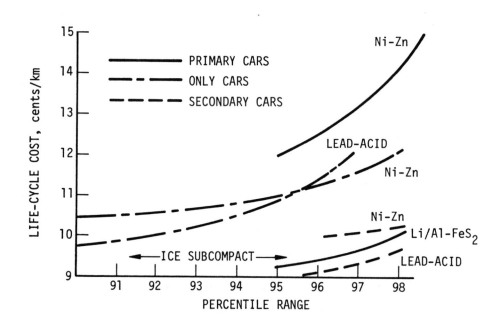

b. Life-Cycle Costs

Figure 8.1. Dependence of Electric Car Costs on Percentile Range

218

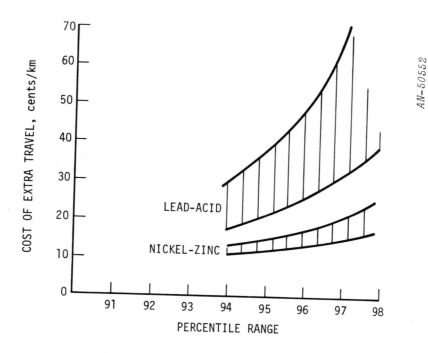

a. Cost per added kilometer of travel

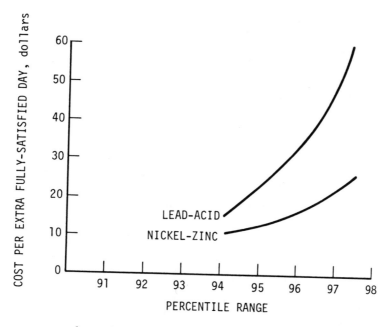

b. Cost per added full travel day

Figure 8.2. Life-Cycle Costs of Extra Urban Travel
(Four-passenger, improved-technology
cars at one-driver households)

a longer-range electric car. Alternatively, he might choose to rent an ICE automobile to accommodate these demanding days. For the lead-acid battery car, renting would surely be a reasonable way to accommodate 96th-percentile days, and would probably be preferable to many motorists for days beyond the 97th or 98th percentile. Thus the 95th and 98th-percentile ranges used as examples in Table 8.1 appear to bracket the likely optimum for the motorist considering renting as an alternative. For the nickel-zinc battery car, extra costs per day are smaller and rise much less rapidly, so that the 98th percentile or even a higher percentile might be the optimum design range.

These sorts of choices for the purchaser of an electric car are illustrated in Table 8.1 by the two nickel-zinc entries for four-passenger only cars at one-car households. With ranges at about the 95th and 99th percentile, they show both the extra costs and the extra capabilities of the higher design range.

8.2 PROJECTIONS OF SALES OF ELECTRIC CARS

No new projections of sales were made in this study for electric cars. Sales were projected, however, by another study based on the representative electric cars described here. At the same time, yet another group independently projected the characteristics and costs of electric cars, and estimated their sales by a sophisticated model based on previous consumer behavior in the automobile market. These projections are briefly summarized here, after review of an earlier projection based on an alternative approach: survey of consumer interest and intentions.

In 1973, a group of faculty and students at the University of Wisconsin surveyed motorists and projected sales of electric cars through 1980. Their marketing-oriented approach and findings were published in 1974 in a book called The Electric Car.[1]

The surveys of consumers made in support of the analysis found an
average "intention to buy an electric car" of 4.5-5 on a scale in which
zero represented absolutely no possibility of purchase, and ten represented
near certainty. Intention to buy was highest among high-income consumers,
owners of compact cars, those who took relatively short work trips, and
those from multicar and multidriver households. The encouragingly high
expressions of intention to buy may have resulted from a description
given of an electric car which seems optimistic. Its features included:

- Subcompact size (four-seater/station wagon)
- Range of 100 kilometers at 80 kilometers per hour (50 miles at
  50 mph)
- Fuel cost only 25% of that for an ICE car
- Batteries rechargeable fully overnight, or 80% in 45 minutes
  with a "quick charge device"
- Initial cost of $2,500, versus $3,000 for an ICE subcompact.

In view of the findings of Sec. 7, the low initial cost for a car of the
size described seems unlikely. Moreover, the implication of very low
operating cost is probably misleading. Respondents in the survey, however,
wanted even more performance and capability at less cost. When asked
which attributes, if improved, would most raise their intention to buy,
they cited range, overnight recharging, size, and cost, in that order.

Though the consumer surveys were made only in Wisconsin, they produced
results resembling those from national surveys and are probably applicable
generally. In a national survey of consumer interest in purchasing electric
automobiles made for the Electric Vehicle Council, high interest was also
noted among younger people with higher income, higher education, urban
residences, and larger households.[2] The survey questions and the responses
by group are reproduced in Table 8.2.

.

TABLE 8.2

RESULTS OF A 1976 SURVEY OF CONSUMER INTEREST

Source: Ref. 2

Here is a question about an electric vehicle. First, let me describe
it, and then I would like to get your opinion.

- The car would be used for shopping, traveling about town, and
  possibly commuting.
- It would have a top speed of 50 miles (80 km/hr) and would go
  about 40 miles (65 km) before the batteries would have to be charged.
  This could be done at home.
- Operating costs would be equal to, or less than a gasoline subcompact
- It would help reduce our dependency on imported oil and eliminate
  the need to buy high-priced gasoline.
- It is quiet and emits no pollutants
- The car would be small, easy to park, and would sell for $3,000
  to $5,000.

Do you think you'd be interested in buying such a car?

	Yes, percent	No, percent	Don't Know, percent
Total US Public	37	56	7
Men	34	60	6
Women	39	52	9
18-29 years of age	45	46	9
30-39 year of age	45	46	9
40-49 years of age	40	53	7
50-59 years of age	29	65	6
60 years or over	24	71	5
Less than high school complete	30	64	6
High school complete	39	53	8
Some college	44	49	7
Professional	53	42	5
Managerial	39	51	10
Clerical, sales	42	51	7
Craftsman, foreman	40	52	8
Other manual, service	34	56	10
Farmer, farm laborer	32	66	2
Rural	34	59	7
Old Suburb	33	59	8
New Suburb	38	56	6
City 1 family	40	54	6
City Multifamily	45	48	7
City Apartment	41	52	7
Northeast	44	50	6
North Central	37	55	8
South	29	63	8
West	42	53	5
Under $5,000 family income	28	66	6
$5,000-$6,999	29	63	8
$7,000-$9,999	37	56	7
$10,000-$14,999	40	52	8
$14,000 or over	44	49	7
No children in household	32	61	7
With children under 18	42	50	8
With teenagers 12-17	37	55	8
Non-metro - Rural	25	67	8
Urban	38	57	5
Metro - 50,000-999,999	38	54	8
1,000,000 or over	42	51	7

In the Wisconsin projections of electric car sales, the primary market
for electric cars was identified as urbanites in upper-income groups who
habitually owned new second cars, only one or two model-years old. Of
66.5 million households in the US at the time of the projections, about
20 million owned two cars, but only a little over 5% of these two-car
households owned second cars which were only one or two model-years old,
1.1 million in all. Of this 1.1 million households, 700,000 were in urban
areas, with incomes over $10,000 per year. The potential primary market
for electric cars was thus estimated at 250,000-350,000 cars per year.

On a much less specific basis, secondary markets were estimated as
shown in Table 8.3. Furthermore, major increases in the secondary markets
were expected by 1980 on account of heightened concern about the ecology,
including air pollution and conservation, plus economic changes working
strongly to the detriment of conventional automobiles. Major increases
in the cost of owning conventional cars were anticipated, while the full
costs of electric cars were apparently underestimated. The conclusion
leading to the increases of Table 8.3 was very favorable to electric cars:
"by 1980 they may cost less than half as much to operate as the least
expensive gasoline fueled alternative."

The total potential market estimated for electric cars in 1980
ranged from under 10% to a little under 20% of US car sales. Projected
sales were based on a 15% penetration of this potential market, to a maximum
of only 3% of the US auto market. For 1977, sales of 17,000 to 36,000
electric cars were forecast, perhaps a hundred times more than actually
recorded, and the forecasted estimate of up to 330,000 for 1980 seems
unlikely.

Sales estimates based on surveys of the intentions of consumers
depend on the assumption that expressed intentions indicate actual future
behavior. An alternative approach which avoids this assumption is based
on models calibrated from actual consumer behavior in past years. No

TABLE 8.3

ELECTRIC CAR MARKET POTENTIAL FOR 1980
(IN THOUSANDS OF UNITS) PROJECTED IN 1973
Source: Ref. 1

Market Segment	1973 Projection	Increase due to: Ecology	Economy	Total
Primary Consumer	250-350			250-350
Secondary Consumer				
1 Car Owners	50-150	25-100	75-250	150-500
2 Car Owners	50-150	25-100	50-200	125-450
Miscellaneous	50-100		35-70	80-170
Industrial/Institutional				
Fleet	70-100	35-75	35-100	140-275
Non-Fleet	30-100	15-75	15-30	60-205
Total	500-950	100-35-	210-640	810-1950

assertions or predictions by individuals about their intentions are necessary under this approach. On the other hand, it is difficult to generalize from consumer behavior in the market for conventional automobiles to that in a future market including electric cars. The reason for this is that conventional cars are not range-limited, so consumers have had no chance to exhibit their degree of willingness to purchase cars with range limitations. Still, examination of this approach is interesting because it suggests that even if the range limitation is inconsequential to consumers, the higher prices of electric cars will limit their sales to a minor fraction of the US auto market.

During the course of the study reported here, electric car sales were projected in a separate study by a group at SRI International.[3] The projection was based on the capabilities and costs of electric cars shown in Secs. 4 and 7, and was made with a model of automotive demand which did not account for the limited range of electric cars. At the same time, a detailed analysis and projection of future electric car sales was made independently by a group at Mathtech, using different assumptions about future batteries, future automobiles, and their relative capabilities and costs.[4]

Overall results are shown in the projections for total electric vehicles in use through the year 2000 shown in Fig. 8.3. The SRI projection follows from an estimated potential market of about 100,000-150,000 electric cars in 1980, rising to about 175,000-250,000 in the year 2000, together with an estimated supply of electric cars based on a detailed analysis of the interests and probable activities of interested parties. The supply scenario considered most likely included the merchandising of mass-produced Japanese electric cars in the late 1980s, followed by entry of the major US manufacturers on a mass-production basis in the 1990s. The Mathtech projections involve considerably larger sales, especially near the year 2000, as a result of assumed technological improvements which far exceeded those underlying the SRI projection. Both the "optimistic" and "pessimistic" Mathtech projections in Fig. 8.3 are based on a degree of technical optimism far beyond that of Secs. 3 and 4.

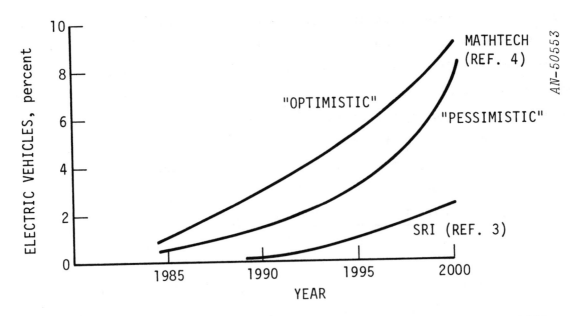

Figure 8.3. Projections of Electric Vehicles in Use, 1980-2000

Underlying the Mathtech sales projections are future electric cars
with the costs described in Table 8.4. The costs themselves are not
unlike those of Sec. 7, but their derivation was considerably different.
Moreover, the batteries projected for these cars provided exceptionally
high performance. The zinc-chlorine battery implicit in Table 8.4 produced 170 watt-hours per kilogram, 50% more than the high-temperature
lithium battery of Sec. 3. The sodium-sulfur battery produced 220 watt-
hours per kilogram, almost 90% more. The life assumed for both batteries
was also greater, 1,000 cycles, but initial costs were assumed to be
essentially no greater. The optimistic and pessimistic projections differed only in that these advanced batteries became available later in
this century under the pessimistic scenario. In both scenarios, both
batteries become available by the year 2000.

An elegant model of market shares was the basis for the Mathtech projections in Fig. 8.3. Explicit, quantitative allowance for the limitation of range of electric cars was incorporated by the method of "stockout costs." The difference between desired travel and travel possible with the electric cars was calculated, much as in Sec. 6. Then a nominal cost of about 15 cents per kilometer was attributed to the distance beyond the capability of the electric cars. This cost, spread over the entire desired travel, is the stockout cost per kilometer shown in Table 8.4. It represents, for example, the cost of renting a car for those trips that are not possible with the electric car; or simply a measure of the "cost" of trips that would not be made. The resultant stockout costs are shown in Table 8.4. They are large for the lead-acid car, with a range of only 30 kilometers, but small for the remaining cars. The other two-passenger cars offered ranges of 100 and 150 kilometers, while the four-passenger cars offered 100 and 200 kilometers. The stockout costs were then capitalized over the life of the car and included in the totals shown in Table 8.4. Thus the limitation of the electric car was incorporated in the model of the automotive market through a cost penalty attached to the electric cars.

Except in the case of the lead-acid car, however, the cost penalties associated with limited range were exceedingly small, at most a few percent of the total. As a result, effects on sales of electric cars estimated by the model were also small.

Because the limited capability of electric cars was given either little or no weight in the projections of Fig. 8.3, they are likely to be on the high side. Even so, they indicate that less than 10% of US autos will be electric in the year 2000.

Viewed another way, both projections show the great importance of the relatively high costs of electric cars. Even if range limitations are inconsequential, these relative costs will apparently keep the market share of electric cars small. In this connection it is interesting

TABLE 8.4

Costs (1975$)	Two-Passenger Urban Runabout			Four-Passenger Suburban Car	
	Pb/Acid	Zn/Cl	Na/S	Zn/Cl	Na/S
Components Cost					
Battery Pack	352	855	802	1,261	1,577
Motor/Controller	1,180	1,125	1,089	1,406	1,351
Other	949	1,323	1,388	2,038	1,923
Total	2,481	3,303	3,280	4,705	4,851
Factory Wholesale Price	3,467	4,289	4,265	5,691	5,863
Price (Plus Taxes & Registration)	4,279	5,232	5,205	6,859	7,028
Stockout Costs (¢/km)	5.7	0.53	.13	.53	.04
Capitalized Costs (¢/km)					
Fixed	4.48	5.48	5.45	7.18	7.36
Operating	12.19	5.16	4.38	5.69	4.58
Total	16.67	10.64	9.83	12.87	11.93

to review the initial price and capitalized costs per kilometer in Table 8.4. They are quite similar to those developed in Sec. 7. Their relation to projected costs for competitive conventional cars was also similar. The Mathtech subcompact for 1985 was priced at $3,720, with a capitalized cost of 9.8 cents per kilometer, figures very close to those for a conventional subcompact estimated in Sec. 7.

SECTION 8 REFERENCES

1. G. M. Naidu, George Tesar, and Gerald G. Udell, The Electric Car: An Alternative to the Internal Combustion Engine, Publishing Sciences Group, Acton, MA, 1974.

2. Press Release, August 27, 1976, by the Electric Vehicle Council, 90 Park Avenue, New York, N.Y.

3. E. M. Dickson and B. L. Walton, A Scenario of Battery/Electric Vehicle Market Evolution, CRESS Report No. 46, SRI International, Menlo Park, December 1977.

4. E. Patrick Marfisi, et al., The Impact of Electric Passenger Automobiles on Utility System Loads, 1985-2000, Final Report, Research Project 758-1, Mathtech, Inc., Princeton, November 1977.

9   COMPARATIVE USE OF FUEL AND ENERGY

Sections 6-8 have compared electric cars with conventional cars solely on the basis of their costs and capabilities for drivers. Costs of fuel and electric energy at current prices were shown to result in little or no advantage for electric cars. Current prices, however, fall far short of indicating the full value and importance of fuels and energy in the United States. The prices of gasoline for conventional cars and of oil for electric utilities are kept artificially low by Federal constraints. Even without these limits, oil and gasoline prices would not fully reflect the political and economic hazards arising in the growing dependence of the United States on foreign suppliers of petroleum and the associated unfavorable balance of international trade. To do justice to the prospective benefits of electric cars, it is therefore necessary to project in detail the effects electric cars would have on the use of fuel and energy in the US.

The use of energy from fossil fuels is projected in Fig. 9.1 for conventional ICE cars and for the representative future electric cars of Table 4.1. This is the starting point for a fuller evaluation of the relative merits of electric automobiles in conserving limited resources of fuel. In Fig. 9.1 and throughout Sec. 9, two basic, simplified cases are compared: in one, all the energy for operating automobiles is derived from petroleum; in the other, all the energy is derived from coal--as synthetic gasoline for conventional cars, and as electric power for recharging electric cars from coal-fired power stations. Actually, of course, electric cars would be recharged both from coal-fired and petroleum-fired power stations, and in addition from nuclear and hydroelectric power as well. The electric power likely to be available from these various sources is projected in Sec. 10, and the proportions which would be used for various levels of electric car use is projected in Sec. 11, along with the net savings of petroleum as conventional cars are replaced by electric cars.

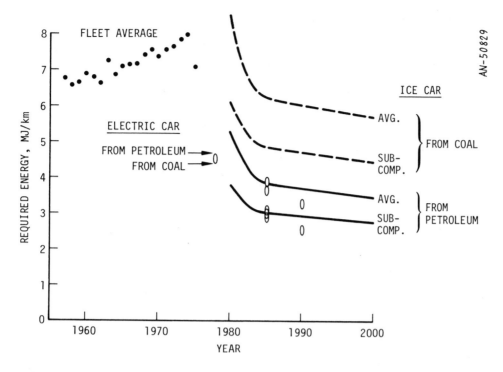

Figure 9.1. Energy Required from Resources of Coal or
Petroleum for Urban Driving (new cars)

In Fig. 9.1, the average energy required from petroleum per kilometer
of urban travel by new cars sold in the United States is shown for the years
1957-75. These averages are based on actual measurements for individual
models of new cars, weighted with the sales of each model. A rising trend
of use is apparent.[1] The projections for future conventional cars, in
contrast, drop sharply through 1985 as required by Federal law imposing
minimum standards for fuel economy.[2] The ovals in Fig. 9.1 indicate projected requirements of energy from coal or oil for the representative future
four-passenger electric cars of Sec. 4. For a given battery and level of
technology, the electric cars with shorter design ranges are competitive
with the conventional subcompacts of the year in which they might become
available.   At longer design ranges, however, the extra weight required
in the electric car leads to substantial additional use of energy.

231

Production of synthetic gasoline from coal is not nearly as efficient as refining gasoline from crude oil. Production of electricity from coal in electric utilities, however, is typically more efficient than from petroleum. As a result, the electric cars require a little less energy from coal than from petroleum for their operation, but conventional cars require much more. Whereas electric cars are merely competitive with conventional cars if fueled from petroleum, they offer major advantages for the use of coal, a much more abundant resource in the United States.

In comparisons such as those of Fig. 9.1, it is clear that the improvement of conventional cars projected for future years is critical. In this section, this improvement for conventional cars is first investigated. Then the relative efficiencies of deriving gasoline and recharge electricity from petroleum and coal are summarized. Finally, direct comparisons are made between conventional and electric cars, and the equivalent fuel economy of electric cars recharged from petroleum is projected.

9.1   FUEL ECONOMY OF FUTURE ICE CARS

The Energy Policy and Conservation Act of 1975 dictates the minimum average fuel economy for passenger automobiles manufactured by any manufacturer in any model year after 1977.[2] These minimums, as detailed by the Secretary of the Department of Transportation for 1981 through 1984 and as specified for other years by the Act, are shown in Table 9.1. While there are minor adjustments possible under the Act, and competition in the market could lead to higher average economies, these minimums form the basis of a reasonable projection for future conventional cars.

Such a projection is illustrated in Fig. 9.2 and detailed in Table 9.2. It entails a number of adjustments to and assumptions about the fuel economies of Table 9.1.

TABLE 9.1

FEDERAL REQUIREMENTS FOR FUEL ECONOMY

Source: Ref. 1

	Minimum Fleet Fuel Economy	
Model Year	Miles per Gallon	Kilometers per Liter
1978	18	7.65
1979	19	8.08
1980	20	8.50
1981	22	9.35
1982	24	10.20
1983	26	11.05
1984	27	11.48
1985	27.5	11.69

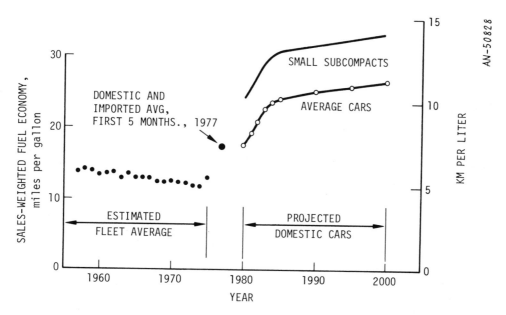

Figure 9.2.   Actual and Projected Fuel Economy for New
Cars in Urban Driving

TABLE 9.2

URBAN FUEL ECONOMY OF PROJECTED NEW ICE CARS, KILOMETERS PER LITER

	1977-1979	1980	1981	1982	1983	1984	1985	1990	1995	2000
Small Subcompact	10.2	10.3	11.0	11.8	12.5	12.9	13.0	13.4	13.8	14.2
Subcompact	8.9	9.0	9.7	10.4	11.2	11.5	11.7	12.1	12.5	12.8
Compact	6.8	6.9	7.6	8.4	9.1	9.5	9.6	10.0	10.4	10.8
Midsize	6.4	6.4	7.2	7.9	8.7	9.0	9.2	9.6	9.9	10.3
Large	6.2	6.2	7.0	7.7	8.5	8.8	9.0	9.4	9.8	10.1
New Car Fleet Average	7.3	7.4	8.1	8.9	9.6	10.0	10.2	10.5	10.9	11.3

1 km/liter = 2.35 mi/gallon

234

First, the projections in Fig. 9.2 are adjusted to apply only to urban driving. The economies of Table 9.1, in contrast, are based on separate Federal test procedures for highway and city driving, which are combined under the assumption that 45% of travel will be highway travel. In 1976, the average ratio of highway fuel economy to city fuel economy was 1.41. From this and the mileage distribution, it may be inferred that urban fuel economy is typically 87% of overall fuel economy as defined in Table 9.1.[2] Thus the new car averages in Table 9.2 are 87% of the minimum requirements in Table 9.1.

Since electric cars are most likely to find service in urban use and are direct replacements only for small cars, fuel economies for the various sizes of conventional cars are separately projected in Table 9.2. For this separate projection it was assumed that the present mix of sizes would remain constant, that is, 50% large and intermediate cars, 20% compact cars, and 30% subcompact and small subcompact. It was also assumed that the difference in fuel economy between large cars and small subcompact cars would remain about 4.7 kilometers per liter (11 miles per gallon), as it has recently. These assumptions essentially imply that all sizes of cars will grow lighter and more efficient in the future, but with the greatest changes in the larger cars. This trend is already manifest in the "downsizing" of standard cars which began with the 1977 model year, in which weight and external size were substantially reduced without loss of passenger accommodations. In smaller cars, there is less opportunity for this kind of improvement.

Finally, an improvement in fuel economy of .09 kilometers per liter was assumed for each year after 1985 in Table 9.2. This assures that average fuel economy in the year 2000 agrees with that projected by the Interagency Task Force on Automotive Goals Beyond 1980, the source of basic projections in Secs. 4 and 7 about electric cars.[3]

It is clear from Fig. 9.2 that the improved fuel economy projected for conventional cars requires a drastic reversal of the longstanding downtrend in the years preceding 1975. Due to minor changes in test procedures over the years, the fuel economies shown for 1957-75 cars differ slightly from those based on the current urban driving cycle implicit in the projections; the down-trend, however, is unaffected.

The total use of fuel by conventional automobiles in the US is projected in Table 9.3. The projection is based on the number of cars available at residences from Table 6.7, average annual driving per car of 16,000 kilometers, and the fuel economies of Table 9.2. Since only new-car fuel economies are shown in Table 9.2, the averages for all cars on the road in Table 9.3 were calculated using the distribution of automobile travel with age shown in Table 9.4.[4] The total required energy from petroleum allows for transportation and refining energy as estimated in Sec. 9.2.

The eventual impact of the Energy Policy and Conservation Act is clear in Table 9.3: a reduction of over 25% in national automotive use of petroleum by the end of the century, despite an increase almost as large in total travel. The prospective benefit from substitution of electric cars is correspondingly less than it would have been in the absence of this major improvement of conventional cars.

There are numerous uncertainties in the projections of Table 9.3. On-the-road fuel economy recorded under similar conditions may differ substantially from the dynamometer tests on which the projections are based. In a recent study, almost half of the cars tested achieved less than 90% of the fuel economy measured in the standard tests. Moreover, many of the actual production cars investigated required significant adjustments, though they were nearly new, to meet manufacturers' specifications for tuning.[5] Beyond this, actual conditions of use may differ substantially from those of the test, leading to considerably lower fuel

TABLE 9.3

PROJECTED USE OF FUEL BY ICE CARS

	1980	1990	2000
Cars available at residences, millions	102	116	126
Annual driving, 10^9 km	1.63	1.86	2.02
Average fuel economy, km/liter	6.5	10	11
Annual fuel consumption, 10^{11} liters	2.5	1.9	1.8
Required energy from crude petroleum, 10^{12} MJ	9.8	7.2	7.1

TABLE 9.4

PERCENT OF TRAVEL BY AGE OF VEHICLE

Vehicle Age	1	2	3	4	5	6	7	8	9	10	11	12	13 and older
Travel Fraction, percent	10.6	14.2	13.3	12.3	10.8	9.2	7.7	6.4	5.0	3.5	2.3	1.6	3.2

economies. The test measurements have been routinely reduced 11% by the US Department of Transportation and 15% by the Federal Energy Administration in estimating national use of fuel.[6] Offsetting these considerations, however, are the potential effects of imported cars, which have consistently offered much higher average fuel economies than those of US manufacturers. If they continue to do so, foreign cars might raise total fleet averages by 5-10% over the values computed for domestic cars alone.

Finally, the assumed annual driving per automobile of 16,000 kilometers may be incorrect. The basis for this assumption, discussed in Sec. 5, is the annual estimate of driving per registered passenger car shown in Fig. 5.8. This estimate, compiled by the Department of Transportation from state data, shows a remarkable stability over the past four decades, despite great improvements in highways and rising speed limits, both of which allowed motorists to travel farther and farther in the time available. In the future, however, today's lower speed limits, much-reduced highway construction, and increasing congestion may even lead to a decline in average driving per car.

9.2 EFFICIENCIES OF CONVERTING PETROLEUM AND COAL TO AUTOMOTIVE FUELS

In the simplest case, both conventional and electric cars might be provided with energy from petroleum via refineries producing gasoline and electric power plants burning oil. To compare overall requirements for petroleum directly in this simple case, the processes of conversion into gasoline and electricity must be included. In Fig. 9.3, efficiencies of transforming crude oil into gasoline or electricity for cars are shown at each stage of the necessary processes.[7] Inputs of additional energy for pumping and transporting petroleum are shown in triangles. To calculate overall requirements from crude oil, these additional inputs may be added to the basic requirement for crude oil at the top of the figure.

238

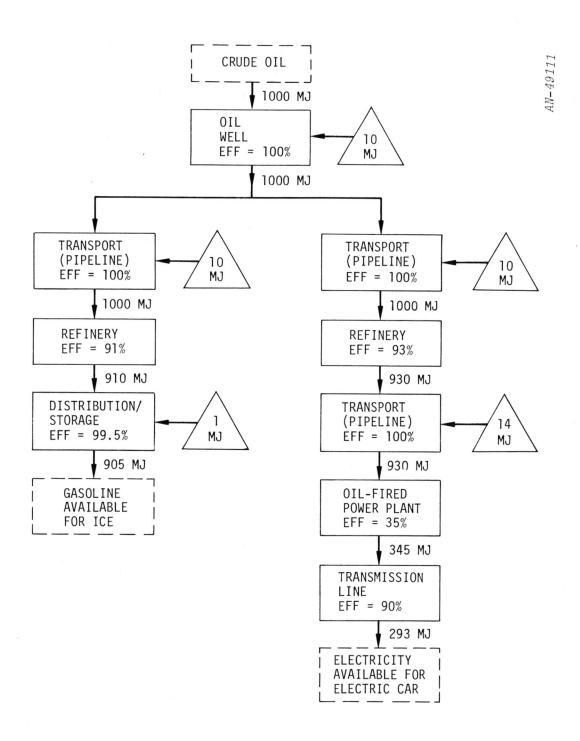

Figure 9.3.   Energy Flows in Preparing Petroleum for Automotive Use
(Source: Ref. 7)

At the other extreme, it would also be possible to derive all energy for both electric and conventional automobiles from coal, a resource of fossil fuel which is far more abundant in the United States. Similar efficiencies and energy requirements are shown in Fig. 9.4 for converting coal into gasoline or electricity.[7]

Overall, there are four possible conversions of fossil fuel for automotive use, with efficiencies (including all inputs of energy) as shown:

Crude oil to gasoline	89%
Crude oil to electricity	28%
Coal to gasoline	55%
Coal to electricity	30%

Conversion of coal to gasoline is not expected to grow much more efficient; the figure shown is already a projection for future years. The production of electricity from both coal and petroleum, however, is given at current average figures, which may be surpassed considerably by future power plants. Modern steam plants reach efficiencies of 38-40%, considerably above the average. Moreover, the use of topping cycles and magnetohydro- dynamic generators could become practical in this century, with efficiencies up to 50%. This could reduce the total energy required from coal for electric cars by as much as 30%; but development times and costs are considerable, so that few such installations seem likely by the year 2000.[8]

The use of diesel rather than gasoline automobiles would increase the refinery efficiencies in Figs. 9.3 and 9.4. Overall, the efficiencies of converting fossil fuel to gasoline would each be increased by 2% as a result. Again, this possible improvement is not assumed in the projec- tions.

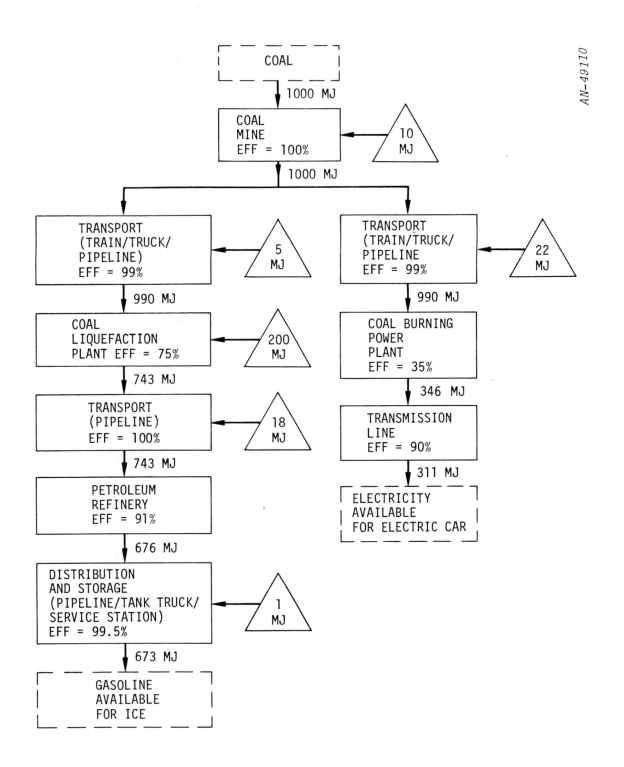

Figure 9.4.   Energy Flows in Preparing Coal for Automotive Use
(Source: Ref. 7)

9.3   AUTOMOTIVE USE OF ENERGY FROM PETROLEUM AND COAL

Tables 9.5 and 9.6 show energy required from primary resources for electric and conventional cars. The electric cars are the representative future cars summarized in Table 4.1. The projected fuel economy of the conventional cars was given in Table 9.2. Figure 9.1 displayed graphically the energy requirements for four-passenger cars from Tables 9.5 and 9.6.

The electric cars utilize either petroleum or coal resources with approximately equal effectiveness. Conventional cars, however, are much less efficient overall if they must operate on synthetic gasoline derived from coal. For a given amount of driving, the use of ICE cars instead of electric cars would require mining 20% to 80% more coal, a serious disadvantage in view of the difficulty of rapid expansion of coal mining and the serious or even irremediable environmental degradation which may result.[9]

Figure 9.5 restates the fuel consumptions of Fig. 9.1 in the familiar terms of fuel economy. Also shown are US fleet averages recorded since 1957, and a range of examples from the 1977 model year for subcompact ICE cars meeting the stringent California emissions standards--standards which will be equaled elsewhere in future years.[10] In Fig. 9.5, all energy is assumed to be derived from petroleum resources for both electric and conventional cars. This allows computation of an effective fuel economy for electric cars such that equal amounts of crude oil would be required for electric and conventional cars with the same fuel economy.

Again, the drastic improvement projected for conventional cars is evident in Fig. 9.5. At the same time, the achievements in the 1977 model year show clearly that this improvement is well within reach. In fact, more could be achieved if even smaller future cars, with lower performance, were acceptable. The implication of the projections shown is that in the US market, buyers will prefer the largest domestic cars which can be built within the fuel economy requirements of the Energy Policy and Conservation Act.

TABLE 9.5

ENERGY REQUIRED FROM PRIMARY RESOURCES FOR OPERATING ELECTRIC CARS

Application	Passengers	Technology	Battery	Range, km	Energy Input to Battery Charger, MJ/km	Energy Use from Resource, MJ/km Petroleum	Coal
Urban extra car	2	Recent	Lead-acid	65	.900	3.21	3.00
Urban secondary car	2	Improved	Lead-acid	75	.662	2.36	3.21
			Nickel-zinc	75	.644	2.30	2.15
		Advanced	Lithium	100	.584	1.98	1.85
	4	Recent	Lead-acid	75	1.307	4.67	4.36
		Improved	Lead-acid	100	.889	3.18	2.96
			Nickel-zinc	100	.835	2.98	2.78
Urban only car	4	Improved	Lead-acid	150	1.062	3.79	3.54
			Nickel-zinc	150	.904	3.23	3.01
General-use car	4	Improved	Nickel-zinc	250	1.138	4.06	3.79
			Lithium	250	.752	2.69	2.51
		Advanced	Lithium	450	.954	3.41	3.18

243

TABLE 9.6

ENERGY REQUIRED FROM PRIMARY RESOURCES FOR OPERATING PROJECTED ICE CARS

Type of Car	Year	Fuel Use, km/liter	Energy Use from Resource, MJ/km	
			Petroleum	Coal
Small Subcompact	1980	10.3	3.80	6.15
	1981	11.0	3.56	5.76
	1982	11.8	3.32	5.37
	1983	12.5	3.13	5.07
	1984	12.9	3.03	4.91
	1985	13.0	3.01	4.87
	1990	13.4	2.92	4.73
	2000	14.2	2.76	4.46
Average	1980	7.4	5.29	8.56
	1981	8.1	4.83	7.82
	1982	8.9	4.40	7.12
	1983	9.6	4.08	6.60
	1984	10.0	3.91	6.33
	1985	10.2	3.84	6.21
	1990	10.5	3.73	6.03
	2000	11.3	3.46	5.60

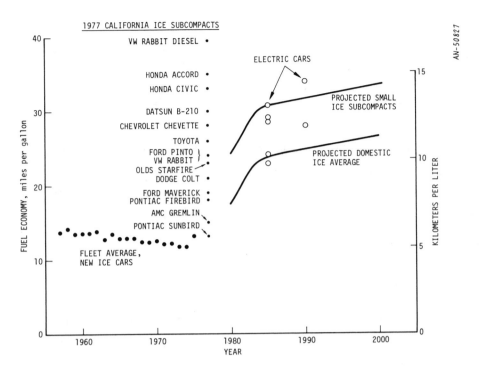

Figure 9.5. Effective Urban Fuel Economy of Electric Cars Recharged From Oil-Fired Power Plants

Despite the projected improvement for conventional cars, the electric cars appear competitive. The effective fuel economy of the electric cars depends strongly, however, on both design range and type of battery. With low design ranges and batteries offering high energy densities, the electric cars are little or no heavier than the conventional small subcompacts, and equal their effective fuel economy. Otherwise, however, they may be considerably heavier and correspondingly less economical of fuel. The 250-kilometer improved-technology electric car with nickel-zinc battery achieved about 9.8 km per liter (23 miles per gallon) equivalent consumption of petroleum. This is much less than the 13.2 km per liter (31 miles per gallon) for the projected 1985 ICE subcompact. On the other hand, the test weight of the electric car was about 75% greater than that of the small ICE subcompact. This extra weight is solely due to the battery and the extra propulsion and structure required to propel and support it. Its effect on energy use is more than enough to account for the difference in the fuel economies of the two cars.

9.4 ENERGY FOR MANUFACTURING

Fuel and energy use in Secs. 9.1-9.3 are for operation only. Substantial additional energy is required for the manufacture of an automobile, as shown in Table 9.7.[11,12,13] For conventional cars, it may be as much as a third of the energy required for operation during the life of the vehicle. Recycling of automotive materials can reduce this requirement by 30% or more, however; as shown in Table 9.8, the energy required to produce new materials is almost two-thirds of that for the completed car, and recycling materials can cut this in half.[13] Recycling is expected to be the usual practice in future years.[14]

Also shown in Table 9.7 are the only estimates available for energy required to manufacture an electric car--in this case, a subcompact with high-temperature lithium battery.[7] The estimate for manufacturing the battery exceeds that for the remainder of the car. It raises the possibility that total energy for manufacturing of electric cars and their batteries could compare unfavorably with that for conventional cars.

The estimate for the battery in Table 9.7, however, is not based on detailed data. No estimates have apparently been made in detail for this or any other type of propulsion battery. Moreover, much of the estimated energy requirement is for production of the necessary materials. Eventually, however, little new material will be needed; most battery materials are scarce and valuable enough to be fully recycled. Though the procedures for recovering materials from used batteries have not yet been developed, at least for the advanced batteries, it is likely their energy requirements will be much less than for producing new materials.

Manufacturing energies are being estimated in current battery development programs sponsored by the US Department of Energy. Until these estimates become available, it is too early to say whether the manufacturing energy required for electric cars will be substantially greater than that for conventional cars.

TABLE 9.7

ESTIMATES OF ENERGY REQUIRED IN MANUFACTURING AUTOMOBILES

| Source of Estimate | Manufactured Item | Energy Required in Manufacture | | Maximum Savings with Recycling, percent |
		Total, MJ	per 1000 kg, MJ	
Berry and Fels, 1973	Average 1967 auto (1,608 kg)	134,000	83,400	30
J.K. Tien, et al., 1975	Typical US car (1,633 kg)	105,000	64,500	37
J.J. Harwood, 1977	1974 Ford (1,633 kg)	129,000	78,800	30
E.E. Hughes, et al., 1976	Subcompact Car (907 kg)	79,100	87,200	–
	Subcompact car for electric drive (726 kg)	62,500	86,200	–
	41-kWh Li/Al-FeS$_2$ battery (259 kg)	84,400	326,000	

247

TABLE 9.8

USES OF ENERGY IN MANUFACTURING A 1974 FORD AUTOMOBILE

Source: Ref. 13

Manufacture of Metallic Materials	66%
Manufacture of Other Materials	5%
Fabrication of Parts and Assembly of Automobile	27%
Transportation of Materials and Assembled Auto	2%
	100%

SECTION 9 REFERENCES

1. T. C. Austin and K. H. Hellman, Passenger Car Fuel Economy--Trends
    and Influencing Factors, Paper No. 730790, Society of Automotive
    Engineers, September 1973.

2. Energy Policy and Conservation Act of 1975, Public Law 94-163, 94th
    Congress of the United States of America, Washington, Dec. 22, 1975.

3. The Report By the Federal Task Force on Motor Vehicle Goals Beyond
    1980, Task Force Report (Draft), US Department of Transportation,
    September 2, 1976.

4. Mobile Source Emission Factors (Draft), US Environmental Protection
    Agency, Office of Transportation and Land Use Policy, Dec. 3, 1977.

5. J. Kelderman, "Are High-MPG Models Really that Gas-Stingy?", Automotive
    News, March 20, 1978.

6. "New-Car Owners' Ire Grows As Mileage Falls Below EPA Estimates,"
    Wall Street Journal, August 31, 1977.

7. E. E. Hughes, et al., Long Term Energy Alternatives for Automotive
    Propulsion: Synthetic Fuels vs. Battery/Electric System, Report No. 5,
    Center for Resource and Environmental Systems Studies, Stanford
    Research Institute, Menlo Park, August 1976.

8. J. C. Corman, et al., Energy Conversion Alternatives Study (ECAS),
    FLD/610 10B, General Electric Corporate Research and Development,
    Schenectady, N.Y., December 1976.

9. E. M. Dickson, et al., Synthetic Liquid Fuels Development: Assessment
    of Critical Factors, ERDA 76-129, SRI Project EGV-4810, June 1976-
    May 1977.

10. 1977 Gas Mileage Guide, US Environmental Protection Agency, September
    1976.

11. R. Stephen Berry and M. F. Fels, "The Energy Cost of Automobiles,"
    Science and Public Affairs, December 1973.

12. John K. Tien, et al., "Reducing the Energy Investment in Automobiles,"
    Technology Review, February 1975.

13. Julius J. Harwood, "Recycling the Junk Car," Technology Review, February
    1977.

14. Robert W. Roig, et al., Impacts of Material Substitution in Automobile
    Manufacture on Resource Recovery, EPA-600/5-76-007, US Environmental
    Protection Agency, Washington, D.C., July 1976.

249

10 AVAILABILITY OF ENERGY FOR RECHARGING

Demand for electricity drops sharply during the late evening in the United States, freeing equipment and facilities which could be used to generate power for overnight recharging of electric cars. Figure 10.1 shows projected energy available for recharging in the contiguous United States on the least-favorable day of the year. This is the day of the annual peak demand, which occasions the greatest use of existing and planned facilities during the year and leaves the minimum capability available for recharging electric cars. Figure 10.1 shows that even in the near future, much of the energy available for recharging would come from coal, not petroleum; in future years, the percentage available from coal and nuclear sources will increase rapidly. Figure 10.1 also shows that even on the least favorable day of the year, the amount of electricity obtainable from facilities which would otherwise be idle would suffice for recharging tens of millions of electric cars. This projected capability far exceeds the requirements of any number of electric cars which could reasonably be put into service during this century.

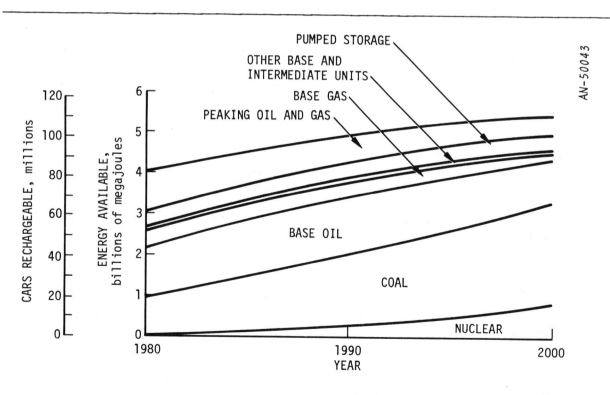

Figure 10.1. Energy Available on Peak Days for Electric Car Recharge

There are many uncertainties in the projections of Fig. 10.1 and in all long-term projections of supply and demand for electric power in the United States. This section begins with the method and assumptions behind Fig. 10.1. Next, it summarizes "baseline" projections of installed capacity and the total supply of and demand for electricity in the absence of electric cars. Finally, it details the projected capacity which might be available for recharging electric cars in future years. The probable mix of fuels for recharging a given number of electric cars is discussed separately in Sec. 11.

10.1 ANALYTIC METHOD

Projections of energy available for recharge begin with today's pattern of demand, which fluctuates so that most of the time considerably less than the full capability of an electric utility is actually being used. Figure 10.2, for example, shows the actual demand for energy, hour by hour, recorded during the weeks of maximum and minimum demand in Southern California in the year 1974. It is clear that even on the days of highest demand, the demand during the hours of late evening and early morning is very much less, leaving idle almost half the capacity required to meet the peak demand of the day. Even after allowance for maintenance and repair, much of the idle capacity could reasonably be put to use for recharging electric cars.

In Southern California, as in most parts of the United States, the hour of annual maximum demand comes in the late afternoon of hot summer days. During the winter there is a secondary maximum resulting from extensive use of electric heating and lighting on cold, dark winter days. Annual minimum demand is typically recorded during the spring or fall, and ordinarily on weekends when commercial and industrial activity is least. Hourly demand for the week of the annual minimum demand is also shown in Fig. 10.1. During this week, as in most weeks of the year, there is a large idle capacity available throughout all hours of the day which could be used for recharging electric cars.

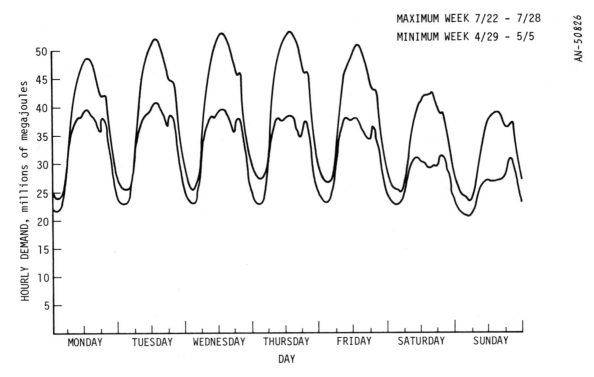

Figure 10.2. Hourly Demand for Energy During the Weeks of the Maximum
and Minimum Demands of 1974, Southern California

To project quantitatively the energy which might be available for
recharge in future years, it is first necessary to project the hourly fluc-
tuations of demand. Figure 10.3 shows such a projection for one utility in
Southern California. The figure includes only the peak day of the year. There
is a major valley in the curve during the early hours of the day during which
a large amount of power is available for recharging electric cars.

To determine how much energy would be available and the fuels which
would be used to generate it, it is necessary to project the capacity
available. This is also shown, again for one utility, in Fig. 10.3.
The capacity shown is net dependable capacity, that which can be sustained for short periods to meet peak demands. The capacity available
to meet demand at other times—including that for recharging electric
cars—is considerably less. To derive available capacity, installed
capacity must be adjusted downward in line with historical records on the

252

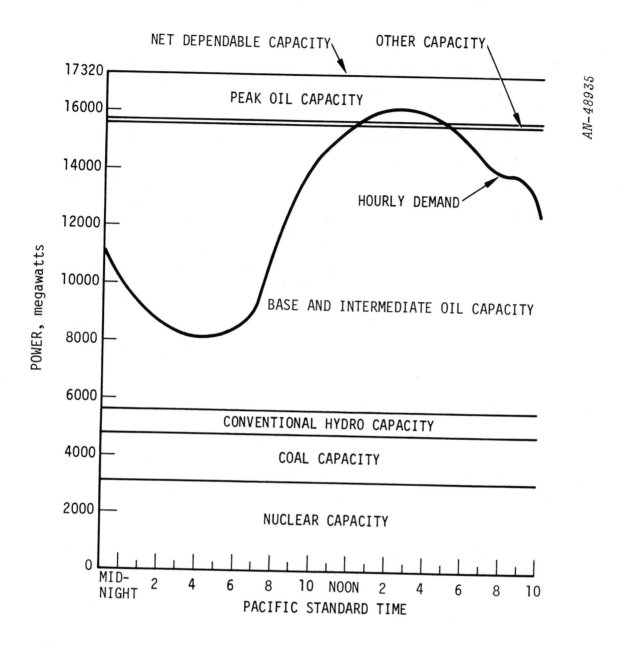

Figure 10.3   Hourly Demand and Net Dependable Capacity for a Single
Utility (Southern California Edison Co., projected peak
summer day, 1985)

actual availability of the different types of generating units after forced, planned, and maintenance outages. In the case of hydroelectric power, a limitation depending on the probable amount of water available is also necessary.

At every utility, a dispatcher determines which generating units will be operated to meet the load at any given time. There are ordinarily many different units available, allowing considerable latitude in choosing which fuels might be used to meet the demand. Within constraints imposed by scheduled and unscheduled maintenance, dispatching procedures are ordinarily tailored to minimize total cost. Since oil is usually more expensive than coal, and coal more expensive than nuclear fuel, it may be expected that nuclear capacity would be used first, followed by coal and oil. This is implied by the placement of the capacity available from different fuels in Fig. 10.3.

It is customary to define three types of generating capacity. The base capacity operates continuously to meet the base load, that is, the load which is present throughout the year. Coal and nuclear plants are used widely for base-load capacity, despite their high initial costs, because their relatively low fuel costs make them least expensive in the long run. Peak-load facilities, in contrast, operate only for those few hours of the year with very high demands. Combustion turbines and jet engines are commonly used for peak capacity despite relatively high fuel consumption per unit of output, because their low initial cost and ease of installation are far more important.

In between base-load and peaking facilities are intermediate facilities. In the Southern California Edison system, these facilities are expected to be oil-fired even in 1985. It is these intermediate-load facilities which are started or stopped to follow changing demands during the day. From Fig. 10.3 it is clear that oil would be used by Southern California Edison to generate additional power for overnight recharging of electric cars on the peak days.

At other utilities the situation may be entirely different. In regions of the country where oil has been relatively expensive, utilities may use only coal and nuclear electricity for recharging. Moreover, the variation of demand during the day and the year may also be quite different. To determine the prospective national use of petroleum and other fuels for recharging electric cars, it is therefore necessary to build up a total from individual analyses of each utility.

Furthermore, it is also necessary to analyze each day of the year separately, since demands for electricity vary considerably with the seasons. Figure 10.4 shows the average weekly maximum and minimum demands for electricity in Southern California during 1974. The variation in maximum demand is considerable, even in this temperate region where relatively little winter heating and summer cooling are necessary.

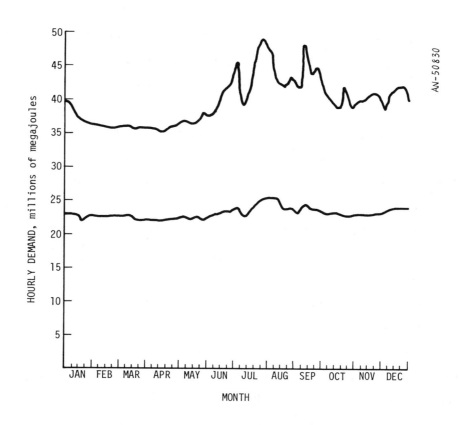

Figure 10.4. Weekly Average Maximum and Minimum Demands, Southern California, 1974

To deal with all the hours of all the days for each major US utility for a whole year is clearly a job for a computer. The computer is especially desirable, moreover, because the necessary data on supply and demand of electricity is already available, on a regularly updated basis, in machine-readable form on computer tape. No existing computer model, however, was capable of the necessary projections and calculations when this study began. A new model was therefore developed.

Figure 10.5 shows the basic functions of the Recharge Capacity Model (RECAP) developed for this study. It processes data obtained from the Federal Power Commission (the FPC, now part of the Department of Energy) and the Edison Electric Institute (EEI), which both collect detailed information on a regular basis from major electric utilities in the United States. The data used describe both recent and projected supply and demand for electric utilities representing about 98% of all generating capacity in the contiguous United States.

The 1975-85 projections of both supply and demand obtained for RECAP from the FPC were originally prepared by each individual utility. The 1985-95 projections were prepared by the nine Regional Councils of the National Electric Reliability Council (NERC). NERC was formed in 1968 to promote effective interconnection and cooperation among electric utilities, in order to enhance reliability and make the best use of available capacity. The hourly demands provided by EEI for 1974 were aggregated by power supply area (PSA), each typically including several major utility companies. The Southern California PSA, for example, reported the total demands shown in Figs. 10.2 and 10.4 from the combined experience of Southern California Edison Company, the Los Angeles Department of Water and Power, San Diego Gas and Electric Company, and several municipally-owned utilities which serve small portions of the area.

Generally, the individual utility was the basis of analysis in RECAP. In some cases, however, several utility companies effectively operate together as a single system or power pool, jointly allocating available

256

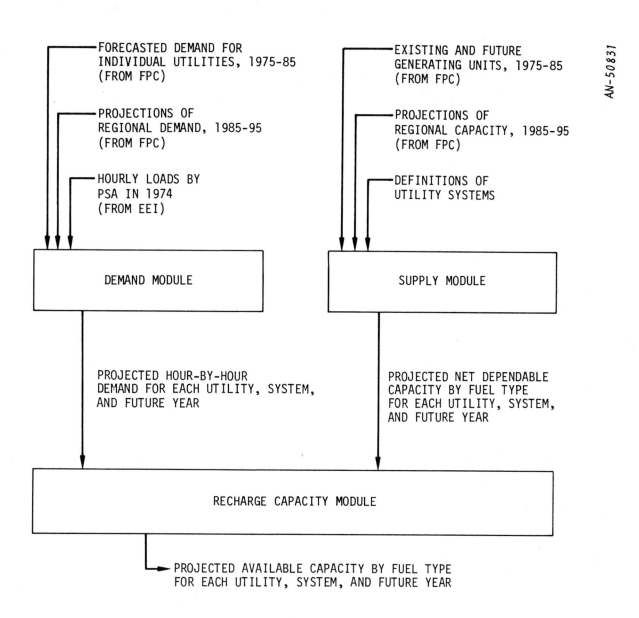

Figure 10.5.   Inputs and Outputs of the Recharge Capacity Model (RECAP)

facilities to meet total demand most efficiently. Additional inputs to RECAP specified such systems. In all, RECAP dealt with 190 utility systems made up of 228 utility companies.

As shown in Fig. 10.5, the Supply Module of RECAP combines the various inputs describing capacity and systems to project net dependable capacity by fuel type for each utility and system in each future year.

The 1975-85 supply of electricity was defined by a complete list of individual generating units showing the capacity and type of each unit, the fuels it could use, and the date of availabilty for new units. A generating unit is an electric generator together with its prime mover; there are often several operable independently at a single power plant. For 1975-85, the capacities of individual utilities were projected by adding up their existing and planned generating units. For 1985-95, regional projections of capacity by fuel type were distributed to individual utilities in the same proportions as for 1985. The data was simply extrapolated from 1995, the last year of the regional projections of capacity, to the year 2000.

The Demand Module of RECAP similarly disaggregates regional demands for 1985-95 into demands for indiviudal utilities, and extrapolates them to the year 2000. The available projections of demand describe only peak hours and annual totals. To obtain the hourly demands required by the analysis, the hourly loads recorded in 1974 were first distributed to individual utilities and systems, and then projected for future years by a scaling procedure which preserves the ratio of forecasted annual peak to average demand.

The Recharge Capacity Module of RECAP combines the hour-by-hour demand projections for each utility with its projected available capacity by fuel type. For each hour of each future year, it calculates and records the capacity for generating power from each fuel type which would be available at each utility and system. In making this calculation, it is assumed that utilities would meet hour-by-hour demands through operation of facilities offering the lowest marginal costs. For hydroelectric facilities, average supplies of water are assumed. Where pumped-storage hydroelectric facilities are available, use is assumed only if coal or nuclear facilities are available during the previous day to provide pumping power.

10.2 ASSUMPTIONS

For many years, growth in the electric utility industry was remarkably predictable. With only minor departures from year to year, overall capacity and peak demand grew about eight percent annually, doubling every eight to ten years. In the 1970s, however, this steady trend was interrupted. Concerns over environmental quality and public safety arising in the late 60s made it difficult or even impossible to obtain sites and construction permits for new power plants, and financing the huge expenditures needed to double capacity every ten years also became a major problem. In the wake of the oil embargo of 1973-74, the growth of demand dropped drastically and utilities cancelled or postponed planned expansion accordingly. The national commitment to develop nuclear electric power faltered, future supplies of nuclear fuel began to appear uncertain, and public initiatives to restrict or prevent construction of nuclear electric power plants appeared in a number of states.

In consequence, confident forecasting of supply and demand for electric power is no longer possible. Conditions have been changing too rapidly, and stability is not yet in sight.

Figure 10.6 shows projections to 1995 made annually since the oil embargo of 1973-74. The projections were made by individual utilities for 1975-85, and by the nine regional councils of the National Electric Reliability

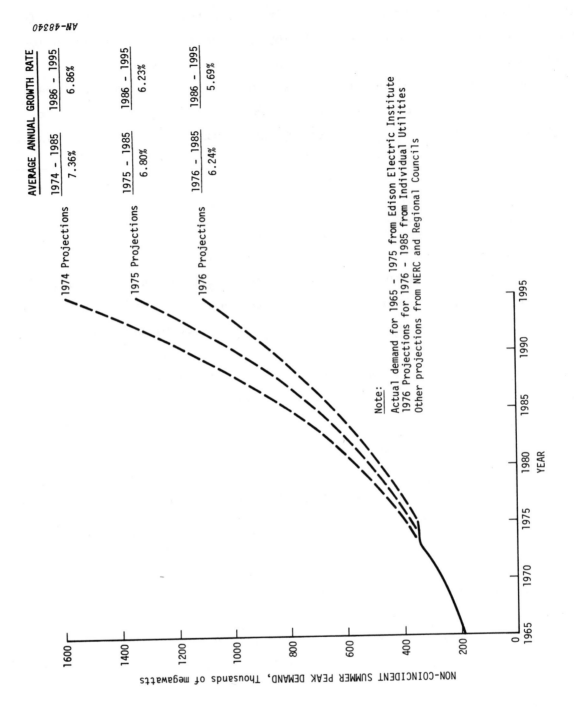

Figure 10.6. Recent Projections of Peak Demand for Electric Power

Council for 1985-95. In Fig. 10.6, the abrupt cessation of growth in peak demand since 1974 is apparent. It is also clear that each annual projection has embodied a lower rate of growth, beginning at a lower level, than anticipated in past years. By 2000, the difference in resultant projections made just two years apart is enormous: over twice the total peak demand actually recorded in 1970.

Beyond uncertainties in overall growth lie additional uncertainties in technological capability and the political environment. Moreover, there are several approximations in the calculations performed by RECAP which affect overall results. As a result, the projections to be advanced in this section and in Sec. 11 could easily be a long way from actuality. Nevertheless, they do reflect detailed treatment of the most recent, complete, and authoritative data available to this study.

The major assumptions behind these projections include the following:

- Overall demand and supply will grow in line with utility and FPC projections made in 1976 (the projection shown in Fig. 10.6). In short, growth rates will be substantially less than in the past or in earlier projections, but still substantial. Since these supply and demand projections are compatible, they imply that there will be no loss of reserve capacity, nor increasing frequency of brownouts and blackouts. This implies that the nation will not demand more electricity than it allows its electric utilities to prepare for and supply.

- The daily and seasonal variation of demand will remain as it was in the past. This is a very uncertain area, largely because electric utilities may, in fact, be unable to build new facilities needed to meet rising demand. In that case, flattening of peak demands is unavoidable. Whether peaks would be reduced in an orderly way, rather than by unplanned blackouts and brownouts, is uncertain. Higher prices for peak-hour electricity and new

261

devices giving utilities remote control over non-essential loads such as air conditioners are possible alternatives.

- Generating units will be operated to minimize the cost of the electricity produced. In RECAP, this is implemented by operating them in accord with the preferences summarized in Table 10.1, either for individual utility companies or for systems of several companies operating as a pool. Additional transfers of power between utility companies beyond those within such systems are not considered.

TABLE 10.1

ASSUMED ORDER OF PREFERENCE FOR
GENERATING UNITS IN A SYSTEM

1. Nuclear (steam turbines)
2. Coal (steam turbines)
3. Oil - base and intermediate (steam turbines and combined cycle)
4. Gas - base and intermediate (steam turbines and combined cycle)
5. Other (methanol, waste heat, refuse, geothermal steam)
6. Oil - peak load (jet engines, combustion turbines)
7. Gas - peak load (jet engines, combustion turbines)

Conventional hydroelectric units are used after coal and before oil units, and use all available water each day. Pumped-storage hydroelectric units are used after base and intermediate oil units, but only if sufficient nuclear or coal power was available earlier in the day for the necessary pumping.

- Generating units capable of burning either oil and coal, or gas and oil, will burn the preferred fuel exclusively.

- Availability during times of electric car recharging will be 85% for generating units that become available after 1985, and 74%-95% for other units, depending on recent experience with forced outages, maintenance outages, and planned outages for existing units of the same type (see App. B, Table B-2).

- All generating capacity within this limit, and beyond that required to meet projected demand, will be usable for recharging electric cars, regardless of the time of day. In practice, this would require battery chargers which could be remotely controlled by the utility, at least for very large numbers of electric cars.

- Major technical innovations will not drastically affect the projections, except as adjuncts to the use of electric cars. Such innovations include batteries with which utilities could meet peak demands without building planned generating units, or selective load control which would allow utilities to reduce peak demands and again omit construction of planned generating units. Both these innovations are assumed to be used in support of electric cars, not as means for avoiding construction of new plants which would be needed for recharging large numbers of electric cars.

10.3 PROJECTIONS OF FUTURE SUPPLY AND DEMAND

Under the assumptions just described, the RECAP model was used to project net dependable capacity from the base year, 1976, through the year 2000. The result, in Fig. 10.7, shows a major decline in the importance of oil relative to other sources of energy. The most rapid growth, an average of over 12% per year, is foreseen for nuclear electric

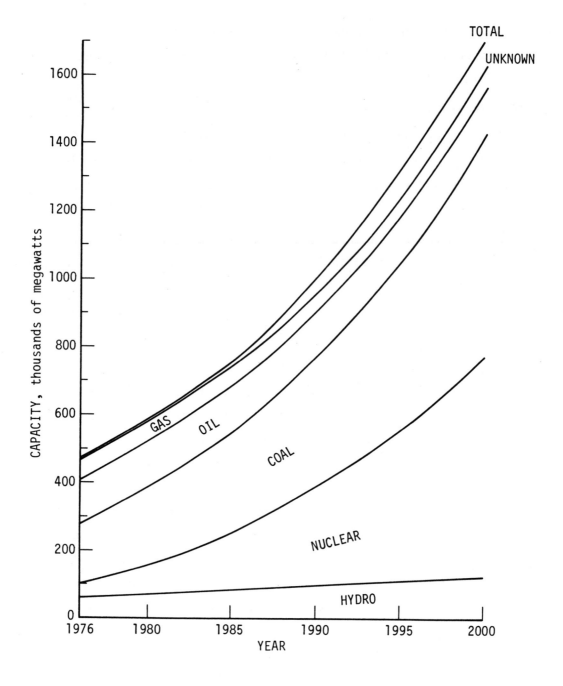

Figure 10.7. Net Dependable Capacity by Type of Fuel,
Contiguous United States, 1976-2000

capacity, followed by coal at an average rate of 5.3% per year. Hydroelectric installations, which already occupy the most favorable sites,
are expected to grow at about 3% per year in terms of total capacity.
Though a moderate growth of oil-fired facilities remains scheduled for
the coming decade, subsequent conversions and retirements will lead to an
average growth in this century well under 1% per year. No growth is
expected for gas-fired facilities. It is assumed that wherever feasible,
oil will be used in place of gas, and coal in place of oil.

Depending largely on the distance to low-cost mines, coal may be
more or less expensive than nuclear power for future generation of electricity.
In consequence, projected expansion of capacity by source of energy differs
sharply in the various regions of the United States. This is shown in
Fig. 10.8 for the nine regional reliability councils of the National
Electric Reliability Council. The boundaries of the regions are shown
in Fig. 10.9, and the relative sizes of the regions are shown in Table 10.2.

The projected generation of electricity is shown in Fig. 10.10. Here
nuclear and coal-fired units are much more important than in the net reliable capacity projection, Fig. 10.7, because these are the units operated
nearly continuously to meet base loads, while the use of oil and gas-fired
facilities is avoided. Despite the recent delays and cancellations of
orders for nuclear generating equipment, nuclear power is still expected
to meet over half of all US demands in the year 2000. On the other hand,
the recent experience suggests that if supply and demand grow less rapidly,
it is the nuclear facilities which will be primarily affected. Given
either lower growth of demand or increased difficulty in constructing
nuclear plants, coal plants would probably become much more important.
The probable use of petroleum for generating electricity, however, would
be relatively little affected.

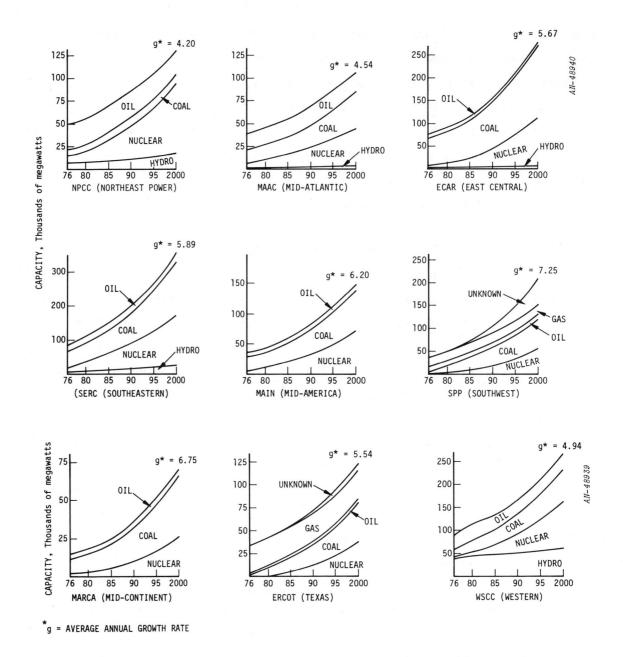

Figure 10.8. Regional Electric Power Capacity Projections

266

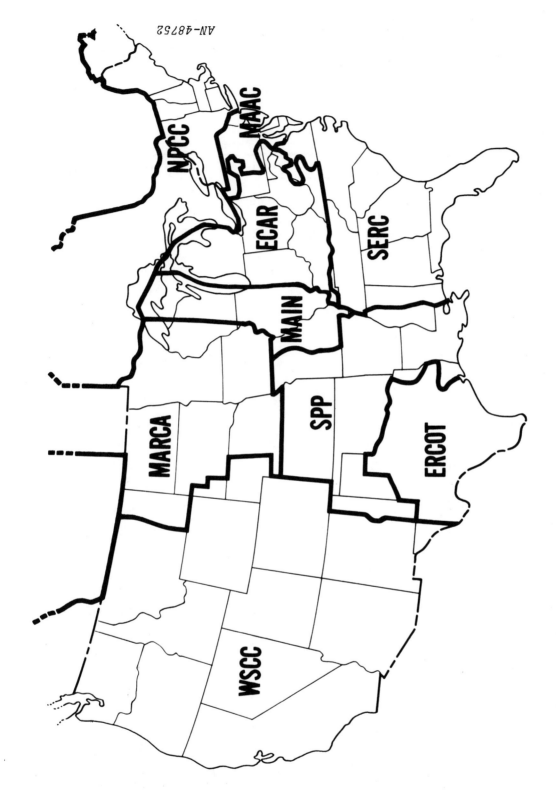

Figure 10.9. National Electric Reliability Council Regions, Contiguous United States

TABLE 10.2

RELATIVE SIZES OF THE NINE RELIABILITY COUNCIL REGIONS

Name	Population, Percent of National Total[*]			Electricity Use, Percent of National Total		
	1980	1990	2000	1980[**]	1990[†]	2000[†]
NPCC--Northeast Power Coordinating Council	13.8	13.8	13.8	9.0	8.0	7.7
MAAC--Mid-Atlantic Area Council	11.6	11.3	11.0	7.8	7.4	7.3
ECAR--East Central Area Reliability Coordination Agreement	14.7	14.8	14.9	17.3	17.4	16.4
SERC--Southeastern Electric Reliability Council	16.2	16.3	16.5	21.4	22.1	22.2
MAIN--Mid-American Interpool Network	9.4	9.2	9.1	7.7	7.7	8.4
SPP--Southwest Power Pool	7.4	7.2	7.0	8.4	9.8	10.7
MARCA--Mid-Contenent Area Reliability Coordination Agreement	4.6	4.5	4.4	3.9	4.0	4.1
ERCOT--Electric Reliability Council of Texas	4.9	5.0	5.0	6.3	6.5	6.7
WSCC--Western Systems Coordinating Council	17.4	17.9	18.2	18.2	17.1	16.6

[*]Population data is approximate.

[**]Percent of electricity demand based on individual electric utility company estimates as reported to the FPC in early 1976 using Form 12E-2, Schedule 5.

[†]Percent of electricity demand based on Reliability Council estimates made in early 1976 as reported to FPC in response to Item 10, Appendix A-1, Order 383-3.

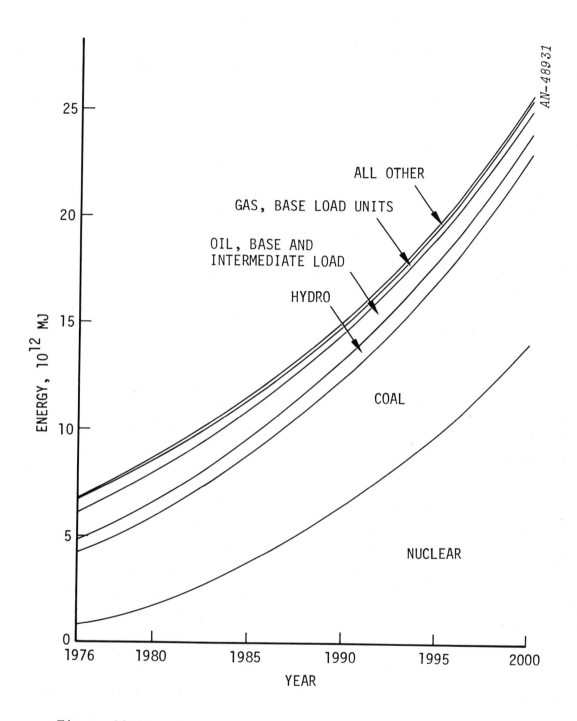

Figure 10.10. Generation of Electricity by Type of Fuel, Contiguous United States, 1976–2000

10.4 CAPACITY AVAILABLE FOR RECHARGING ELECTRIC CARS

The energy which could be generated by the projected supply system to supply a load added to the projected demand is shown in Fig. 10.11. Since nuclear and coal plants are largely tied up by base loads, they could provide relatively little additional electric energy, at least until after 1985. Of the total energy available, considerably more is available in the late night and early morning than during the day, as shown in Fig. 10.12, but daytime availability is still very large. The portion of energy available in the year 2000 from different fuels is shown in Fig. 10.13. Both these figures show the annual total of the energy available during a given hour of each day from all US utilities. Much more energy is available late at night, of course, than during the day. Annual totals for daytime and early evening hours are still large, however, even though little or no energy might be available in these hours on days of peak demands.

The total energy available for recharge on the peak day alone was shown in Fig. 10.1. The number of cars which could be recharged on this day is based on recharge requirements of 1 MJ per km and average travel of about 16,000 km per year (44 km per day).

Though the proportions of the various fuels from which energy is available vary little from hour to hour in Fig. 10.13, they differ greatly in the different regions of the United States. This is shown in Fig. 10.14 for the regions defined in Fig. 10.9 and described in Table 10.2. The electric energy available per car also differs, leading to the maximum percentages of electric cars in Table 10.3.

The fuels which would actually be used to recharge electric cars depend both on the total number of cars and on the region or regions in which they are operated. This is the subject of Sec. 11. Before turning to it, however, it is important to note that the total capacity available for recharge is very large, even at its minimum on the peak-demand day of the year. As shown in Fig. 10.1, tens of millions of cars

270

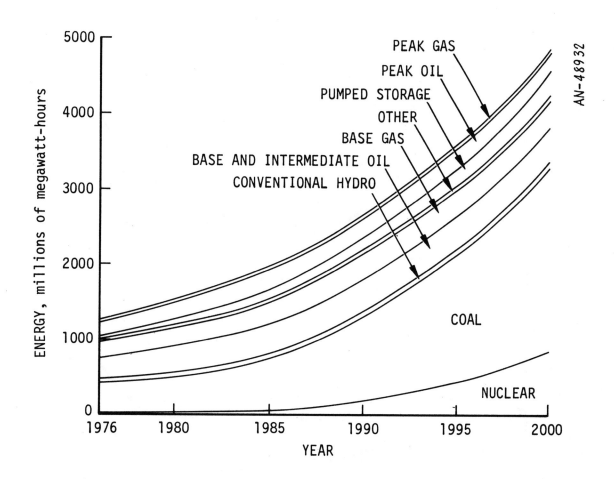

Figure 10.11.   Annual Capacity Available for Generating Recharge
Energy by Type of Fuel, Contiguous United States,
1976–2000

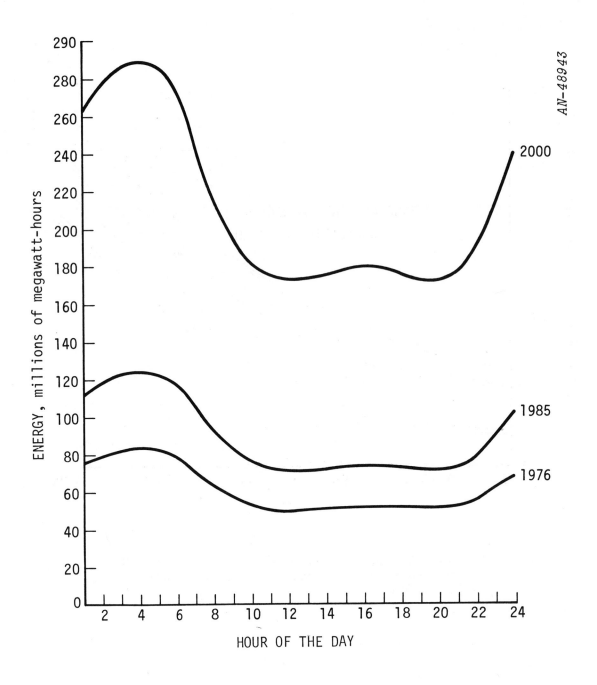

AN–48943

Figure 10.12.   Total Annual Energy Available for Electric Car Re-
Charge by Hour of the Day, Contiguous United States

272

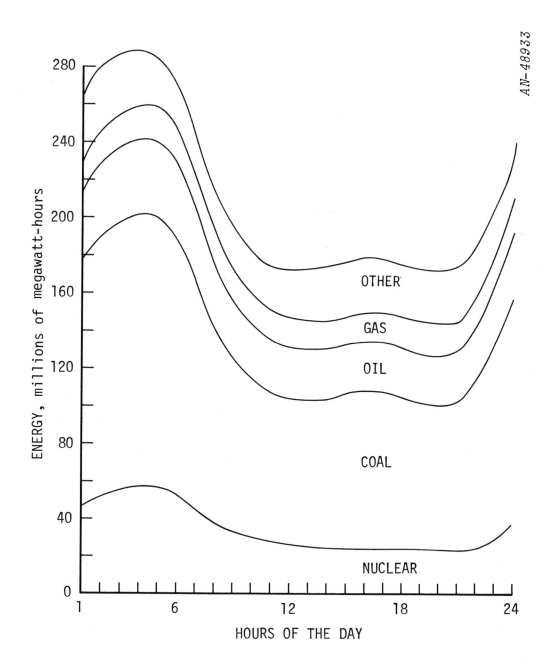

Figure 10.13.   Annual Energy Available in 2000 by Fuel Type, Contiguous United States

273

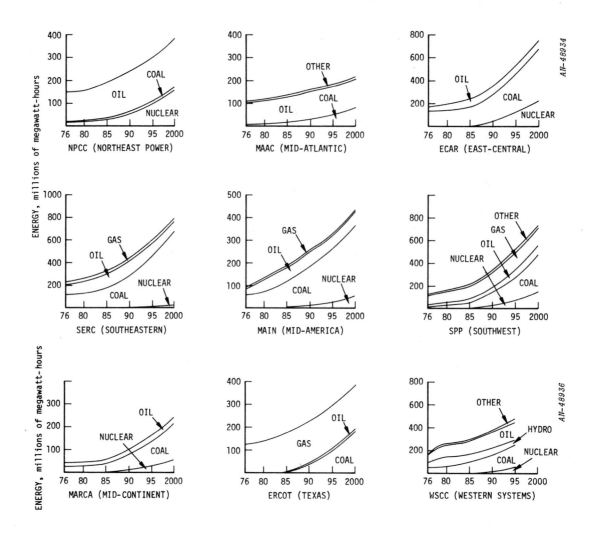

Figure 10.14.   Annual Energy Available by Region, Year, and Fuel Type

274

TABLE 10.3

NUMBER OF ELECTRIC CARS THAT CAN BE RECHARGED ON PEAK DAY

Region*	Total Personal Cars, millions			Rechargable With Peak Units, percent			Rechargable Without Peak Units, percent		
	1980	1990	2000	1980	1990	2000	1980	1990	2000
NPCC	15.3	17.4	18.9	68	59	49	52	48	44
MAAC	11.6	13.2	14.4	95	100	100	43	41	63
ERAC	17.0	19.4	21.0	75	82	86	70	79	85
SERC	13.3	15.2	16.5	95	96	81	69	74	75
MAIN	9.8	11.2	12.2	84	94	95	59	92	93
SPP	7.2	8.2	8.9	84	80	80	79	76	77
MARCA	4.0	4.5	4.9	55	69	74	31	68	72
ERCOT	4.3	4.9	5.3	100	88	76	82	87	76
WSCC	19.5	22.1	24.0	61	80	87	52	65	83
Total	102.0	116.0	126.0	78	83	81	59	68	74

*See Fig. 10.9 and Table 10.2 for boundaries, names, and sizes of regions.

could be recharged even without using any peaking units. Moreover, the total energy shown as available on the peak day assumes that recharging can only be done when total load is below about 85% of net dependable capacity. For one or a few days of the year, this requirement might be relaxed. Furthermore, full recharge for all driving on the peak day is not absolutely necessary, since most electric cars would be driven only a fraction of their total range on the peak day and could meet the needs of most drivers on the following day without any recharge at all.

In short, the availability of electricity for recharge is unlikely to limit the use of electric cars, nor would a rapid conversion to electric cars require any major additions to the utility system already planned. This is important because the US utility system is so large and valuable that major expansion becomes very difficult. The value of utility structures and equipment is almost 10% of the total value of all business structures and equipment in the United States. The electric utility industry is the most capital-intensive in the nation, with an investment of over four dollars per dollar of annual sales, seven times that in the automobile industry, and dollar sales of electricity exceed those of motor vehicle manufacturers.

11   IMPACTS ON USE OF FUELS AND ENERGY

Because relatively little oil-fired generation of electricity would be required for recharging electric cars, immense quantities of petroleum could be saved if conventional cars were replaced by electric cars. Figure 11.1 shows how the use of petroleum by conventional cars would decline if they were somehow replaced by electric cars in the near future. It also shows the petroleum which would be required for recharging, and the net use of petroleum for automotive transportation. In later years, 1990 and 2000, even less petroleum would be used for recharging, and savings of petroleum in 2000 would be relatively larger.

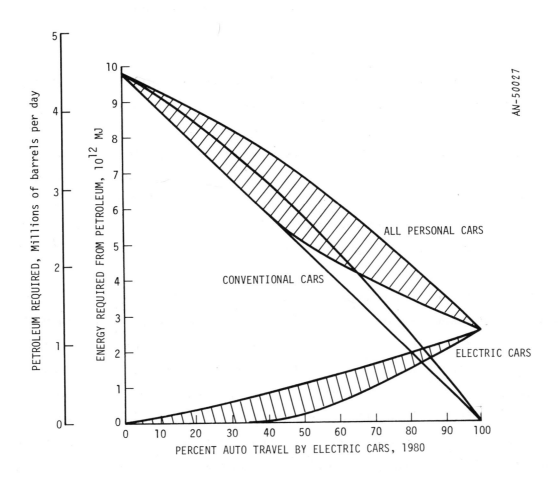

Figure 11.1.   Required Petroleum for Personal Cars Versus Use of Electric Cars, 1980

At each level of electric car use in Fig. 11.1, a band of possible usages of petroleum is shown for both electric and conventional cars. For electric cars, the upper edge of the band corresponds to a uniform distribution of electric cars among residential customers of electric utilities. The lower edge, in contrast, corresponds to distribution of electric cars first among customers of those utilities that use the least petroleum for recharge. Over 30% of automotive travel could thus be electrified with virtually no use of petroleum for recharge. For conventional cars, the band of usage shown in Fig. 11.1 depends on which cars are replaced by electrics. If average cars of average fuel economy were replaced, the use of petroleum would fall at the lower edge of the band. If the cars with highest fuel economy were replaced first by electric cars, use would fall at the upper edge of the band.

The most likely use of petroleum for all personal cars is probably near the center of the band indicated in Fig. 11.1. The range of possibilities is considerable: if electric cars replaced average cars in areas where power for recharge required no petroleum, then automotive use of petroleum could be reduced 30% if electric cars were used for 30% of automobile travel. If the same number of electric cars were distributed uniformly in the nation, however, and replaced efficient small cars rather than average cars, savings might be 15%, only half as much.

As shown in Sec. 9, electric cars are similar to conventional cars in overall efficiency so long as gasoline is derived from petroleum rather than coal. As a result, use of electric cars has little effect on the national use of energy, and savings of petroleum due to electric cars will be matched by increased use of energy from other fuels. The maximum possible shift from oil to other fuels is shown in Fig. 11.2, assuming total replacement of conventional cars with electric cars. Most of the decrease in oil use would be matched by increases in coal use. Relatively little energy for automobiles would be obtained from nuclear power, which would already be operating near its maximum possible level to meet utility

278

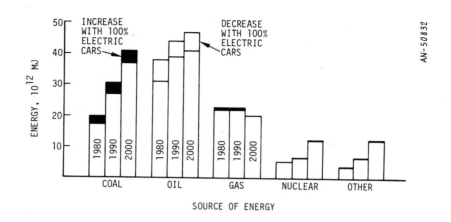

Figure 11.2. National Annual Use of Energy With and Without Electric Cars

base loads. Relative to the total national use of coal and oil for all purposes, changes due to complete electrification of automotive travel would be relatively small because automobiles use a relatively small amount of all oil and energy used in the nation.

As shown in Sec. 10, electric utilities are not expected to have sufficient capacity available for 100% electrification of US automobiles, even in 2000, on the peak-demand day of the year. On almost all other days of the year, however, it would be possible. The case of 100% electrification therefore remains an interesting and useful upper bound on the effects of electric cars. In actual fact, it would probably require either small additions of capacity, or modest rescheduling of travel and recharging away from days near those of the annual peak demand.

In this section, the available capacities for recharge derived in Sec. 10 are transformed into results such as those of Figs. 11.1 and 11.2. Where possible, the use of electric cars is treated as a parameter ranging from 0% to 100%. First, the fuels which would be used for recharging at each level of electric car use are detailed by year and geographic region. Next, net savings of petroleum are projected by combining recharge fuels with estimates from Sec. 9 for use of petroleum by conventional automobiles. Then effects on national use of energy from all fuels are tabulated. Finally, the sensitivities of the projections for fuel and energy use to major alternative assumptions about growth and electricity demand are discussed.

11.1 FUELS FOR RECHARGING

Figure 11.3 shows the fuels which would be used for generating additional electricity required by electric cars in 1980, 1990, and 2000. These projections are based on the capacity available for recharging projected in Sec. 10. It was assumed that the generation of power for recharge would follow the rules for use of different generating units and fuels assumed in Table 10.1, and that cars would be distributed uniformly. No restriction was imposed on the time of day at which recharging could be accomplished. At low and medium levels of electric car use, virtually all recharging could be done late at night. At very high levels of electric car use, however, increasing amounts of recharging during daytime hours would be necessary, particularly at utilities with relatively little variation in demand during the day. The maximum daytime recharging would occur with 100% use of electric cars; it is illustrated in Fig. 11.4. In no case, of course, was any utility system assumed to operate above available capacity (about 85% of net dependable capacity) in order to recharge electric cars. In some utilities on one or a few high-demand days of the year, this made it impossible to meet the entire demand for recharging at the assumed level of electric car use. The loss in travel is small, however, as would be the additional use of fuel required for producing this recharge power. One hundred percent electrification of automobiles, then, remains a useful upper limit to consider.

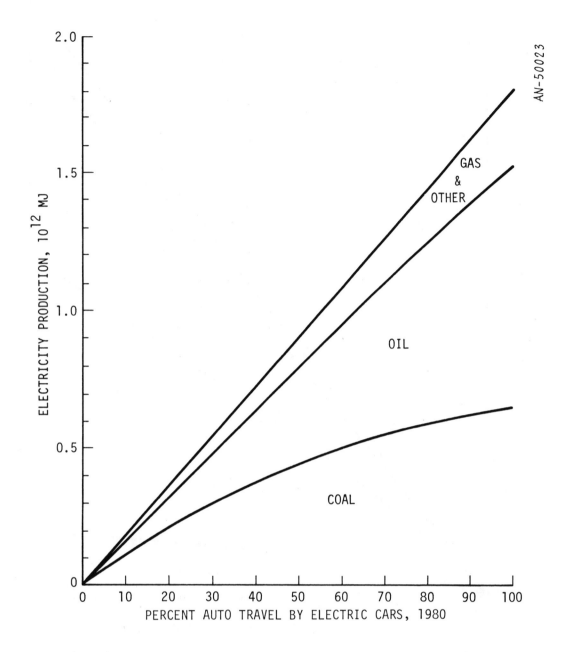

a. 1980

Figure 11.3. Projected Use of Fuels for Recharging
Electric Cars

281

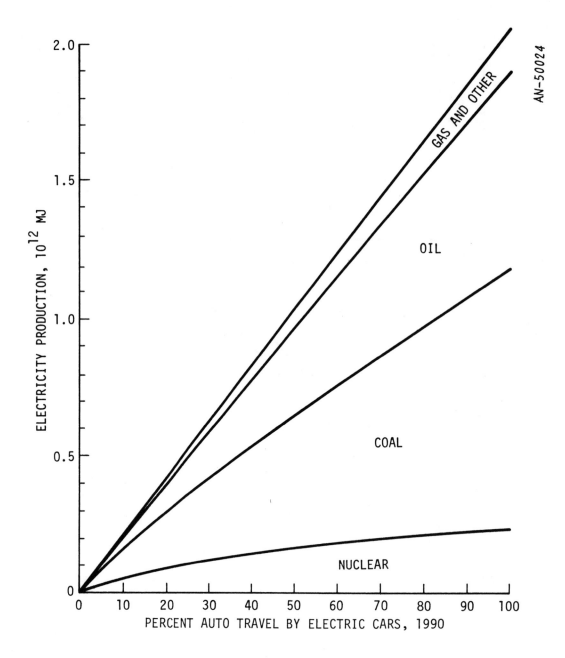

b. 1990

Figure 11.3. (Continued)

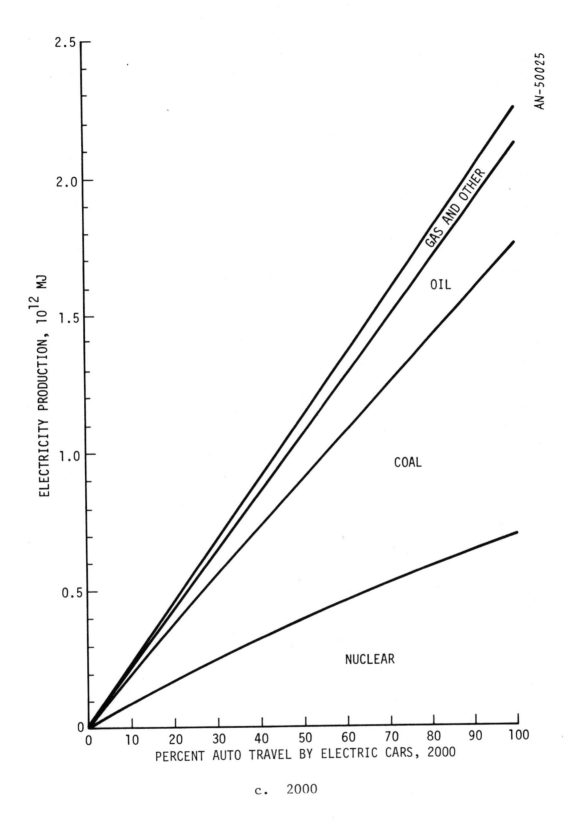

c. 2000

Figure 11.3. (Continued)

283

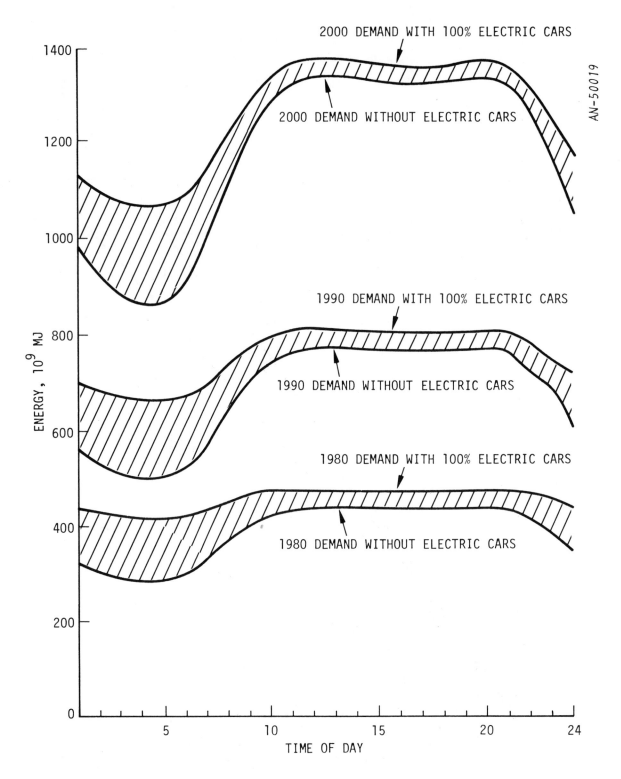

Figure 11.4. Yearly Demand by Hour of the Day, Contiguous United States

Figure 11.5 summarizes the projected use of fuel for recharging electric cars at this upper limit. The rapid decline of oil and the rapid rise of nuclear power are particularly striking. For lower levels of electric car use much less oil and gas would be employed, since these are the fuels of last resort.

In different regions of the United States the mix of fuels for recharging would differ greatly, as shown in Fig. 11.6. (The names and descriptions of these regions appear in Table 10.2.) Petroleum would be most important for recharging electric cars in New England, and least important in the middle US states that rely heavily on coal for generating electricity. In the giant western region, the use of petroleum for re-charge would be concentrated in Southern California, while in the mountain states coal and nuclear power would be much more important, and hydropower would also be a factor in the abundantly-endowed Pacific Northwest.

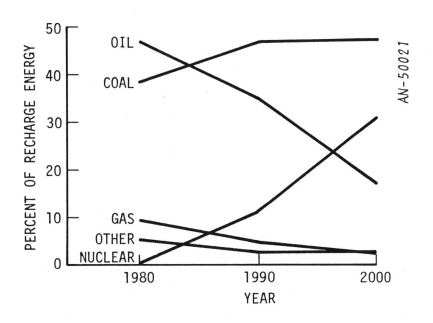

Figure 11.5. Projected Use of Fuel for Recharging, 1980-2000, 100 Percent Electric Cars

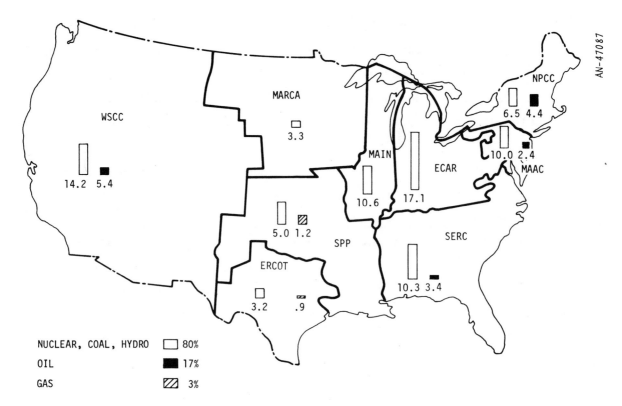

Figure 11.6. Fuel Mix by Region Required for Recharging in
the year 2000, With 100 Percent Electric Cars

The regional differences in Fig. 11.6 suggest that to conserve
petroleum, electric cars should be first employed in areas able to use
other fuels for recharge. The extent to which this policy could reduce petroleum requirements for recharging is shown in Fig. 11.7. The upper limits of
the bands shown for 1980 and 2000 correspond to uniform distributions of
electric cars, that is, replacement of conventional cars at a uniform
rate independent of geographic location. The lower edge of the band, in
contrast, corresponds to use of electric cars first in areas requiring the
least petroleum for generating recharge power. To avoid confusion, the
band for 1990 is not shown; it would lie between those appearing in
Fig. 11.7.

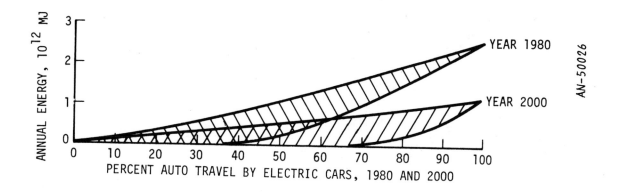

Figure 11.7. Energy Required from Petroleum for Recharging
Electric Cars

11.2 NET USE OF PETROLEUM

Figure 11.8 shows how the petroleum required for fueling conventional automobiles would decrease as the use of electric cars increased. It is assumed here that each conventional car replaced is driven 16,000 kilometers per year, about the national average. If the cars most economical of fuel were replaced first, the resultant use of petroleum would be at the upper boundary of the shaded region for each year in Fig. 11.8. If each car replaced were average in fuel economy, the use of petroleum would fall at the lower boundary of the shaded region. Because the overall cost of an electric car tends to be substantially higher than that of a comparable conventional car, as shown in Sec. 8, it seems likely that electric cars will tend to be smaller than conventional cars have been. As a result, they come nearest to being direct replacements for compact and subcompact conventional cars, which are well above average in fuel economy. Fuel use near the upper edges of the bands in Fig. 11.8 thus seems most likely.

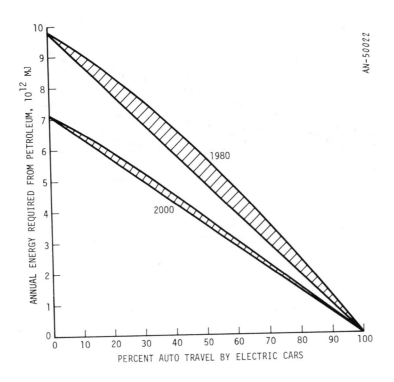

Figure 11.8. Petroleum Required for Conventional Cars
Versus Use of Electric Cars

Annual net requirements of energy from petroleum as a function of
use of electric cars were shown for 1980 in Fig. 11.1, and are shown for
1990 and 2000 in Fig. 11.9. The net requirement is the sum of the petroleum required by conventional cars, as in Fig. 11.8, and that required for
recharging electric cars, as in Fig. 11.7. This sum, as well as its
individual components, is illustrated in Figs. 11.1 and 11.9. The range
of possible net savings shown in these figures is considerable; it is due
partly to the range of fuel economies of conventional cars replaced (as
in Fig. 11.8), and partly to the range of petroleum required for recharging
depending on region (as in Fig. 11.7).

Two points are of special interest in Figs. 11.1 and 11.9: the
maximum use of electric cars which could be achieved without any use of
petroleum for recharge, and the maximum possible savings of petroleum if
all cars were electric. These are illustrated separately in Fig. 11.10.

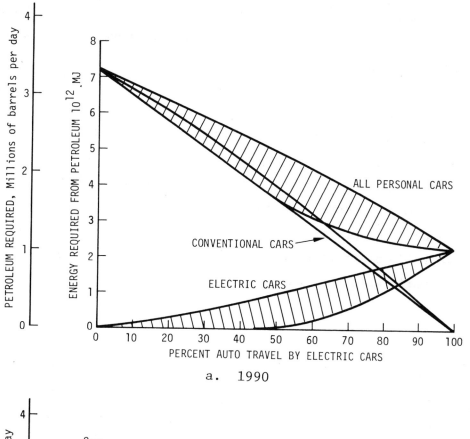

a. 1990

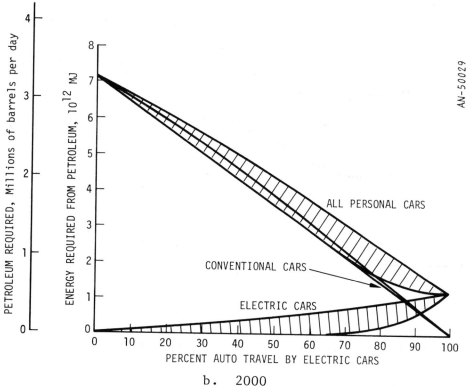

b. 2000

Figure 11.9. Petroleum Required for Automobiles Versus Use
of Electric Cars, 1990 and 2000

289

The decrease from 1980 to 1990 in maximum possible savings of petroleum is due to the rapid decline in fuel consumption of conventional cars projected during this period.

11.3 NATIONAL USE OF ENERGY

The maximum possible effects of electric cars on national energy use are shown in Table 11.1. In this table, the total national use of energy from various sources is broken down by source, assuming either no electric cars or 100% use of electric cars. National energy use in the absence of electric cars was obtained from projections which were current at the Energy Research and Development Administration in early 1977.[2] The figures shown apply to an assumed scenario with moderate prices for energy.

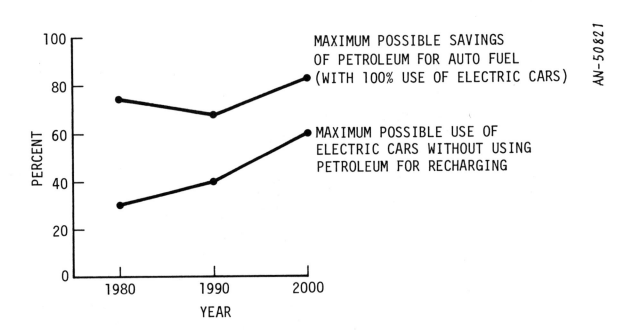

Figure 11.10. Maximum Possible Petroleum Savings and Use of Electric Cars Without Recharge from Petroleum

TABLE 11.1

NATIONAL USE OF ENERGY WITHOUT ELECTRIC CARS AND WITH ONLY ELECTRIC CARS

(in units of 10^{12} MJ)

Primary Resource	1980			1990			2000		
	Without*	With	Percent Change	Without*	With	Percent Change	Without*	With	Percent Change
Coal	17.7	19.8	+12	27.3	30.3	+11	37.1	40.9	+9
Oil	38.3	31.1	-19	44.1	39.1	-11	46.9	41.0	-13
Natural Gas	23.2	23.8	+2	23.2	23.7	+2	20.2	20.4	+1
Nuclear	5.3	5.3	0	14.9	15.7	+5	30.1	32.3	+7
Other	3.7	3.9	+7	6.5	6.8	+5	12.1	12.3	+2
Total	88.2	83.9	-5	116.0	115.6	0	146.4	146.6	0

*Source: Ref. 1

291

In 1980, the total use of energy would be somewhat reduced by the use of the assumed future electric cars. In 1990 and 2000, however, the total would be effectively unchanged. The decrease in 1980 results from replacing conventional automobiles which will be relatively inefficient with electric cars. By 1990, when future standards for fuel economy and the retirement of older automobiles will have eliminated inefficient conventional cars from use, the advantage of the electric cars disappears.

Though complete electrification of the US auto fleet is a very drastic change, it would nonetheless affect national use of petroleum relatively little, reducing it only 19% in 1980 and even less in subsequent years. The reason for this is that only a modest portion of petroleum is used by automobiles. Table 11.2 shows the consumption of petroleum by sector in the United States in the year 1974.[2] Though 53% was consumed in the transportation sector of the economy, passenger cars alone accounted for only about half this, or 28% of the national total. The rest was divided between other modes of transportation as shown in the table. Total elimination of automotive consumption could thus have reduced petroleum consumption in 1974 by at most 28%. While reduced automotive consumption may be very desirable and important, then, it can only begin to solve the overall problems of petroleum use in the United States.

In the future, the use of petroleum by automobiles is expected to fall even lower in relation to the national total. Several representative projections are summarized in Fig. 11.11. The "moderate prices" projection made by ERDA is that implicit in the figures of Table 11.1.[2] The projection by Brookhaven National Laboratory (BNL) is basically an extrapolation of earlier trends; it shows a higher level of automobile consumption, but a virtually identical downward trend in the fraction of national use.[3] The other three projections were independently developed in a Ford Foundation study which investigated drastically different alternatives for the future.[4] The three projections illustrated in Fig. 11.11

TABLE 11.2

CONSUMPTION OF PETROLEUM BY SECTOR, 1974

Source: Ref. 2

Household and Commercial		18%
Industrial		18%
Electrical Generation		10%
Transportation		53%
Cars	28	
Trucks	12	
Buses	.4	
Railroad trains	1.9	
Airplanes	4.2	
Ships	2.4	
Pipelines	2.1	
Other gasoline	1.3	

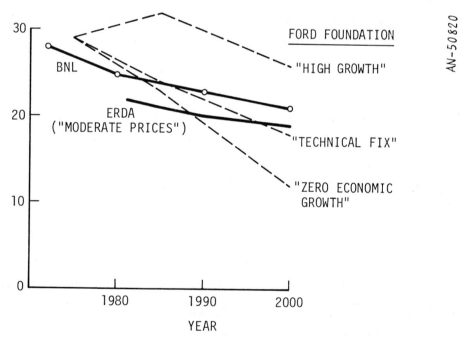

Figure 11.11.   Various Projections of Petroleum Use by Automobiles as a Percentage of US Petroluem Use (from Refs. 1, 3, 4)

293

may reflect very different alternatives but they all have a common feature: by the end of this century, the proportion of petroleum used by automobiles will be less than in the mid-1970s.

11.4 SENSITIVITY TO CHANGES

The projections of fuel and energy use in Secs. 10 and 11 rest on a number of uncertain assumptions which were described in Sec. 10.2. Among the most important were that the overall growth of supply and demand would continue at a lower pace than in recent years, but still at a relatively high rate, and that the hourly variation of demand in recent years would remain little changed. Most of the projections are relatively insensitive to the first of these assumptions, and relatively sensitive to the second.

So long as supply and demand remain in balance as they have been historically, changes in overall growth affect the projections relatively little. As shown in Fig. 10.1, the number of electric cars which could be recharged increases only 30% from 1980 to 2000. With slower growth, the increase would be even less, but capacity for recharge would still be sufficient for electrifying over half of US automobiles. This is far more than are likely to be electrified by 2000, as shown in Sec. 8.

If there is lower growth, there are likely to be fewer new coal and nuclear facilities, with an attendant protraction of dependence on petroleum. Again, the effect is relatively unimportant because over 30% of US autos could be electrified in the near future without any use of petroleum at all.

Changes in the shape of the hourly demand curve, however, could drastically alter the projections of Secs. 10 and 11. The use of fuel and the availability of recharge power in these projections depends on the historical late-night dip in demand experienced by most US utilities. Were the dip to decrease, available capacity for recharge would be diminished and petroleum use would be increased.

Several factors work towards a reduction of the late-night dip in
demand. During the last decade, electric utilities have had great difficulty
in adding capacity. Had growth in demand proceeded at historical rates
after 1972, shortages might already be imminent. It happens, however, that
after the oil embargo of 1973-74 and during the serious economic downturn
at about the same time, demand growth was much less than in most past years.[5]
It may return to levels approaching those of former years, however, and if
it does, shortages seem likely in the mid-1980s.

An official study during 1976 by the Federal Power Commission warned
that there could be significant regional shortages of electricity by 1985.[5]
The prospective shortages were attributed to a number of factors, including
current and prospective requirements under the Clean Air Act, restrictions
on strip mining of coal, modification and delay in constructing nuclear
power plants, and opposition on environmental grounds to new facilities
for producing and distributing electric power.

On the other hand, actual increases in demand may remain low in
comparison with years past. A study at the Oak Ridge National Laboratory
in 1975, for example, showed that whereas an extrapolation of past trends
indicated a 6.9% per year growth to 1985, an econometric model reflecting
the changing patterns of consumption in US households led to growth rates
of only 3.8 to 4.1% per year.[6]

Nevertheless, demand has recently been rising and may again reach growth
rates recorded in the past. Furthermore, planned new electric plants
may be successfully opposed by proponents of environmental protection,
conservation of resources, public safety, or even a general slowing of
industrial growth. As a result, capacity could become insufficient to
meet demand. There is no assurance that opposition to new power plants
will be matched by public frugality in the use of electric power.

The first effects of inadequate capacity would probably be felt during periods of very high demand, when equipment failure would be most likely to leave utility systems with insufficient generating capacity to avoid blackouts and brownouts. The catastrophic effects of blackouts in large areas for long periods could be avoided by deliberate "rolling blackouts," in which service would be interrupted for an hour or two to each of a succession of small regions so as to keep total demand within available capacity. Some combination of selective load control and disincentives to peak-hour use of power, however, seems preferable.

In selective load control, utilities install electronic devices for the remote control of electric water heaters, air conditioners, and other large loads. These make it possible to interrupt service if available capacity becomes inadequate. Imposing a higher price at times of peak demand is the usual disincentive to peak-hour use of electricity. It is often combined with selective load control in order to provide positive protection against demands exceeding available capacity. Higher prices in the late afternoon may alone be insufficient to discourage the operation of air conditioners on extremely hot summer days, for example, even though they are effective on other days.

Selective load control and peak pricing both tend to displace demand for electricity from peak to off-peak hours. The effects can be dramatic, as illustrated by the actual experience of the Hamburg electric works, shown in Fig. 11.12.[7] Through imposition of peak pricing and selective load control, this German utility virtually eliminated its late-night dip in demand in just five years. It also made more effective use of its existing facilities and thereby reduced the additions needed to meet the total demand for electric energy.

At the same time, of course, it considerably reduced the capacity which would be available for recharging electric cars.

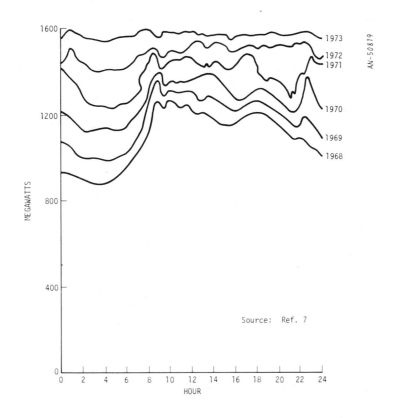

Figure 11.12. Load Serviced by the Hamburg Electric Works on a Typical
January Day (from Ref. 7)

In Hamburg, a major portion of residential space heating is electric.
The imposition of selective load control and peak pricing gave consumers
an incentive to purchase electric heaters with thermal storage: bricks
or reservoirs which were well-insulated, heated late at night by electric
power, and then drawn upon for heat during the next day. Similar systems
have been widely used in England and Wales.[7]

If the growth of demand exceeds the growth of capacity in the US,
selective load control and peak pricing are the probable alternatives to
brownouts and blackouts. Should they be as effective as in Europe in
shifting demands from peak to off-peak hours, flattening the daily load
curve, they could significantly reduce both the present and projected
capability of US utilities for recharging electric cars.

SECTION 11 REFERENCES

1. Analysis of Alternative Energy Futures, ERDA, Office of the Assistant
    Administrator of Planning and Analysis, February 4, 1977.

2. D. B. Shonka, A. S. Loebl, and P. D. Patterson, Transportation
    Energy Conservation Data Book: Edition 2, ORNL-5320, Oak Ridge
    National Laboratory, October 1977.

3. M. Beller, Ed., Sourcebook for Energy Assessment, BNL-50483, Brook-
    haven National Laboratory, Upton, N.Y., December 1975.

4. A Time to Choose: America's Energy Future, Final Report by the
    Energy Policy Project of the Ford Foundation, Ballinger Publishing
    Company, Cambridge, Mass., 1974.

5. Factors Affecting the Electric Power Supply, 1980-85: Executive
    Summary and Recommendations, Bureau of Power, Federal Power Commission,
    Washington, D.C., December 1, 1976.

6. W. S. Chen, et al., Estimating Future Electricity Demand in an Era
    of Increasing Energy Scarcity, presented at the American Nuclear
    Society Winter Meeting, San Francisco, November 1975.

7. J. G. Asbury and A. Kouvalis, Electric Storage Heating: The Experience
    in England and Wales and in the Federal Republic of Germany, ANL/ES-50,
    Argonne National Laboratory, Argonne, Illinois, May 1976.

12   IMPACTS ON URBAN AIR QUALITY

Widespread use of electric cars would make major changes in the emissions of air pollutants by automobiles and electric utilities, two important sources of air pollution in the United States. Electric cars themselves emit no pollutants (except particulates due to tire wear), so each electric car which replaces a conventional car reduces total vehicular emissions accordingly. Generation of recharge power for electric cars, however, produces additional emissions from electric utilities, at least to the extent that fossil fuels are used. The additional pollution thus depends very much on the mix of fuels used for recharge in different geographic regions. It also depends on the actual location of the generating stations, which may be hundreds of kilometers distant from the cars being recharged.

The net effects of electric cars on emissions of air pollutants in urban areas are projected in Fig. 12.1. The changes shown are an upper bound, assuming the electrification of all automobiles. For the pollutants emitted primarily by automobiles, carbon monoxide and hydrocarbons, electrification could substantially reduce total emissions in the urban areas of the projection. Emissions of sulfur oxides, to which power plants significantly contribute, would be substantially increased, since there are almost no sulfur oxide emissions from conventional automobiles to be eliminated by electrification. Pollutant emissions to which both autos and power plants contribute, particulates and nitrogen oxides, would be relatively little affected.

As in the case of petroleum use, the effect of electric cars depends very strongly on the future performance of conventional automobiles. Here again, stringent regulations are in effect: by 1981, emissions of air pollutants by new cars will have been reduced some 90% from the levels prevalent in 1970. The perspective benefits of electric cars are accordingly limited. On the other hand, stringent regulations are also being applied to emissions from electric power plants, reducing the added pollution electric cars would cause from this source.

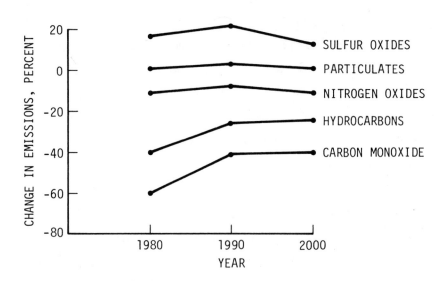

Figure 12.1. Effect of 100% Use of Electric Cars on
Emissions of Urban Air Pollutants
(Population-Weighted Averages for
24 Regions)

Meanwhile, there remain many important sources of pollution which are unaffected by electric cars. The future of emissions from these sources is uncertain, but in the projection of Fig. 12.1, only modest improvements are foreseen. As a result, they tend increasingly to mask the potential improvements due to electric cars.

The projection of Fig. 12.1 was derived from the results of Sec. 11, and from a host of other sources of material, by applying a computer model to twenty-four individual urban regions. This section begins with a discussion of the analytic approach and the model itself. It then presents baseline projections of emissions in the absence of electric cars and the levels of air quality associated with them. Next, it presents the changes in emissions and pollution which would result from 10% or 100% electrification of automobiles. Finally, it discusses the major uncertainties in the projection, which primarily arise in future regulatory actions. The discussion is limited to urban air pollution, since electric cars are most likely to be applied in urban driving and the majority of people adversely affected by air pollution live in urban areas.

12.1 METHOD OF ANALYSIS

The three major steps in the analysis are summarized in Table 12.1. It was necessary to go through all three for each urban area, since each differs significantly from the others. Meteorological conditions, the importance of other sources of pollution, the location of power plants, and the fuels used by power plants all differ significantly from region to region.

In order to deal individually with the two dozen largest urban areas in the United States, existing computer systems were used to the maximum feasible extent as tools in the analysis. These are also shown in Table 12.1.

TABLE 12.1

ANALYTIC STEPS AND TOOLS

Step	Tool
1. Establish base-year emissions and air quality, 1974	NEDS (National Emissions Data System) SAROAD (Storage and Retrieval of Aerometric Data) System
2. Project baseline emissions and air quality, 1980-2000	REPS (Regional Emissions Projection System) "Linear rollback," "Appendix J"
3. Project emissions and air quality with 10% and 100% electric cars, 1980-2000	(Same as in Step 2)

301

Data for the base year, 1974, on emissions and air quality were obtained from two systems developed and operated by the US Environmental Protection Agency.[1] These are standard sources for such data and are regularly updated and improved. For projecting emissions, the Regional Emissions Projection System (REPS), also developed by EPA, was used.[2] Owing to various difficulties with REPS, EPA terminated its further development after the beginning of the study reported here. Since no alternative model was either available or in prospect, however, REPS was placed in operation at General Research Corporation, debugged and improved, and then modified to work in concert with the RECAP model described in Sec. 10.

To relate air quality to emissions, the primary tool used was "linear rollback." This is a very simple formula based on the assumption that the concentration of pollutants is proportional to the emissions of pollutants. "Rollback" is a reference to the original application of this assumption, in estimating the percentage reductions of emissions required to roll back concentrations of air pollution to levels prevailing in some former year, levels deemed acceptable and desirable.

The standard rollback formula is

$$R = \frac{(PAQ) - (DAQ)}{(PAQ) - (B)} \qquad (12.1)$$

where

      R = fractional reduction in emissions

  PAQ = present air quality (highest concentration recorded)

  DAQ = desired air quality

     B = background concentration of pollutant (concentration unavoidably present due to natural causes)

Since the purpose here is to estimate future air quality (DAQ) given the current air quality (PAQ), the background level (B), and the fractional reduction in emissions (R), it is necessary to solve Eq. 12.1 for DAQ:

$$DAQ = PAQ(1 - R) + (R)(B) \qquad (12.2)$$

R is estimated from

$$R = 1 - \frac{E_k}{E_{1974}} \quad ; \quad k = 1980, 1990, 2000$$

where E_k are the emissions projected for the year k.

The simplicity of linear rollback makes it plainly inadequate to deal with local variations in concentration of pollutants; it is generally applied to total emissions for a considerable area. Rollback is also inadequate to deal with oxidants, pollutants which are not emitted directly but instead are produced by photochemical reactions involving emissions of hydrocarbons and nitrogen oxides. In the last decade, elaborate computer models have been developed for dealing with both these complexities. Application of such models for two dozen separate urban areas, however, would be far beyond the resources available to this study, and might not even be possible without quantities of detailed data which are not generally available. Furthermore, the validity of even the most detailed models has frequently been questioned, and even challenged in court.[4] Finally, a previous study of the effects of electric cars in Los Angeles compared results obtained from rollback with those obtained through exercise of a detailed model which included both photochemistry and meteorology.[5] The differences were so small that the effort and expense of more detailed modeling appear unjustified.

Linear rollback is acceptable today in the official plans of the individual states to control air pollution in compliance with Federal regulations.[6] In using rollback to estimate changes in oxidant concentrations, it is customary to assume that they are proportional to changes in emissions of hydrocarbons alone, ignoring changes in nitrogen oxides. An alternative is to use an empirical, non-linear relation between oxidant concentrations and hydrocarbon emissions which is referred to as the method of "Appendix J," the portion of a document officially prescribing this as an acceptable alternative to linear rollback.[3] In this study, both methods were employed; since results differed by only 10%-20%, only the results of the rollback calculations are presented in the following pages.

Given pollutant concentrations proportional to emissions, future emissions become all-important in projecting impacts of electric cars on air pollution. The Regional Emissions Projection System used to make these projections is summarized in Fig. 12.2. Working from detailed demographic and economic data, as well as base-year emissions and projected future controls, REPS provides detailed inventories of future emissions for a given area.[2] In this study, the areas were the twenty-four Air Quality Control Regions (AQCRs) in the United States that include the largest urban populations. REPS projected for each AQCR the total emissions, in metric tons per year, in the categories shown in Table 12.2. Only four of these categories, those marked with asterisks, would be affected by a shift from conventional to electric automobiles.

National economic and demographic projections were derived from two established sources. The first is the Strategic Environmental Assessment System, which was developed by EPA to make national projections of environmental quality. To support these projections, the system includes the most elaborate input-output model of the US economy which is available for use. To disaggregate national totals projected for future years, regional data were obtained from the OBERS 1972 projections.[8] Again, these projections were developed for another purpose: they were provided by the US Departments of Commerce and Agriculture for use by the US Water Resources Council.

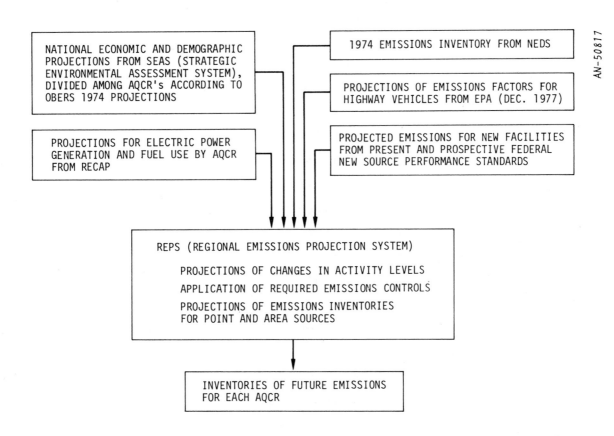

Figure 12.2. Inputs and Outputs of REPS

305

TABLE 12.2

CATEGORIES OF EMISSIONS PROJECTED BY REPS

Fuel Combustion

    External Combustion

        Residential

        Electricity Generation*

        Industrial

        Commercial/Institutional

    Internal Combustion

        Electricity Generation*

        Industrial

        Commercial/Institutional

        Engine Testing

Industrial Processes

Evaporation

Solid Waste Disposal

Transportation

    Highway Vehicles

        Light Duty Gasoline*

        Heavy Duty Gasoline

        Heavy Duty Diesel

    Off-Highway Vehicles

    Aircraft

    Vessels

Miscellaneous (Area)

    Gasoline Handling Evaporation Loss*

    Solvent Evaporation Loss

---

*Subcategory that will be affected by electric cars

The projections of electric power generation made in Secs. 10 and 11 are far more detailed than those available elsewhere for REPS. Accordingly, REPS was revised to accept the detailed projections from the RECAP model. Base-year emissions were obtained from NEDS, and projected reductions in emissions due to regulatory controls were taken from Federal regulations and supporting calculations for highway vehicles and for new sources of pollutants.[9]

No projections were included for additional controls to be imposed by individual states. This is discussed in Sec. 12.4 as one of the major uncertainties in projecting emissions and air quality.

12.2 BASELINE PROJECTIONS OF URBAN POLLUTANT EMISSIONS AND AIR QUALITY

The twenty-four air quality control regions with the largest urban populations in the United States are shown in Fig. 12.3. Their populations and base-year levels of air pollution are shown in Table 12.3. The total population of these regions is 92.4 million, well over half of the entire urban population of the United States in 1974. The levels of air pollution shown are the maximum concentrations of the five pollutants for which National Ambient Air Quality standards have been established. The concentrations are expressed as a percent of the relevant primary national standard, the standard for protection of human health. In 1974, every area exceeded the standard for at least one pollutant, and most areas substantially exceeded the standards for three or four pollutants.

The national standards themselves are summarized in Table 12.4, together with nationally-occurring background concentrations. The standards are defined on a worst-case basis; that is, they are not to be exceeded at the place and time of worst air pollution in a region. Moreover, they were chosen to avoid adverse effects on health not just for average persons, but also for that minority which is more susceptible, either through age or other infirmity, to detrimental effects. Failure of a region to attain compliance with the national standards, then, does not imply that most

307

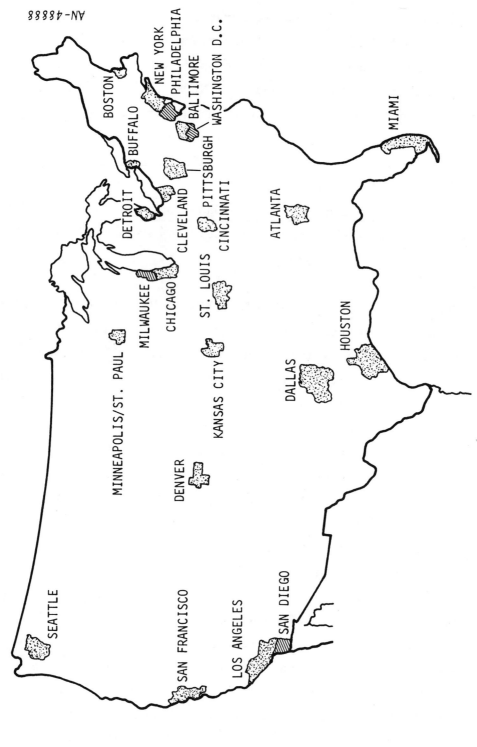

Figure 12.3. The Twenty-Four Air Quality Control Regions in the United States Containing the Urbanized Areas With the Largest Populations

TABLE 12.3

1974 POPULATION AND AIR POLLUTION IN THE
TWENTY-FOUR LARGEST AIR QUALITY CONTROL REGIONS

Air Quality Control Region	1974 Population, millions	Maximum 1974 Air Pollution (percent of national ambient air quality standards)				
		Particulates	SO_2	NO_x	Oxidant	CO
New York	18.0	177	110	99	441	443
Los Angeles	10.6	197	79	141	661	328
Chicago	8.0	204	75	160	499	171
Philadelphia	5.8	264	76	94	576	225
San Francisco	4.9	93	34	76	331	193
Detroit	4.5	193	92	52	105	120
Boston	3.9	117	55	70	244	197
Cleveland	3.5	241	132	113	272	116
Washington	3.0	184	72	68	184	1,149
Pittsburgh	2.9	235	176	67	207	221
Dallas	2.8	117	4	52	229	24
Miami	2.6	111	37	50	97	67
St. Louis	2.5	204	62	76	612	248
Houston	2.4	172	85	68	286	133
Baltimore	2.1	179	96	67	86	144
Minneapolis-St. Paul	2.0	120	151	65	122	149
Seattle	2.0	136	84	94	159	231
Atlanta	1.8	112	50	90	159	139
Milwaukee	1.8	125	67	65	351	125
Cincinnati	1.7	216	51	85	186	103
Kansas City	1.5	156	36	66	626	119
Buffalo	1.4	163	160	61	181	110
San Diego	1.4	119	17	50	392	116
Denver	1.3	189	30	88	306	226
Population-Weighted Average		178	82	94	375	266
Percent of Regions in Compliance		4	79	88	8	8

TABLE 12.4

BACKGROUND CONCENTRATIONS AND PRIMARY NATIONAL AMBIENT AIR QUALITY STANDARDS

	Background Concentrations	Primary Standard[1]
Particulates	10 μg/m^3 [10]	75 μg/m^3 (annual geometric mean)
Sulfur Dioxide	0 [11]	80 μg/m^3 (annual mean)
Nitrogen Oxides	10 μg/m^3 [12]	100 μg/m^3 (annual mean)
Total Hydrocarbons	1 mg/m^3 [13]	*
Photochemical Oxidants	20-100 μg/m^3 [14]	160 μg/m^3 (one hour not to be exceeded more than once a year)
Carbon Monoxide	1 mg/m^3 [15]	10 mg/m^3 (8-hour average)

---

*There is no standard for total hydrocarbons. The standard for hydrocarbons less methane is 160 μg/m^3 (maximum 3 hour concentration (6-9 am) not to be exceeded more than once a year).

---

people in most parts of the region are in immediate danger. On the other hand, attainment of clean air as represented by the standards is an important national objective for several reasons, among which health is only one. Reduction of the effects of air pollution on animals, vegetation, and structure is important and of immense monetary value. Improving the amenities of the urban environment may be equally important.

Annual rates of population growth averaging about one percent are projected for the regions of Table 12.3, along with annual growth in economic activity of about 3.2%. These follow from the SEAS and OBERS projections.[7,8] Growth of automotive travel in proportion to population was assumed. Generation of potential air pollutants increases correspondingly. Under federal, state, and regional regulations, however, actual emissions of pollutants must be controlled to an increasing degree as the years pass.

The best-known controls have been applied to automobiles, requiring reductions of their individual emissions by well over 90% in the fifteen-year period ending in 1981. Rates of emissions assumed for automobiles in new condition in this study are shown in Table 12.5. These are average levels recorded in the past for new automobiles, or expected of them in the future under requirements of the Clean Air Act Amendments of 1977. They were subsequently adjusted upward by factors depending on age, model year, and pollutant emitted in order to calculate total emissions from all automobiles on the road in a given future year.[9] They were further adjusted for proportions of travel in stop-start city driving and at higher sustained speeds on highways. The percentage emissions in Table 12.5 do not reflect an earlier reduction approaching 50% in emissions of hydrocarbons, which was achieved from 1963 to 1968.

TABLE 12.5

EMISSION RATES FOR NEW LIGHT-DUTY VEHICLES

(except California, high-altitude areas)

Source: Refs. 9, 16

| | Emission Rates | | | | | |
| | g/mi | | | percent of pre-1968 value | | |
Model Year	HC	CO	NO_x	HC	CO	NO_x
Pre-1968	4.45	68.30	3.58	100	100	100
1968-72	2.43	31.14	4.43	55	100	124
1972-74	2.43	31.14	2.98	55	100	83
1975-76	1.13	18.60	2.42	25	60	68
1977-79	1.13	18.60	1.50	25	60	42
1980	0.12	3.00	1.50	2.7	9.6	42
1981 and thereafter	0.12	1.40	0.29	2.7	4.5	8.1

More stringent controls than those of Table 12.5 were assumed for automobiles in California, which has led the nation in the regulation of emissions from automobiles and still imposes stricter standards than those applied elsewhere.[9] Special controls were also applied to autos at high altitudes, as required by Federal regulation.[9]

The Clean Air Act Amendments of 1970, which imposed the Federal limitations on automobile emissions, also required limits on new sources of air pollution. There are hundreds of categories of such new sources, each potentially emitting one or more of the five principal air pollutants. The Environmental Protection Agency was designated to develop performance standards appropriate for each industrial category and pollutant. Because the consequences can be enormous, the standards must be carefully derived, and the burden of doing so is immense.[17] To date, only a fraction of prospective standards have actually been promulgated. All proposed and promulgated standards were included in REPS for this study. Among the most important in this context are those affecting emissions by electric utilities, which are major generators of pollutants and are also growing rapidly, so that new (or modified) sources may be relatively more important than in other industries in future years. Table 12.6 shows the degree of control required for coal-fired and oil-fired electric plants, almost all of which are large enough to fall in the categories shown.

TABLE 12.6

ASSUMED NEW SOURCE PERFORMANCE STANDARDS
AFFECTING ELECTRIC UTILITIES

Source Category	Effective Year	Required Control Efficiency, percent	
		Particulates	SO_x
Coal-fired steam generators (over $6.3 \cdot 10^7$ kg-cal/hr)	1975	98	90
Oil-fired steam generators (over $6.3 \cdot 10^7$ kg-cal/hr)	1975	98	70

Source: Emissions Standards and Engineering Division, EPA Office of Air Quality Planning and Standards

To promote air quality, electric utilities were ordered in critical cases in the early 1970s to convert to natural gas or low-sulfur oil in boilers designed to be fired by oil or coal. Since the oil embargo of 1973-74 and subsequent shortages of natural gas, however, utilities have been required to convert or reconvert facilities so as to shift from natural gas to oil, and from oil to coal where possible. In this study, it was assumed that plants capable of using oil or gas would use oil, and those capable of burning oil or coal would burn coal. This has important implications for emissions, since it involves shifts to fuels of higher sulfur content.

Emissions of individual air pollutants projected for 1980-2000 by the use of REPS as just described are shown in Fig. 12.4. The emissions are expressed as a percentage of the level in the base year, 1974, and are averages for the urban regions of Table 12.3. Here and in subsequent averages for the twenty-four regions, regional populations were used as a weighting so that the results are a better measure of the exposure of the total urban population to pollution. Otherwise, levels projected for areas with small populations would affect the average as much as those for areas with populations ten to fifteen times larger.

Projected reductions in emissions appear in Fig. 12.4 only for carbon monoxide, hydrocarbons, and nitrogen oxides. These are the three main pollutants emitted by automobiles, and the reductions are the result of strict Federal regulations. Emissions of stationary sources in general are not projected to decline, and for particulates and sulfur oxides, which have no diminishing component due to automobile improvement, considerable increases are projected. The situation may change due to state and Federal regulations not included in the projections; this is discussed in Sec. 12.4.

The levels of pollution associated with the emissions projected in Fig. 12.4 are shown in Fig. 12.5. Pollution levels are expressed

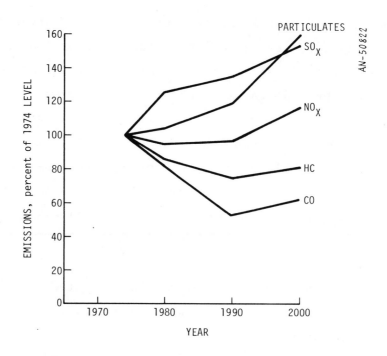

Figure 12.4. Projected Emissions of Air Pollutants
in Urban Regions

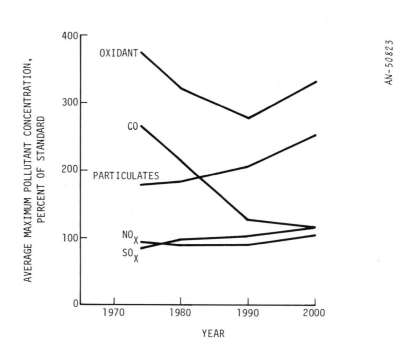

Figure 12.5. Projected Air Pollution in Urban Regions

314

in terms of the national standards of Table 12.3 and are averages with weighting for population. Again, the major improvements (in oxidant and carbon monoxide) are attributable to cleaner automobiles. Especially after 1990, there is a trend to degradation of air quality in these projections.

So far as electric cars are concerned, it is significant that in the projections the relative importance of both automobiles and power plants declines. This is shown is Fig. 12.6. As the emissions of conventional cars decline, the further improvements which might be achieved by electric cars are reduced. Moreover, since little improvement in stationary sources is expected, further improvement has a decreasing relative effect on total pollution. The percentages in Fig. 12.6a amount to upper bounds for improvements due to electric automobiles. Even without any pollution from generating recharge power, electric cars could at most eliminate the percentages of regional emissions shown. These percentages decline considerably in the future, and they have already declined significantly from past years, in which automobiles were the dominant source of air pollutants in major urban areas.

12.3 EFFECTS OF ELECTRIC CARS

The maximum effects of electric cars, assuming complete electrification of the automobile fleet, are shown in Table 12.7. The table shows total emissions of air pollutants as a percent of the baseline emissions without electric cars for each of the twenty-four urban regions. Also shown are population-weighted averages for each type of pollutant.

These results were computed by reducing emissions from conventional autos in proportion to the number of electric cars, and increasing electric generation at power plants in each region in accord with projections from the RECAP model for generation of the required recharge energy.

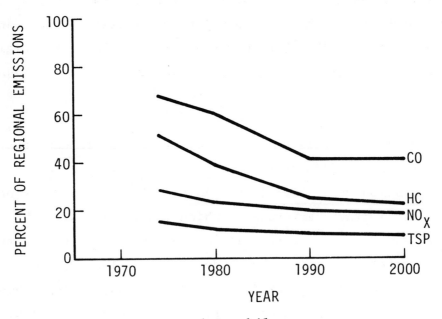

a. Automobiles

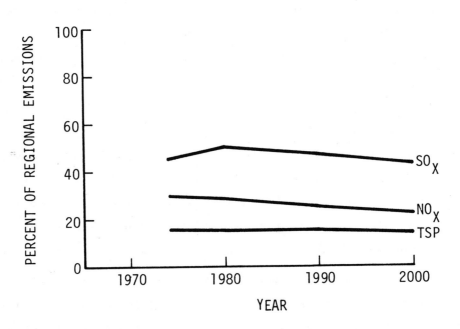

b. Electric Power Plants

Figure 12.6.   Importance of Automobiles and Power Plants
in Urban Air Pollution

TABLE 12.7

EFFECT OF ELECTRIC CARS ON URBAN EMISSIONS
OF AIR POLLUTION IN MAJOR AQCRs, 1990

Air Quality Control Region	Percent of Baseline Emissions with 100% Use of Electric Cars				
	Particulates	SO_x	NO_x	HC	CO
New York	101	119	93	68	42
Los Angeles	101	118	88	74	45
Chicago	102	125	97	86	95
Philadelphia	103	114	93	79	62
San Francisco	110	167	83	68	55
Detroit	107	133	105	79	89
Boston	101	118	89	75	40
Cleveland	102	117	84	80	65
Washington	109	129	94	55	39
Pittsburgh	110	118	105	57	57
Dallas	99	100	76	86	57
Miami	101	118	86	59	54
St. Louis	103	118	101	81	73
Houston	100	104	82	96	88
Baltimore	100	115	103	86	39
Minneapolis–St. Paul	103	122	95	85	86
Seattle	97	101	85	71	63
Atlanta	102	112	95	62	67
Milwaukee	131	157	95	92	61
Cincinnati	100	119	104	72	55
Kansas City	100	107	88	80	70
Buffalo	98	100	84	71	57
San Diego	105	171	98	57	51
Denver	100	108	91	62	59
Population-Weighted Average	103.0	121.8	92.4	74.1	58.9

The results in Table 12.7 vary considerably from region to region. They reflect different mixes of fuels used for recharging electric cars in the regions, as well as different locations of power plants and different concentrations of pollution-producing industries. These are, of course, among the important reasons why air pollution is best analyzed for each individual region rather than in terms of national totals.

The trends of emissions with time are indicated in Table 12.8, for both 10% and 100% use of electric cars. The figures for 100% use represent a maximum effect, an upper bound on what might be the result of using electric cars. They were shown graphically in Fig. 12.1. The deviations from 100% (the baseline without electric cars) are not simply ten times the deviation with 10% electric cars, because the fuels used for recharging electric cars change as the total number of electric cars increases. Even in the year 2000, of course, 100% electrification is unlikely. The 10% level is probably more realistic and representative of benefits within reach. The increases are relatively small in Table 12.8, but one of them--for particulates--is for a pollutant which is typically above the national standard and also projected to increase in the future. The major reductions, of hydrocarbons and carbon monoxide, are in emissions which are projected to decline in relative importance, but nonetheless result in air quality falling far short of the national standard.

Overall, it appears that the effects of electric cars will be rather modest in 1990 and 2000, when emissions from conventional automobiles will be fully controlled. As in the case of overall national petroleum consumption, overall air pollution is relatively insensitive even to total electrification of automobiles. Underlying this conclusion is the assumption employed in projecting overall levels of pollution that urban air pollution will not be greatly reduced in the next ten years, despite existing legislation to the contrary. If compliance with the national air quality standards had been projected instead, emissions from stationary sources would be much less and the percentage changes due to electric cars would be much larger.

TABLE 12.8

OVERALL EFFECT OF ELECTRIC CARS ON URBAN AIR POLLUTION

	Emissions, Percent of Baseline Average					
	10% Electric Cars			100% Electric Cars		
Pollutant	1980	1990	2000	1980	1990	2000
Particulates	100.6	100.4	100.1	101.2	103.0	101.5
Sulfur Oxides	102.6	102.0	101.1	117.0	121.8	113.4
Nitrogen Oxides	98.9	99.0	98.8	89.1	92.4	89.0
Hydrocarbons	96.0	97.4	97.6	59.7	74.1	76.1
Carbon Monoxide	94.0	95.9	96.0	40.0	58.9	60.2

This is illustrated in Table 12.9, in which changes due to electric cars are shown in relation not to the projected level of pollution, but to an absolute value: the national standards themselves. Here the effect of 10% use of electric cars is considerably larger. In some cases, in fact, the changes relative to the standard are larger than 10%. This results from elimination of pollutants from conventional automobiles which alone would cause violation of the standard by a considerable amount, even in the absence of any other source of that pollutant.

The changes in air pollution which might be caused by electric cars are of the same order of magnitude as changes which were actually recorded in the US in the early 1970s. These are shown in Fig. 12.7. The change in air quality from the wide use of electric cars might be expected to be roughly as significant to the average individual as those actually achieved from 1970 to 1974.

TABLE 12.9

PERCENT CHANGE IN URBAN AIR POLLUTION
WITH TEN PERCENT ELECTRIC CARS

	Change in Pollutant Concentration, Percent of Standard		
	1980	1990	2000
Particulates	+1	+1	+0.5
Sulfur Oxides	+2	+2	+1
Nitrogen Oxides	−1	−1	−1
Oxidant	−12	−6	−7
Carbon Monoxide	−13	−5	−5

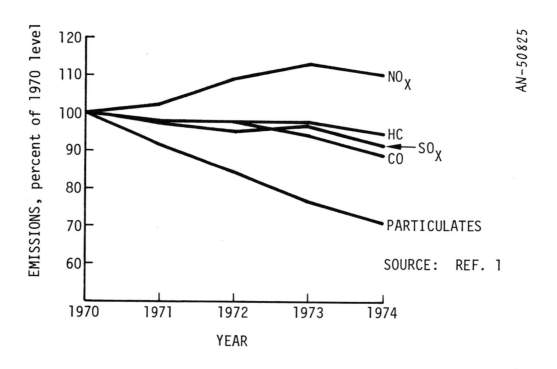

Figure 12.7. National Emissions of Air Pollutants, 1970-74 (from Ref. 1)

12.4 UNCERTAINTIES

The effect of future regulatory action on emissions of air pollutants is the principal uncertainty in the projected effects of electric cars. Emissions from conventional cars which would be replaced, and from power plants which would supply recharge electricity, may be projected with relative confidence. As shown in Tables 12.5 and 12.6, they are specifically and stringently controlled under existing regulations. Only in the case of existing, unmodified power plants do the regulations allow any uncertainty at all. Most of the uncertainty about emissions concerns other sources, and the extent to which they will overshadow emissions from power plants and automobiles in the future.

Projecting these other emissions of pollutants is difficult and uncertain partly because appropriate regulations have not been developed, partly because many regulations are developed and enforced by individual states, and partly because regulatory action in the past has not led to legislated goals, which were sometimes unrealistic. Whether the most recent legislative goal, compliance with national air quality standards by 1983 (or 1987, if that is impossible), will be attained remains to be seen.

The original Federal Clean Air Act was passed in 1963.[18] By that time, air pollution was widely acknowledged to be a severe problem in a number of urban areas in the United States. In California, air quality standards were being adopted and regulatory controls of both stationary and mobile sources of pollution had already been imposed. This was largely in response to the plight of Los Angeles, where poor ventilation and abundant sunshine led to levels of photochemical smog which were nationally notorious.[19] By that time, the origin of the oxidants in photochemical air pollution had been traced to emissions of hydrocarbons, emissions of nitrogen oxides, and their chemical interactions in the sunshine. Both catalytic and direct-flame afterburners for automotive exhausts had been invented and tested, and controls of emissions from

stationary sources were well advanced, having been practiced in many
localities over the years. The Clean Air Act of 1963, in recognition of
this basis for action, allocated funds for training and control as well
as research, with special attention to auto exhaust and to sulfur in
fuels. These are both problems which remain crucial today, fifteen years
later.

Among the several amendments of the Clean Air Act, those of 1970
have been most important.[4] In these amendments, the Congress directed
that National Ambient Air Quality Standards be adopted which would protect
human health, and required that the individual states plan and implement
compliance with the standards by 1975. The standards eventually adopted
are those of Table 12.4; but as Table 12.3 shows, actual air quality was
far from meeting these standards on schedule. The necessary state implementation plans were completed, as required by the Amendments, by 1973, but
in many cases, they did not realistically provide for implementing compliance by 1975 or even by some year much further in the future. The
reason was often that possible cures for air pollution would have been
far worse than the disease. In Los Angeles, for example, the Environmental
Protection Agency was eventually driven to preparing its own plan for
Los Angeles to replace the inadequate state plan, and in this plan EPA
included the outright elimination of gasoline sales in the Los Angeles
area during the smoggy months of the year.

Though the goals of the Clean Air Act Amendments of 1970 were
not achieved, the adoption of national standards was an important step
forward, as were two sets of Federal emissions standards also resulting
from the Amendments. Because it was deemed inappropriate by Congress for
manufacturers of automobiles to meet different emissions requirements
in every state, Federal emissions standards for automobiles were imposed
except in the case of California, which had special problems and its own
stiff standards to cope with them. Standards requiring levels of emissions

322

complying with the overall goal of the Congress, a 90% reduction of automotive emissions, were promulgated in the early 1970s, but the automobile industry successfully argued that it could not and should not meet their final, most demanding levels of control in 1975-76. The other area of Federal controls covered new sources of pollutants. To deter the establishment of poorly-controlled plants and factories in remote areas with few existing pollution problems and few regulatory constraints, the Congress required that standards for emissions from new stationary sources of pollutants be developed by the Environmental Protection Agency, for nationwide application. This is the source of the controls required of new electric power plants shown in Table 12.6. As yet, however, all the standards needed for attainment of national air quality objectives have not been developed. There are over 200 different industries, each emitting up to a half-dozen separate pollutants. Establishing reasonable levels of control for each of these cases is an enormous task, one which has not yet been accomplished.

In response to these difficulties with state implementation plans, reduction of emissions from automobiles, and establishment of new Source Performance Standards, the Clean Air Act Amendments of 1977 make important changes.[20,21] They delay the dates for attaining the national standards for air quality to 1983 or, where that is infeasible, to 1988. They direct an immediate assessment of conditions and revisions of plans by the states to achieve these goals. They stretch out the original schedule for reduction of automotive emissions so that the final levels are achieved in 1981, not 1975, and they hold out an opportunity for raising the allowable emission of nitrogen oxides by a factor of two and a half. They direct the Environmental Protection Agency to complete the promulgation of new source performance standards by 1983 (or 1988, if the earlier date is infeasible). They also introduce new levels of complexity in control of emissions. In response to court action in the wake of the 1970 Amendments, the 1977 Amendments identify so-called "PSD" areas: areas in which national standards of air quality are already met, and--under court ruling--"prevention of significant deterioration" is required. Different controls are required in these areas than in all other areas, which are called non-attainment areas because they have not attained compliance with the standards. Furthermore, requirements for control of existing sources are strengthened and various types of control are identified: "reasonably available control technology," "best available control technology," "best available retrofit technology." In addition, a new emissions requirement is defined for non-attainment areas and new or modified sources, the "lowest achievable emission rate," and the various technologies and rates are defined in a way which makes them interdependent. The Amendments themselves extend to 112 pages, and their full implication is far from obvious today.[20]

It is clear that some previous legislative goals were neither optimum nor actually achieved. To achieve current goals, major reductions in emissions from stationary sources will be necessary. The projections of this section, however, include relatively little improvement in emissions from most stationary sources. Even if, as in the past, future control of these sources is insufficient to meet the legislative goals, it does seem likely that their emissions may be less than projected here.

To the extent that total emissions are lower, the relative effects of electric cars will be larger. Whether they will also be more important, however, is uncertain. The regulation of air pollution, after all, is largely based on the proposition that below some threshold most pollutants have no effect on health (or, at a possibly different level, on animals, vegetation, or structures). As air pollution approaches this threshold, doubtless the benefits of changes of a given magnitude decrease. To the extent that national standards for air quality are met or approached without electric cars, further reductions from use of electric cars may be unnecessary or unimportant.

SECTION 12 REFERENCES

1. Monitoring and Air Quality Trends Report 1974, Environmental Protection Agency, EPA-450/1-76-001, February 1976.

2. Regional Emission Projection System, System Documentation, Booz, Allen, and Hamilton, Inc., Report No. 9075-014, April 1, 1975.

3. "Appendix J, the Requirements for Preparation, Adoption, and Submittal of Implementation Plans," 36 F.R. 15486.

4. Noel de Nevers, "Enforcing the Clean Air Act of 1970," Scientific American, June 1973.

5. W. F. Hamilton, et al., Impact of Future Use of Electric Cars in the Los Angeles Region, Vol. III: Task Reports on Impact and Usage Analyses, EPA-460/3-74-020-C, US Environmental Protection Agency, October 1974.

6. "The Requirements for Preparation, Adoption, and Submittal of Implementation Plans," 36 F.R. 15486.

7. Peter House, Trading Off Environment, Economics and Energy: A Case Study of EPA's Strategic Environmental Assessment System, Lexington Books, Lexington, Mass., 1977.

8. Regional Economic Activity in the U.S., 1974 OBERS Projections, developed by the US Departments of Commerce and Agriculture for the US Water Resources Council.

9. Mobile Source Emission Factors, Draft Document, Environmental Protection Agency, Office of Transportation and Land Use Policy, December 3, 1977.

10. Air Quality Criteria for Particulate Matter, National Air Pollution Control Administration, AP-49, January 1969.

11. Air Quality Criteria for Sulfur Oxides, National Air Pollution Control Administration, January 1969.

12. Air Quality Criteria for Nitrogen Oxides, Environmental Protection Agency, AP-84, January 1971.

13. Air Quality Criteria for Hydrocarbons, National Air Pollution Control Administration, AP-64, March 1970.

14. Air Quality Criteria for Photochemical Oxidants, National Air Pollution Control Administration, AP-63, 1970.

15. *Air Quality Criteria for Carbon Monoxide*, National Air Pollution Control Administration, AP-62, March 1970.

16. Frank P. Grad, et al., *The Automobile and the Regulation of its Impact on the Environment*, University of Oklahoma Press, Norman, Oklahoma, 1975.

17. L. J. Habegger, R. R. Cirillo, and N. F. Sather, *Priorities and Procedures for Development of Standards of Performance for New Stationary Sources of Atmospheric Emissions*, EPA-450/3-76-020, US Environmental Protection Agency, Office of Air and Waste Management, Research Triangle Park, North Carolina, May 1976.

18. Seymour Tilson, "Air Pollution," *International Science and Technology*, June 1965.

19. A. J. Haagen-Smit, "The Control of Air Pollution," *Scientific American*, January 1964.

20. *Clean Air Act Amendments of 1977*, Public Law 95-95, 95th Congress, United States of America, August 7, 1977.

21. B. J. Goldsmith and J. R. Mahoney, "Implications of the 1977 Clean Air Act Amendments for Stationary Sources," *Environmental Science and Technology*, February 1978.

13   IMPACTS ON URBAN TRAFFIC NOISE

The importance of noise pollution and its control have been recognized in recent years in legislation at all levels of government. In particular, the Federal Noise Control Act of 1972 established as a national policy the control of emissions of noise that are detrimental to the human environment. The Act notes that "...the major sources of noise include transportation vehicles and equipment," and is the basis for the regulation of vehicle noise which is now in progress.[1]

Electric propulsion of automobiles is inherently quiet. Although noise data is scarce for electric cars, it suffices for the preliminary estimate of the potential benefits of electric cars in reducing urban traffic noise which is illustrated in Fig. 13.1. EPA figures show that almost one hundred million people were exposed in 1975 to significant urban traffic noise. The noise reductions already required for future trucks, buses, and motorcycles will reduce the impact of traffic noise to about 57% of the recent level, even if car noise is unchanged. Though noise emission standards have not yet been adopted for automobiles, quieting of conventional cars could produce an additional reduction of impact, to about 41% of the recent level. Substitution of increasing numbers of electric urban cars, which will be substantially quieter during acceleration than the improved conventional cars, could further reduce noise impact to 27% of the 1975 level.

Current urban traffic noise, regulatory goals for the future, and resultant changes in noise impacts were recently investigated by the Interagency Task Force on Motor Vehicle Goals Beyond 1980.[2] The report of the Task Force is the basis for the discussions of community noise

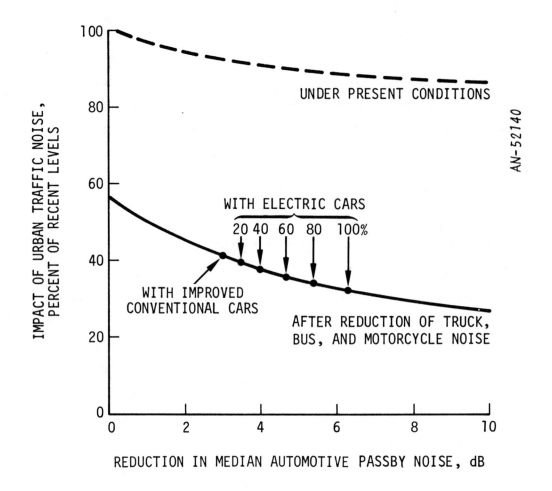

Figure 13.1. Effects of Electric Cars on Urban Auto Noise
and Traffic Noise Impact

and baseline traffic noise (in the absence of electric vehicles) which
begin this section. Next, prospective noise emissions from quiet conventional cars and electric cars are appraised, and finally the resultant
potential reductions in noise impacts are found for assumed levels of future
use of electric cars.

13.1 COMMUNITY NOISE

Measures

The customary measures of community noise are presented in Table 13.1. The A-weighted sound level, which ordinarily varies considerably with time, is indicated directly by standard sound level meters. The A weighting emphasizes sounds in the middle frequencies to which the human ear is most responsive. In quiet areas at quiet times of day, A-weighted sound levels may be as low as 30-40 dB(A), while in very noisy areas, they may exceed 100 dB(A).

Average community noise through the 24-hour day is described by L_{dn}, the day-night equivalent sound level. As Table 13.1 shows, this level is calculated by averaging the minute-to-minute readings of an A-weighted sound level meter. Between the hours of 10 **PM and 7 AM, the A-weighted** level is increased by 10 dB in this averaging, reflecting the heightened sensitivity of the community during the usual hours of sleep. Though the day-night equivalent sound level, L_{dn}, is defined in a manner which is partly arbitrary, in practice it serves as a useful and informative measure of community noise.

TABLE 13.1

MEASURES OF COMMUNITY NOISE

$L_A(t)$ = A-weighted sound level in **decibels** at time t

L_{dn} = day-night equivalent sound level, dB

$$L_{dn} = 10 \log_{10} \frac{1}{24} \left\{ \int_{7\text{ AM}}^{10\text{ PM}} 10^{L_A(t)/10} \, dt \right.$$

$$\left. + \int_{10\text{ PM}}^{7\text{ AM}} 10^{(L_A(t)+10)/10} \cdot dt \right\}$$

Effects

Noise may be defined as unwanted sound. When excessive, it interferes with many human activities. The resultant annoyance is related to day-night equivalent sound level as shown in Fig. 13.2, which is drawn from several studies of airport and other community noise.

An important source of annoyance with noise arises in its interference with communication. At a 65 dB(A) noise level, for example, relaxed conversation is fully intelligible to a listener only within one foot of the speaker, while a raised voice enables easy communication only to a distance of about six feet.[*] An outdoor noise level of 75 dB(A) is typically reduced to 65 dB(A) indoors. It is easy to see, then, why outdoor day-night noise levels of 75 dB might produce annoyance, complaints, and vigorous community action as illustrated in Fig. 13.2.

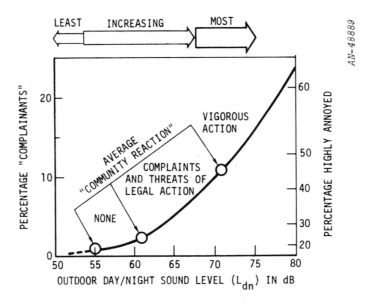

Figure 13.2. Summary of Annoyance Survey and Community Reaction Results (Fig. 6-1 of Ref. 2)

---

[*]See Ref. 2, Fig. 6-2.

Excessive noise on a regular, continuing basis has been shown to jeopardize physical and mental welfare. Adverse effect on normal sleep becomes increasingly noticeable at ambient noise levels above about 35 dB(A).[3] Arousal by noise may induce muscular tension interfering with needed delicate movements or physical relaxation. Excessive background noise, as well as intermittent noise, has been cited as a causative factor in stress-related physical changes such as dilation and constriction of blood vessels, rise in blood pressure, changes in heart rhythm, dilation of the pupils of the eyes, additional endocrine secretion into the blood stream, ulcers and gastro-intestinal problems, migraine headaches, and other metabolic changes.[2] The EPA found that exposure to urban environmental noise levels for which L_{dn} exceeds 70 dB may be harmful to health, especially when combined with intermittent exposures to higher noise levels during travel, work, and recreation.[4]

Sources

The importance of major sources of community noise is indicated by Table 13.2. In the nationwide survey reported in Table 13.2, motor vehicles were judged to be over three times as important as any other source of noise in noisy neighborhoods.

The EPA strategy under the Noise Control Act of 1972 calls for the reduction of noise from all sources. Nevertheless, it appears that urban traffic will remain the most important source of community noise through-out this century.[3] In the remainder of this paper, only urban traffic noise will be considered further. Reductions in the impact of traffic noise will be assumed desirable without regard for the possible predominance of noise from other sources.

TABLE 13.2

PERCENT CONTRIBUTION OF EACH SOURCE IDENTIFIED BY
RESPONDENTS CLASSIFYING THEIR NEIGHBORHOOD AS NOISY

(72% of 1200 Respondents)

Source: Ref. 2, Table 6-1.

Source	Percentage
Motor Vehicles	55
Aircraft	15
Voices	12
Radio and TV Sets	2
Home Maintenance Equipment	2
Construction	1
Industrial	1
Other Noises	6
Not Ascertained	8

13.2 BASELINE TRAFFIC NOISE

Measures of Impact

The customary measure of the impact of urban traffic noise is computed from outdoor day-night equivalent sound levels as shown in Table 13.3. The computation combines the level of traffic noise with the number of people exposed at that level. It assumes that adverse effects of noise begin at a specific criterion, 55 dB, and that they reach a 100% level at 75 dB. At the heart of the impact calculation is a parameter called fractional impact, which varies linearly from 0 at 55 dB to 1 at 75 dB day-night equivalent noise level. The fractional impact is used to weight exposed subpopulations in arriving at a total equivalent population 100% impacted.

At day-night equivalent sound levels of 55 dB outdoors, indoor levels may be near 45 dB, allowing 100% intelligibility for all types of speech material. After a 20 dB increase above this level, intelligibility begins to drop very rapidly with further increases, supporting the assumption in the impact calculation that few people would be adversely impacted at 55 dB, while at 75 dB virtually everyone would be adversely affected.

Extent of Traffic Noise Exposure

Table 13.4 shows populations exposed to urban traffic noise at various levels. These figures, estimated by EPA for 1975, may be used to calculate the impact measure of Table 13.3 for current conditions. Furthermore, reductions in impact may be found for assumed reductions in total urban traffic noise, as shown in Table 13.5.

The reduction in noise impact from Table 13.5 is plotted versus reduction in traffic noise in Fig. 13.3. The solid curve in Fig. 13.3 shows that the reduction in noise impact is most rapid for the initial reduction in traffic noise when noise impact units (reduction in total equivalent people impacted) are used. For comparison, the dashed curve

TABLE 13.3

MEASURES OF COMMUNITY NOISE IMPACT

L_c = Criterion for outdoor day-night equivalent noise level (level at which adverse impacts are considered to begin)

L_i = Outdoor day-night equivalent sound level exposure for population P_i

FI_i = Fractional impact of noise on population P_i

$$FI_i = \begin{cases} 0.05 \, (L_i - L_c), & L_i > L_c \\ \\ 0, & L_i \leq L_c \end{cases}$$

P_{eq} = Noise impact units (equivalent population 100% impacted)

$$P_{eq} = \sum_i P_i \cdot FI_i$$

Δ = Percent reduction in noise impact units

$$\Delta = 100 \, \frac{P_{eq} \,(\text{before}) - P_{eq}\,(\text{after})}{P_{eq}\,(\text{before})}$$

TABLE 13.4

ESTIMATED NUMBER OF PEOPLE SUBJECTED TO URBAN TRAFFIC NOISE

Source: Ref. 2, Table 6-4.

At or Above Outdoor L_{dn}	People, Millions
55 dB	93.4
60	59.0
65	24.3
70	6.9
75	1.3

TABLE 13.5

NOISE REDUCTION RESULTS

Source: Ref. 2, Table B-1

| | Recent Conditions | | L_{dn} Noise Reduction in Decibels | | | | | | | |
| | | | 0 | | 5 | | 10 | | 15 | |
L_{dn} dB	Population exposed to higher L_{dn}, millions	P_i, millions	FI_i	FI_iP_i, millions	FI_i	FI_iP_i, millions	FI_i	FI_iP_i, millions	FI_i	FI_iP_i, millions
55	93.4	34.4	0.125	4.3	0	0	0	0	0	0
60	59.0	34.7	0.375	13.0	0.125	4.3	0	0	0	0
65	24.3	17.4	0.625	10.9	0.375	6.5	0.125	2.2	0	0
70	6.9	5.6	0.875	4.9	0.625	3.5	0.375	2.1	0.125	0.7
75	1.3	1.2	1.125	1.4	0.875	1.1	0.625	0.8	0.375	0.5
80	0.1	0.1	1.375	0.1	1.125	0.1	0.875	0.1	0.625	0.1
Total Equivalent People Impacted, P_e (millions)				34.6		15.5		5.2		1.3
Percent Reduction in Impact, Δ				0		55		85		96

335

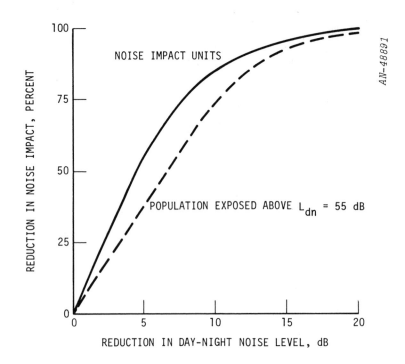

Figure 13.3. **Reduction of Urban Traffic Noise and Its Impact**

---

in Fig. 13.3 shows percent reduction in total population exposed above the 55 dB level. This reduction also rises most rapidly for the initial reductions in traffic noise, but not quite so rapidly as the reduction in noise impact units.

The "complainants" curve of Fig. 13.2 is in basic agreement with the dashed curve of Fig. 13.3. If the percentages of complainants indicated at 55 and 75 dB day-night levels are taken to represent 0 and 100% impact, then the percentage impact reduction versus noise reduction from 75 dB in Fig. 13.2 coincides with the dashed curve in Fig. 13.3.

In the following, the solid curve of Fig. 13.3 will be used in calculating the effects on noise impact of quieter conventional vehicles and of quiet electric cars. This is more conservative than use of the dashed curve would be: it will attribute more of the projected impact reductions to improved conventional cars and less to quiet electric cars.

Baseline Levels of Vehicular Noise

To determine the changes in vehicular noise and noise impacts which may result from the use of electric cars, it is first necessary to determine baseline levels of noise and noise impacts for conventional traffic. In Table 13.6, median "passby" noise levels at 15 meters (50 feet) are presented for conventional vehicles. These passby noise levels are composites which average emissions during cruise and acceleration conditions representative of urban driving. In all cases, cruise speed was taken to be 43 kilometers per hour (27 mph). Levels of acceleration were not necessarily maximums achievable, but rather those typical of urban conditions. Autos were assumed to be accelerating 17% of the time, while other vehicles were assumed to accelerate 20% of the time.

TABLE 13.6

VEHICULAR NOISE LEVELS AND TRAFFIC MIX

Source: Ref. 2, Tables 6-5 and 6-6.

| | Median Passby Noise Level at 15 m, dB(A) | | Percent of Urban Traffic |
	Present	After Regulation	
Heavy Duty Trucks	85	71	1.0
Medium Duty Trucks	77	71	6.0
Buses	79	75	0.5
Motorcycles	82	78	1.0
Automobiles	65	(to be determined)	91.5

In Table 13.6, present passby noise levels are those presently measured and computed. Levels after regulation are those expected to be achieved in the 1990's, after standards recently promulgated for trucks, buses, and motorcycles have been in effect long enough for older, noisier vehicles to disappear from use. A Federal standard has not yet been established for automobiles.

The traffic mix shown in Table 13.6 is used in calculating overall traffic noise level. Noise powers corresponding to the decibel levels in the table are weighted by the mix percentages in order to determine total noise power for the typical traffic mix.

Future reductions in overall urban traffic noise will depend on the future level of automobile noise, whether from conventional or electric cars. In the absence of a standard for automobiles, impacts are first estimated here for a range of automotive noise levels. Specific possible levels for future conventional and electric cars are considered in Sec. 13.3.

Impact of Urban Traffic Noise

The impact of urban traffic noise in 1975 is shown in Table 13.5, i.e., 34.6 million equivalent people impacted. Hereafter, this level will be taken as the baseline relative to which percentage reductions will be found (as in Table 13.3) as overall traffic noise levels are reduced by the admixture of quieter conventional vehicles and quieter electric automobiles.

Figure 13.4 shows how the impact of traffic noise decreases with reductions in automotive passby noise. The dashed curve in Fig. 13.4 shows impacts given present levels of truck, bus, and motorcycle noise. Evidently, quieter automobiles at present would reduce impact relatively little because of the dominance of these other sources of traffic noise. The solid curve in Fig. 13.4 shows that after current regulations have had their effects on the truck, bus, and motorcycle

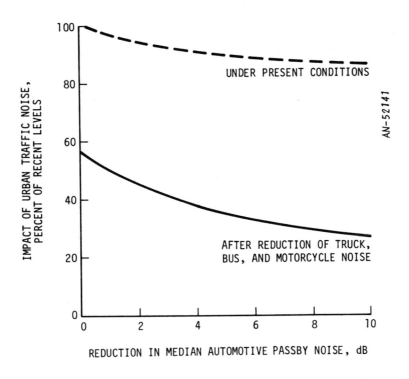

Figure 13.4. **Effect of Reductions in Auto Noise**

population in use, traffic noise impact will be reduced 43% even if automobiles are not quieted at all. Under these conditions, automotive
quieting can make a much more important contribution to further reduction
of traffic noise impact.

The impact levels in Fig. 13.4 for zero reduction of automotive noise
were calculated from Tables 13.6 and 13.5. Changes with reductions in automotive noise were calculated by first finding the reduction in day-night
noise level for the traffic mix and other conditions of Table 13.6, and then
determining the reduction in impact at this noise level from Fig. 13.3. The
results presented in these figures are similar to those sketched in
Scenarios A and C of Ref. 2.

To determine the effects of electric car use, it is next necessary to investigate the sources of automotive noise, the prospective quieting of conventional automobiles, and the likely noise levels of well-engineered electric cars of the future.

13.3 REDUCTIONS OF AUTOMOTIVE NOISE

Current Sources of Automotive Noise

Noise from current automobiles emanates principally from five sources:

- Exhaust
- Fan
- Engine
- Air intake
- Tires

For most automobiles, exhaust noise predominates at cruise speeds under roughly 60 kilometers per hour (35 mph). At higher speeds tire noise becomes equally significant. During acceleration, exhaust and other engine-related noises increase drastically. The automobile passby noise level in Table 13.6 is a composite of 60 dB(A) at 43 kilometer per hour cruise (27 mph) and 72 dB(A) during urban acceleration (noise during maximum acceleration would be much higher). In the composite 65 dB(A) figure of Table 13.6, acceleration noise contributes considerably more to the total than cruise noise, so reductions in acceleration noise will be critical for the eventual reduction of noise impact.

Noise Levels for Future Conventional Cars

Engine and engine-related noises may be reduced by improved design. Tire noise is then likely to dominate, at least during cruise, limiting the maximum reductions from the current 60 dB level of urban cruise noise. Tread vibration is the primary contributor to passby tire noise, and tread design can be changed only within limits which ensure adequate control and braking for safety. As one authority observes, "The structure of the pneumatic tire is basically fixed by the many functions it must perform. Significant further tire noise reduction will be very difficult without changing this basic structure."[6]

As shown in Fig.13.5, taken from coast-down tests at a sideline distance of 7.5 meters (25 feet), tire noise is currently about 65 dB(A) at 48 kilometers per hour and varies with the fourth power of speed.[6] At 43 kilometers per hour, this figure would be reduced to 63 dB(A). Doubling the sideline distance to 15 meters would reduce the reading by about 5 dB, leading to a level of 58 dB for tire noise in urban cruise.

This suggests a maximum reduction from the current 60 dB(A) cruise noise of only two decibels, even if engine and engine-related noise are almost entirely eliminated. In fact, they will not. be perfectly controlled, but tire noise may be reduced moderately in compensation.

Overall, it seems reasonable to assume a future cruise noise of 58 dB(A), due primarily to tire noise.

It should be noted that tire noise depends considerably on many factors. Different pavement surfaces account for variations of 5 to 7 dB. Wet pavement may increase noise 10 dB. Tread wear may increase noise 2 dB. Variations of 1 dB are produced by 30% under-inflation or over-inflation. Changes in tire loading may, for certain tread patterns, change noise by 1 dB. Low-aspect-ratio tires, desirable in some designs for energy efficiency, may increase noise 2 dB.[2,7]

In urban acceleration, present cars are 12 dB(A) noisier than in urban cruise. This noise is primarily engine-related, and in consequence may be reduced more than cruise noise because it is nearly independent of tire noise. A reduction in acceleration noise twice that for cruise noise, 4 dB, is assumed. This would leave acceleration noise at 68 dB, 10 dB above future cruise noise. A 10 dB differential is assumed in the projected scenarios of the Task Force on Automotive Goals for the 1980s.[2]

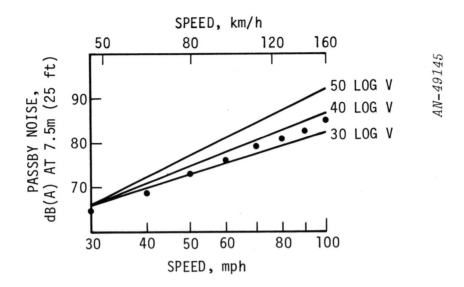

Figure 13.5. Tire Noise Versus Speed (from Ref. 6)

The assumed cruise and acceleration noise levels result in a weighted composite of 62 dB(A) for future conventional cars, 3 dB below the present value.

Noise Levels for Future Electric Cars

Electric cars do not have an engine, radiator fan, air intake, or exhaust. Instead, they have only an electric motor and controller, which are typically much quieter than the components they replace in the internal combustion automobile. Experimental data indicating quantitatively the quietness of electric cars is scarce, however.

In the "Intercollegiate Clean Air Car Race" held in 1970, noise levels were measured for several electric automobiles. The quietest

electric car, designed from the ground up for electric propulsion, produced passby cruise noise of 58 dB(A) at 48 kilometers per hour (30 mph)
and about 15-meter (50 feet) sideline distance.[*]

Noise from an electric car developed at Cornell was measured and
compared with measured noise from 35 other experimental cars with internal
combustion engines.[8] The electric car was 12 dB quieter than the average
of the internal combustion vehicles (64 dB versus 76.3 dB, for 48 kilometer per hour cruise at 7.5 meter sideline distance). Doubling the
sideline distance typically decreases measurements 5 dB, suggesting a
59 dB sound pressure level at 15 meters. Since the Cornell measurements
were not A-weighted, however, this level is not directly comparable to
the 58 dB(A) figure above. The 12 dB differential relative to conventional
cars, however, clearly suggests that electric cars are advantageous.

Noise measurements on vehicles with gasoline and electric propulsion
were recently reported by the Japanese Government in a paper describing the
Japanese program of electric vehicle development.[9] Figure 13.6, reproduced
from the paper, shows noise comparisons under four conditions which unfortunately are not described in any further detail in the published paper.
Here the noise levels are stated in phons, a unit of noise measurement
with frequency weightings corresponding to those of the human ear. They
differ from A-weighted sound levels largely in that the weighting varies
with the total amplitude of the sound. The variation in weighting over
the range from 60 to 80 phons is not great, however, so the differences
between gasoline and electric vehicles in Fig. 13.6 are indicative of the
differences in A-weighted sound levels which might be expected.

---

[*]Private communication, Mr. Charles Dietrick, Bolt Beranek and Newman, Inc.

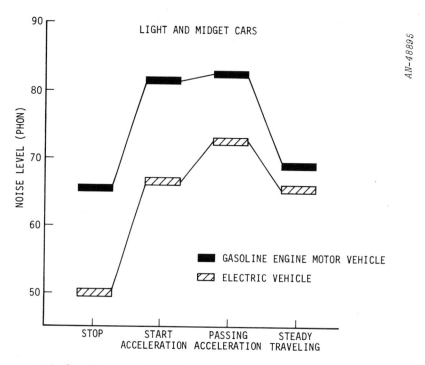

Figure 13.6. **Measured Noise of Japanese Test Cars** (from Ref. 9)

In view of the above, it will be assumed here that the cruise noise of the electric car in urban driving will be about 58 dB(A), due primarily to tire noise. This is in line with the measurements above, and with current findings on tire noise. During acceleration, the noise of the electric car will be taken as 61 dB(A). This corresponds to a 3 dB(A) increase during urban acceleration, or a doubling of noise power. The resultant composite noise level for the future electric car is 58.7 dB(A), corresponding to a reduction of 6.3 dB(A) from the current composite of 65˙dB(A) for conventional automobiles.

Effective control of noise is assumed for this electric car, just as in the case of the quiet future conventional car which it would replace. In particular, the penetrating whine emitted by some recent electric cars is assumed to be eliminated or drastically reduced. This whine appears to result from chopper control of large armature currents and resultant magnetostrictive effects in the motor and any external inductor required. Use of field control, battery switching, and other types of motors are all possible remedies. So also are special acoustic enclosures, which have proven effective in attenuating magnetostrictive noise from electrical transformers.

13.4   EFFECTS OF ELECTRIC CARS ON TRAFFIC NOISE IMPACTS

Figure 13.1 is a reproduction of Fig. 13.4 in which noise level reductions are indicated for improved conventional cars, and for electric cars at various levels of use. Passby noise levels were assumed as described in Sec. 13.3:

	Urban Cruise	Urban Acceleration	Composite
Conventional Car			
Current	60 dB(A)	72 dB(A)	65 dB(A)
Future	58	68	62
Electric Car	58	61	59

As Fig. 13.1 shows, desirable reductions in the future impacts of traffic noise are likely with the wide use of electric cars. Even though conventional cars are expected to be considerably quieter in the future, substitution of electric cars could reduce the future level of noise impact by as much as one-third. Quieting of other vehicles--trucks, buses, and motorcycles--in accord with adopted standards is a prerequisite for this benefit; otherwise, the noise from passenger cars will remain a minor factor in the overall impact of urban traffic noise.

SECTION 13 REFERENCES

1. Noise Control Act of 1972, Section 2.

2. "Air Quality, Noise and Health," report of a panel of the Interagency Task Force on Motor Vehicle Goals Beyond 1980, US Department of Transportation TAD-443.1, March 1976.

3. Wilson, et al., Transportation Noise: Impacts and Analysis Techniques, Argonne National Laboratories, 1973.

4. A. F. Meyer, Jr., "EPA's Implementation of the Noise Control Act of 1972," Sound and Vibration, December 1975.

5. J. E. Roberts and J. O. Borthwick, "Florida's Approach to Motor Vehicle Noise Control," Sound and Vibration, December 1975.

6. M. G. Richards, "Automotive Tire Noise - A Comprehensive Study," Sound and Vibration, May 1974.

7. Ralph K. Hilquist and Phillip C. Carpenter, "A Basic Study of Automobile Tire Noise," Sound and Vibration, February 1974.

8. J. L. Posson, "Cornell's Electric Car," Engineering: Cornell Quarterly, Vol. 8, No. 4, Winter 1974.

9. Research and Development of Electric Vehicles in Japan, Agency of Industrial Science & Technology, Ministry of International Trade & Industry, and Society of Automotive Engineers of Japan, Inc., 1977.

346

14 OTHER IMPACTS

Though air pollution and noise are more important, there are many other ecological effects of using electric cars instead of conventional cars. Singled out for specific attention in this section are four areas of lesser effect which have been subjects of particular public concern in the past:

- **Thermal pollution** by large power plants, which use of electric cars would increase

- **Impairments of public health and safety** due to coal and nuclear power plants, which use of electric cars would increase

- **Abandonment of automobile hulks**, which would tend to be reduced by long-lived electric cars with high salvage value

- **Dumping of waste oil**, which would be reduced by use of electric cars having no crankcase oil to be periodically changed

Though the importance of these effects is difficult to estimate, especially in the case of risks from nuclear reactors, fuels, and wastes, all appear to be only minor factors in the overall desirability of electric cars.

14.1 THERMAL POLLUTION

Electric cars were shown in Sec. 9 to be about as efficient overall as conventional cars fueled from petroleum, if typical losses in electric utilities are included. They would thus have little effect on total energy used and eventually released as heat into the environment. In conventional cars, however, almost all this heat is evolved when and where the cars are driven. In electric cars only about a third of the total heat would be released this way. The remainder would be evolved at a relatively few power plants during recharging, and concentrated releases of heat can potentially produce significant environmental disturbances.

In the past, "once-through" cooling has been customary for power plants because it has been the cheapest way to disperse the heat energy from the fuel which cannot be converted into electricity. In once-through cooling, river or ocean water is pumped through a heat exchanger in the plant in such volume that its temperature rise is acceptable. In the future, however, neither river water nor coastal sites are likely to remain readily available for cooling power plants. Protection of coastal resources has become an important goal on both the Atlantic and Pacific seaboards, river flows are insufficient to accept much more heat with acceptable increases of water temperature, and a study of power plant cooling concludes that few sites for once-through cooling will remain available after 1990.[1]

As a result, cooling of new power plants will shift to systems employing lakes, spray canals, and wet or dry cooling towers. In any of these means, the effective area in which waste heat is released is greatly reduced. For the moment, resultant atmospheric effects appear acceptable, but predictive models are poor and their results are correspondingly uncertain.[2]

In the long run, dry cooling towers will probably be necessary because insufficient water will be available to make up the evaporative losses in lakes and wet cooling towers. Lacking evaporative cooling, dry towers must provide for roughly five times greater air flow, and consequently may pose the most serious environmental problems. Dry cooling towers employ either natural convection or huge fans to move an enormous volume of air past heat exchangers through which a heated fluid or gas from the power plant is circulated. They may add 5% or more to the life cycle cost of a power plant. Because few dry cooling towers have been built in the past, little experience is available from which to determine either optimum design or probable environmental effects. The flow of heated air from the cooling tower could trigger thunderstorms and high winds in the immediate vicinity of the power plant, if large enough. Furthermore, the local heating could change the general pattern of precipitation. A detailed study for a hypothetical dry-cooled nuclear energy center in an arid region (Nevada) has been made, however, which indicates that dry cooling is feasible, and that even at a multiple-unit energy center with a capacity of about 15 gigawatts of electric power, atmospheric effects will be acceptable.[3]

Another analysis, nonetheless, reached a preliminary conclusion that still larger centers, producing over 20 gigawatts of electricity, will cause "unacceptable disturbances" including modification of rain and cloud patterns, and triggering of "severe weather events."[4] Whether electric energy centers of this size, including several power plants at the same location, will ever be built is uncertain. No such concentration of generating facilities exists today, but the shortage of acceptable sites for new plants may necessitate such centers if demand for electric power continues to grow rapidly.

Beyond this possibility of local problems lies a general potential problem of atmospheric heating which is sometimes discussed. In the last hundred years, there has been a gradual warming of the climate of the earth.[5] This may be in part due to discharges of pollutants from fossil fuels into the atmosphere; sulfates are particularly important, and emissions of sulfates would be increased by electric cars. On the other hand, carbon dioxide is also important in establishing the heat balance of the earth, and any shift towards nuclear power for recharging electric cars tends to reduce the total emissions of carbon dioxide.

14.2 HEALTH AND SAFETY

Large-scale use of electric cars could potentially affect public health and safety through changes in auto accidents, through conditions of workers in the battery and automobile industries, and through the increased generation of electric power. Since electric cars will probably meet the same safety standards as conventional cars and will equal the lower-performance conventional cars in acceleration, their overall effect on auto accidents should be small. If the lower capability of electric cars encourages more prudent driving, in fact, there may be positive benefits from their use. In manufacturing, protection of health is required by the Occupational Safety and Health Administration, which is presently seeking costly changes in battery manufacturing to reduce the exposure of battery workers to lead.[6] There remain the effects of increased generation of electric power, which appear to be considerably more consequential.

The extra amounts of coal and nuclear energy shown in Table 11.5 are upper bounds on requirements for electric cars. They result from the assumption that all personal cars in the United States will be electric. Though these changes in total power generation from coal and nuclear fuel seem modest on a relative basis, on an absolute basis they are only describable as immense. Even indirect and highly attenuated effects are potentially significant for these magnitudes of extra power generation.

The detrimental effects of power plants on public health and safety have been repeatedly analyzed in recent years, largely because of the fierce public debate over the desirability of nuclear power. The analyses show clearly that nuclear plants are not alone in presenting risks to health and safety; coal plants are also detrimental.[7,8,9] While some parts of these analyses are relatively secure, other very important parts require assumptions which are little more than guesswork. It has therefore been impossible to conclude whether nuclear plants are preferable to coal plants. It is clear, however, that use of electric cars would increase whatever the problems of nuclear and coal plants may be.

Tables 14.1-14.4 and Figs. 14.1-14.2 summarize the situation. They are reproduced from a document prepared as a basis for discussion in a symposium devoted to comparing coal and nuclear plants.[5] Though both the methods and the findings appearing in these charts are clearly tentative at best, they illustrate the major assumptions and the major ways in which use of electric cars might increase risks to public health and safety.

TABLE 14.1

SOCIAL AND ECONOMIC COSTS OF ALTERNATIVE COAL-ELECTRIC

FUEL CYCLES IN THE NEW YORK AREA, mills per kWh

Source: Ref. 5

	Plant Configuration		
Cost Elements	Appalachian Minemouth (High Sulfur Coal)	New York Location (Low Sulfur Coal)	New York Location (High Sulfur Coal and Flue Gas Desulfurization)
Economic:			
Capital	12.1	12.1	14.6
Operating	0.6	0.6	1.5
Fuel	6.5	8.5	6.9
Transportation	(AC line) 5.8	(unit train) 1.1	(unit train) 1.2
Economic Cost	25.0	22.3	24.2
Social:			
Sulfur oxide	4.1	3.2	1.1
Other consequences (Table 14.2)	0.44	0.56	0.56
Social Cost	4.5	3.8	1.7
TOTAL COST	29.5	26.1	25.9

TABLE 14.2

COAL FUEL CYCLE: SOCIAL COST ESTIMATES

Source: Ref. 5

Fuel Cycle Element	Social Cost, mills per kilowatt-hour
● Deep Mining	
– Subsidence and mine wastes	0.10
– Acid drainage	0.04
– Occupational hazards	0.11
Subtotal	0.25
● Surface Mining	
– Land disruption	0.10
– Acid drainage and water pollution	0.04
– Occupational hazards	0.02
Subtotal	0.16
Average for mining (36% Deep, 64% Surface)	0.19
Rail transportation	0.12
Power plant, excluding sulfur oxide emissions	0.25
Total social cost, excluding sulfur oxide emissions	0.56 m/kWh

Sulfur oxide emissions (no scrubbers):

Urban location	Low Sulfur	3.1
	High Sulfur	11.5
Rural location	Low Sulfur	1.3
	High Sulfur	4.1

TABLE 14.3

NOMINAL POLLUTION COSTS:

HIGH-SULFUR COAL IN APPALACHIAN PLANT

Source: Ref. 5

Cost of sulfur oxide emissions: representative calculation for remote plant emitting 16,700 kg of SO_x per hour (161.5×10^6 pounds of sulfur per year)

Costs computed based on 0.24 $\mu g/m^3$ ambient increase in sulfate and 0.58 $\mu g/m^3$ ambient increase in sulfur dioxide in metropolitan areas with a population of 50 million

Health Effects (computed at ambient level of 16 $\mu g/m^3$)

42,800 cases of chronic respiratory disease × $250 per case	$10.7 million
428,000 person-days of aggravated heart-lung disease symptoms × $20	8.6
84,000 asthma attacks × $10 each	0.9
10,400 cases of children's respiratory disease × $75	0.8
23 premature deaths × $30,000	0.7
Total Health Costs	$21.7 million

Materials Damage

$11.3 million per $\mu g/m^3$ of SO_4 × 0.24	2.7 million
$3.0 million per $\mu g/m^3$ of SO_2 × 0.58	1.7
Aesthetics ($0.034 × 161.5 × 10^6 lb)	5.5
Acid rain ($0.015 × 161.5 × 10^6 lb)	2.3
Total Emissions Costs	$33.8 million
Emissions Cost Per Pound of Sulfur	21¢

Social Cost of SO_x Emissions = 4.83 mills per kWh

TABLE 14.4

SOCIAL AND ECONOMIC COSTS OF THE NUCLEAR-ELECTRIC FUEL CYCLE

(Mills per kWh)

Source: Ref. 5

Fuel Cycle Element	Total Economic Costs	Total Social Costs	Itemized Social Costs						
			Radiation Related					Nonradiation Related	
			Accident	Pu Diversion	Sabotage	Low Level	Occupational Hazards	Accidents	Occupational Hazards
Mining and Milling	1.14	.007					.0007		.006
Conversion	.10	.001							.001
Enrichment	.66	.001							.001
Transportation (above elements)	.0007	.0007						.0006	.0001
Fuel Fabrication	.32	.007	.00002	.0004	.006				.001
Fuel Transport	.001	.001		.001	.000004			.0002	.00003
Reactor	20.20	.04	.0006		.04	.00003	.001		.0001
Spent Fuel Transport	.14	.0005	$<10^{-7}$	.0002	.00001	.00001	.00001	.0003	.00005
Reprocessing (fuel credit)	.53 (-.441)	.003	.000002	.0004	.001	.00002	.0006		.0007
PuO$_2$ Transport	.0007	.001	$<10^{-9}$	.001	.00008				
High-Level Waste Transport	.01	.0002	$<10^{-7}$	.00007	.00001	.00006		.00004	.00001
High-Level Waste Disposal	.038		~ 0						
TOTAL (mills/kWh)	22.7	.06	.0006	.003	.05	.0001	.002	.001	.01

354

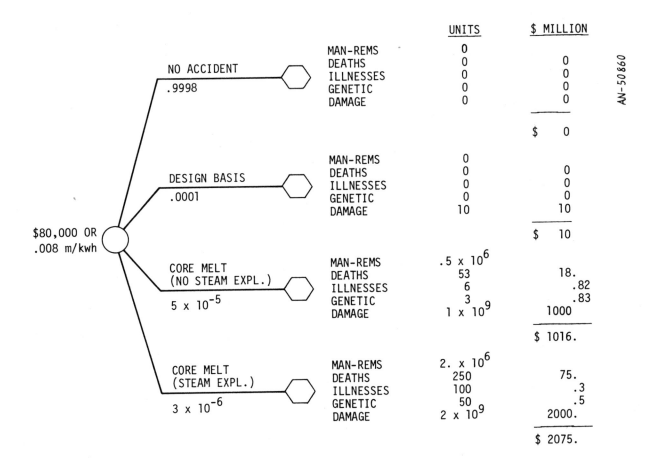

*SOCIAL VALUES FOR SAFETY DECISIONS

DEATH	$300,000
ILLNESS	3,000
GENETIC	10,000

Figure 14.1. Reactor Accident Summary (from Ref. 5)

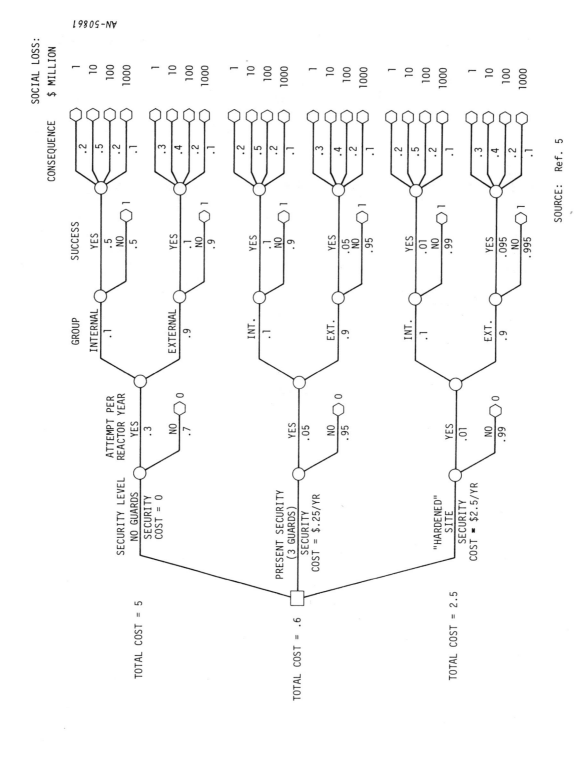

Figure 14.2. Simple Model of Reactor Sabotage

SOURCE: Ref. 5

356

Table 14.1 summarizes economic and social costs for coal-fired electric generation in the New York area, a particularly difficult region because of the high concentration of people exposed to emissions of air pollutants from regional power plants. Even with the assumption of scrubbers eliminating 90% of sulfur oxide emissions, it is these emissions which account for most of the social costs for each of the three different plant configurations shown.

The contributions to social cost from various factors are shown in Table 14.2; they reveal the care taken in the analysis to account for all aspects of environmental degradation and impairment of public safety and health. Table 14.3 illustrates steps in the estimation of the social costs of sulfur oxide emissions for one power plant. It shows both the incidence of health effects and the valuations attached to each, both of which are very uncertain.

To some extent, of course, the increased social costs of sulfur oxides emissions due to electric cars should be offset by reduced social costs from automotive emissions of hydrocarbons and carbon monoxide. A comprehensive attempt to evaluate the costs of losses due to all air pollutants, however, found 44% of the national total to be due to sulfur oxides and only 9% to oxidants (which result largely from hydrocarbons), while no value at all was established for costs of carbon monoxide, the pollutant most reduced by a switch to electric automobiles.[10] Apparently, then, the social costs of increased sulfur oxide emissions from power plants are much more important than the social costs eliminated for emissions reduced by electric cars.

Table 14.4 summarizes social and economic costs of nuclear electric energy. Again, a comprehensive approach is taken to the complete fuel cycle, and to the various economic and social costs associated with each step in the cycle. Here, however, the nature of social costs is very different. Whereas the primary social cost of the coal system resulted

357

from long-term exposure of large numbers of people to polluted air, the principal social cost for the nuclear system is attributed to reactor sabotage, a relatively infrequent event with potentially disastrous consequences if it occurs. Figures 14.1 and 14.2 suggest the origins of the social costs arising in unlikely but potentially serious circumstances: reactor accidents and reactor sabotage. In both cases, the assumed probabilities shown at each stage of the analysis are difficult at best to estimate, and in the case of sabotage they apparently defy quantification. In the discussion that followed the presentation of this material, participants in the symposium flatly concluded that "it is not possible to quantify the likelihood of sabotage attempts per year".[5]

Though Table 14.4 attributes relatively little social cost to the potential diversion of plutonium, many analysts have regarded it with great concern. Plutonium-239, the isotope of greatest importance, is used in atom bombs and constitutes at least 70% of the total plutonium produced in power reactors. About 20,000 kg of plutonium are produced each year at present, mostly remaining unprocessed in spent fuel rods from nuclear reactors. By the year 2000, worldwide production could be ten times as large.[7] Only six kilograms are necessary in metallic form to produce a fission explosion. Inadvertent chain reactions or diversion of plutonium by terrorists to clandestine bombs are possibilities which might lead both to local devastation and to dispersion of plutonium in the environment. Plutonium is comparable in toxicity to the potent biological toxins. Unlike them, however, it is not unstable and does not lose its activity in a few minutes of boiling. It remains a hazard for periods up to twenty times its half life, or about half a million years.[7]

The important problem of long-term nuclear waste is not even addressed in Table 14.4, though it has been a focus of public concern and remains an unresolved issue in the production of nuclear power. Largely from production of nuclear weapons, a large legacy of high-level radioactive wastes already exists, to which power plants are now adding significantly. The wastes are now stored in temporary facilities because efforts to devise permanent storage have not yet been successful. Since the temporary facilities can probably be maintained and managed indefinitely so as to assure public safety, the risks of these wastes are primarily for generations yet unborn. The wastes remain dangerous for over a hundred thousand years, a period so long that continued maintenance of "temporary" facilities to ensure safe storage cannot be guaranteed. A variety of techniques for permanent disposition of the wastes has been investigated: terrestrial disposal in geologically stable formations on land, or in the sea bed, or in ice sheets; rocketing the wastes into space; and transmutation into less hazardous elements.[11] As yet, no method has been shown to be acceptable. Proving that such proposed repositories as salt mines in Kansas will safely contain the wastes for one hundred thousand years or more is plainly difficult, and insistence on absolute assurances may be unrealistic. On the other hand, it has been observed that the history of waste management to date shows a frightening legacy "...which resulted from many small, past actions, premised on limited vision and constrained by few resources, severe time pressure, and overwhelming competing priorities."[12]

Overall, there seems little question that by requiring added generation of electricity, electric cars will detract from public health and safety. The effects, however, will surely be far less than proportionate to the extra electric energy required by electric cars. Since no new facilities will be needed, electric cars need not cause an increase in the number of nuclear reactors subject to accidents. Moreover, where diversion of plutonium and sabotage of reactors are the serious risks, they may not be increased significantly by electric cars. If reactors are already numerous and shipments of nuclear materials among them are already frequent, additional shipments may have little practical consequence for would-be terrorists or saboteurs already presented with abundant opportunities for action. Even if nuclear reactors were eliminated from the United States, as some groups have advocated, the rest of the world will continue to provide such opportunities. Rapid growth of nuclear power is expected abroad, especially in nations with few resources of the coal which is so abundantly available in the United States. In West Germany, for example, over 80% of electric energy in the year 2000 is expected to come from nuclear power plants.[7]

14.3 AUTO HULKS AND WASTE OIL

Disposal and discharge of solid and liquid wastes into the environment has been extensively regulated during the past decade. Continued promulgation and enforcement of such regulations ensures, for the most part, against adverse impacts on the environment arising from the manufacture and use of either electric or conventional automobiles.

Historically, however, there are two areas in which regulation has been or would be ineffective: the abandonment of worn-out automobiles, and the dumping of used crankcase oil from automotive engines. Both have been nationally recognized as significant problems, and both could potentially benefit significantly from a switch to electric cars.

Abandoned Automobiles

From 1958 to 1970, the estimated number of automobile hulks abandoned to the environment increased from one to thirteen million. In urban areas abandoned automobiles were removed by local authorities, but in rural areas rusting hulks accumulated by roadsides and in impromptu automobile graveyards. A number of studies were undertaken and abandoned automobiles were publicized as a national environmental problem.

Electric cars should be considerably more valuable as hulks and will therefore offer increased incentive for recovery and recycling rather than abandonment. Two thorough recent studies, however, indicate the problem of abandoned automobiles is rapidly disappearing, and furthermore is unlikely to recur despite the rapidly changing materials composition of conventional automobiles.[13,14] Thus there are likely to be few further benefits from introduction of electric cars.

The problem of abandoned automobiles was essentially economic in origin. During the last two decades, the open-hearth furnace has been replaced to a large degree by the basic oxygen furnace in producing iron and steel in the United States. As shown in Table 14.5, the basic oxygen furnace is operated with a much lower percentage of scrap in the feed. The result was an excessive supply of scrap, a low price for scrap, and a low value for automobile hulks. Retrieval of scattered hulks in rural areas was unprofitable, and they accumulated wherever they were abandoned.

More recently, however, the value of automobile hulks has been greatly increased by two innovations: automobile shredders, large machines which more effectively separate the materials composing an automobile hulk to yield a higher grade of steel scrap; and electrical furnaces for steel making, which are operated with nearly 100% scrap feed. A considerable regional steel industry has grown up around the electrical furnace, the demand for auto hulks has risen accordingly, and prices have reached levels at which retrieval of hulks long abandoned to the environment is underway. The situation is summarized in Fig. 14.3, which shows that the number of hulks processed has probably exceeded the number being retired for several years.

In the future, changes in the conventional automobile are projected to accentuate the demand for automobile hulks. Future automobiles will be smaller, and provide a smaller percentage of ferrous scrap as aluminum and plastics are more extensively employed to improve fuel economy. The overall result will be a reduction in the total supply of ferrous scrap, probably to be followed by intensified competition among the operators of shredders for automobile hulks, with higher prices which will make recycling even more advantageous.

A shift to electric cars would result in junked automobiles of even higher value. The propulsion battery will contain materials adding considerably to the value of the hulk, and as shown in Sec. 4, the weight and size of the batteries will make their removal and separate abandonment

TABLE 14.5

RELATIVE IMPORTANCE OF IRON-AND-STEEL-MAKING

FURNACES AND THEIR SCRAP UTILIZATION

Source: Ref. 14

Furnace Type	Average Content of Scrap Feed (1974), percent	Percent of Total Iron and Steel Production in United States		
		1966	1970	1974
Basic Oxygen Furnace	28.5	21.4	41.6	46.1
Open Hearth Furnace	46.0	51.9	31.9	20.6
Electrical Furnace	96.8	10.0	13.9	19.1
Cupola Furnace	88.0	10.3	8.9	8.8
Miscellaneous	N/A	6.4	2.7	5.4

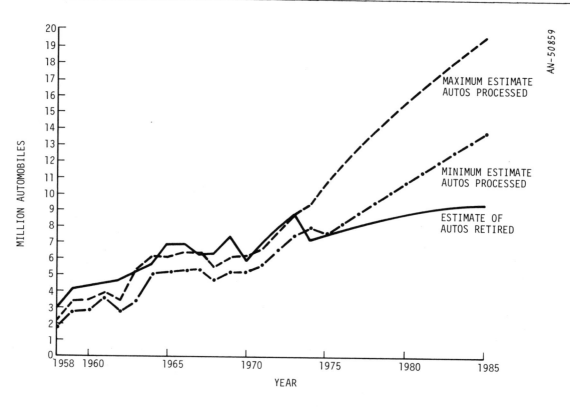

Figure 14.3. Estimates of Automobiles Retired and
Automobiles Required for Processing
by Shredders and Balers (from Ref. 13)

difficult. The present value of a hulk is about $100; at the current price for junked lead-acid batteries, a little over 10¢ per kilogram, a lead-acid propulsion battery would add over fifty percent to its value.[14] Moreover, the electric motor and controller are both likely to be in excellent condition at the end of the life of the ordinary automobile. Both motors and controllers are now designed for lifetimes which may exceed the typical 3000-5000 hours of internal-combustion engines by factors of ten or more. Quite apart from the considerable value of the copper in the motor, which alone may approach that of the conventional automobile hulk, the motor and controller should be as operable as when new and therefore correspondingly valuable. In consequence, electric cars seem even less likely to be abandoned in future years than conventional cars. The problem of abandoned automobiles, however, is disappearing so rapidly that there will be little benefit left to be obtained by substitution of electric for conventional cars.

Waste Oil

Lubricating oil in the crankcases of automotive engines is periodically drained and replaced with clean oil. The old oil is often collected and used as fuel, for road oiling, for asphalt, and for other purposes. Nevertheless, substantial quantities of oil are more or less indiscriminately dumped into the environment, particularly in rural areas where collection is presently unprofitable. A substantial amount of oil from automobiles is discarded by do-it-yourselfers, who buy about a third of all engine oil sold for automobiles. A survey found that of the waste oil drained from crankcases by do-it-yourselfers, 58% was haphazardly discarded: 33% in backyards, 11% in sewers, 11% in public dumps, and 3% in vacant lots.[14]

Electric cars have no crankcases and require no periodic changes of crankcase oil. To the extent they were used, the problem of discarded oil from automobiles would be eliminated. Accomplishing this objective by other reasonable means may be unlikely.

In 1964, a law controlling the disposal of lubricating oil was passed in West Germany, and legislation to the same end has been considered widely in Europe, attesting to the seriousness of the problem. In the United States, the Federal Water Pollution Control Act Amendments of 1972 directed the Environmental Protection Agency to determine the extent of problems resulting from waste oils and the effect of various disposal techniques on the environment.[14]

The findings of the subsequent study performed by the Environmental Protection Agency were reported to Congress in 1974.[15] They fell short, however, of conclusively determining either the quantity of waste oil "surreptitiously" dumped into the environment, or the environmental effects which resulted. A supporting study for the EPA report noted that "little is known about the disposal of used oil in America," and "the environmental damages resulting from these disposal practices are of uncertain magnitude."[14] Nevertheless, the EPA report to Congress does demonstrate that used oil and its contaminants are toxic to various forms of life, and that the quantities discarded into the environment are considerable, even if imprecisely known.

Figure 14.4 summarizes the estimated flows of lubricating oils in the United States to original users, to various losses and recoveries, and finally to disposal by "other means," generally in landfills, in storm and sanitary sewers, and on vacant land.[15] Proportionately, less automotive waste oil is recovered than waste oil from industry, aviation, and government. About a third of the estimated 821 million liters per year of discarded automotive waste oil comes from do-it-yourselfers. In this figure, "automotive" oils include those used for trucks, buses, and other motor vehicles besides passenger automobiles.

For lack of more detailed data, the rationale summarized in Table 14.6 served as the basis for estimating quantities of waste oil shown in Fig. 14.4.[15] The importance of assumptions, as opposed to documented

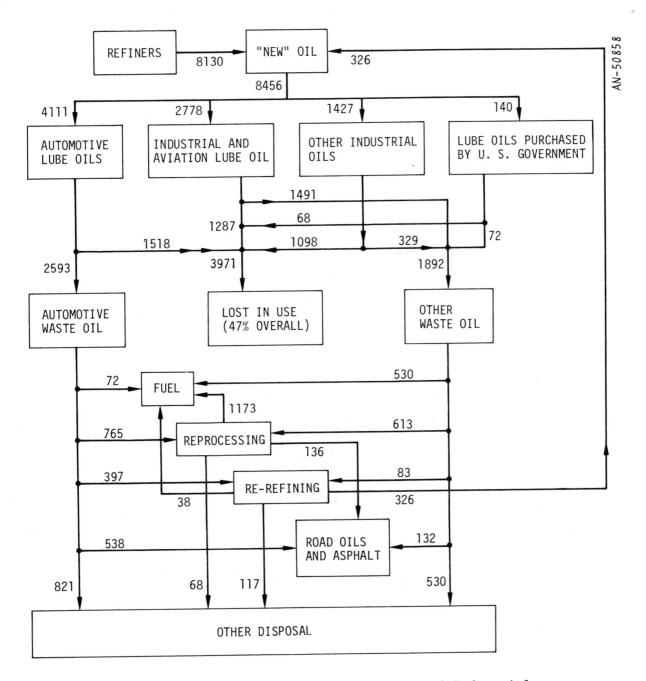

Figure 14.4. Principal Flows of Lubricating and Industrial
Oils, 1972 (in millions of liters)

365

TABLE 14.6

ESTIMATE OF FACTORS FOR CONVERTING AUTOMOTIVE SALES
TO WASTE OIL QUANTITIES

Source: Ref. 15

Service Stations

70% of oil sold is used for changes.
Oil drained is 90% of filled capacity.
70% × 90% = 63% of oil sold = waste oil generated.

Garages and Auto Supply Stores

Assume average is same as service stations (63%).

New Car Dealers

100% of oil sold is used for changes.
Oil drained is 90% of filled capacity.
100% × 90% = 90% of oil sold = waste oil generated.

Retail Sales for Commercial Engines

Assume same as service stations (63%)

Automotive Fleet and Other Lube Oil Uses

Assume 50%, allowing for two-cycle engines and internal use,
e.g., fuel, by commercial and governmental fleets.

Factory Fills, Automotive and Farm

Assume 90% recovery as in automotive service centers.

Oil Bought at Discount Stores

Assume same as service stations (63%).
Assume 35% of waste oil generated finds its way to service stations.
63% × 35% = 22% of oil sold = waste oil generated at service stations.

observations, is considerable. Perhaps the most important of these is
the general assumption that some 50% of all lubricating oils are "lost in
use" and therefore never enter the category of waste oils. To the extent
that less oil might be lost in use, the oil reaching the "other disposal"
category would be increased. Since the "lost in use" estimate is so large,
any change in this assumption would change the "other disposal" figure
by over three times as great a percentage.

Though electric cars would significantly reduce the quantities
of automotive waste and discarded oil, they would be least able to do so
in the rural areas where collection of used oil is now most difficult and
least effective. Because the situation is changing rapidly, moreover, it
is difficult to make projections for the future. On the one hand, recommended
intervals between oil changes for passenger automobiles have been steadily
increasing for many years: for 1978 models, intervals are for as long as
twelve months and 16,000 kilometers, three times what they often were just
a decade ago. Synthetic lubricants may allow them to be doubled again, or
even more.[16] Their effects if discarded in the environment, however, may
be quite different. Meanwhile, the growing popularity of do-it-yourself
automotive maintenance and discount merchandising tends to increase the
fraction of waste oil from automobiles which is dumped in yards, drains,
and sewers, potentially offsetting decreases in the total amount of waste
oil due to less frequent changes.

Overall, electrification of all automobiles in the United States would
eliminate the use of about 2 billion liters of oil per year for automobile
crankcase oil. This amounts to almost 59% of all automotive demand for
lubricating oils, 28% of all demand for lubricating oils, 1% of all use
of petroleum by automobiles, and a quarter of a percent of all US use of
petroleum.

SECTION 14 REFERENCES

1. D. E. Peterson, J. C. Sonnichsen, _Assessment of Requirements for Dry Towers_, HEDL-TME-76-82, Hanford Engineering Development Laboratory, Richland, Washington, September 1976.

2. J. E. Carson, _Atmospheric Effects of Evaporative Cooling Systems_, ANL/ES-53, Argonne National Laboratory, Illinois, October 1976.

3. _Technical, Environmental, and Socioeconomic Factors Associated with Dry-Cooled Nuclear Energy Centers_, BNWL-1985, Battelle Pacific Northwest Labs, Richland, Washington, April 1976.

4. L. R. Koenig, and C. M. Bhumralkar, _On Possible Undesirable Atmospheric Effects of Heat Rejection From Large Electric Power Centers_, R-1628-RD, The RAND Corporation, Santa Monica, CA, December 1974.

5. R. Bernardi, et al., _Quantitative Environmental Comparison of Coal and Nuclear Generation: Workshop Summary_, NSF/OEP-76-003, Mitre Corporation, McLean, Virginia, September 1975.

6. "Making Lead as Costly as Gold," _Business Week_, Jan. 24, 1977, p. 26.

7. E. E. El-Hinnawi, _Review of the Environmental Impact of Nuclear Energy_, IAEA-CN-36/361, International Atomic Energy Agency, Vienna, Austria, 1977.

8. L. D. Hamilton, _Energy and Health: The Health Impacts of Present and Alternative Energy Sources and Policies_, BNL-21395, Brookhaven National Laboratory, Upton, New York, 1976.

9. C. D. Brown, et al., _The Environmental Effects of Using Coal for Generating Electricity_, NUREG-0252, Argonne National Laboratory, Illinois, May 1977.

10. Thomas E. Waddell, _The Economic Damages of Air Pollution_, EPA 600-5-74-012 W74 11798, Washington Environmental Research Center, May 1974.

11. _High-Level Radioactive Waste Management Alternatives_, WASH-1297, US Atomic Energy Commission, Washington, D.C., May 1974.

12. T. LaPorte, et al., _Space Disposal of Nuclear Wastes_, N77-24924, University of California, December 1976.

13. R. W. Roig, et al., _Impacts of Material Substitution in Automobile Manufacture on Resource Recovery_, EPA-600/5-76-007, US Environmental Protection Agency, Washington, July 1976.

14.   William A. Irwin, et al., <u>Used Oil in the United States and Europe</u>, EPA 600/5-74-025, US Environmental Protection Agency, Washington, July 1974.

15.   <u>Waste Oil Study: Report to Congress</u>, US Environmental Protection Agency, Washington, April 1974.

15   SUPPLIES AND RESOURCES OF KEY MATERIALS

Because automobiles are manufactured in enormous quantities, their
demands for materials are formidable. In the US, for example, auto manufacturing accounts for 17% of all iron and steel, 33% of all zinc, and 59%
of all synthetic rubber used each year.[1] If the electric cars envisioned
in Sec. 4 were to replace conventional cars, most of the required materials
would be little affected. The significant changes would be in battery
materials, and to a lesser extent in copper required for windings of the
electric motor.

To electrify 10% of US automobiles, a reasonable upper bound by
2000 in the absence of drastic changes in the marketplace, considerable
increases in production of materials would be necessary. They are probably
feasible, however, and recoverable reserves are sufficient to supply them.
To manufacture propulsion batteries for all US automobiles expected on the
road in 2000, however, identified reserves of materials in the US or in the
entire world are barely adequate, and in practice complete extraction of these
reserves is unlikely. New discoveries of material resources, however, could
considerably improve prospects.

This situation is summarized in Table 15.1 for the active materials
of the representative batteries selected in Sec. 3 (excepting sulfur, which
is plentiful). The table shows the ratios of resources to the cumulative
demands projected for 1974 through 2000. The cumulative demands include
provision of lead-acid, nickel-zinc, or lithium-sulfur batteries for all
126 million personal cars projected to be available in the United States in
2000. Separate ratios are shown for US resources and demand, and for
resources and demand in the entire world. In the latter case, however,
only the US cars (roughly a third of the world total) are assumed to be
electrified. Material requirements per car are averages of the maximum
and minimum values required for the representative electric cars of Table
4.1. Resource estimates and demand projections come from US Geological
Survey and Bureau of Mines publications.

TABLE 15.1

RESOURCES OF BATTERY MATERIALS IN RELATION TO CUMULATIVE DEMAND, 1974-2000, INCLUDING ELECTRIFICATION OF ALL US AUTOMOBILES

Material	Ratio of Resource to Cumulative Demand, 1974-2000					
	Recoverable Reserves		Identified Resources		Potential Reserves	
	US	World	US	World	US	World
Lead	.8	1.0	1.7	1.8	.8	17
Nickel	–	1.4	.7	2.7	7.1	53
Zinc	.7	1.0	1.7	6.4	4.4	33
Lithium	.11	.23	.3	.7	1.3	42

The first pair of columns in Table 15.1 shows the ratio of recoverable reserves to cumulative demand. Recoverable reserves are those portions of identified resources (specific bodies of mineral-bearing material which are relatively well known) which could presently be extracted economically and legally. In Table 15.1, it is clear that the US has insufficient recoverable reserves of any of the four battery materials to meet cumulative demands through 2000 including electrification of all US passenger cars. World reserves would be barely sufficient for cumulative demands including electrification of US autos for the lead-acid and nickel-zinc batteries, but not for the lithium-sulfur batteries. For comparison, world reserves of petroleum are about equally large: just sufficient to cover cumulative world demand through the year 2000.

Identified resources of battery materials are much bigger, of course, than the recoverable reserves estimated in 1974 and used as a basis for the first columns of Table 15.1 The identified resources in the middle columns of Table 15.1 are as well-known as recoverable reserves and include

371

them, but they also include subeconomic resources which could be economically extracted only at higher prices than those recently prevailing. Except in the case of lithium, identified resources are more than sufficient for electrifying all cars in the United States by 2000.

Finally, a much more speculative category of resources, potential reserves, is shown at the right of Table 15.1. Potential reserves include not only the presently known recoverable reserves, but also potential new discoveries that would become recoverable reserves--i.e., the material could be economically extracted at recent prices. Estimates of potential reserves are based on the relative abundance of the elements in the earth's crust, and the assumption that equal fractions of each element are actually recoverable at current prices. The implication is that the portion which has so far been specifically identified as recoverable reserves depends primarily on the effort which has been expended in prospecting and exploration. Since the recoverable reserves of lead are larger in relation to crustal abundance than those of any other material, they are assumed to represent the degree to which intense exploration for any material could be successful in locating recoverable reserves. In Table 15.1, then, there is no difference between potential reserves and recoverable reserves of lead in the United States, which has already been intensively explored. In the world, however, potential reserves of lead are much larger than 1974 recoverable reserves. For nickel, zinc, and lithium, potential reserves are very much greater than either identified resources or recoverable reserves, and worldwide they are vastly more than would be required for electrification of all US automobiles.

Beyond potential reserves, there are presumably other undiscovered resources which are subeconomic at present prices with present methods of extraction. Eventually, they also could provide battery materials. Thus there are encouraging prospects for new discoveries which would be more than adequate to electrify all the world's automobiles. Presently identified reserves of most battery materials for electric cars, however, are no more abundant worldwide than reserves of petroleum for meeting future needs.

15.1 MATERIALS REQUIRED FOR AUTOMOBILES

The representative electric cars described in Sec. 4 require the same manufacturing procedures and materials as future conventional cars, except for the electric motor and propulsion battery. A shift to electric cars would therefore only affect the production and resources of materials to the extent that the electric motor and the battery differ from the internal combustion engine system of the conventional car.

Typical requirements for materials in recent and projected US automobiles are shown in Table 15.2. The future automobile requires considerably less material overall, with higher proportions of light materials such as aluminum and plastics.[2]

The electric motor which replaces the gasoline engine will be largely iron and steel, like the conventional engine. It will, however, include windings of copper wire weighing perhaps 25 kilograms for a typical 150-kilogram motor.[3] This is considerably more than the copper content of present automobiles, which is largely in the radiator. It might double the copper content of each car. The US auto industry now uses only 8% of all US copper, however, so the maximum effect of a complete shift to electric cars would be to increase copper demand less than 10%. If accomplished over a period of years, this would have little effect either on production or on reserves and resources, so it will not be considered further in this section.

Materials required for batteries, however, are a major addition to the typical materials shown in Table 15.2. Materials required for the representative batteries of Sec. 3 are shown, per unit of battery capacity, in Table 15.3. Total requirements per car, depending on range and battery type, are shown in Table 15.4 for the representative electric cars projected in Table 4.1. For materials such as lead and zinc which are already used in cars, the amounts required for batteries are far larger than in Table 15.2.

TABLE 15.2

MATERIALS IN TYPICAL US AUTOS, 1975 AND 1995
Source: Ref. 2

Material	Weight, kg 1975	Weight, kg 1990	Percent 1975	Percent 1990
Steel	953	621	61.2	54.2
Cast Iron	253	91	16.2	7.9
Aluminum	45	136	2.9	11.9
Copper, Brass	15	6	1.0	.6
Zinc	13	4	.8	.3
Lead	10	8	.7	.7
Other Metals	4	16	.3	1.4
Rubber	72	58	4.6	5.0
Glass	38	32	2.4	2.8
Plastic	54	105	3.5	9.2
Other Non-Metal	101	68	6.5	6.0
	1559	1144	100.	100.

TABLE 15.3

POTENTIALLY SCARCE MATERIALS FOR BATTERIES

Battery Type	Nominal Capacity, Wh/kg	Material Required per kWh of Capacity, kg							
		Lead	Antimony	Nickel	Zinc	Cobalt	Lithium	Molybdenum	Yttrium
Recent Lead-acid	27	22	.5						
Improved Lead-acid	46	12	.2						
Nickel-zinc	77			3.3	3.5	.056			
Lithium/aluminum-iron sulfide	115					.10	.42	.30	.055

TABLE 15.4

BATTERY MATERIALS REQUIRED FOR REPRESENTATIVE ELECTRIC CARS

Car Range, km	Battery Type	Nominal Capacity, kWh	Material Required per Car, kg							
			Lead	Antimony	Nickel	Zinc	Cobalt	Lithium	Molybdenum	Yttrium
75	Lead-acid	23.6	520	12						
100	Lead-acid	18.8	230	3.8						
150	Lead-acid	30.6	370	6.2						
150	Nickel-zinc	26.0			86	88	1.5			
250	Nickel-zinc	51.2			169	180	2.9			
250	Lithium/aluminum-iron sulfide	36.7					3.7	15	11	2.0
450	Lithium/aluminum-iron sulfide	69.0					6.9	29	21	3.8

The projected requirements for the various battery materials are approximate, of course, and could differ considerably in the battery designs which may eventually prove most satisfactory. This is particularly likely for supporting materials as opposed to active materials. The antimony used to harden lead grids in lead-acid batteries, for example, may be totally replaced by more abundant materials as calcium. The cobalt added to the active electrode materials in nickel-zinc and lithium-sulfur batteries could conceivably be replaced, as could molybdenum current collectors and high-temperature insulators based on yttrium. For the active materials themselves, there are also other possibilities, as noted in Sec. 3. Sulfur is not included in Table 15.3 because it is already abundant and supplies are expected to increase rapidly as flue gases from power plants are desulfurized to comply with environmental regulations. The principal problem now facing the sulfur industry, in fact, is that huge quantities of sulfur which must be recovered to comply with environmental regulations "may be dumped on the market regardless of production costs."[4]

15.2 BASELINE PROJECTIONS FOR BATTERY MATERIALS

The starting point for estimating effects of electric cars on materials supplies and resources is a projection for the case in which few or no electric cars will be used. Such projections are regularly made by the US Bureau of Mines and reported in Mineral Facts and Problems. The fifth and most recent edition, published in 1976, deals systematically and in detail with all minerals of commercial importance, devoting a detailed analysis to each in its 1200 pages.[4] Its projections and estimates for battery materials are summarized in Tables 15.5-15.7.

In Table 15.5, primary demands for battery materials for 1974, 1985, and 2000 were taken directly from Mineral Facts and Problems. Figures for 1980 and 1990, years of particular concern in this analysis, were obtained by linear interpolation. Only primary demand is included, that is, demand for new materials. It is this demand which will be initially affected by electric automobiles. After electric automobiles have been in use long

TABLE 15.5

PRIMARY DEMAND FOR MATERIALS IN THE ABSENCE OF ELECTRIC CARS

Source: Ref. 4, pp. 28-29

Annual Demand, Millions of Kilograms

Material	1974 US	1974 World	1980 US	1980 World	1985 US	1985 World	1990 US	1990 World	2000 US	2000 World
Lead	845	3,077	978	3,952	1,089	4,681	1,189	5,410	1,388	6,867
Antimony	18	70	23	84	28	96	33	107	44	128
Nickel	199	704	219	850	236	971	274	1,128	349	1,442
Zinc	1,328	5,806	1,653	7,014	1,923	8,020	2,204	9,081	2,767	11,203
Cobalt	10.4	31.3	11.4	34.7	12.2	37.6	14.6	45.8	19.5	62.1
Lithium	4.5	7.3	5.5	9.8	6.4	11.8	8.5	16.6	12.7	26.3
Molybdenum	34.5	90.7	41	117	46.3	139	60	181	87.5	266

TABLE 15.6

RESERVES AND RESOURCES OF MATERIALS
Source: Ref. 4, pages 32-33

Material	1974 Reserves,[1] Millions of kg		Identified Resources,[2] Millions of kg	
	US	World	US	World
Lead	53,500	150,000	108,000	300,000
Antimony	91	4,161	118	5,060
Nickel	--	54,000	13,600	112,000
Zinc	45,000	236,000	118,000	1,500,000
Cobalt	--	2,450	764	4,280
Lithium	297	675	840	1,910
Molybdenum	2,700	5,900	16,000	29,000
Yttrium	3.2	35	41	176

[1]A reserve is that portion of an identified resource from which a usable mineral can be economically and legally extracted at the time of determination.

[2]Identified resources are specific bodies of mineral-bearing material whose location, quality, and quantity are known from geological evidence supported by engineering measurements, and include reserves and subeconomic resources.

TABLE 15.7

SUPPLY OF MATERIALS IN THE ABSENCE OF ELECTRIC CARS

Source: Ref. 4, pages 27, 28, 29

Material	Ratio of US Primary Production to US Primary Demand*					Ratio to Cumulative Demand, 1974-2000, of:			
						Recoverable Reserves		Identified Resources	
	1974	1980	1985	1990	2000	US	World	US	World
Lead	.71	.65	.60	.61	.63	1.9	1.2	3.8	2.4
Antimony	.065	.055	.046	.047	.05	.1	1.6	.2	2.0
Nickel	.064	.24	.38	.49	.70	-	2.1	2.1	4.2
Zinc	.34	.31	.28	.31	.36	.9	1.1	2.3	6.9
Cobalt	~0	.26	.48	.63	.93	-	2.1	2.1	3.7
Lithium	>1	1.07	1.07	1.07	1.07	1.5	1.7	4.3	4.9
Molybdenum	1.47	1.75	1.99	1.99	1.99	2.0	1.4	>10	7.0

*From domestic resources

enough so that batteries are being retired from service, recycling will begin and there will be major effects on secondary supply and demand for materials. Since recycling will probably be well over 90% efficient, however, associated additional demand for primary production will be relatively small.

The reserves and resources of battery materials estimated in 1974 are shown in Table 15.6. In Table 15.7, the ratio of US primary production from domestic resources to US primary demand is first shown. Again, figures for 1980 and 1990 are linear interpolations between values obtained directly from Ref. 4. Where these ratios are greater than one, the US is an exporter of primary material; where they are less, the US must import. Some lead and most antimony are projected to be imported, in proportions near those of recent years. Though almost all nickel and cobalt have been imported recently, the projections envision rapid expansion of US production to account for most US primary production by 2000, with a consequent lessening of dependence on foreign suppliers for these battery materials. The US is expected to continue exporting lithium and molybdenum.

The ratios of recoverable reserves and identified resources to cumulative demand from 1974 to 2000 are also shown in Table 15.7. Aside from a notable US lack of antimony (which accounts for the high assumed imports through 2000), US and world reserves are only modestly greater than cumulative projected demand in the remainder of this century. This is a common situation for most materials, probably because there is little incentive for exploration so long as identified reserves are enough to last for 30, 40, and 50 years or more. The existence of substantial additional identified resources which are not recoverable at current prices also lessens the need for further exploration.

Except in the case of antimony, US identified resources are more than sufficient to accommodate cumulative US demand through 2000. US recoverable reserves, however, are considerably less. The increasing domestic production in Table 15.7, particularly of nickel and cobalt, follows from the projection that world prices will rise sufficiently to convert presently subeconomic

resources into recoverable reserves from which the US can obtain materials
at less expense than by importing.

15.3 EFFECTS OF ELECTRIC CARS

Initially, manufacturing electric cars in large quantity may tax the
capacity of plants for primary production of battery materials. Over the
years, the batteries in electric cars may come to contain a major portion
of the known resources of these materials. In the following, these two
potential effects are separately illustrated through simple quantitative
examples.

Eventually the size of the electric car fleet would stabilize, and
then additional primary production and resources would be necessary only
to the extent that materials were lost in recycling and remanufacturing
used batteries. Recycling processes have yet to be developed for most
future batteries, but they are expected to be very efficient for scarce
materials. In consequence, the eventual effects of recycling losses on
primary production and on resources would be relatively small and are not
considered further here.

The projected effects of manufacturing one million electric cars
per year on the demand for materials are shown in Table 15.8. The assumed
electric cars cover the various levels of technology and driving range
embodied in the representative cars of Table 4.1. The lower and upper
limits of tabulated increases correspond to the lower and upper design
ranges for the cars. The percentage increases are based on the quantities
of material per car shown in Table 15.4, and the demands in the absence
of electric cars shown in Table 15.5.

In Table 15.8, the increases in primary demand are particularly large
for nickel and lithium, though at least one material for each of the three
battery types is substantially affected. The huge increases in lithium
demand, despite the small amount of lithium required per car, are due to
the very small size of the lithium industry at present.

TABLE 15.8

INCREASED DEMAND FOR MATERIALS FROM MANUFACTURING

ONE MILLION ELECTRIC CARS PER YEAR

Percent Increase in Primary Demand for Materials

Car	Battery Material	1980		1990		2000	
		US	World	US	World	US	World
Recent (75 km)	Lead	53	13	44	9.6	37	7.6
	Antimony	52	14	36	11	27	9.4
Improved (100–150 km)	Lead	24–38	5.8–9.4	19–31	4.3–6.8	17–27	3.3–5.4
	Antimony	17–27	4.5–7.4	12–19	3.6–5.8	8.6–14.1	3.0–4.8
Improved (150–250 km)	Nickel	39–77	10–20	31–62	7.6–15	25–48	6.0–12
	Zinc	5.4–11	1.3–2.6	4.0–8.0	1.0–2.0	3.2–6.5	.8–1.6
	Cobalt	13–25	4.3–8.4	10–20	3.3–6.3	7.7–15	2.4–4.7
Advanced (250–450 km)	Cobalt	33–61	11–20	25–47	8.1–15	19–35	6.0–11.1
	Lithium	270–530	150–300	180–340	90–170	120–230	57–110
	Molybdenum	27–51	9.4–18	18–35	6.1–12	13–24	4.1–7.9

Demands for materials to manufacture a million electric cars per year would probably appear over several years rather than all at once. Over a decade, building up to this level of production would mean yearly increases not much greater than now projected in production of each material except lithium. Lithium production, however, is relatively easy to expand because it begins from so low a base. Supplying the increases in demand in Table 15.8, then, appears possible without major increases in prices or far-reaching effects from building new production facilities.

The materials for the batteries in ten million electric cars are shown in relation to reserves and resources in Table 15.9. Ten million electric cars on the road would be the approximate eventual result of continued manufacture of a million cars per year. It is also near the maximum projection for US populations of electric cars discussed in Sec. 8.

In relation to reserves and resources, the major problems appear to be adequacy of antimony, lithium, and yttrium. US reserves and resources of antimony are very small, but those of the world are large and the necessary materials might be obtained through importation. It is also possible that other materials could be substituted for antimony in the lead-acid batteries. In the high-temperature lithium battery, obtaining yttrium for ten million cars is probably too much to expect, but other insulators not requiring yttrium may be developed. The lithium for the battery, however, is essential. Outfitting ten million electric cars with lithium batteries would so seriously tax reserves and resources in the US and the world that considerable price increases are likely (with resultant additional exploration, and development of methods to extract lithium economically from currently subeconomic resources).

The figures of Tables 15.8 and 15.9 are proportional to the assumed productions and populations of electric cars, at least for moderate levels of production and population. Generally, it appears that up to 10% of US automobiles could be replaced in the 1990s with relatively minor effects on production and resources of materials, excepting possibly in the case of the lithium battery. It is commonly expected, however, that world

TABLE 15.9

MATERIALS FOR TEN MILLION ELECTRIC CARS
IN RELATION TO RESERVES AND RESOURCES

Car	Battery Material	Material as Percent of 1974 Reserves*		Material as Percent of Identified Resources**	
		US	World	US	World
Recent (75 km)	Lead	9.7	3.5	4.8	1.7
	Antimony	132	2.9	102	2.4
Improved (100–150 km)	Lead	4.3–6.9	1.5–2.5	2.1–3.4	.8–1.2
	Antimony	42–68	.9–1.5	32–53	.8–1.2
Improved (150–250 km)	Nickel	–	1.3–2.5	5.0–9.6	.6–1.2
	Zinc	2.4–5.0	.5–1.0	.9–1.9	.1–.2
	Cobalt	–	.6–1.2	2.0–3.8	.4–.7
Advanced (250–450 km)	Cobalt	–	1.5–2.8	4.8–9.0	.9–1.6
	Lithium	51–98	22–43	18–35	7.9–15
	Molybdenum	4.1–7.8	1.9–3.6	.7–1.3	.4–.7
	Yttrium	630–1200	57–108	49–93	11–22

* A reserve is that portion of an identified resource from which a usable
  mineral can be economically and legally extracted at the time of determination.
** Identified resources are specific bodies of mineral-bearing material whose
   location, quality, and quantity are known from geological evidence supported
   by engineering measurements, and include reserves and subeconomic resources.

resources of petroleum will be sufficient for present styles of living
only a little beyond the year 2000. It is thus relevant to investigate the
adequacy of resources for batteries to electrify all US automobiles, not
just ten percent, by the next century. From Table 15.9, it is apparent
that the necessary increases, over ten times those shown in the table,
would tax identified resources heavily.

15.4 ADEQUACY OF RESERVES AND IDENTIFIED RESOURCES

In Table 6.7, 126 million cars were projected to be available at US residences in the year 2000. In 1975, the number of cars in Europe was approaching that in the United States, and in the entire world there were about two and a half times as many cars as in the United States.[1] Since car populations are growing elsewhere much faster than in the United States, there may be three times as many cars in the world as in the US by the year 2000, or almost 400 million. Inspection of Tables 15.8 and 15.9 makes it evident that immense changes would be necessary to electrify car fleets of this order of magnitude. Given time, of course, orderly expansion of the industries producing the necessary materials should be possible--so long as reserves and resources permit. The crucial question, then, is the extent to which resources would suffice for electrifying most autos in the US or the world.

Table 15.10 shows the effects on cumulative demand through 2000 of providing propulsion batteries of a given type (lead-acid, nickel-zinc, or lithium-sulfur) for all US automobiles. Table 15.11 shows the ratios of resources to cumulative demands which include those for the battery materials stated in Table 15.10. These may be compared directly with the ratios presented in Table 15.7. The decreases in the ratios are considerable, and are drastic in the case of lithium. Nevertheless, world reserves of materials for both lead-acid and nickel-zinc batteries are nominally sufficient, and beyond this lie considerable resources available at higher prices.

It is interesting to compare the ratios of Table 15.11 with those presented in Table 15.12 for fuel resources. The ratios in Table 15.12 assume few or no electric cars, and summarize the resource problem the world now faces for fuels used in transportation, heating, industry, and other purposes. It is notable that the ratio for petroleum is 1.0, the same as the ratios for lead and zinc in Table 15.11. In one sense, however, the situation for electric cars is more difficult: the ratio for petroleum includes operation of all the world's automobiles, whereas the ratios for electric

TABLE 15.10

EFFECT OF ELECTRIC CARS ON CUMULATIVE PRIMARY
DEMAND FOR KEY BATTERY MATERIALS, 1974-2000

(billions of kg)

	Cumulative Demand, 1974-2000		Requirement to Electrify all US Autos in 2000	Ratio of Cumulative Demands With and Without Electric Cars	
	US	World		US	World
Lead	28	123	29.0-46.6	2.03-2.66	1.23-1.38
Nickel	6.4	26	10.8-21.3	2.71-4.35	1.41-1.81
Zinc	51.7	217	11.1-22.8	1.21-1.44	1.05-1.11
Lithium	.20	.39	1.89-3.65	10.6-19.6	5.85-10.4

TABLE 15.11

RATIOS OF RESOURCES TO CUMULATIVE DEMANDS, 1974-2000,
INCLUDING ELECTRIFICATION OF ALL US AUTOS

	Ratio of Recoverable Reserves to Cumulative Demand		Ratio of Identified Resources to Cumulative Demand	
Material	US	World	US	World
Lead	.7-.9	.9-1.0	1.4-1.9	1.7-1.9
Nickel	∿0	1.2-1.5	.5-.8	2.3-3.0
Zinc	.6-.7	1.0-1.0	1.6-1.9	6.2-6.6
Lithium	.08-.14	.16-.29	.22-.41	.47-.84

TABLE 15.12

RATIO OF FUEL RESOURCES TO CUMULATIVE DEMAND,

1974-2000, WITHOUT ELECTRIC CARS

Source: Ref. 4, p. 32, p. 160

Material	Ratio of Recoverable Reserves to Cumulative Demand		Ratio of Identified Resources to Cumulative Demand	
	US	World	US	World
Coal	17	8.7	154	123
Natural Gas	.5	1.3	.8	NA
Petroleum	.2	1.0	.4	NA
Uranium	.3	.4	.3	.7

NA - Not Available

---

cars assume electrification of less than half of these automobiles. Competition from other nations attempting electrification of cars could considerably reduce the supplies of materials available to the US.

Table 15.12 makes clear that immense resources of coal are available to provide energy for electric cars into the indefinite future. Resources of uranium, on the other hand, are surprisingly limited; but breeder reactors could increase the effective utilization of uranium resources by a factor of a hundred.

15.5 ADEQUACY OF POTENTIAL RESOURCES

Especially in the case of lithium, identified reserves and resources seem likely to be only a small fraction of deposits actually available in the earth's crust. Known reserves of lithium at just one area--the Kings Mountain region of North Carolina--amount to at least a 100-year supply at current US production rates.[5] Incentives for exploration, then, are small and it may be expected that relatively little of available resources has been identified.

To some extent, this may be true of other battery materials for which the ratios of reserves and identified resources to cumulative demand have been higher than in the case of petroleum. It is important, then, to appraise as best possible the undiscovered resources which may be located and exploited in the future if there are large demands for electrification of automobiles.

So far in this section, only identified resources have been considered. The relation of identified resources to all resources is suggested in Fig. 15.1. The quantity, quality, and location of identified resources are known from specific measurements and supporting geological evidence. Recoverable reserves are specific materials in identified resources which can be economically (and legally) extracted at current prices. The identified resources tabulated in this section include both recoverable reserves and subeconomic reserves, which will be economically recoverable only with higher prices or improved methods of extraction. Beyond identified resources lie all other resources actually present at reasonable depths in the earth's crust, the "undiscovered" resources in Fig. 15.1.

One method of estimating quantities of undiscovered resources is based on actual discoveries of particular minerals which have been extensively sought in the past. Lead, copper, zinc, silver, gold, and molybdenum fall in this category. For an intensely explored area such as the United States, it is possible to estimate the total amount of a mineral at reachable depths

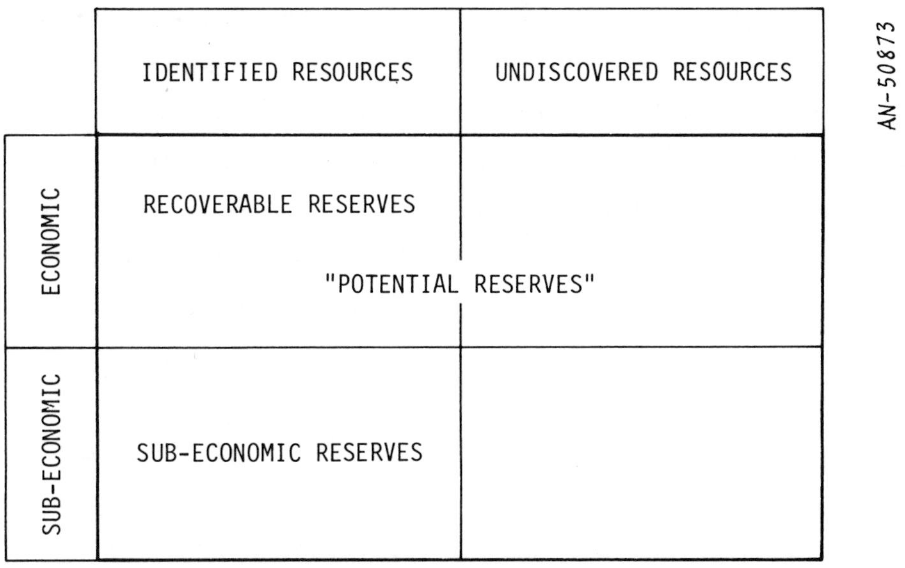

	IDENTIFIED RESOURCES	UNDISCOVERED RESOURCES
ECONOMIC	RECOVERABLE RESERVES "POTENTIAL RESERVES"	
SUB-ECONOMIC	SUB-ECONOMIC RESERVES	

AN-50873

Figure 15.1. Categories of Resources

in the earth's crust, say 1 kilometer, and compare that with identified reserves in the area. This suggests the fraction of a material in the crust which might eventually be located through intensive exploration.

In the United States, reserves of lead and molybdenum are higher in relation to estimated total lead and molybdenum at a depth of one kilometer or less than are reserves of any other metals. If it is assumed that intensive exploration would be equally successful in locating undiscovered resources of other metals, it is possible to estimate what may be called "potential resources." This estimate applies to resources from which the metals may be recovered economically at current prices; in the literature, "potential resources" apparently include already identified resources.[6]

Table 15.13 shows potential resources of basic battery materials in relation to known reserves in 1970.[6] Also shown are the underlying estimates of average abundance in the earth's crust in parts per million. Because the basis for the calculation is the amount of lead found in the United States to date, potential resources for lead are the same as known reserves. For all other materials, however, in Table 15.13, potential resources are much greater. This is especially true for lithium worldwide, apparently because there has been relatively little worldwide exploration. There is also a large potential reserve of nickel in the United States, where the kind of rocks from which nickel is usually recoverable at recent prices are seldom present, at least on the surface.

Additional discoveries of lead are possible and even likely, despite the ratio of one shown in Table 15.13. In fact, though surface exploration of most of the US has been thorough, there may be large subsurface deposits which, if located, would greatly increase reserves. A major deposit of this type was recently discovered in Southeast Missouri through exploratory drilling.[7]

The potential reserves in Table 15.13 do not include undiscovered subeconomic resources. Again, vast quantities of material may eventually be produced from such resources.

Table 15.14 shows how the inclusion of potential reserves would affect the ratios of reserves to cumulative demand tabulated in Table 15.11. There is no change in the case of US lead, since this is the standard of achievement on which the potential reserves were calculated. Worldwide, however, the ratios suggest there could be sufficient lead at recent prices for electrifying US cars, and a relative abundance of nickel and zinc for this purpose. US lithium would be barely adequate, even including potential reserves, for electrifying all US automobiles, but worldwide lithium might be relatively as abundant for electrifying cars as any of the other battery materials.

TABLE 15.13

POTENTIAL RESOURCES OF MATERIALS

Material	Abundance in Earth's Crust, parts per million	Ratio of Potential Reserves to 1970 Known Reserves	
		US	World
Lead	12	1	18
Nickel	89	830	40
Zinc	94	6.3	32
Lithium	21	12	180

Source: Ref. 6, p. 22-24

TABLE 15.14

RATIOS OF POTENTIAL RESERVES TO CUMULATIVE DEMANDS,
1974-2000, INCLUDING ELECTRIFICATION OF ALL US AUTOS

	US	World
Lead	.7-.9	16 - 18
Nickel	5.4-8.7	46 - 59
Zinc	3.9-4.8	32 - 33
Lithium	.9-1.7	30 - 53

One possible alternative to importation of lithium for electrifying cars would be production from sea salt. Traces of over seventy-five of the first ninety-two elements have been identified in sea salt, and the concentration of lithium is relatively high, as shown in Table 15.15.[8] The amount of lithium in the ocean, as the table shows, is immense in relation to identified reserves, unlike that for lead, nickel, or zinc. The great obstacle to extraction of lithium from sea water is cost: processing of huge volumes of water and salt would be necessary. Even the very high dollar values of gold and silver, which are present in lesser concentrations, have been insufficient to warrant their extraction. Bromine, however, is presently extracted directly from sea water, but its concentration is 67 parts per million in sea salt, over a hundred times that of lithium.

TABLE 15.15

MATERIALS IN WATERS OF THE OCEANS

Source: Ref. 8

| Material | Amount in Sea Salt | | Identified Resources, 10^9 kg | Ratio of Ocean Content to Identified Reserves |
	Parts per million	10^9 kg		
Lead	.00003	.0839	300	.0003
Nickel	.007	19.55	112	.174
Zinc	.011	30.72	1,500	.02
Lithium	.17	474.8	1.91	249.

Based on: Volume of oceans: $7.77 \cdot 10^{16}$ m^3

Density of ocean water: 1030 kg/m^3

Salt content of ocean: 3.49%, or $2.793 \cdot 10^{18}$ kg

Lithium brines are generally considered to be a more promising source than the ocean. Though they are not included in the identified resources of Table 15.6, there are oil well brines in Texas and Arkansas estimated to contain over ten billion kilograms of lithium. Because of the potential demand for lithium for fusion reactors, resources of lithium have been repeatedly reviewed in recent years. One such review is reproduced in Table 15.16; even without the Texas oil well brines, it shows identified resources several times those of Table 15.6.[9]

15.6 COMPETING DEMANDS FOR BATTERY MATERIALS

Massive demands for battery materials to support electrification of automobiles could drive up costs and reduce supplies of materials for other applications. Conversely, major new demands for materials not envisioned in the projections presented in this section could reduce the availability of materials for electrifying cars. Table 15.17 details forecasted demand through 2000 from Ref. 4 to show something of the various applications of battery materials and their relative growths. The projections are for total US demand, which includes both new material and recycled material. Demand for new material in Table 15.5 is the difference between total forecasted demand and projected secondary supply, which in turn depends on recovery rates from the various end uses.

The principal uses of lead in Table 15.17 have been in transportation, mostly in storage batteries for starting, lighting, and ignition (SLI); in antiknock compounds added to gasoline; and as sheathing for electrical cable. Because lead is being phased out of gasoline, major decreases of this use are projected for 2000. In transportation, a considerable allowance is made for propulsion batteries as well as SLI batteries. A large quantity of this allowance is recycled into secondary production, however, and consequently primary demand is only modestly affected. Recycling of lead from automotive batteries has been estimated at over 80%.

TABLE 15.16

IDENTIFIED RESOURCES OF LITHIUM IN THE WESTERN WORLD

Source: Ref. 9

Country	Location	Type of Deposit	Total Identified Resources (tonnes Li)	Identified Resources	
				Proven and Probable Reserves (tonnes Li)	Possible Additional Reserves (tonnes Li)
US	Kings Mountain, North Carolina	Large pegmatites	313,000	441,000	560,000
US	Black Hills, South Dakota	Small pegmatites	Not Specified		10,000
US	Other areas	Small pegmatites	Not Specified		1,000
US	Silver Peak, Nevada	Underground brine (300 ppm Li)	553,000	454,000	2,000,000
US	Searles Lake, California	Surface brine (70 ppm Li)	50,000	10,000	30,000
US	Great Salt Lake, Utah	Surface brine (60 ppm Li)	707,000	Not Specified	Not Specified
USA	Salton Sea, California	Underground geothermal brine (210 ppm Li)	1,000,000		1,000,000
USA Total (rounded)			2,600,000	900,000	3,000,000
Canada	Barante, Quebec	Medium pegmatites	86,000	76,000	
Canada	Bernic Lake, Manitoba	Medium pegmatites	73,000	41,000	
Canada	Other areas	Pegmatites	317,000	117,000	180,000
Canada Total (rounded)			476,000	117,000	180,000
S.W. Africa	Walvis Bay	Small pegmatites	17,800	4,000	
Rhodesia	Bikita tinfield	Medium pegmatites	83,900	82,000	
Zaire	Manono and Kittdo	Large pegmatites	1,000,000 (inferred)		1,000,000
Africa Total (rounded)			1,100,000	86,000	1,000,000
W. Australia	Coolgardie	Small pegmatites	15,000	Not Specified	Not Specified
S. America	Salar de Atacama	Underground brine	1,300,000	1,000,000	1,000,000
Western World Total (rounded)			5,000,000	1,100,000	5,800,000

7,000,000

TABLE 15.17

CONTINGENCY FORECASTS FOR US MATERIALS DEMAND
(in millions of kilograms)
Source: Ref. 4

Material	End Use	Demand in 1973	Projections for 2000 Low	Probable	High
Lead	Gasoline additives	249	45	100	272
	Transportation	635	1,089	1,451	1,905
	Construction	79	91	109	181
	Paints	99	118	136	181
	Ammunition	73	64	91	181
	Electrical	122	100	136	200
	Other	192	109	181	272
	TOTAL	1,450	1,615	2,204	3,193
Nickel	Chemicals	35	79	100	109
	Petroleum	21	48	64	66
	Fabricated metal products	24	32	42	45
	Transportation	49	73	83	115
	Electrical	30	54	91	100
	Household applicances	16	18	20	23
	Machinery	16	30	33	36
	Construction	21	23	36	54
	Other	21	24	31	32
	TOTAL	259	381	499	581
Zinc	Construction	484	726	998	1,270
	Transportation	333	363	454	816
	Electrical	163	272	454	635
	Machinery	127	181	272	363
	Paint	34	27	54	82
	Chemicals	54	45	136	181
	Rubber products	118	136	181	290
	Other	183	200	354	499
	TOTAL	1,496	1,950	2,903	4,137
Lithium	Aluminum production	1.27	3.18	5.62	5.62
	Ceramics and glass	.91	1.63	2.45	2.81
	Lubricants	.44	.47	.60	.71
	Air conditioning	.23	.36	.64	.64
	Other	.65	1.81	3.76	18.14
	TOTAL	3.49	7.36	13.06	27.92

Nickel is widely used to make alloys which are strong, corrosion-resistant, and useful over a wide temperature range. Such materials are particularly important in the chemical and petroleum industries. There are substitutes for nickel in almost all its uses, but they are generally more expensive or less effective.

Zinc is third among non-ferrous metals in terms of world consumption, following only copper and aluminum. It is used for alloying, protective coatings (galvanizing), and in making rubber and paints.

Lithium metal has accounted for only a tenth of total lithium demand in recent years. Lithium compounds, notably lithium carbonate, are used in the electrolyte of aluminum cells, and also in ceramics, glass, and lubricants. The metal itself is in demand for the manufacture of synthetic rubber, vitamin A, and anodes for premium primary batteries offering very high energy density and long shelf life. Though lithium demand is presently small, well under one percent of that for lead or zinc, much more rapid growth in demand is projected. Moreover, there is much more uncertainty: in Table 15.17, the high projection for 2000 is almost four times the low projection for lithium, whereas for lead, nickel, and zinc, the high and low projections differ by approximately a factor of two.

The demand projections for lithium include allowances for lithium secondary batteries by the year 2000, but these are not large in relation to requirements for electrifying a substantial fraction of US automobiles. Moreover, the projections for lithium make no allowance for its prospective use in generation of power through nuclear fusion.

Use of lithium in nuclear fusion could be enormous during the first portion of the next century. Requirements by 2030 for fusion alone have been estimated as near today's total identified resources.[5,9] Furthermore, substitution of other materials seems unlikely.

Current efforts to develop fusion reactors are based on the reaction between two heavy isotopes of hydrogen, deuterium and tritium. Though deuterium is obtainable in abundance from the ocean, tritium is not. It is radioactive, decays with a half-life of 12.6 years, and is not found in nature in any significant quantity. It must be bred from lithium by capture of a neutron, and so prospective fusion reactors are planned from the outset as breeders to produce the tritium they require. 92.6 percent of natural lithium is the isotope of atomic weight seven; only the remainder is the isotope of weight six which can be converted to tritium.[5]

Two designs of thermal nuclear reactors for deuterium-tritium fusion are considered likely. One requires about ten times as much lithium as the other: about a million kilograms (a thousand tonnes) per gigawatt of power output. The design requiring most lithium uses it in liquid form as a coolant to remove heat from the thermonuclear reactor and transfer it to the electric generating system. It also uses a blanket of lithium around the core of the reactor as a neutron absorber to breed tritium. The design using less lithium employs a solid blanket around the core which must be enriched to about 90% Li-6. Obtaining this enriched lithium requires access to almost as much natural lithium as the other design, but once the light isotope has been separated, the remainder of the lithium is available for other uses.

Which of these arrangements for developing power through nuclear fusion will succeed remains to be seen. Even for the reactor needing the higher amount of lithium, however, one investigation suggests that the western world's resources of lithium are sufficient through the year 2030, even with growth in demand for other purposes ranging up to 10% per year.[9] It does not also suffice, however, for general electrification of automobiles.

15.7 OTHER BATTERIES

The batteries discussed so far in this section were those selected as representative of the future possibilities in Sec. 3. There are other promising prospects--in particular, those of Table 3.3--which are under active development and could provide performance ranging from that of the advanced lead-acid battery to that of the lithium-sulfur battery.

Of these alternatives, the nickel-iron, zinc-chlorine, and zinc-air batteries would require materials which have already been discussed, in roughly the same quantities as the representative batteries addressed so far. The sodium-sulfur battery, however, requires none of these materials and could provide exceedingly high performance. It may be that this or the sodium-chlorine battery, another possibility under less intensive development, could obviate problems of material scarcity for batteries.

Sodium is not only abundantly available from sea salt, but from enormous mineral deposits on land. The trona deposits of Wyoming contain sufficient soda ash, for example, to meet the 1974 level of demand for another 3800 years. This trona is a mixture of soda ash (sodium carbonate), sodium bicarbonate, and water deposited by evaporation of an ancient lake. At present, demand for metallic sodium is much less than for soda ash. If the metallic sodium were extracted from the Wyoming trona, however, about 90,000 kilograms could be obtained for each of the automobiles expected to be available in the United States in the year 2000.[10] Obviously all the world's cars could be electrified many times over from this single resource with sodium-sulfur or sodium-chlorine batteries.

Recoverable reserves of sulfur in the United States are only about half of projected cumulative demand for 1974-2000. Identified resources, however, in the US alone are four times cumulative US demand. Moreover, as noted earlier, future supplies are expected to be derived principally from desulfurization of flue gases rather than natural deposits. The approximate sulfur content of coal resources in the United States is almost seven trillion kilograms, eighteen times the cumulative demand of the United States to the year 2000, or about 50,000 kilograms per car expected in the US in the year 2000.[11]

SECTION 15 REFERENCES

1. *Motor Vehicle Facts and Figures* '76, Motor Vehicle Manufacturers Association, Detroit, 1977.

2. R. W. Roig, et al., *Impacts of Material Substitution in Automobile Manufacture on Resource Recovery* - Vol. 1: Results and Summary, EPA-600/5-76-007a, US Environmental Protection Agency, Office of Research and Development, Washington, July 1976.

3. W. Hamilton, *Impact of Future Use of Electric Cars in the Los Angeles Region,* Vol. II, EPA-460/3-74-020-b, US Environmental Protection Agency, Alternative Automotive Power Systems Division, Ann Arbor, Michigan, October 1974, pages 1-78.

4. *Mineral Facts and Problems*, 1975 Edition, Bureau of Mines Bulletin 667, US Government Printing Office, Washington, 1976, p. 1075.

5. A. L. Hammond, "Lithium: Will Short Supply Constrain Energy Technologies?" *Science*, Vol. 191, 12 March 1976.

6. D. A. Brobst and W. P. Pratt, Editors, *United States Mineral Resources*, Geological Survey Professional Paper 820, US Government Printing Office, Washington, 1973, pages 21-25.

7. Ref. 4, page 597.

8. *Encyclopedia Brittannica*, 1968 edition, Vol. 16, p. 847.

9. N. Walton and E. Spooner, "Lithium and Nuclear Fusion," *Nature*, Vol. 261, June 17, 1976.

10. Ref. 4, p. 1020.

11. Ref. 4, p. 160

16   ECONOMIC IMPACTS

The most important economic impact of electric cars is probably
the higher cost for motorists discussed in Sec. 7. Associated with
higher cost, however, would be an overall increase in the economic activity
required to manufacture, sell, and service automobiles. Furthermore, there
would be important changes even where overall levels of activity remain
constant: employment in the manufacture of internal combustion engines,
for example, would decline while employment in the manufacture of electric
motors and controllers would expand about equally. In this section, the
impacts on employment and payroll are projected for industries which would
be directly affected either by changes in total activity or changes in type
of activity.

An upper bound on the economic impacts of electric cars on employment
in the US is shown in Fig. 16.1. Baseline employment in affected industries,
in the absence of electric cars, is shown as a dashed line. The solid lines

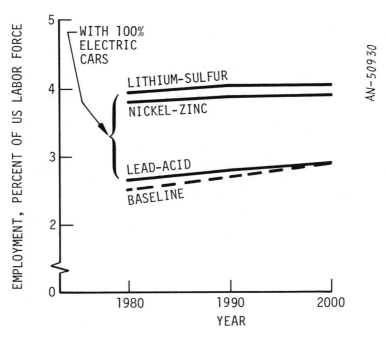

Figure 16.1.   Employment in Affected Industries With
and Without Electric Cars

above it show employment in these industries which would be required if all automobiles in the US were electric, using one of the three representative future batteries described in Sec. 3. In each case, the longest-range versions of the future electric cars in Table 4.1 are assumed; these require the largest batteries and consequently produce the greatest changes in related economic activity.

The changes in Fig. 16.1 are largest for the cars with nickel-zinc and lithium-sulfur batteries and ranges of 250 and 450 km, which require batteries of proportionately high capacity and cost. While these changes would increase activity in affected industries by a relatively large amount, almost half, they still total only about one percent of all projected US employment. Adding employment in auto-related economic activity implies removing it from other activities and thus reducing production of non-automotive goods and services. There would be corresponding changes, of course, in consumption: after paying more for automotive travel, families with electric cars would have less money available for other purchases.

Even a very rapid shift from conventional to electric cars would take decades. Spread over such time periods, the employment impacts in Fig. 16.1 would result in very small annual changes. Annual losses of old jobs or gains of new jobs would amount to only about a tenth of a percent of US total employment, a figure insignificant in comparison with typical rates of unemployment. Furthermore, it appears that although some national impacts would be moderately concentrated in a few specific regions, no regional impacts would be severe. Finally, any imports of battery materials necessary in the transition would be more than offset by reduced imports of petroleum over a very few years.

16.1 BASELINE PROJECTIONS

Economic activity potentially affected by use of electric cars is summarized in Table 16.1.[1] Overall, only 3.75% of US employment in 1974 was in potentially affected industries, with payroll only 4.5% of the national total. Even if all this employment were affected or even eliminated by use of electric cars, over a period of twenty years the annual changes would be very small. Not all of it, however, would be affected. Motor vehicle distribution and sales, for example, may be relatively little impacted, since selling electric cars may be very similar to selling conventional cars. It is noteworthy that more people were recently employed in vehicle distribution and sales than in vehicle manufacturing, where at least the activity related to the propulsion system would be impacted by a switch to electric cars.

Because major new activities are required for electric cars, the assignment of resultant impacts among existing industries in Table 16.1, or to new industries not yet defined and classified, is in part arbitrary. The major new activities required are manufacturing electric controllers and propulsion motors, manufacturing propulsion batteries, and distributing and selling propulsion batteries. For this analysis, the manufacture of controllers was assigned to the electrical controls industry. The manufacture of propulsion motors was assigned to a relevant sector of motor vehicle manufacturing: that involved in making starter motors, generators, and other electrical equipment for conventional automobiles. Finally, the distribution and sales of propulsion batteries were assigned to a new industry which was defined and projected for this purpose.

In practice, of course, distribution and sales of propulsion batteries may eventually be regarded as a part of the overall distribution and sales of automobiles. This analysis is clarified and simplified, however, by segregating it as a separate entity. Then the part of auto distribution and sales which would be little affected, that associated with the car independent of its propulsion battery, need be considered no further, and

403

TABLE 16.1

ECONOMIC ACTIVITY POTENTIALLY AFFECTED BY ELECTRIC CARS, 1974

Industry	Standard Industrial Classification	Employment Persons	Employment Percent[*]
Mining and Smelting of Battery Materials		31,721	.04
Lead and zinc mining	1031	7,068	
Cobalt, nickel, molybdenum mining	1061	5,352	
Other mining (antimony, yttrium)	1099	1,416	
Lead smelting	3332	4,761	
Zinc smelting	3333	5,054	
Other non-ferrous metals smelting	3339	8,070	
Storage Batteries	3691	25,438	.03
Electrical Equipment Manufacturing		160,799	.19
Electric motors (heavy)	3621	97,546	
Electrical controls (heavy)	3622	63,253	
Motor Vehicle Manufacturing		806,542	.94
Carburetors, pistons, rings	3592	30,661	
Electrical equipment	3694	60,104	
Vehicle bodies	3711	292,245	
Vehicles and parts	3714	423,532	
Motor Vehicle Distribution and Sales		893,386	1.04
Wholesale vehicle distribution	5012	107,989	
New and used cars	5511	746,250	
Used cars	5521	39,147	
Petroleum Distribution and Sales		704,239	.82
Petroleum, wholesale	5171-2	130,423	
Service stations	5541	573,816	
Vehicle Maintenance		598,944	.70
Wholesale parts distribution	5013	257,956	
Auto supply stores	5531	185,992	
Auto repair	7538-9	154,996	
TOTAL		3,221,069	3.75

[*] Percent of total US employment in 1974 (85,936,000 persons)

404

attention may be focused on battery distribution and sales. This activity is important because, as in the existing auto industry, employment in distribution and sales of batteries will exceed that in their manufacture.

Baseline projections of employment and payroll in the absence of electric cars are shown in Table 16.2 for the potentially affected industries selected from Table 16.1. For most of these industries the projections were made by least-squares regression analyses of historical employment and payroll data which appear in Ref. 1. For mining of individual materials for the different batteries, however, another approach was necessary. Separate payroll and employment data for each battery material were unavailable, but separate impacts were to be estimated for each battery. Accordingly, production per man-year of employment in mining each material was first estimated from production and employment data given in Ref. 2. Then future employment was estimated from this and projected future production of the material, also given in Ref. 2. Finally, future payrolls were calculated from future employment and the annual average payroll per employee, which was estimated from data for the relevant mining and smelting industries shown in Table 16.1.

In one case only, that of automotive service stations, the basic projections derived from historical data were adjusted to account for major innovations within the industry. A nationwide shift to self-service operation is underway at service stations which will reduce employment below that implied by the historical data. For 1980, a decrease in employment of 17% from the 1974 level was projected based on published estimates of fewer service stations and lower average employment per station, together with an assumed future mix of station types (10% no-service, 50% full-service, and 40% split-island).[3,4] A small further reduction was included due to the reduced frequency of routine maintenance being recommended for present and future cars. Resumption of the historical growth trend was assumed for subsequent years, after the transition to self-service operation has run its course.

TABLE 16.2

BASELINE PROJECTIONS FOR INDUSTRIES AFFECTED BY ELECTRIC CARS

Standard Industrial Classification	Industry	Employment, Thousands			Payroll, Millions of 1977 Dollars		
		1980	1990	2000	1980	1990	2000
3592	Carburetor, piston, valve manufacturing	35.9	45.1	54.3	507.3	661.1	815.0
3622	Electric controls manufacturing	71.2	92.2	133.2	910.6	1199.3	1488.1
3694	ICE electrical equipment manufacturing	67.9	81.6	95.3	1007.0	1305.2	1603.4
3711,3714	Motor vehicle body and parts manufacturing	822.5	913.8	1005.2	14798.3	18773.0	22747.7
5012	Motor vehicle parts distribution	125.0	153.3	181.7	1875.4	2415.7	2957.0
5171,5172	Petroleum wholesalers	181.8	197.8	213.7	2660.0	3080.2	3500.5
5531	Automotive supply stores	223.0	290.5	358.1	2137.9	2860.9	3583.9
5541	Automotive service stations	474.1	565.2	661.0	2813.0	3406.2	4030.1
7538,7539	Automotive repair shops	194.4	245.0	297.4	1590.3	1974.6	2376.3
3691	Storage battery manufacturing	26.5	31.9	37.2	357.7	445.3	533.0
1031,3332	Lead and zinc mining, plus lead or zinc smelting	12.0	15.2	20.1	162.4	221.5	314.2
–	Nickel and cobalt mining	1.6	2.4	4.1	29.7	58.8	153.1
–	Lithium mining	.4	.6	1.0	7.7	15.2	33.4
–	Molybdenum mining	3.2	5.2	8.0	59.0	128.8	266.2
All	TOTAL US	88,536	97,144	105,248	1,496,457	2,103,610	3,036,096

406

16.2 MAXIMUM EFFECTS ON EMPLOYMENT AND PAYROLL

The economic impacts of electric cars would be maximum if all new cars manufactured were electric, if all cars on the road were also electric, and if all these electric cars offered the maximum possible design range. These are the assumptions under which the changes in employment and payroll in Table 16.3 were estimated. For any level of production and use less than 100%, the figures in Table 16.3 may be adjusted downward proportionately.

The individual industries in Table 16.3 are divided into five groups. Impacts on industries in the first group would be essentially independent of the type of battery used in the electric cars. Impacts on industries in the four remaining groups depend strongly on the type of battery. In each of the four groups, a different representative battery from Table 3.1 is assumed to be used in all the electric cars being manufactured and operated.

To obtain total impacts on employment and payroll for cars with a particular type of battery, it is necessary to add the subtotal from Table 16.3 for the battery-independent industries in the first group to the subtotal for one of the battery-dependent industry groups. The results of this addition for each of the four possible battery types are shown in Tables 16.4 and 16.5. The percentage changes in employment from Table 16.4 for cars with future batteries were illustrated in relation to baseline employment in Fig. 16.1.

In Tables 16.3-16.5, the net impact of cars with improved lead-acid batteries is very small. This results from the relatively low costs associated with the battery. The battery weights and costs assumed are those for the longest range four-passenger cars of each battery type in Table 4.1. In all four cases of Table 16.3, the weights are similar. The capacities of the batteries, however, span a four-to-one range in accord with their capacities per unit weight from Table 3.1. The overall result is a range of four to one (or more) in initial battery cost. The case with

407

TABLE 16.3

IMPACTS OF 100% USE OF ELECTRIC CARS ON
EMPLOYMENT AND PAYROLL, BY INDUSTRY

Standard Industrial Classification	Industry	Employment Change, thousands			Payroll Change, millions of 1977 dollars		
		1980	1990	2000	1980	1990	2000
(independent of battery type)							
3592	Carburetor, piston, valve manufacturing	-24	-31	-37	-345	-450	-554
3622	Electric controls manufacturing	33	38	41	425	497	459
3694	ICE electric equipment manufacturing	15	14	11	425	230	187
3711,3714	Motor vehicle body and parts manufacturing	-56	-57	-54	-1000	-1173	1227
5012	Motor vehicle parts distribution	-57	-55	-84	-854	-819	-1360
5171,5172	Petroleum wholesalers	-35	-22	-28	-505	-339	-455
5531	Automotive supply stores	-67	-87	-107	-640	-858	-1075
5541	Automotive service stations	-293	-350	-410	-1741	-2112	-2499
7538,7539	Automotive repair shops	-93	-118	-143	-757	-948	-1141
	SUBTOTAL	-576	-667	-810	-5191	-5972	-7665
(recent lead-acid batteries)							
1031,3332	Lead and zinc mining, smelting	103	122	150	1,395	1,768	744
3691	Storage battery manufacturing	483	529	559	6,519	7,398	8,005
-	Battery distribution and sales	1,011	1,066	1,096	13,476	15,340	16,662
	SUBTOTAL	1,597	1,717	1,805	21,390	24,505	27,005
(improved lead-acid batteries)							
1031,3332	Lead and zinc mining, smelting	73	86	107	994	1,254	1,665
3691	Storage battery manufacturing	196	214	224	2,648	2,985	3,212
-	Battery distribution and sales	432	454	467	5,753	6,536	7,099
	SUBTOTAL	701	754	798	9,395	10,775	11,976
(nickel-zinc batteries)							
1031,3332	Lead and zinc mining and smelting	55	60	57	744	868	892
-	Nickel and cobalt mining	43	37	35	796	915	1,332
3691	Storage battery manufacturing	518	587	622	6,996	8,197	8,903
-	Battery distribution and sales	1,084	1,140	1,172	14,438	16,404	17,818
	SUBTOTAL	1,700	1,823	1,887	22,973	26,384	28,946
(lithium-sulfur batteries)							
-	Nickel and cobalt mining	14	11	11	248	280	408
-	Lithium mining	22	25	27	389	595	863
-	Molybdenum mining	10	11	12	181	275	402
3691	Storage battery manufacturing	601	659	699	2,206	9,212	10,005
-	Battery distribution and sales	1,217	1,280	1,317	16,215	18,423	20,010
	SUBTOTAL	1,863	1,986	2,066	25,140	28,785	31,694

TABLE 16.4

IMPACTS OF 100% USE OF ELECTRIC CARS ON TOTAL
EMPLOYMENT IN INDUSTRIES DIRECTLY AFFECTED

Type of Battery Used in Electric Cars	Employment Change in Affected Industries					
	Thousands			Percent US Employment		
	1980	1990	2000	1980	1990	2000
Recent Lead-Acid	1,022	1,049	995	1.15	1.08	0.95
Improved Lead-Acid	126	87	-12	.14	.09	-0.01
Nickel-Zinc	1,124	1,156	1,077	1.27	1.19	1.02
Lithium-Sulfur	1,287	1,319	1,255	1.45	1.36	1.19

TABLE 16.5

IMPACTS OF 100% USE OF ELECTRIC CARS ON TOTAL
PAYROLL IN INDUSTRIES DIRECTLY AFFECTED

Type of Battery Used in Electric Cars	Payroll Change in Affected Industries					
	Millions of 1977 Dollars			Percent US Payroll		
	1980	1990	2000	1980	1990	2000
Recent Lead-Acid	16,199	18,534	19,340	1.08	.88	.64
Improved Lead-Acid	4,204	4,803	4,311	.28	.23	.14
Nickel-Zinc	17,782	20,412	21,281	1.19	.97	.70
Lithium-Sulfur	19,949	22,813	24,029	1.33	1.08	.79

recent lead-acid batteries has much larger impacts, despite low initial costs, than that for improved lead-acid batteries because the recent batteries are short-lived and must be frequently replaced. The cases with nickel-zinc and lithium-sulfur batteries have higher impacts than that for improved lead-acid batteries because of the high initial costs of their batteries. Though the capacity of the assumed nickel-zinc battery in each car is less that that of the lithium-sulfur battery, its cost per unit capacity is somewhat greater. In all cases except that of recent lead-acid batteries, average daily driving would be only a small fraction of maximum range, average discharge depth of the battery would be correspondingly low, and battery life would be the eight-year maximum projected in Sec. 3. There would be no difference, then, in requirements for replacement batteries.

In all cases, the car itself (without battery) was assumed to be the weight-conscious four-passenger subcompact described in Fig. 4.10. Elsewhere in Sec. 4 and in this study, long-range cars with recent lead-acid batteries and lithium-sulfur batteries differed somewhat from this car. The differences, however, appeared insufficient to warrant separate calculations of impacts for the first group of industries in Table 16.3.

The car implicit in Table 16.3 weighs 1083 kg without battery, about 20% more than the comparable ICE subcompact which is also described in Fig. 4.10. Because of this additional weight, its cost without battery is only slightly less than the average price recently paid in the US for cars of all sizes.[5] After adjustment for inflation, the difference was 5.4%. In Table 16.3, the projected impacts in the battery-independent industries were calculated under the assumption that the electric subcompact replaced all sizes of conventional automobiles. Part of the reductions shown in employment and payroll are simply due to its lower value (without battery), not to its electric drive. Other important decreases for battery-independent industries in Table 16.3 stem from the low maintenance of electric cars, which reduces activities both in replacement parts and in service. Finally, the largest reduction of all in these industries, that for automotive service stations, results from the elimination of sales of fuel for personal automobiles.

Among impacts in Table 16.3 for the different types of battery, there are increases for mining, manufacturing, distribution and sales which generally exceed the reductions projected for battery-independent industries. In line with current practice in the automobile industry, more employment was assigned to distribution and sales than to manufacturing the batteries.

In any transition to electric cars, the loss of jobs in individual industries may be more important than the net increase in jobs after new jobs are added. Even on this measure, however, the impact of electrifying all US autos over ten to twenty years would be relatively small: the total losses of jobs in Table 16.3 are only 0.7-0.8% of projected future US employment.

Motor Vehicle Manufacturing

Three of the first four industries of Table 16.3 are now involved in conventional motor vehicle manufacturing. Not all motor vehicles, however, are personal automobiles which would be replaced by electric cars. Automobiles have recently fallen below 80% of all motor vehicles produced in the US.[5] This is partly due to the growing popularity of personal trucks and vans; but in the future, as more stringent regulations are applied to pickup trucks and vans for both fuel economy and pollution control, the new popularity may subside. In view of this and the higher average value of motor vehicles other than automobiles, it was estimated that 68% of activity in motor vehicle industries was required for personal automobiles and therefore subject to changes due to substitution of electric cars.

In the carburetor, piston, ring, and valve manufacturing industry, almost all activity for personal cars would be eliminated if all personal cars

411

were electric. Accordingly, 68% reductions in baseline employment and payroll are shown as impacts in Table 16.3.

In the electric controls manufacturing industry, baseline activity would be increased to cover the manufacture of controllers for new electric cars. The number of new electric cars was estimated as 10% of the fleet projected in Table 6.7. The average price per controller sold by the industry was estimated at $176, in line with estimated average motor cost of $309 and the total cost indicated in Sec. 7.1 for both motor and controller. The ratio of total controller sales to baseline sales was used to factor up baseline employment and payroll, yielding the changes shown in Table 16.3. Baseline sales were estimated from baseline employment and an available projection of industry sales per employee.[6]

In the ICE electric equipment manufacturing industry, activity was first reduced 68% due to elimination of personal ICE cars. Then industry sales of motors for electric cars were estimated from the price per motor of $309 and unit sales equal to 10% of the personal car fleet projected in Table 6.7. Baseline employment and payroll in the industry were increased in accord with the ratio of motor sales to baseline sales. As for the electric controls industry, baseline sales were estimated from baseline employment and an available projection of sales per employee.[6]

In the motor vehicle body and parts manufacturing industry, 68% of baseline employment was estimated to be engaged in manufacture of conventional cars. Because the electric cars were 5.4% less expensive on the average, the reduction in total manufacturing employment due to substitution of electric cars was estimated to be 5.4%. Not all of manufacturing employment is in the motor vehicle body and parts manufacturing industry, however; some would be in the three other manufacturing industries just discussed. Accordingly, the employment reduction due to electric cars in the motor vehicle body and parts manufacturing industry was chosen so that the total change in manufacturing employment, including those just projected for the

other three industries, would be 5.4%. Payroll in the motor vehicle body
and parts manufacturing industry was reduced in proportion to this change
in employment. The resultant reductions shown in Table 16.3 are a little
larger than 5.4% of the baseline, owing to the net increases projected for
the other three manufacturing industries at the top of the table.

Motor Vehicle Fuel, Parts, and Service

Major reductions were projected in all these industries due to the
low maintenance of the electric car and its independence of petroleum fuel.
Sixty-seven percent of activity in the motor vehicle parts distribution industry was estimated to be related directly to internal-combustion engines, in
line with Table 7.5 after exclusion of tires. This portion of the industry
activity was reduced 68% to account for elimination of engine-related
parts sales for personal cars. Activity of petroleum wholesalers was
reduced by the percentage of petroleum consumption which would be eliminated
through 100% electrification of automobiles, as shown in Table 11.1.
Forty-four percent of the auto supply store industry was estimated to be
engaged in selling ICE-related parts, in accord with Table 7.5. Activity
in this portion of the industry was reduced 68% to account for elimination
of engine-related parts sales for personal cars. Ninety-one percent of
sales at automotive service stations were estimated to be ICE-related:
in a recent year, 82% of all sales were sales of gasoline, and half of
the remainder were sales of parts and services related to the ICE system.[6]
The 91% of activity related to internal-combustion engines was reduced
68% to account for elimination of personal ICE cars. Finally, 70% of
automotive repair shop activity was assumed to be ICE-related, as discussed
in Sec. 7. This ICE-related activity was reduced 68% to account for
elimination of personal ICE cars.

Propulsion Batteries

The retail prices of Table 3.1 were applied to all propulsion batteries.
The total battery capacities to which these unit prices were applied were
summarized in Table 15.4. As discussed in Sec. 3, a 50% markup to the retail

price was assumed. The implication is that a correspondingly large new
activity, similar to present-day automobile distribution and sales, would
appear to distribute and sell new and used propulsion batteries.

The baseline projections for mining and smelting of materials were
simply scaled up in line with the increased requirements for electric cars.
Both new and replacement batteries were included. In the long run, of
course, some of this activity would shift to recovering and recycling
materials from used batteries.

Activity in storage battery manufacturing was first decreased to
reflect loss of battery production for conventional cars, and then increased
to cover production of propulsion batteries. Ten percent of the industry
baseline was assumed to be unaffected, allowing for manufacture of batteries
other than for motor vehicles.[7] The remainder was decreased 68% to account
for elimination of ICE personal cars. The activity required to manufacture
propulsion batteries was then estimated by combining projected retail
prices of Table 3.1 and the battery capacities of Table 15.4 to obtain
retail sales of batteries. These were reduced by one-third, the markup
to retail, to obtain the value of the manufactured product. Fifteen percent
of this value was estimated to be labor cost and used to project payroll.
Associated employment was estimated from baseline payroll per employee.
The labor content of 15% was based on informal discussions with industry
personnel and agrees reasonably with the careful analysis for lithium-
sulfur batteries of Ref. 8. The total number of batteries produced for
propulsion includes both new and replacement batteries. Annual production
of new batteries was estimated to be one-tenth the total number of personal
cars in use in Table 6.7. Replacements were found from the number of personal
cars in use divided by battery life.

Activity in battery distribution and sales was taken to be proportional
to the markup to retail on all new batteries sold. In line with recent
figures for the automobile distribution and sales industries, 60% of this

markup was estimated to go to payroll. Payroll per employee was assumed to be the same as in automotive distribution and sales.

16.3 REGIONAL CONCENTRATIONS

Though the national effects of electric cars are relatively small, this is no insurance against concentrations of effects in a few regions. There are three kinds of regional concentrations of potential consequence. The first is in existing manufacturing which would be eliminated by shifting to electric cars. The second is in new manufacturing required by electric cars, which might or might not be regionally concentrated. The third is in mining and smelting of materials for batteries, which must generally be located wherever resources are found.

Table 16.6 shows major regional concentrations of existing manufacturing which would be affected by a switch to electric cars. To obtain these figures, automotive plants of major manufacturers were located from listings in Ref. 3. Then employment in counties containing the plants was obtained from Ref. 1. In some cases, large percentages of county employment would be affected by electric cars, and by changes in the particular industry under consideration. Even over periods of ten to twenty years, the declines in employment for the upper-bound case of total electrification of cars could be significant: two to four percent per year in the worst case.

Potential declines could be offset, however, by location of new manufacturing for electric cars in the affected areas. With facilities and skilled labor available, it is reasonable to expect that manufacture of electric motors and possibly controllers would replace at least part of the manufacture of ICE equipment no longer needed by electric cars.

There remain the potential increases in activity in areas with major resources of future battery materials. Much of the new mining and smelting required may be concentrated in a few places. Almost half

TABLE 16.6

REGIONAL CONCENTRATIONS OF AFFECTED MANUFACTURING

Concentrated Industry (percent change)	Area of Concentration		Area Employment		
	State	County (city)	Total	Percent Affected by Electric Cars	Percent in Con-centrated Industry
Motor Vehicle Bodies, Parts, Accessories Manufacturing (-18%)	Michigan	Wayne (Detroit)	865,832	12	10
		Genesee (Flint)	122,481	40	38
		Ingham (Lansing)	80,904	24	24
		Oakland (Pontiac)	311,506	10	8
		Washtenaw (Ypsilanti)	82,735	36	26
	New York	Erie (Tonawanda)	336,413	7	5
	Ohio	Cuyahoga (Cleveland)	673,756	5	3
		Montgomery (Kettering)	218,857	9	8
		Allen (Lima)	39,876	21	19
Carburetor, Piston, Ring and Valve Manufacturing (-68%)	Michigan	Washtenaw (Ypsilanti)	82,735	36	9

of US lead, for example, is derived from the large resources in Missouri, and over 80% of US lithium is produced at Kings Mountain, North Carolina. The increased activity associated with electrification of all cars could be very large: employment in lithium mining, for example, can be seen from Tables 16.2 and 16.3 to increase from 1,000 to 28,000 in the year 2000. The result, even spread over twenty years, would be relatively rapid growth in mining areas, though the total number of people involved is not large. Lesser changes would be required for other materials, ranging to an increase of less than six times in the employment for lead and zinc mining and smelting.

16.4 IMPORTS

Because reduction of oil imports is a major motivation for any shift to electric cars, a possible requirement to import materials for batteries deserves special attention. There are many uncertainties, notably in the extent to which increased demand due to electric cars would lead to increased prices for such materials and the extent to which additional demands beyond the baseline projections would be met by additional imports. Under simple assumptions, however, as in Table 16.7, it is possible to indicate the order of magnitude of imports which might result.

In Table 16.7, the proportion of imports for the base case (from Ref. 2) is simply assumed to apply to all additional imports, and recent prices are also assumed to prevail. Under these assumptions, the imported lead required in electrification of all US cars with improved lead-acid batteries would cost 12.6 billion dollars, while the imported nickel and zinc for electrification of all US cars with nickel-zinc batteries would cost forty-one billion dollars. This is to be compared with a twelve-billion-dollar annual reduction in imports of petroleum which would result from a saving of a billion barrels of oil annually (as in Table 11.1) valued at $12 each, the current price of imported oil.

TABLE 16.7

NOMINAL COST OF IMPORTED MATERIALS

TO ELECTRIFY ALL US CARS BY 2000

Material	Requirement, billions of kg	Nominal Imports,[*] percent	Nominal Price,[**] dollars per kg	Cost of Imports, billions of dollars
Lead	46.6	37	.73	12.6
Nickel	21.3	30	4.59	29.4
Zinc	28.4	64	.65	11.6

[*]Projected in Ref. 2 in the absence of electric cars
[**]Prices as of April 1978

It thus appears that although initial requirements for imported material might add considerably to US imports, their value would be recouped in a few years through reduced imports of oil. For the lithium-sulfur battery, no imports would be needed since the US is an exporter of lithium and is expected to obtain immense amounts of sulfur from flue gas desulfurization to meet environmental objectives.

There is great uncertainty, of course, in all these figures. Imports of nickel might be very much less than in Table 16.7 because the US is expected to reduce its dependence on nickel imports in coming years, as shown in Sec. 15, and additional demand due to electric cars might be entirely accommodated through more rapid expansion of new US production. World prices for any of the materials might be considerably higher than at present, especially if there were large demands for propulsion batteries. The cost of imported petroleum is similarly uncertain. With decreasing reserves worldwide, much higher prices may eventually be inevitable, but the stability of the cartel which now maintains oil at several times its 1972 price is not assured.

SECTION 16 REFERENCES

1. *County Business Patterns 1974*, National Summary and Volumes for Individual States, US Department of Commerce, Bureau of the Census, 1977.

2. *Mineral Facts and Problems, 1975 Edition*, Bureau of Mines Bulletin 667, US Government Printing Office, Washington, 1976.

3. *Automotive Manufacturing and Maintenance*, Report of a Panel of the Interagency Task Force on Motor Vehicle Goals Beyond 1980, US Department of Transportation, Washington, March 1976.

4. *1977 National Petroleum News Factbook Edition*, McGraw-Hill, Inc., New York.

5. *Motor Vehicle Facts and Figures '77*, Motor Vehicle Manufacturers Association, Detroit, Michigan, 1977.

6. W. Hamilton, et al., *Impacts of Future Use of Electric Cars in the Los Angeles Region: Vol. III*, EPA-460/3-74-020c, US Environmental Protection Agency, Ann Arbor, Michigan, October 1974, pp. 9-23 through 9-62.

7. *Annual Survey of Manufacturers 1974: General Statistics for Industry Groups and Industries*, M74(AS)-1, US Department of Commerce, Bureau of the Census, November 1976.

8. W. L. Towle, et al., *Cost Estimate for the Commercial Manufacture of Lithium/Iron Sulfide Cells for Load-Leveling*, ANL-76-12, Argonne National Laboratory, Argonne, Illinois, March 1976.

17   CONCLUSIONS

This study has examined in detail the major prospects for future electric cars. It began at their technology and performance, their capabilities in relation to the needs of typical drivers, and their costs in relation to those of competitive conventional cars. It ended with the impacts which large-scale use of future electric cars might have on petroleum consumption, environmental quality, materials resources, and the national economy. Its objective has been not to judge electric cars, but to provide quantitative projections of their advantages and disadvantages at various possible levels of use.

Though no final judgment is intended, a number of intermediate conclusions may be drawn from the quantitative projections. In fact, they are so strongly implied that they can scarcely be overlooked. All are subject, of course, to the uncertainties which beset any such effort to project future conditions. They are also subject to the particular limitations of this study, which has been confined solely to personal battery-electric passenger cars and has not considered commercial or hybrid-electric vehicles.

First, the benefits generally envisioned for electric cars are substantiated by the quantitative projections of this study. Future electric cars could make most auto travel independent of petroleum. They could substantially reduce the noise of urban traffic, which is a serious environmental problem. They could also bring improvements in urban air quality, though cleaner conventional cars will already have eliminated most automotive air pollution. The capacity already planned by the electric utilities of the nation could recharge enormous numbers of electric cars, and resources of battery materials will probably be forthcoming in sufficient quantity.

Second, successful battery research and development is essential to make electric cars a reasonable alternative to the conventional auto. Batteries have long been the major obstacle to practical electric cars. Expected advances in the next decade should increase useful range several times over, and at the same time cut costs significantly.

Third, despite these advances, electric cars will still be limited in range, so their use would entail a modest sacrifice of mobility. They will also be more expensive than competitive conventional cars unless designed for relatively short range, so long as gasoline remains relatively inexpensive. Neither technological advances in batteries nor in the remainder of the electric car are likely to reverse this situation. If US gasoline prices double or triple, reaching levels common in most other industrialized nations, the cost disadvantages of electric cars would be substantially eliminated--but the limitation on range would remain.

Fourth, electric cars would be most effective and economical if used as secondary cars at multi-car households. Electric cars designed to meet the modest demands typically placed on secondary cars could be relatively light and inexpensive. About a third of US cars are secondary cars, but relatively few are purchased new, so the market potential for electric second cars is limited.

Fifth, if gasoline remains as cheap and available as it has been since 1975, only a small minority of US cars are likely to be electric in this century. Their contribution to petroleum conservation and environmental quality will be correspondingly small unless steps are deliberately taken to ensure wider use.

Through governmental action, of course, higher usage of electric cars could be encouraged or required in order to reduce petroleum consumption and enhance the environment. To further these objectives, conventional cars are already required to meet demanding standards for emissions of air pollutants and consumption of petroleum. Yet problems of air pollution and oil imports remain serious. A deliberate shift to higher use of electric cars would be one partial remedy. Whether this would be desirable depends on whether the advantages of the electric cars would outweigh their disadvantages--and whether some other alternative appears more favorable.

In judging the overall desirability of encouraging or requiring the use of electric cars, oil appears to be the critical motivating factor. Substantial independence of petroleum appears to be by far the most important benefit of electric cars. If future supplies of petroleum were sufficiently likely to be scarce, uncertain, and expensive, the use of electric cars could be justified despite their limited range and higher cost.

INDEX

423